The Biological Bases of Human Behavior

The Biological Bases of Human Behavior

Geoffrey G. Pope

William Paterson University

Allyn and Bacon

Boston ■ London ■ Toronto ■ Sydney ■ Tokyo ■ Singapore

Series Editor: *Sarah L. Kelbaugh*
Editor-in-Chief, Social Sciences: *Karen Hanson*
Series Editorial Assistant: *Jennifer DiDomenico*
Marketing Manager: *Brooke Stoner*
Composition and Prepress Buyer: *Linda Cox*
Manufacturing Buyer: *Julie McNeill*
Cover Administrator: *Jenny Hart*
Editorial-Production Service: *Modern Graphics*
Electronic Composition: *Modern Graphics*

Library of Congress Cataloging-in-Publication Data

Pope, Geoffrey Grant.
      The biological bases of human behavior/ Geoffrey G. Pope.
          p.   cm.
      Includes bibliographical references and index.
      ISBN 0-205-27993-7
      1. Genetic psychology.   2. Behavior evolution.   3. Psychology,
Comparative.   4. Sociobiology.   I. Title.
BF701.P67 1999
155.7—dc21   99-35084
                                                                       CIP

Printed in the United States of America

10   9   8   7   6   5   4   3   2   04   03   02   01   00

CONTENTS

PREFACE

Where have I been? Nay, how now!
Where are you?

—William Shakespeare

This book was written out of necessity, frustration, and fascination. The need for this text grew out of years of teaching a class entitled "The Biological Bases of Human Behavior." After more than a decade of teaching this subject in various institutions around the globe, it became clear that there was no systematic integration of biological and cultural anthropology. It also became obvious that the rapid advances in psychology, the neurosciences, and other behavioral sciences were not being integrated into an evolutionary framework. Like other instructors, I had to compile a reader containing bits and pieces of information drawn from a variety of fields. Although the articles on human origins were highly evolutionary, articles on modern human behavior contained little if any reference to evolution and natural selection. From my viewpoint, the major paradigm of the universe, which is directly relevant to the mystery of human existence, was not being applied to attempts to understand why we do what we do. Students found the reader of different articles that I assembled incomprehensible as a whole without the aid of class lectures. Though class attendance is essential to comprehending any academic subject, I was disappointed that there was no written comprehensive and authoritative treatment of the interplay between the biology and behavior of humans that students could read at home. The studious reaction to the various readings was usually, "What does it all mean?" Though many texts have appeared that purport to treat human beings in a holistic manner, few actually do.

The frustration encountered in producing this book has taken the form of realizing that no single volume can possibly cover the immensity of the subject of evolutionary psychology. The field as a whole is still being born, and each subheading in the text could not be completely covered by several texts. Many critics of this new science have equated evolutionary psychology with "pop science." In some cases this criticism is deserved; in others it simply reflects the fact that infinitely complex phenomena (human behavior) do not have easily comprehensible "laws" that explain them. Unfortunately, both the popular and legitimate scientific press as well as academics have come to realize through experience that simplistic explanations and "breakthroughs" are much more likely to receive attention (and future funding) than plodding explorations of uncertainties. The most frustrating aspect of trying to draw together all the alleged facts of the biological bases of human behavior is the certain knowledge that any attempt will be inadequate. Thus, it is only possible to make a beginning. Every critic of this attempt will surely note that there is a lack of depth to each exploration. This is inevitable in a scientific climate where specialization is prized and generalizations are eschewed. Nonetheless, I believe that characterizations of the human species based on evolutionary theory will be the mainstay of future attempts to understand human nature.

The lack of standardized methodology for studying human behavior is also frustrating (Chapter 1). All fields of relevant inquiry are constantly changing their methodologies. A very new approach such as evolutionary psychology has only the past to guide it. Inevitably, it will come to rest on genetics, Darwinian evolution, sociobiology, statistics, and anthropology. However, all of these fields have their own internal and ongoing debates. Any new science must pick and choose among competing paradigms. Therefore, any adopted methodology for evolutionary psychology will unavoidably be idiosyncratic. This volume also contains anecdotal evidence that, despite the bent of most scientific philosophy, has a role to play in understanding our species.

Despite the fact that culture is learned, the categories of things that are learned are virtually identical among humans living anywhere on the planet. Any science eventually arrives at the question of *why*? For the study of human behavior, *why* usually has been answered from the polarized perspectives of experience or genes. We are finally beginning to conclude that both are important. But the ultimate and many proximate answers to *why* can be answered only with reference to the evolutionary past (Chapters 2 and 3). There is no alternative when dealing with organisms. To understand humans, it is also essential that we understand the development of that unique human behavior known as culture. This is possible almost exclusively through an understanding of the evolution of archaeology and anatomical changes associated with new modes of adaptation (Chapter 3).

Whether compared with other animals, other cultures, or other individuals, human beings are fascinating organisms. A major part of this fascination is the limitless variation of cultural and individual behavior. All human beings are mind readers. Without this ability, we cannot feed ourselves, reproduce, or exist. Other animals are also mind readers, but on this planet, humans are by far the best at it. We need to understand what each other is thinking, and we do it through a variety of ways. Linguistic communication and "body language" allow an intense communication of brains that no other species has developed to the same degree. Cultural universals (Chapter 4) link both hunters and gatherers and agricultural populations across the planet. The anatomical structure of the modern human brain (Chapter 5) reflects not only our vertebrate legacy of hundreds of millions of years, but also the unique human capacity and need for language (Chapter 6). Just as we need food and water, we also need to communicate with each other to mature and function normally. A central *why* question is the need to understand why humans communicate so intensely when other organisms have found no evolutionary need to "improve" their own systems of interaction. (And by the way, this book contains a great many long Greek and Latinate words, which are defined in the glossary. It also contains terms and words that are found in any adequate English dictionary. Any good student needs a good dictionary. Humans as a species frame their world on words with meanings that must be mutually agreed on.)

Human reproduction is also a highly fascinating subject, especially to other humans (Chapter 7). Unlike other organisms, most of human mating does not result in reproduction. This is a highly unlikely evolutionary development. Furthermore, we have extended aspects of sexuality into diverse components of our social life. Humans have merged play, economics, and cultural and individual behaviors into a prolonged cycle of sexual activity and interest that is unprecedented in other organisms. As a result, human males and females reproduce like few other animals. Many scholars over the centuries and millennia have gone so far as to speculate that a concern with sex permeates our daily existence.

Whatever humans think about sex, they think a lot in general. Questions surrounding the definition of intelligence and consciousness will no doubt continue to occupy us for the rest of human existence (Chapter 8). By any standard, humans are the most intelligent organisms on the planet. There is, as yet, no consensus about what intelligence is. However, there is a growing consensus that it is not a single entity. Much that is blatantly wrong and racist about intelligence has been written and believed. Like other attempts to deal with human behavior, opinions about the bases of intelligence have oscillated over the decades between genetic and experiential explanations. Yet comparisons with other closely and distantly related species suggest that humans are not just best at being humans, but rather fundamentally unique in their ability to respond to different stimuli and situations. We are not just more intelligent about understanding ourselves, we are also more intelligent in our ability to understand complex physical phenomena whose nature has never "crossed the mind" of other species. This text audaciously seeks to link the concept of intelligence to "behavioral plasticity," which in turn is linked to the nature of our evolutionary anatomy. I specifically suggest that what we humans recognize as intelligent behavior is made possible by the physical ability to manipulate the environment with prehensile appendages (hands). Intelligent animals are prehensile animals, though dolphins and whales may have arrived at a notable intelligence through a different evolutionary path. This approach makes the bold prediction that if we are not alone in the universe, other intelligent life will have appendages with manipulative capabilities similar to ours. Similarly, they will also recognize the concept of consciousness.

Dreams during sleep are one of the fundamental characteristics of higher life on this planet (Chapter 9). Invertebrates and lower vertebrates do not dream. Dreams are part of the various body rhythms and cycles of most vertebrates, but their function remains highly controversial. Furthermore, there is little agreement about what dream content has to do with consciousness, language, or other aspects of human behavior. However, there is widespread agreement that dreams, like sleep, are essential to human well-being. Deprivation of either results in severe dysfunctional states. From a cultural perspective, dreams are always accorded a unique nature in most if not all societies. Modern medicine is increasingly aware of the importance of human wake–sleep cycles in clinical situations.

The final chapter presents what I believe is currently "the bottom line" (Chapter 10), that is, what we can presently say about human behavior and the interplay between human evolutionary biology and the modern world. A main theme of this concluding section is that most human behaviors are genetically circumscribed because of their evolutionary history. At the same time, the specific details of human behavioral categories comprise a vast array of cultural details that are always changing. Like all species, we have species-specific characteristics, some of which we consider good and some of which we consider evil. Mating, parental investment, and social structures we share in common with our close primate relatives, though in each of these cases, humans have elaborated on these behaviors far more than other mammals have. Other features such as language, culture, art, and morality (to name but a few) are unique human qualities that cannot be readily identified in other organisms. This chapter strongly suggests that human species-specific characteristics are not easily changeable. In this sense, evolutionary psychology has a very applied aspect, which strongly suggests that attempts to change certain aspects of human behavior are doomed to failure. Socioeconomic and political "engineering," if it is to be successful, must be built on top of human propensities and not around them. Many of the conclusions of evolutionary psychology are common sense. While it seems that such conclusions are pedantic, it is important to realize that our species' long history of human tragedy and frustration has almost always resulted from institutions and individuals that ignored human nature.

Above all, the study of human behavior should be fun. At the same time, the subject is so complex that students inevitably will be led to new sources of knowledge they had rarely thought about. The words and terms in **bold** are those found in the glossary. Students should also consult the recommended readings that appear at the end of each chapter. In turn, students in class should call the attention of their instructor to subjects that are of particular interest to their own lives. "Sex, drugs, and rock 'n' roll" are legitimate topics for discussion, especially when considered from an evolutionary perspective.

Finally, all of us have an innate interest in the human condition. To understand where we are going and where we are as the next millennium dawns, we must understand where we have been. Historians know this, but as individuals, each of us rarely stops to comprehend the immensity of what we are about. In this volume, I have tried to do just that. Evolution is a fact of the universe. By knowing facts and truths, we can more accurately make our way in the world that we have created and that has created us.

ACKNOWLEDGMENTS

I wish to thank and acknowledge the help of many insitutions and individuals around the world who contributed invaluable editorial assistance to making this book possible. I especially thank S. Keates (Oxford), L. La Regina, J. J. Trobriano, N. Galimi, K. Russell-Henning, E. Woodruff (New Jersey), K. Sender (Florida), K. Nakabunlang and S. Nakabunlang (Thailand), and J. Pope and T. Pope (Arizona) for their help. F. Spencer (New York) graciously provided some of the illustrations. Over the years, funding for this project was provided by William Paterson University, The Holt Family Trust Foundation, The L.S.B. Leakey Foundation, The National Science Foundation, and The National Geographic Society. Also over the years, students have provided essential input both in the form of reactions to various versions of the text and in the form of fascinating questions and animated discussions. I also wish to express my sincere gratitude to the many foreign colleagues who have helped to make fieldwork and the presentation of results in many countries possible: in China (Huang Weiwen, Jia Lanpo, Liyi, Wei Qi, Wu Xinzhi), in Kenya (Jack Harris, Phillip Tobias), in Taiwan (Yang Lianzhu), in Thailand (Somsak Prmankij, Vadhana Subhavan, Supaporn and Kai Nakbunlung, David Frayer), in Australia (Peter Bellwood, Jack Golson, Johann Kamminga, Allan Thorne), in Canada (Richard Shutler), in Indonesia (Teku Jacob, Riley Seiver), in England (Christopher Stringer), in France (Marielle Santoni, Francois Semah), in Germany (Jens Franzen, Gunter Brauer), and many other countries. I would like to thank the following reviewers for reading the manuscript: Kenneth A.R. Kennedy, Cornell University; Michael F. Gibbons, Jr., University of Massachusetts at Boston; and Frank Spencer, Queens College of the City University of New York. Finally, over the years, I have benefited from interaction with my mentors and friends: F. Clark Howell, Herbert Phillips, Donald Savage, Sherry Washburn (U.C. Berkeley); Bernard Campbell (U.C. Los Angeles); Christie Turner III, Geoffrey Clark (Arizona State University); Kenneth Kennedy (Cornell University); and many other friends.

ACKNOWLEDGMENTS

1 Goals and Foundations

Since the ancients (as we are told by Pappus), made great account of the science of mechanics in the investigation of natural things; and the moderns, laying aside substantial forms and occult qualities, have endeavored to subject phenomena of nature to the laws of mathematics, I have in this cultivated mathematics so far as it regards philosophy.

—Sir Isaac Newton

Find a paradigm for which you can raise money, and attack with every method of analysis at your disposal.

—E. O. Wilson

For first, I propose a natural history that does not so much charm with its variety or gratify by the immediate fruit of experiments, as provide light for the discovery of causes and supply the first mother's milk to the infant philosophy.

—Francis Bacon

Why do we do what we do? How is it that humans came to be the very strange way that they are? The question continues to puzzle humankind but no longer needs to. It is imperative that humans should come to understand themselves in the context of the natural world that created them. As a species, we are difficult to understand in part because we have evolved a complex and often confusing way of coping with the world, which requires an infinitely complex interaction between biology and experience. In fact, human behavior is so complex that no single discipline has yet developed a comprehensive approach or even a terminology for exploring what it is that we mean by humanity.

Thus, this text is forced to attempt the task of integrating a number of traditionally disparate and distinct approaches that have developed over the thousands of years of human history. The task is daunting and requires the development of a perspective that is historical, scientific, and philosophical. Students of the subject of human evolution and behavior and readers of this text will quickly realize that one is forced to become a jack of all trades to truly develop even a rudimentary understanding of the basics of the interplay between biology and behavior. In addition to mastering terms and concepts from various scientific fields, it is also essential to contemplate humans in time in space. Just as physicists and astronomers must deal with natural phenomena in a multidimensional framework of creation, which explains the spatial and temporal distribution of change, so must students of humans learn to see themselves as a product of ongoing processes that have been at work since the beginning of time.

As with any science, the language and complexity of mutual understanding must be agreed on and readily comprehensible to people interested in the same things. Thus, definitions and conceptual frameworks presented in this chapter are explored below. Because **evolutionary psychology** is a new approach that owes its origin to many other approaches, students must "retool" the way they think about things. Retooling is not easy and requires a new kind of imagination that has not previously existed as a whole way of looking at things. As a species, we need a new way of looking at our place in the natural order of things because we have an immense potential for creation and destruction. Too often as cultures, societies, and individuals, we contend with the world in ill-considered ways. Our cities, lifestyles, achievements, and failures evince repeated patterns that cry out for explanation and understanding. We need to know how to make life better for the inhabitants of our planet, and the only way to do that is to figure out what we are and how we got that way. This means that we must understand evolution, one of the irreducible facts of the universe. We are evolution, and evolution is us. To see humanity in any other light is to form an inappropriate notion of reality. The path to this decidedly nonmystical form of enlightenment is complicated and fraught with historical accidents, but it is possible to make a sound beginning.

The time has long since passed when the behavior and biology of human beings can be treated as separate subjects. Evolutionary psychology is a recent concept that has been applied to attempts to synthesize a number of traditionally distinct biological and social sciences in the framework of the **theory of natural selection.** Like **Charles Robert Darwin's** (1809–1882) own theory, it grows not out of a stunning eureka-type discovery but out of the accumulation of data from a number of fields. Although natural selection theory represented a **paradigm** shift, evolutionary psychology has not yet achieved this status, but it is much closer to this objective than it was ten years ago. As a whole, the new perspective is historical (in Ernst Mayr's sense of the word), descriptive, and very predictive. Only organisms behave, and therefore, their behavior must have a biological basis. Like any other organism, humans have been shaped by **evolution** resulting from natural selection. Legitimate scientific debates about human nature, behavior, and thinking have focused not on the fact of organic evolution but on the degree to which human behavior is circumscribed by innate biological structures.

The **nature versus nurture debate** continues unabated in modern social and biological thought. In attempts to understand humans, the modern form of this debate has usually been translated into experience–environment versus genes (often race). Neither extreme has or, in my opinion, will ever triumph over the other. At the same time, it is now increasingly possible and useful to make a decision about which factor is more important in any given set of behaviors. This is the boldest claim of evolutionary psychology. Scientists, politicians, and even the public at large have historically abused the study of human behavior by adopting extreme positions at either end of the behavioral spectrum. Just as it is impossible to understand the mind without understanding the brain, it is equally impossible to understand the brain without understanding the human body and its evolutionary history.

The aim of this text is to synthesize information from the evolutionary and social sciences in a modern interdisciplinary framework that explores the biological bases of human behavior. The sources of these kinds of data are necessarily wide-ranging. In fact, the database relevant to this task is so vast that each subheading could be the subject of many volumes. Each chapter could easily encompass the life work of hundreds of scholars and still be only a sampling of the possibilities for understanding human behavior. The compartmental divisions of this book are arbitrary but reflect general divisions of anthropology, biology, and psychology as they might be consensually recognized today. The general approach is unavoidably "a mile wide and an inch deep." My greatest defense of this method is that I had no choice but to make a first attempt at formally defining evolutionary psychology.

Human behavior, especially when an evolutionary time depth of millions of years is added, is so complicated, that an even more holistic approach would currently resemble philosophy or religion. In the modern Western world, even the narrowest specialist realizes that every system influences or directly affects some other system. There are no closed systems in nature. The same is true at the level of the organism. Every scientist should support this conclusion.

In the past, many kinds of psychology have treated behavior quite separately from the organic substrates that must underlie behavior. I believe that one of the really encouraging achievements of twenty-first-century behavioral studies will be the final abandonment of the **brain–mind dichotomy.** All thoughts are stored and processed as electrochemical phenomena. There is no alternative to this conclusion without reference to a "ghost in the machine." Similarly, while the behaviorist-environmental approach to human behavior is highly useful, it alone is powerless to explain universal human traits.

The psychological sciences began in the first decades of the twentieth century embroiled in a nature–nurture dichotomy that evolved from the racist nature of preoccupations in Europe and the United States. **Behaviorism** increasingly became a response to genetics and racism. Psychoanalysis was an odd mix of the two extremes, which postulated that all people were born with the same kind of universal psychological problems that they tried to resolve according to their environmental experiences. Like most highly educated men of his time, the neurologist Sigmund Freud (1856–1939) understood the contentions of evolution. Also, like most of his contemporaries, what he did not grasp were the behavioral ramifications of natural selection: Animals evolve in such a way as to pay attention to (consciously or unconsciously) and adjust to conditions that are important to them.

The social sciences (anthropology, history, sociology, and economics) and the human biological sciences concerned with behavior traveled down very different paths. Though both purported to incorporate Darwinism as they misunderstood it, in fact, both groups essentially ignored the details of natural selection theory. From its inception, biological anthropology was predominantly racist in its concerns and conceptions. The reaction to the rise of biological racism in places like Germany and later the United States was so strong that the social sciences abandoned biology and genetics almost completely. Early **physical anthropologists** concentrated on documenting physical differences and linking them to intellectual capacity, moral character, and social "achievements." In comparison with the human biological sciences, the social sciences took on a more difficult task. These fields of studies adopted the goal of both understanding and predicting the behavior of groups of the behaviorally complex human organism. Individual human behavior, though quantifiable in groups, has proved hard to predict at any level. Although economists have seemingly been much less successful than the minds of Madison Avenue, the sciences of prediction and manipulation have very little explanation of why people do what they do.

Ernst Mayr has pointed out that scientists and students of science divide the scientific world into sciences that are "soft" and those that are "hard." The social scientist produces statements of low predictability, and, to paraphrase Mayr, the more social a science the softer it is. Hard sciences produce highly replicable results. Although nonreplicable results are produced in both sciences due to techniques and mistakes, these kinds of problems actually result from the nature of the objects of study themselves. Simply put, living organisms (especially complex ones) present a set of variables that even the most powerful computer cannot adequately deal with. To predict the behavior of atomic particles, it is necessary to stipulate far fewer circumstances than would be necessary to predict what any given human being will do in the course of a single day. In spite of the complexity of predicting human behavior, humans make thousands of predictions a day about the behavior of other people with an accuracy that usually allows them to achieve and maintain complex social relationships. The increasing successes of the soft social sciences, though they are still few, are in large part due to the rise of computers. The same could be said of weather forecasting. Computers are also crucial to observation and interpretation.

There is virtually no field of human scholarship in which computers have not been crucial. Along with statistics, computers have become essential to an understanding of human behavior. However, there are at least two prices that we pay for the new advantage. One is a dream that originally began with the rise of physics (see below) and came to fruition with the digital age. That is the belief that quantification is equal to understanding. Few scientific journals will publish articles without numbers (read *data*).

The other price that we pay began as a rather obscure essay by Willie Henning in the 1930s. It languished in obscurity until the dawn of the PC age. The essay was on **taxonomy** (Gk. *tax*=to order+*onomy*=name). Sitting at their computers wrapped in their statistics, many scholars accepted the idea that existence was dichotomous and that objects could be described in base two. In fact, both philosophers and many other social scientists have suggested through the millennia that human thinking is basically dichotomous in its organization and processes. The new approach was called **cladistics** (Gk. *clado*=to split). Splitting is a good description of exactly what cladistics did to many subfields of biology. By the 1980s, it reached out of biology to fields such as linguistics. It took on the characteristics of a crusade or holy war complete with zealots and infidels who gathered at conferences around the world to preach.

In biology and especially in **paleontology,** any object can theoretically be described with reference to its quantifiable distance from any two other objects. The usefulness of this approach is discussed below. But for now, the point to be taken—and taken seriously—is that it thoroughly encourages a renaissance of polarized interpretations of the organic world. Questions that linger today include **Eve versus regional continuity debate** about the evolution of modern humans, the punctuated equilibrium versus gradualism debate about the evolution of life in general, the brain versus mind debate, and the humanism versus scientific debate about why we study human culture and behavior at all. Today we are still hotly contesting whether the human brain is basically organized in a dichotomous way. One could make a case from history that this is undeniably true. The most perennial debate is the nature versus nurture debate. It is not that the debate is new, only that the scientific climate is once again ripe for resuming the great dichotomous argument—but this time with digital data.

One unfortunate effect of these kinds of debates is the understanding of evolutionary science not only by educated and uneducated laypeople, but also by other scientists in only distantly related fields. The public often interprets arguments between evolutionary biologists as arguments about whether evolutionary theory is accepted at all. Unfortunately antievolutionists, especially **creationists,** are nearly always waiting in the wings to seize an opportunity to proclaim that many scientists doubt the theory of evolution.

Evolution, the idea that things change through time, is perhaps the only theory that unites all truly scientific investigation. It is certainly at the core of biological science. However, most biologists are not directly concerned with tracing evolution of organisms. Most texts in biology, psychology, and even the "soft" social sciences acknowledge evolution as a valid description of the organic world. However, I have always found it strange that the space devoted to evolution in most biology texts is minute. This is especially true of psychology texts.

After years of questioning students about their biology classes at both the secondary and tertiary level, I realize that they, like I, were taught biology with very little reference to evolutionary theory. The reason for starting with earthworms and ending up with cats or pigs was almost always given as representing a transition from simple to complex, from the "primitive to advanced." Actually, the distinction between higher and lower and primitive and advanced is not scientific because these terms imply moral connotations that date back at least to the Greco-Roman, Judeo-Christian view of the world. Instead, paleontologists use terms that avoid these pejorative descriptions. Paleontologists and biologists in general tie their modern terms to the paleontological concept of time and space.

The first step is to begin the education of students with a number of indisputable facts:

1. Organic evolution is a theory in exactly the same way as Newton's laws of motion are. To believe that it is a highly implausible theory, which many scientists do not believe, is to be unscientific. Philosophically and technically, all scientific laws are only theories. That is, they are probability statements.

2. Scientists do argue a great deal about evolution. However, no real scientist argues about the reality of organic evolution. What they do legitimately argue about is the mechanism of evolution. Darwin was not the first to propose evolution. He was one of the first to propose a highly plausible mechanism of evolution that could be and has been scientifically tested. Many legitimate scientists today think Darwin may not have stumbled onto the correct details of the mechanism. Scientists debate the details, not the notion that organisms change through time.

3. The total range of modern human behavior is an amalgamation of past behavioral tendencies that evolved in a way of life that we no longer follow. Our physical anatomy is similarly the result of adaptations to lifestyles that most of us no longer pursue. The details of our heritage are so complex and expressed in so many dimensions that a single conventional science has difficulty making sense of the human animal as a whole. The single clue that can hold the mental and physical organism together as a whole is evolution. The evolution of human behavior can be studied from a unique perspective that is not available to students of other forms of animals. This avenue is **archaeology,** which encompasses the study of the evolution of cultural behavior. Recent theoretical developments in archaeological theory have provided insights that not only allow us to organize our thinking about archaeology, but that are also useful in organizing observational data and conclusions in general.

Philosophical and Scientific Approaches to the Study of Human Behavior

Scientists, like lawyers, athletes, clergy, or just about any members of a group, operate under a particular set of laws, rules, and assumptions that all of the group's members share. In the 1960s, Thomas Kuhn, a historian and philosopher of science, proposed the term *paradigm* to refer to the common worldview and methodologies under which scientists operate when carrying out what he called **normative research.** Normative research questions are those that are generated by testing the paradigm. The direction of research is usually determined by past discoveries and the assumptions and conclusions that come from them. In the course of normative research, anomalies are sometimes discovered. The explanation of anomaly is one way in which research proceeds. Research can also proceed from the replication of previous experiments or the confirmation of widely held paradigms. Frequently, even when a paradigm is confirmed, other anomalies, some that may or may not be related to the normative paradigm, often arise. The history of science is frequently a series of **paradigm shifts.** It is through these shifts that scientific knowledge expands and diversifies. It is probably safe to say that most scientific research confirms previous paradigms and often elaborates on the details of the previous theories.

Theories are **hypotheses,** or tentative explanations, that need further testing and confirmation. Scientific philosopher **Karl Popper** contended that real theories in the true scientific sense of the word must be falsifiable. He pointed out that no theory can actually be proved because every prediction is technically only a **probability statement.** Just because every time a rock is dropped it falls down does not mean that it won't fall up the next time. Real theories are only falsifiable. Some theories have been replicated so many times and for so long with the same results that normative research has moved on to other tests. Performing the experiment one million more times is unlikely to reveal any new anomalies or novel ways of confirming the paradigm. In the practical world of research, this means that few people are likely to accord any more research money to such a project.

Evolutionary Biology

It is both useful and necessary to introduce a number of the basic terms that paleontologists, evolutionary biologists, and archeologists use to order and examine the natural world. A great deal of these ideas are based on evolutionary theory as originally developed by Charles Darwin and later modified by geneticists and evolutionary biologists. Darwin solved the problem of how new species arise. The modern **synthetic theory of evolution** combines and synthesizes what geneticists have discovered about **genes, DNA (deoxyribonucleic acid),** and **chromosomes** with the viewpoint paleontologists and biologists have developed from observing changes in structure and function in animals (including humans) over time. The modern synthetic theory recognizes that evolution proceeds at both the genetic and **species** levels. Genes are codes carried by the molecule DNA that specify a portion of the forms and behaviors of an organism. Among animals, only the category *species* has an objective biological reality that can be tested through observation. Species are **reproductively isolated populations** that only mate with their own kind to produce **viable offspring.** Viable offspring are descendants that can in turn reproduce. The two fields of study have been synthesized to produce a general approach to the study of animals that realizes that the data from one branch of the science must also be consistent with data from other sciences. Evolutionary biology studies organic change over time. All natural scientists agree that species change over time, but they often disagree on exactly how this happens.

There are common terms and ideas that any evolutionary biologist uses to think, describe, and explain the behavior and morphology of animals. Of particular importance is the paradigm of **natural selection** and our modern understanding of how it works. Darwin put this theory together after decades of worldwide personal observation, knowledge of other people's views on life, and years of contemplation. Although Darwin knew nothing of chromosomes, DNA, or genes, he put forward a theory that, among other things, explains why there is a correlation between fossil forms and living forms of life. His ultimate conclusion, deduced from his own and others' observations, is that all life evolves in relation and response to the environment it exists in. This is an extremely subtle but useful concept. The clear implication of Darwin's theory was that human beings are also subject to the **selection pressures** that the environment places on them.

The Growth of Natural Selection Theory

Natural selection theory is the basic paradigm of biology, paleontology, genetics, and all other interrelated fields that study organisms. Darwin's great contribution to biology was not that he discovered that animals change over time; this idea had been sporadically defended for thousands of years before Darwin. Even diametrically opposed French scholars such as Jean Lamarck (1744–1829) and Georges Cuvier (1769–1832) agreed that fossils showed clear changes over time. What they disagreed bitterly about was why and how they changed. Lamarck favored a natural process as opposed to a supernatural process (the direct intervention of a divine being). Cuvier favored a process of repeated creation and destruction controlled by God. Lamarck believed in what is now called the theory of **acquired characteristics.** This is the belief that traits acquired in an individual's lifetime through repeated use are passed on to offspring. The classic example usually given is that giraffes developed long necks from stretching to eat higher and higher vegetation.

Darwin's great contribution was his ability to synthesize a number of diverse ideas, which led him to propose a mechanism of evolution that was natural and not supernatural. Although Lamarck's mechanism of change was wrong, it resembled Darwin's explanation by rejecting direct supernatural intervention. The reaction of certain segments of the church to his idea was based on the literal interpretation of the Bible and the inescapable conclusions that if animals had changed through time, then humans were subject to the same natural forces of change. Furthermore, according to literal biblical interpretation, the earth was young and only as ancient as the Bible said it was according to some people.

Thus, in Europe, Archbishop Ussher (1581–1656) was able to add up the generations of humankind as reported in the Bible and to conclude that the earth began in 4004 B.C. The possibility of the special creation of each of the millions of species was much more probable on a young Earth. Ironically, many of the ideas that influenced Darwin and helped to form the core of his theory were those of very religious men. It was a number of the ideas of his predecessors and contemporaries that formed key parts of his argument for natural selection.

These people observed nature in the tradition of **natural theology,** a movement that held that natural phenomena (including animals) were governed by laws similar to the ones that the infant science of physics had discovered. For natural theologians the study of nature and her laws was tantamount to studying God. This was because the study of a world created by God was a direct means of understanding the Creator. Philosophically and historically, this tradition descended from clerics such as the Jesuits and Franciscans. It is important to emphasize that all the natural theologians were religious men.

The early astronomers, philosophers, and physicists such as Nicolaus Copernicus (1473–1543), Galileo Galilei (1564–1642), Johannes Kepler (1571–1630), Sir Isaac Newton (1642–1727), and René Descartes (1596–1650) explored "**mechanics**" and discovered "laws" and order in the creations of God. To study nature then was to study the workings of the perfect machine that God, "The Great Watch Maker" had set in motion. One of the conclusions of this viewpoint was that creation was a kind of machine that, once set in motion, did not require divine intervention. Processes at work on the earth could therefore be natural and still be the work of a divine being.

The split between the church and natural theologians eventually arose as the result of observations motivated by natural theology. Inadvertent discoveries were to prove contradictory, and many were completely unexpected. The discovery of the New World and the invention of the microscope revealed whole constellations of living things that had never been mentioned in the Bible. Not only was the New World populated by strange people, plants, and animals that the Bible had never mentioned, but another microscopic world also literally existed under one's nose. The increased interest in observation of the natural world almost inevitably led to the need to rethink the idea that organisms had not changed since their creation.

The desire to organize an understanding of the biological world led to a comprehensive classification of organisms into a **systema naturae** of classification undertaken by the Swedish biologist Carolus Linnaeus (1707–1778). Linnaeus believed and helped popularize the idea that species had not changed since the biblical Creation. Although he was a staunch defender of the "fixity of species," his later work raised the possibility that species do change through time. At the end of his life, the great classifier of the biological world was deeply disturbed by the implications of what he could no longer conveniently deny.

One other development made the questioning of the church's interpretation of creation inevitable. This was the eventual realization that the earth was far older than anyone had imagined. The theoretical aspects of "mechanics" were eventually transformed into the Industrial Revolution. To run the machines of production, fuel and iron were needed. That meant a fledgling science of geology was needed to locate ores and coal. Men such as William "Strata" Smith (1769–1839) and especially Charles Lyell (1797–1875) began carefully observing the details of geology from the perspective of investigators who believed that there was order in the earth. Smith deduced that fossils in the ground occurred in a particular sequence from top to bottom, which allowed one to predict the location of resources such as coal and iron. Previously, fossils were regarded as "sports of nature," the result of lightning strikes, or, even more terrifying, the works of the Devil.

Lyell's book *Principles of Geology* (1830–1833) had a great influence on Darwin. He read it during his many years of observations in the field. Lyell, who never did come to accept human evolution, popularized the concept of **uniformitarianism.** This doctrine concluded that the forces that had acted on the earth in the past were the exact same ones that are active on the earth today. The forces were uniform in that forces such as erosion, volcanism, wind, rain, and ice could explain the features of the land as they existed today. There was no need to believe in divine interventions such as worldwide floods or divinely generated catastrophic forces of the kind that Cuvier had proposed. Lyell's theory had a very important and inescapable conclusion with regard to the probable age of the Earth. Uniformitarian forces were for the most part so subtle and of such low energy that the Earth must be much older than previously supposed. Taken to its logical conclusion, it meant that supporters of the idea that populations of animals changed had a lot more time to work with. All of these conclusions arose from a fusion of the need for industrial technology with natural theology. All of the forerunners that contributed to Darwin's theory worked in the mainstream of the tradition of natural theology.

The Industrial Revolution also set the tone of Dickensonian England. Here a cleric named Thomas Malthus (1766–1834) was so impressed by the "struggle for existence" among the industrial poor, that he wrote his "An Essay on the Principle of Population." The essay, which both Alfred Russell Wallace (see below) and Darwin read, maintained that populations inevitably outbreed their food supply if left unchecked. This was a key part of Darwin's theory.

The ideas that Darwin inherited from his predecessors can be listed as follows in conjunction with their proponents:

1. Animals change through geologic time (Lamarck). The earth was not static.
2. Environmental forces are uniformitarian. The forces at work today are the same as those that have always been at work on the earth. These forces are natural and not the result of repeated divine intervention (Lyell and other natural theologians).
3. The earth is very old (Lyell).
4. Populations outbreed their food supply, which results in a struggle for existence (Malthus).

The origin and details of Darwin's own observations have now been explored in numerous scholarly works. Here we present a distillation of his own field observations. In fact, the conclusions that Darwin came to all could have been reached without ever leaving England. As with **Alfred Russell Wallace** (1823-1913), the cofounder of natural selection theory, the study of island faunas and their comparison with mainland continental faunas provided a natural laboratory that accentuated patterns that related certain behaviors and anatomies to specific geographic conditions. One of the great triumphs of natural selection theory is the incorporation of subtle observations in a theory of dynamic change that embraces all life. Darwin's own observations can be summarized as follows:

1. Individuals vary. All individuals (excluding identical twins) are different in their morphology.
2. Form fits function. Traits of individuals can be observed to have a utilitarian function.
3. Populations vary in relation to their geographic isolation from one another.

Darwin sought a mechanism for change that was natural. The mechanism not only had to be mechanical and free of the necessity of divine intervention, but it also had to be why competition was translated into biological change. In many ways Darwin was the culmination of thinking that had been developed under the auspices of natural theology.

In the end, both Wallace and Darwin concluded that the environment selects those individuals whose lineages will survive to produce their own **viable offspring.** Viable offspring in turn must be able to reproduce. In the years since Darwin published *On the Origin of Species* (1859), **Darwinian fitness** has become defined as represented by those individuals that left the most offspring. **Differential reproduction** is another way of viewing the process of reproduction. By definition, those individuals that leave the most offspring are the most fit. Survival of the fittest does not necessarily refer to those individuals that are stronger, faster, bigger, or more aggressive, though many of these qualities may have a direct influence on a species' Darwinian fitness. The same is true of cooperation, docility, and avoidance of direct physical competition. As Darwin and his contemporaries knew, some matings that produced sterile offspring are irrelevant to the process of evolution. Although at first Darwin dealt with anatomical traits, it is clear from all of his works that he also considered behavior and the implications of the interrelationship between behavior and biology.

The Mechanism of Natural Selection

At this point, it is imperative to fully understand the basics of natural selection. The triumph of Darwinian theory was that it explained changes through time as the result of a mechanism that did not require divine intervention. If a divine being was behind this change, then that being worked through natural selection. Natural selection can be summarized as follows:

1. All individuals are different (differences are physical, physiological, mental, and so on).
2. Those differences that by chance are better adapted to the environment give the animal a reproductive advantage (it leaves more viable offspring). It has the most Darwinian fitness.
3. If the advantages are continually passed down from generation to generation, the number of animals with the adaptive advantage become more numerous and eventually replace those lineages without the advantage.
4. Over time, anatomical form comes to function better in the environment.

5. Because new forms are always being born and because the environments are always changing, evolution never stops.

Darwin's work culminated in one of the most scientifically important deductions of this or any other century. Although he never understood where new original variation came from, his work made it abundantly clear that organisms changed as the environments of the earth changed. Nature is constantly selecting new forms. The process of natural selection was slow, subtle, and like the earth itself, far more ancient than anyone had suspected before Darwin's time. Fossils embedded in great thicknesses of rock can be related to living forms because they share a common ancestry. In fact, all life on Earth has a common ancestry. There has been a process of modification that continues today. Perhaps the most socially disturbing aspects of Darwin's work was the scientifically inescapable conclusion that humans were subject to the same environmental selection pressures as other organisms.

The Modern Synthetic Theory of Evolution

Darwin and Wallace never knew about genes, much less about DNA. Darwin never solved the mystery of where original individual variation arose from in the first place. We now know that **mutations,** or mistakes in the genetic code, are the source of all original variation. Recombination of existing traits did not pose a great problem for Darwin. The agricultural breeding of plants and animals made it obvious that once separate characteristics could be combined through artificial selection. The synthesis of genetics, and more recently molecular biology with paleontology and **ethology,** led to the formulation of modern evolutionary theory. At the core of modern theory is the observation that the environment selects certain phenotypes, which are determined to a large extent by the genotype of an individual. The **genotype** is the genetic code that, except in the presence of mutagens (that is, radiation and certain chemicals), does not change in an individual's lifetime. The **phenotype** is the result of the environment and the genotype. In trying to understand the evolution of both morphology and behavior, it is always desirable to separate the phenotype from the genotype. In humans, this has been the subject of intense debate. For instance, an organism may have a genetic code that specifies a certain adult height, but environmental stress in the form of inadequate individual nutrition may result in an individual of only half the specified height. Isolating the factor that accounts for most of the variance of a trait can be exceedingly difficult. In our example, for instance, determining what part of someone's height is due to genes and what proportion is the result of diet becomes difficult. The question is further complicated by the concept of **polygenic traits.** What is perceived by a researcher as a single trait in fact may be coded for by a number of genes. With the exception of a comparative handful of traits studied in laboratory animals, human traits are poorly understood at the genetic level. This is especially true of behavioral traits.

The key to modern genetic theory is the organic molecule DNA. All known organisms and their cells contain DNA. In environments that allow organic chemical reactions, the creation of DNA is probably inevitable. The constituents of the DNA molecule, sugars, phosphates, and four bases are complimentary in that they only combine with each other in certain ways. The permutations and variation in size of DNA make possible combinations almost infinite. However, certain repeated codes have been selected over billions of years of evolution, and all DNA shares the same basic functions.

One function is **replication.** This is the process that DNA uses to copy itself. The second function is **recombination,** in which strands of DNA from one individual recombine to form a new genetic code with strands of another individual. The last function of DNA is **protein synthesis,** in which the code directs the construction of proteins from which to carry out a vast number of functions in the organism.

In carrying the function of replication and protein synthesis, DNA can make mistakes known as mutations. These mutations are random in that they can occur anywhere in the DNA molecule. In terms of their evolutionary significance, mutations may be **deleterious, neutral,** or **beneficial.** Although it is arguable, most geneticists view the vast majority of random mutation as deleterious to the organism. Sudden random change to an organismal system that has evolved over billions of years is unlikely to be beneficial. A useful analogy is that of an automobile engine. The chance of enhancing the performance of an engine by randomly altering its components is low. Other scientists have argued that neutral mutations, those that have no effect on how the environment "reads" the phenotype that DNA helps to construct, are much more common than has been generally thought. Perhaps the rarest mutations are those that are beneficial. Whatever viewpoint a scientist emphasizes, the inescapable conclusion is that organic evolution has been at work for a very long time. It is also important to remember that what is deleterious, neutral, or beneficial is determined solely by the environment. Furthermore, environments are always changing. Therefore, what was once beneficial may become deleterious and vice versa.

It is important to emphasize that mutations are selected for or deleted only after they have occurred. Mutation may precede or follow the selection pressures that test it. The modern synthetic theory of natural selection explains the physical changes from generation to generation as the result of random mutations that tend to favor one individual over another. According to the way Darwin and modern biologists have viewed fitness, only the number of viable offspring determine whether one individual is more "fit" than another. Darwinian fitness also depends on the fact that every individual is unique (with the exception of identical twins, who have exactly the same genetic make-up). Therefore, given any particular environment or any change in environment, one individual will always be better or less adapted to a particular set of environmental conditions.

It is very important to emphasize that what a particular individual desires has nothing to do with the determination of Darwinian fitness. Animals can behave in a certain way without realizing that they are doing something that helps or hinders that chance of leaving offspring in the next generation. Thus, **nonvolitional behavior** (not wanting to accomplish an objective) can have a profound effect on whether a particular lineage of organism survives into the next generation. The simple yardstick of whether a particular behavior, part of the body, or combination of the two survive is determined simply by whether it gives a particular animal an advantage over others of its own species.

All of the diversity of life has arisen from the accumulation of mutations resulting either from the mistakes of DNA or from damage to DNA caused by the environment. Recombination of DNA strands through sex or other means also produces new forms, but the reshuffling of new possibilities would never be possible without the changes introduced by mutations. Biologists study humans and other organisms at many levels. Geneticists map the structure of DNA, which provides the blueprint for the physical structures of the body that we can see. These blueprints can now be compared directly through a number of different techniques. These techniques are very accurate and have succeeded in establishing which species are more closely related and which are more distantly related. On another level, scientists also study the products such as proteins that DNA codes for. Such studies are one step removed from the direct study of sequence differences in the DNA. At an even more removed level, some scientists study the **comparative anatomy** of organs and skeletons of various animals.

The field of paleontology seeks to document the physical changes in organisms and their phylogenetic relationships as they can be deduced from fossils, most of which exist in the form of chemical casts of the hard parts of an animal's body. Though seemingly far removed from modern behavior, paleontological data can offer an opportunity to understand when and where and in relation to what environments anatomy evolved in support of particular behaviors. For instance, we have recovered ancestral horse fossils spanning nearly 60 million years. From a comparison of the changes in horse skeletons over the years, we are certain that horses got bigger and faster over the years. As their original five digits were lost, the feet were eventually transformed into a single digit with a hoof. We conclude that running became increasingly important to the survival of horses. When we study the evolution of their teeth, we conclude that they became higher and wider to more efficiently chew grass and other tough foliage. By combining these types of information with modern observations about horse behavior and their habitats, we can conclude that horses became increasingly more adapted to living in social groups that occupied grasslands.

Sociobiology

In the last few decades, traditional Darwinian evolution has been challenged by what many biologists term **"the new synthesis."** As mentioned previously, Darwin never discovered the source of original variation because he did not know about genes or DNA. Today it would be unthinkable to study the biology of any organism without reference to DNA. Our knowledge of the biomolecular nature of genes led some scientists to argue that Darwin was wrong when he identified the individuals of a species as the unit of selection that the environment works on. **E. O. Wilson** and several other biologists proposed a new approach called sociobiology, which recognizes that DNA is the unit of selection. According to sociobiology, it is not Darwinian fitness (the number of viable offspring left to each generation) but **inclusive fitness** that is the basic unit for understanding evolution. Inclusive fitness refers to how much DNA (not necessarily offspring) is included in each generation.

The idea of inclusive fitness grew out of Wilson's study of ants. In ant colonies it seemed that only the DNA of the queen was passed on to the next generation. The rest of the colony devoted their entire existences to protecting, feeding, and helping the queen reproduce. What puzzled Wilson was how such a system could have evolved if the unit of selection was in fact the individual. Put another way, what was in it for the ants that did not reproduce? Eventually, it was discovered that all members of the colony shared essentially half of their DNA with each other and the queen.

From this observation, Wilson and others realized that inclusive fitness had far-reaching implications for genetically based behavior in general. Sociobiologists recognized that there were ways of including one's own DNA without actually reproducing. According to sociobiology, the only thing that matters in evolution is how much DNA is passed on. Furthermore, there are several paths to reproduction that make use of inclusive fitness.

Returning for a moment to Darwinian evolution, we can observe that there is a broad spectrum of strategies for reproduction. At one end of the spectrum are animals that leave a large number of eggs to develop into offspring. This so-called "**shotgun theory**" relies on sheer numbers to ensure that at least a few offspring will survive. This type of reproduction involves very little **parental investment** of time and energy in the offspring. Insects, fish, and many reptiles are a good example of this type of reproduction.

At the other end of the scale are so-called **rifle** strategies in which at least one of the parents invests heavily in the offspring. This type of reproduction involves only one or just a few offspring, which usually take longer to mature in comparison to shotgun parents. Primates and large mammals employ this approach. Instead of numbers, rifle-adapted species rely on curation and protection to raise their young to adulthood. Yet other species have adopted strategies in between the two extremes. Bird species are highly variable. Some birds rear only one nestling, while others will have a number of eggs and care for them until the offspring are old enough to fend for themselves. The cuckoo bird adopts the comparatively rare (among vertebrae) strategy of widely dispersing its offspring (r-strategy) and letting other species shower parental investment (k-selected) on the chick.

However, the ants that Wilson studied employed yet another constellation of the two extremes. In ants and other communally living insects, a number of offspring are produced simultaneously and/or continuously. Ants are organized in effect so that members of the colony all contribute to the raising of offspring.

This type of reproduction and communal rearing has been described by sociobiologists as **eusocial** (Gk. *eu*=true+social). Sociobiologists further suggest that all species can be assessed according to these criteria. Species that are organized in this cooperative manner are referred to as k-selected (for "kinship"). K-selected species are groups such as primates, that raise only one or a few offspring at a time. Species that use the so-called shotgun approach of leaving a number of offspring are referred to in sociobiological jargon as r-selected (for "relatedness").

Sociobiologists maintain that the degree of eusocial cooperation in a species can be assessed according to a simple equation:

$$K = 1/r$$

The above equation not only describes the degree to which species are K- or r-selected, but it also by implication describes the reproductive relationship between members of the same species. Furthermore, it predicts the amount of cooperation between individuals. The equation predicts that closely related DNA will help each other. In sociobiology this is referred to as reciprocal altruism. The word *altruism* is used differently than it is usually used in English. Real altruism connotes helping others with no expectation of reward. As the word is used in sociobiology, it denotes helping other DNA to receive help. Because of this, the alternative term **bioaltruism** has been used to convey the idea that selfishness not selflessness is the relationship that is being described. In fact, sociobiologists have often referred to what they call the selfish gene. One popular maxim that has come out of sociobiology is the observation that "you are just DNA's way of making more DNA."

If DNA is the only unit of selection, then all of the behavior that goes on between generations of genes has, or will ultimately, evolve in relation to your DNA's furtherance of itself. Taken to its logical extreme, selfish gene theory implies that genes that do not code for selfish behavior will be deleted from the population. This leads to a number of implications and in many cases unavoidable conclusions about the evolution of behavior. When applied to humans, it theoretically has implications for all human behavior. One of the unavoidable corollaries of this position is that behavior is under, or will completely come under, genetic control or else the behavior would not exist for a span of millions of years.

If the selfish gene theory is correct in its implication that more closely related individuals will give each other more mutual assistance, then there must be some way for closely related individuals to identify each other. Indeed, sociobiologists have postulated many such recognition strategies, which are subsumed under the concept of **kin recognition.** Once kin is recognized, the strategy must be to help one's kin at the expense of others. This concept has interesting and ominous implications for human behavior.

In defense of kin recognition, it is true that human cultures have mechanisms, some of which are highly elaborate, for recognizing kin. However, when we look at actual kinship in humans, it will become obvious that kinship terminology is just as likely to ignore relatedness as it is to follow it. For human beings, the clear implication is that people who do not physically resemble each other should not help each other. In other words, the logical conclusion is that **racism** is biologically based and that it is adaptive for one's own DNA. **Ethnocentrism** is often confused with racism.

In all sexually reproducing species, the individuals most closely related to an individual are one's parents and siblings. One shares half of one's genes with any other member of the nuclear family. However, it is important to remember that the degree of relatedness is simply a statistical concept, and the actual percentage can be much less or much more with family members. Kin recognition does predict that people will give most assistance to one's immediate family members.

Theoretically, there are many ways to help your close relatives leave more of their DNA in the next generation. Some strategies do not involve one's own personal reproduction. For instance, every time your sibling has a child, an average of 25 percent of one's own DNA will be present in the offspring. If one reproduces oneself, one ensures that statistically 50 percent of one's DNA will be included in the next generation. Alternatively, if an individual does not reproduce, but instead commits his or her resources to a sibling so that the sibling has three children, then 75 percent of one's DNA will be passed on. Sociobiologists maintain that there are situations in which this is a more evolutionarily sound approach than straightforward reproduction.

A Brief Critique of Sociobiology

Sociobiology has been used to explain such wide-ranging behaviors as homosexuality, female "coyness," male "promiscuity," morality, virtue, art, and virtually all supposedly innate human behaviors. In fact, sociobiology can theoretically explain all behavior with reference to inclusive fitness. However, in some cases, sociobiology must invoke special circumstances that strain credibility. For example, suicide has been explained as a way of reducing the strain of resources and competition for one's siblings and parents (who have other children). Homosexuality has been explained the same way. Some other examples will help to make the point I am trying to get at. How does one explain madness that interferes with all the relatives' reproduction? Sociobiologists admit the possibility of aberrant nonadaptive behavior and simply say that such genes are constantly selected out and are constantly being introduced by new mutations.

What about saving a drowning stranger who obviously does not belong to one's race? Here reciprocal altruism can be invoked. If the morality of a population dictates saving strangers, then the more people that follow the morality, the greater the chance that one will someday benefit from a similar action. What about saving a stranger with no possibility of repayment? One could say these kinds of genes are selected out and that most individuals do not behave that way.

What about criminals (**cheaters** in the parlance of sociobiology) and the cuckoo bird? Any well-organized system has the potential for cheating, and a few individuals will inevitably be selected in this direction. If cheating is profitable enough, the cheating will spread until cheating ceases to be cheating because all individuals adopt the system.

Virtually any human behavior can be "explained" on the basis of sociobiological theory. With the addition of cheaters and mental illness to the concepts of reciprocal altruism and kin recognition, it becomes possible to see why sociobiology does not fulfill the definition of a theory. First and foremost, it is not falsifiable. Adherents cannot specify the conditions, which will force abandonment of the theory. The same is not true of gravity or organic evolution.

In terms of usefulness or heuristic value, it may work well for groups like insects that have very stereotyped behavioral repertoires. It is a fairly good description of ant reproduction and social behavior. For humans with an incomparably wider behavioral range, it may describe and predict some behaviors. The actual effects of behaviors like homosexuality are very different than the biological role that sociobiology must postulate for them. It may in fact "predict" the general phenomena of human kinship, but it cannot predict the variability of kinship systems that often transcend close biological relationships. Furthermore, sociobiology becomes strained to the point of breaking in trying to replicate and explain such human behaviors as language, art, music, and dozens of other human phenomena that have no comparable counterparts among nonhuman species.

Although sociobiology has some useful concepts, which we will consider later, especially those that relate to sexuality, it cannot account for the evolution of that uniquely human behavior known as culture. In many ways it is also a **reductionist** argument that allows us to conclude that DNA are bones' way of making more bones. Additionally, replacing the individual Darwinian organisms with sociobiological DNA does not increase our understanding of human evolution. In both Darwinian evolution and sociobiological evolution, behavior need not be volitional. The problem that this poses for the evolutionary study of human behavior is that human behavior seems to be uniquely characterized by a tremendous increase in volitional behavior. The great question is not just what is the relation between genes, behavior, and selection, but the specific factors that selected the malleable and labile set of capacities known as culture. Sociobiology inherently predicts that behaviors should have come under increasingly greater and greater genetic control as stereotyped behaviors. This is the opposite of what we mean when we speak of the so-called higher vertebrates.

Evolutionary Biology in Time and Space

Ernst Mayr introduced two extremely useful concepts for understanding the "meaning" of particular features of organisms, which also turn out to be extremely useful in understanding the behavior and biology of organisms as a whole. He has pointed out that biological phenomena can be examined with regard to whether a particular trait is teleonomic (Gk. *teleos*=end, distant+*nomic*=law, custom) or teleomatic (Gk. *matic*=to move). As used in this book, the definitions are somewhat different. Teleonomic traits are those whose function is reasonably obvious and well understood. For instance, we have little doubt about the function of eyes. It is therefore possible to make very accurate guesses about what selection pressures may have acted and still act on an organ that senses light and movement. We expect that nocturnal animals will be different from diurnal animals and that these differences will be evident in their structures. Teleomatic traits are another matter. Mayr regards teleomatic functions as being specific processes with specific end results resulting from physical laws. There are, in my opinion, some traits that do not have an obvious function but that may be genetically related to traits that do have important functions. **Pleiotropy** embraces a similar concept in that there may be a commonly shared genetic structure to two or more seemingly unrelated traits. Traits may be genetically linked, but one manifestation of the trait has no discernible function but varies in relation to a trait that is crucial to the survival of the organism. The theory of natural selection is so useful that relatively few traits seem to be teleomatic.

One such trait may be eye color. We know that in general there is a good correlation between people with dark skin, dark eyes, and dark hair. We are confident that dark skin with more active pigment is directly related to the need to protect the skin from strong ultraviolet light, which causes skin cancer. It may be that the gene or gene complex that controls for the adaptively important skin color is also responsible for hair and eye color. If the skin color is dark, so is the color of the hair and eyes. In other words, the color of hair and eyes may be of little importance, and they may just be genetic "baggage" that is neutral as far as natural selection is concerned. In the same way, many "unimportant" human behaviors may be of comparatively little adaptive significance. On the other hand, features may be viewed as insignificant when in fact they have an important but subtle function. The human appendix and tonsils are classic examples that anyone who has been to a family doctor is familiar with. In fact, both of these "unnecessary" organs may play a vital role in the body's defense mechanisms. The jury is still out. A popular pseudoscientific piece of folklore used to hold that "we only use ten percent of our brain." The research of the last decade has steadily increased our knowledge of the brain. It is now impossible to view 90 percent of the brain as teleomatic. Today we may understand the basic outlines of as much as 30 to 60 percent of the brain, depending on how one quantifies brain functions. It is safe to say that, as with other organs, the more we study a particular biological structure, the more we are impressed that very few of our body parts are teleomatic in their function. A timescale of billions of years predicts this conclusion.

In another example, it is clear that secondary sex characteristics and the shape traits, such as breast development, body shape, hair distribution, voice, and other external characteristics, are mediated by hormone levels that ultimately insure reproduction. It is less clear exactly how external appearances support the ultimate goal of sexual reproduction. It is possible that these sexually dimorphic characteristics are "evolutionary accidents" that are unimportant in the context of natural selection. Once again, the immense time depth of organic evolution suggests otherwise.

One of the primary objectives of paleobiologists (which paleontologists are) is to continually reorganize their findings into geological trees of descent or **phylogenies** (Gk. *phylo*=tribe, race+*genesis*=birth, development). In attempting to do this, they have devised certain concepts and rules for classifying extinct organisms in order to define the relationships between more closely related and less closely related groups.

Principles of Paleobiology

Lamarck and others once contended that organs could be lost through disuse. Some feel that this concept is hard to reconcile with evolutionary theory because selectively neutral traits are theoretically "not read" by natural selection. However, it is possible that traits that have no function still require energy for upkeep. The anthropologist Loring Brace has argued for a **probable mutation effect** in which once adaptive traits become neutral principally because of a change in the environment. He argues that there should be a "reduction" of traits that are now useless. Though this view has not found support from the majority of geneticists, it may offer some insights to certain enigmatic traits. It is reasonable to suppose that neutral traits that require energy and material for upkeep should be selected against. The maintenance of traits with no function should be maladaptive. Furthermore, although a trait is adaptively neutral, the trait (for example, an eye, the skin) still is subject to injury, which would be deleterious to the organism as a whole. This seems logical and is supported by evolutionary studies in general.

Some of what we know of modern cave fauna may possibly be interpreted in this "lack of light." In caves throughout the world, organisms that once dwelt on the surface have often been trapped for one reason or another in underground worlds where no light penetrates. After successive generations, many of these organisms lose their pigmentation and/or exhibit atrophied or vestigial visual systems, in which nonfunctioning eyes are a part. Theoretically, pigment and eyes should be adaptively neutral in a cave. At the very least, they become teleomatic. Yet, they may in fact illustrate the principle of **"use it or lose it."** One can reason that the maintenance of eyes in complete darkness becomes a liability because they can still be injured and thus cause harm to the organism as a whole. Thus, selection would favor individuals who reduced their risk of injury to the eyes. The loss of pigment is more difficult to understand but may be related to the loss of a visual feedback system that controls melanin, or melanogenesis, which is responsible for pigmentation. Changing color in response to environmental colors is a well-known phenomenon in many species as illustrated by chameleons. On the other hand, maintaining pigmentation requires energy, and energy spent on useless traits is maladaptive. One recent and so far unexplainable discovery has been that some deep-sea creatures maintain bright colors even in an essentially lightless environment. The maintenance may be an evolutionary happenstance or it may serve some function we do not yet understand.

In the chapters that follow, we will see that sorting out the adaptive, non-adaptive, and adaptively neutral traits and separating teleonomic traits from teleomatic traits is often difficult. This is especially true of animals like humans who display an open-ended number of behavioral traits. The greatest challenge to evolutionary psychologists is the task of relating perceived traits to the pressures of natural selection.

Classification and Taxonomy

Classification is the science of organizing groups or organisms according to their phenotypic similarities. The basic unit of sameness is actually based on the observation of extant or living creatures. In classifying any object with another, the criteria for classification is always a matter of opinion unless one can devise an iron-clad characteristic that either is or is not present. The concepts of such qualities as *large, furry, brown,* or *thin* are inherently subjective. To accomplish classification, paleontologists must rely on the science of taxonomy, which encompasses the principles and procedures or rules of classification. For observation of the biological world, scientists have agreed that the only category of classification that has an objective reality in nature is a species. All other groupings of animals are a matter of personal opinion (and, some would argue, prejudice).

Volumes have been written and will continue to be written about classification and taxonomy. As we have seen, cladistics is one approach to taxonomy that arose in our digital age. Whatever the method used, it is important that species receive formal, agreed-on names so that scientists will know exactly what is being referred to in discussions. The process of clarifying and naming is so important and complex that there exists an International Congress of Zoological Nomenclature that meets periodically to clarify and debate procedures and the validity of new taxa.

Since the publication of the last edition of Carolus Linnaeus's *Systema Naturae* in 1758, this work has been the agreed-on authority for applying a system of **binomial (two names) nomenclature** to taxa. Under this system, each species is assigned to a genus and given a generic name, and a species within that genus is given a specific name. The generic name is always capitalized; the species name never is. Furthermore, both words must be underlined (separately) or italicized. Thus, our nomenclatural designation is *Homo sapiens*. Under the strict rules of the system, neither *Homo* nor *sapiens* should be used alone. However, there are some exceptions and modifications. If, for instance, one is sure about the genus but unsure about which species, it is permissible to write *Homo sp.* or *Homo spp.* if the specimen may belong to a number of possible species or if one is referring to more than one species. The genus may also be abbreviated as *H. sapiens* if the genus has already been used in its full form previously in the same article.

The importance of knowing at least something of these rather tedious procedures is to understand the importance of bringing order to scientific discussions. In the past history of paleontology, the species under discussion have often been confused or lost in blizzards of lackadaisically applied names. This is especially true in paleoanthropology. Knowing these rules also helps students to gauge the professionalism of the science of which they are reading.

When organisms are classified, they are placed into a **hierarchy** of groups. Thus, species are grouped together in genera, and genera are grouped in subfamilies, which in turn make up a family. As we have noted previously, the use of the word *human* represents a value judgment. In fact, our immediate ancestors and ourselves are scientifically classified as members of the family **Hominidae.** From now on we shall refer to these creatures colloquially as hominids. The Hominidae have been variously divided by various workers in various ways. There is as yet no consensus about exactly how the Hominidae should be parceled out. In fact, there is no consensus about exactly whether the Hominidae should actually be included in the *Pongidae*, which contains the great apes. However, there is now a general consensus about how to recognize a hominid in terms of its morphology and at least some of the family's behavior. We will take this up in the next chapter.

The classification into various hierarchies is a matter of opinion. With the exception of the species, there is no objective definition of any taxonomic group. Most students of the fossil record, however, do feel that groups, no matter what size, should have certain common evolutionary characteristics. Groups should be **monophyletic,** that is they should all have a relatively recent common ancestor from which contemporary kin all descend. How long ago this ancestor should have lived is also a matter of opinion and debate. The determination of inclusion or exclusion should be based on homologies shared in common. Groups should reflect biological reality and have a common evolutionary history. Putting all winged animals in the same group would not reflect their evolutionary history. Putting all animals with backbones (that is, vertebrates) in the same group does reflect a common evolutionary history.

In evolutionary psychology, arguments about the evolutionary origins of human behavior depend heavily on paleontological arguments about the appearance and duration of traits. Paleontological arguments depend on knowing what legitimately constitutes a "natural" fossil group. Rules of procedure are crucial to scientific communication. When one scientist refers to the group known as "apes," it is important that another scientist has the same group in mind, otherwise chaos often ensues. In the modern biological world and in the past, only species have objective reality, and even this is frequently challenged by new observations.

The Species Concept in Time and Space

The species concept is vital to understanding evolution. Among living organisms, it can be readily tested through simple observation. However, as many students of animal behavior and morphology have noted, just because animals look physically different does not mean they cannot produce viable offspring. "Species" of cats or dogs are excellent artificial examples that can look very different and yet still produce viable offspring. However, in the wild, such profound differences are much more commonly indicative of separate species.

Usually, a reproductively isolated population shares certain characteristics that help identify it to others of its own kind and to other species. In other words, if members that produce viable offspring all share a certain shape of antler, there is a very good chance that when one encounters an animal in the field with the same kind of antler, it belongs to that species' population. However, one thorny problem introduced by this kind of standard is that every individual is different. Darwin recognized that all animals differ in their form. Individual variation is the part of Darwinian theory that necessarily leads to differential reproduction.

All organisms that are alive today and all organisms that have ever lived can be classified in a number of ways. There is no absolute consensual agreement about how to best classify life. However, there are significant guidelines. One of these is the concept of **grade.** By grade we mean the level of evolutionary complexity or anatomical organization that an organism exhibits. Although some biological anthropologists object to this kind of division, it is very useful for both organizing discussion of organic evolution and for recognizing the historical sequence of evolutionary development. This recognizes the somewhat prejudicial concept that some animals are more complex than others. The reason that students begin their introductory biology class with the dissection of an insect and then move on to a fish or frog and finally to mammals is that the course of instruction takes them through a sequence that mirrors the order in which grades of animals appeared on earth. Each dissection involves an animal that is more complex than the previous one. This approach recognizes, for instance, that you are much more complex than an earthworm. Groups of organisms, whether fossil or extant, can be organized in just such a way. Both anatomical structure and behavior can be divided by grade. Grades of mammals and primates (our own "order") are presented in the next chapter.

Another way in which the evolutionary history of living and extinct animals can be organized is according to their lineage. In the more easily recognizable case of **cladogenic evolution,** species diverge from their common ancestor and pursue different adaptations (separate ancestor–descendent relationships) (Figure 1.1). Each of the lines produced by cladogenesis is referred to as a **clade.** This term comes from the Latin word *clado,* which means to cut or split. Every birth potentially represents the founding of a new ancestral line as the result of branching. New species that arise by this method are examples of cladogenic evolution (literally birth through splitting).

There are a number of ways in which these splits come about. The ultimate reason for the appearance of a new species is that some members become reproductively isolated from others of their own kind. In order to mate, animals must occupy the same time–space coordinates. Species must be alive at the same time, or synchronic, to mate. Paleontologists by definition deal with the dimension of time. It is a truism that animals could not have mated with each other if they lived at different times.

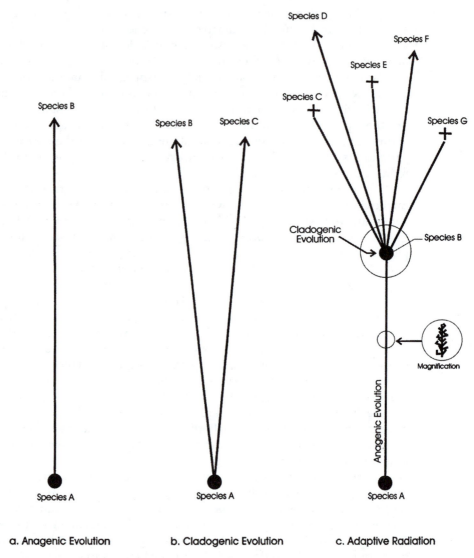

a. Anagenic Evolution   b. Cladogenic Evolution   c. Adaptive Radiation

FIGURE 1.1   *Diagrammatic representation of species evolution: a. anagenic evolution; b. cladogenic evolution; c. adaptive radiation.*

Identifying the beginning of a new species in the fossil record is difficult, if not impossible, because we are dealing with **paleospecies.** Paleospecies are groups of organisms represented by fossil collections (usually incomplete) that are judged to have been sufficiently morphologically distinct from other fossils to have been unable to produce viable offspring with other groups. Ultimately, the degree of morphological, geographical, and inferred behavioral differences to be used as a yardstick depends on analogies drawn from extant populations. A major problem is that the range of variation accommodated in one breeding isolate can vary tremendously from species to species. In the end, paleontologists must rely on their own judgments while making references to modern analogies.

The modern synthetic theory recognizes a number of different mechanisms of speciation. One of the mechanisms that Darwin recognized was geographic isolation. This very common isolating mechanism of speciation occurs when individuals cannot mate with each other because they do not occupy the same space. This eventually produces a new species. Like animals, geophysical environments are also constantly evolving. New rivers, oceans, mountains, deserts, or other changes in the landscape may act as barriers to animals that once freely mated with each other. Even without a change in the landscape, some members of a breeding population may simply migrate across distances that are too great for continued mating. Most paleontologists believe that changes in the landscape commonly lead to speciation. Changes in climate can also isolate potentially reproducing pairs. The Sahara Desert, for example, is a geologically recent climatological development that has come to form an almost impenetrable barrier between sub-Saharan species and those of Europe and Asia. Fossil faunas of Africa and Asia were once so common that they were placed in the same faunal realm. All these types of mechanisms are geographic isolating mechanisms. Furthermore, all of these arguments are frequently invoked in modern attempts to chart human origins.

When populations are isolated, mutations insure that the gene pool will accumulate new genotypes, and therefore phenotypes, that will diverge from the parent population in a process known as **genetic drift.** The fact that the new population is isolated increases the chance that selection pressures will also be different. As mentioned previously, this is why the study of island faunas had such a strong influence on Darwin and Wallace.

There are even more subtle ways in which a new species can begin. Populations that occupy the same habitats can also become reproductively isolated. When organisms become distributed in different geographic areas and eventually become reproductively isolated as new forms, it is referred to as **allopatric speciation** (Gk. *Allo*=other+*patria*=country). We refer to the geographic overlap of species as **sympatric** (Gk. *sym*=together+*patria*=country). Creatures may alter their behavior resulting in behavioral isolation. A classic example is an adaptive shift from being active in the day (diurnal) to becoming active only at night (nocturnal). Thus, although two individuals might live in the same place, they rarely encounter each other because one is always sleeping while the other is awake. In this case, the organisms occupy the same space coordinates but not the same temporal (time) coordinates. Speciation is, in this case, initiated by a change in behavior. Species may be sympatric or even living in the same tree, but one spends most of its time in the canopy while the other spends most of its time in the lower branches. Different species concentrate on different resources, which may require different behavioral repertoires.

Temporal isolating mechanisms refer to the fact that organisms must be alive at the same time to mate. Fossil species separated by sufficient amounts of geological time are referred to as **chronospecies.** The exact boundary of chronospecies is almost always debatable with regard to a concise upper and lower boundary in time. Chronospecies also arise when one species evolves into another through the straight-line process of **anagenic evolution** (Gk. *ana*=no+*genesis*=creation, birth) (Figure 1.1), literally no genesis. Anagenic evolution is really a misnomer in that new species are actually generated over time. Some clades may undergo their own rapid evolution, quickly passing from one chronospecies to another (for example, horses); others may remain relatively unchanged over time (for example, cockroaches). Like other aspects of classification, the decision as to what constitutes a chronospecies will always remain a matter of opinion.

Sometimes a different clade becomes a new grade. That is, sometimes behavioral and/or morphological change is so great that a lineage reaches a new level of evolutionary organization or complexity. Therefore, sometimes a new lineage is not only a new clade, but it is also a new grade that contrasts markedly with its ancestor. Suppose an essentially ratlike animal gives birth to four offspring. Through isolating mechanisms these four offspring turn out to be the beginning of four new clades that eventually become different enough from their parents and from each other to be designated as four species. Although they have changed just enough that they can no longer mate with each other, all of them live essentially like rats. That is, their way of "making a living" is essentially similar. In this scenario, let us further suppose that only three of the clades lived essentially like rats; that the fourth clade exhibited a major mutation that took the form of wings. In this case, the change is so great that we can say that the winged rat is so different that it represents a fundamentally different grade. In this case a different clade has become a different grade that has departed substantially from the rest of the members of its rat family. Although this fanciful example seems to be a good example of "who cares?," it is exactly just this kind of situation that seems to characterize our own evolution.

Ecology and Evolution

In the study of human evolution and the evolution of life in general, we are not only interested in finding out how and when a new species appeared but also why. We generally approach these questions in terms of ecological theory. **Ecology** (Gk. *ekos*=house) is the study of how an animal makes a living in the wild and of the relationship between organisms and their environments. Ecology entered the public consciousness in the 1960s, though it was often understood as being synonymous with conservation. In fact, ecology is a subfield of biology in its own right. Modern ecological studies examine the way in which living things utilize energy and interact with other organisms and the environment. A key concept in understanding organisms and living communities is the concept of niche (Fr. *niche*=shelf) or **econiche** (Gk. *eco*=house). These terms refer to the particular way in which an organism utilizes or exploits its environment. In ecological studies, the habitat is an organism's address and the niche is its occupation or means of survival.

All organisms are part of structured communities. Communities can be stable or at equilibrium or mature. Alternatively, they can be unstable or disturbed. Stable communities are organized into a **food chain.** At the base of the food chain are plants that are consumed by herbivores, who are themselves consumed by carnivores. In stable communities, the organisms being consumed always outnumber the consumers. Thus, there is more grass than buffalo and more buffalo than wolves. It is useful to think of this structure as a community or ecological pyramid.

Although some ecosystems remain virtually unchanged for long periods of time, none are static. One ecological rule of thumb is that empty niches eventually become filled. New niches also evolve out of old ones. A corollary of this idea is the often-quoted saying that "when something evolves, something else will evolve to eat it." As Darwin noted, individuals and species as a whole are always in competition for resources. When there is little or no competition for a necessary resource, animals will naturally move into an empty niche. This idea helps explain a number of aspects of the fossil record. Each of the grades of life on earth were produced as the result of adaptive radiations into unfilled niches. New forms are also produced as the result of competition. Every organism is almost automatically in competition with other organisms. Because natural selection will always select for the most fit, one organism will eventually be driven extinct or at least forced into another niche. This is the principle of competitive exclusion. This principle refers to the fact that two species cannot compete indefinitely for the exact same resource. Organisms that have occupied a particular niche for millions of years will eventually, through natural selection, get very good at housekeeping in that niche. The longer the occupant has been there, generally the more difficult it is to move it out.

However, a compromise solution is also possible that allows two different species to live in the same habitat if it is not exactly the same niche. This arrangement is called a **niche partition** or **niche division.** Although organisms cannot compete indefinitely for the exact same resource, they may divide the organisms they utilize in different ways. Among primates, for example, one primate may exploit the leaves of the same tree that produces fruit utilized by another species. Both niche partitioning and competitive exclusion have been implicated in hominid evolution. Modern ecological studies make it possible to reconstruct the past and relate it to the present. Lyell's principal of uniformitarianism allows students of the present to determine the environments of the past. The application of uniformitarianism to fossils also allows us to reconstruct past lifeways.

Recognizing Species in the Fossil Record

The adjustments that an animal makes over time in exploiting the resources of its environments are referred to as **adaptations.** Sometimes a single breeding pair will give rise to a number of offspring that radiate into a number of new environments and rapidly develop a number of new forms and ways of existence. When a fundamentally different form of existence evolves, we refer to it as an

adaptive shift. When this process occurs over a short period of time, it is referred to as an **adaptive radiation** (Figure 1.1). This rapid diversification of a species into many clades has happened countless times over the history of life on earth. This process continues today. Such "events" can be depicted in phylograms, which represent an explosion of new forms radiating out from a single ancestral node, which designates the point of origin in space and time of any clade. The past radiations of life on Earth are so distinctive that we name periods of the paleontological record for the kinds of animals that existed and flourished at a particular time. Over the course of the last several hundred million years, we can discern the Age of Reptiles (Mesozoic) followed by the Age of Mammals (Cenozoic). Both ages saw major adaptive radiations of terrestrial vertebrate communities.

As wondrous as these explosions of life are, the fate of most lineages in all adaptive radiations is the same. The new lineages eventually decrease through time, and most become extinct. Where there were once hundreds of separate clades, there will one day be only a few or none. In fact, most paleontologists believe that all the lineages may go extinct. However, all of the extant animals of the world are the descendants of at least one lineage that made it through successive radiations, or they would not be here.

For the paleontologist, the problem of identifying distinct species becomes, "How different do the structures or traits of an animal have to be before we conclude that they belong to a different species?" For the field biologist studying extant animals, the problem is easier. If the animals are observed to mate and produce viable offspring, then they belong to the same species. If they mate, but produce sterile offspring, they are not a single species. Any healthy modern human being can mate with any other human being of the opposite sex and produce viable offspring. Therefore, all humans belong to a single species regardless of the fact that different geographical groups differ from one another in appearance. The external physical characteristics tend to be a good guide to species recognition, although maturational and seasonal changes may sometimes confuse species identification. External characteristics are also very important in identifying species to one another. Such physical traits and behaviors not only identify **conspecifics** but also such important qualities as sex, age, dominance, and "mood."

Because paleontologists have no opportunity to observe the behavior and exterior characteristics of the ancient animal, they must essentially rely on Cuvier's law of correlation. Cuvier noticed that certain structures are associated with certain ecological adaptations. For instance, slicing knife-shaped teeth are found in carnivores, and grindstonelike teeth are found in herbivores. The paleontologist's problem arises from the necessity of looking at a fossil and determining how different it must be before declaring it representative of a unique species. For instance, how long can a thigh bone be before it is considered too long to belong to a species with a shorter thigh bone? There is no objective way to solve this problem. However, there are two general guidelines that guide paleontologists.

One approach that is commonly used is to refer to living species with a similar morphology. In other words, if I dig up the thigh bone of what is obviously a fossil monkey (something you can only know after years of studying monkey bones), I can compare the range of morphological variation to that of living monkeys. This is logical and straightforward, but a number of problems arise that have to do with the way that natural selection operates. It may be that past environments once tolerated a greater range of variation within reproductively isolated populations. Alternatively, it may be that the environmental selection pressures tolerated less variation.

Another guideline for helping to solve the problem of species recognition is the concept of diachronic proximity. Simply put, this means that the nearer in time a fossil animal is to its closest living relative, the more that the range of variation should be employed as a yardstick for determining the species of an animal. The problem is that there is no good evidence that ranges of variation evolve at a predictable and uniform rate. In fact, the tempo and mode of evolution is a fundamental debate that continues today in evolutionary studies. What is at issue in this debate is whether evolution typically proceeds in a slowly and smoothly changing mode or rather proceeds as a series of jumps between steps. The **punctuated equilibrium** (Figure 1.2) model holds that rapid morphological change (the vertical part of the step) is followed by periods of morphological and evolutionary stasis (the horizontal part of the step).

At the heart of the debate is a discussion about how Darwinian evolution proceeds in general. It is important to remember that all evolutionary biologists agree that organic evolution is a fact. Despite frequent press citations, no reputable scientist doubts that animals have changed over time. They do, however, argue about how change has proceeded. One group believes that evolution precedes in a steplike manner. This theory is referred to as punctuated equilibrium because it maintains that long periods of no evolutionary change (stasis or equilibrium) are punctuated by geologically rapid periods of dramatic change in which new species come into being. The opposing theory of **gradualism** suggests that the evolution of an organism is essentially a gradual process of slow and steady change. If one were to graph change over time (Figure 1.2), the contrast of the theoretical curves are obvious and have important implications when applied to the evolution of our own species. A third, though decidedly less volatile, school exists that thinks that evolution along a single lineage may sometimes proceed in a punctuated manner and at other times proceed in a gradualistic manner.

Another important development in the way we look at the evolution of a species comes directly out of the digital computer age. This approach, generally referred to as cladistics, maintains that any physical form (in this case fossils) can be classified in relation to any other two forms (fossils) with regard to whether it is closer to one of the other fossils. This process of course depends on what aspect of a form one is studying. If one is dealing with a feature such as bone length, then one of the three bones being considered will be closer to one or the other of the bones to which it is compared. The bone may theoretically be exactly halfway in length between the two reference specimens, but this rarely arises in the natural biological world. The concept that this approach uses is referred to as morphocline polarity. **Morphocline** refers to the fact that shapes show a gra-

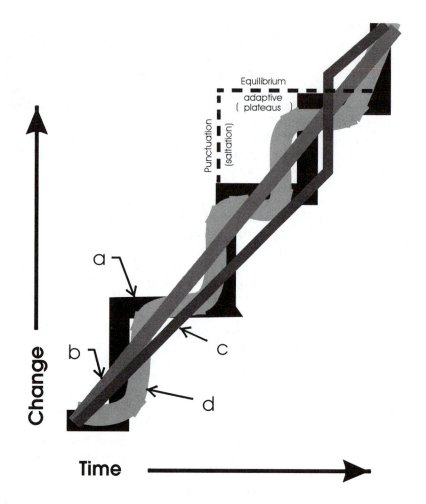

a. Punctuated Equilibrium Model
b. Gradualism Model
c. Intermediate or Combination Model
d. Sigmoid Model (less abrupt transitions)

dation of shapes or forms or development. Polarity refers to the idea that the degree of any particular development can be digitized as closer or farther from another parable specimen. Despite this simple and seemingly elegant theoretical development in classifying fossils, the fact remains that the approach has produced no consensus on how we should classify our fossil ancestors. So much of the debate centers around which characteristics are important. Which are teleonomic and which are teleomatic?

A geometric example once used by Franz Weidenreich (1873–1948) can be used to illustrate this point. If one is comparing a cube, a pyramid, and a sphere, how does one decide which the cube is closer to? Is the quality to be considered volume, sphericity, angularity, color, or some other characteristic? While this kind of philosophical argument seems far removed from illustrating the biological bases of human behavior, it is exactly these kinds of approaches that have been used in classifying and revealing our evolutionary history as it can be deduced from the "bones and stones" of our distant past. Deciding which aspects and traits of what we dig up is so difficult that no consensus about the way to proceed has yet been reached.

In the defense of cladistics, two very useful concepts have come into common usage, at least partially as the result of arguments about how to understand and reconstruct the phylogeny of organisms. As mentioned previously, the cladistic approach emphasizes that every birth is a cladogenic or splitting event. Cladogenesis refers to the process by which contemporary species split into at least one new lineage as the result of isolating mechanisms. Organisms that exhibit the original form of a trait are referred to as possessing **plesiomorphic** characters (Gk. *plesio*=near, everything+*morph*=form). The offspring that is more removed, or derived, from the original ancestral condition is termed **apomorphic** (Gk. *apo* =to remove). These long polysyllabic terms are actually quite useful in dealing with the task of clarifying the diversity of life.

Depending on the particular trait or system of traits that we are dealing with in a particular animal, it is possible to conclude that some parts are more like the original ancestral condition than others. Furthermore, it soon becomes clear that animals are a mosaic of different parts, some of which have changed greatly from the ancestral condition, and some of which have not. To establish the closeness of a relationship between two animals (either living or extinct), animals that share derived characters should be concluded to be more closely related to each other. If they merely share common characters that have been in existence for a long time, then there is no reason for viewing them as particularly closely related. An extension of this principle can be used to suggest that a single species or paleospecies is best defined on the bases of characters that it and only it possesses. Such characters are referred to as **autapomorphic** (Gk. *auto*=self; unique morphologies). Autapomorphic characters are unique characters that are only found in one species. Many taxonomists have argued that autapomorphic characters are the best way of recognizing extinct species. If no other animal living or dead possesses the character, then it was never passed on because the organism became extinct. We shall see that this concept has resulted in heated debates when it is applied to the hominid fossil record. Sometimes organisms share plesiomorphic characters in common. If this is the case, they are said to be **symplesiomorphic** (Gk. *sym*=together; shared original). Alternatively, two different species may also share a few unique characters that indicate they have a relatively recent common ancestry. Such shared unique characters are referred to as **synapomorphic** (Gk.

syn=to join) characters. Whether a character is apomorphic or plesiomorphic depends on what the character trait is being compared to. Symplesiomorphy and apomorphy are always relative to other traits.

For example, with regard to number of digits, all vertebrates are symplesiomorphic in the number of digits they originally possessed. That number is five. Many vertebrates have, however, lost digits and are thus farther removed from the original ancestral condition. The single-toed modern horse is apomorphic with regard to the number of digits, which has been reduced to one. The fact that horses share this character with rhinoceroses, tapirs, and some other extinct relatives indicates a common past ancestor. The fact that all birds have wings constructed of arm bones is also an apomorphic character that unites all birds and sets them apart from all mammals who still retain the symplesiomorphic state of the ancestral vertebrate ancestry that gave rise to both groups. By making these comparisons in this framework, we are able to develop taxonomic groupings that fit evolutionary history.

In fact, no organism, with the possible exception of the very first one, is all plesiomorphic or all apomorphic in their traits. Organisms are an amalgamation of plesiomorphic and apomorphic traits. This phenomenon is embodied in the concept of **mosaic evolution.** All animals are a combination of traits that have evolved at different rates in relation to different selection pressures. Humans are no exception. Understanding modern humans and their phylogenetic history is to a large extent a process of sorting out plesiomorphic and apomorphic traits of our species. Our continued possession of five digits is plesiomorphic, while our large brains are apomorphic. In fact, our brains are so uniquely large that we may regard it as an autapomorphic character. The framework of mosaic evolution is also very useful for making sense of the archaeological residues that hominids have left over the course of the last four million years. Both physically and behaviorally, humans manifest ancient and new traits that interact and influence each other in a complex fashion. The terms and concepts of evolutionary biology provide a direct means of communication for students of the human animal.

One difficult and not always reliable approach to understanding human behavior involves the assumption that the older a particular behavior is the greater the chance that genetic and physical complexes will have evolved to support the consistent performance of that behavior. Behaviors or physical traits that are common to two or more species are frequently present because the animals share a relatively recent evolutionary past. It is therefore tempting to assume that the more widespread a particular trait is the older it is. **Parallel evolution,** in which closely related animals develop along similar lines, and convergent evolution, in which distantly related species develop similar problems in response to similar ecological problems, can be differentiated by comparing homologous structures, which have a common evolutionary origin. Homologous structures are those structures that no matter how much they have changed and no matter how different their functions may be are formed from the same ontological and embryonic sources. In other words, they have a common ancestral origin indicating parallel evolution. Analogous structures are those that serve similar functions but are actually derived from unrelated parts of the organism and indicate convergent evolution. The classic example is that of bat and bird wings. The wing of the bat develops from finger bones, while the wing of a bird develops from arm bones. Both structures have converged on similar morphologies to solve the problem of flying. The bat and bird wings are examples of convergent evolution. Conversely, a horse's hoof with its distinctive morphology and function is homologous to the digits or toes of other mammals. It is an example of divergent evolution because it has diverged away from the ancestral condition of all mammals, which originally had five digits on each limb. Other homologies include feathers and scales, all of which have the same embryological origin.

Parallel evolution cannot only involve separate traits but also separate species and even separate orders. The classic example is that of Australian marsupial mammals and non-Australian placental mammals. In this case, similar econiches have produced similar appearances and adaptations. For instance, the natural fauna of Australia includes animals that closely resemble cats, dogs, and mice in their appearance and ecological adaptations. There are herbivores and carnivores. Once again, organisms respond to similar problems in similar ways. Although marsupials and placentals have a common ancestor, the common link is far more ancient than the common ancestor of any placental feline and canine.

One danger of the assumption that widespread common behaviors indicate a great antiquity or common evolutionary past can be appreciated in what I call the **"Coca-Cola principle,"** which implies that this soft drink has a long history in most human cultures because it is so widely spread. In fact, proponents of "punctuated cultural evolution" can point to a number of features that have been rapidly disseminated through a process of **diffusion,** the spread of one behavior or idea through intercultural contact. **Independent invention** may also account for similarities in culture, but, as with the differences between convergent and parallel biological evolution, a careful survey of detailed difference will usually establish which is which.

Paleoanthropology

Much of the data that this book deals with is drawn from the science of paleoanthropology. Paleoanthropology is a subfield of anthropology. Perhaps more than any other subfield of anthropology, paleoanthropology is interdisciplinary and multidisciplinary. Though each paleoanthropologist has his or her own definition of the field, most would agree on the following: Paleoanthropology integrates human paleontology and **archaeology** to reconstruct the origin and evolution (including behavior) of the extinct and extant members of the human family.

Like all other paleontologists, human paleontologists study fossils. Fossils are any trace left of organisms. Most fossils are actually casts of a part or parts of animals or plants that have survived because the organic material has been replaced by nonorganic minerals. Some fossils, such as coal, still contain organic material. The fossils that paleoanthropologists study are usually bones of extinct members of our biological family the Hominidae. The first hominids appeared in the fossil record at least 4.5 million years ago. Subsequently, a number of species evolved. All but one species, ourselves, are now extinct. In addition to establishing the age and phylogenetic relations of these extinct forms, paleoanthropologists are interested in the evolution of behavior and past ecological adaptations.

Paleoanthropology is one of the most controversial fields of natural science for a number of reasons. One of the most important reasons lies with the nature of the material being studied. Fossil hominid bones are relatively rare in comparison with other mammals. They are more often than not broken, distorted, and incomplete. Although it is usually experienced anatomists that study the fossils, scientists with equally extensive training and experience can examine the same bone and come up with very different conclusions. That means that all measurements, descriptions, and especially conclusions are subjective. Inevitably, disputes about competence arise. These have led to very personal and very public displays of disagreements. Nonhominid paleontologists have the same kinds of disagreements, but they are not dealing with something as emotionally charged as the search for our ancient ancestors. Today, all over the world, people care passionately about their pasts and their origins. Paleoanthropological arguments are frequently followed by the press, where eureka-type announcements are much more interesting than esoteric accounts of fragmentary bones. One other very important factor in paleoanthropological disputes is that the discoverers of fossils frequently have not been trained adequately. To a great extent, finding fossils is still dependent on luck.

Archaeology is also subject to the same kinds of disputes. Laypeople often assume that people who recover bones from excavation sites are archaeologists. In fact, archaeology (literally the "study of old things") is concerned with the study of **artifacts.** Artifacts can be defined as any artificial trace of human behavior. Tools are much more difficult to define. One working definition is that they were artifacts that were fashioned with a purpose in mind or utilized to perform a certain task or tasks. The artifacts need not have been made intentionally. In fact, most Stone Age archaeological sites are composed of discarded unused materials.

The context of archaeological finds is just as important as the finds themselves. The associated animals (if any) provide important clues to paleoenvironments and paleoclimates, which in turn allow us to speculate on paleobehavior and the selection pressures that produced it. In modern archaeology, few aspects of a find are left unstudied. In archaeology, finds can become meaningless without considering them in relation to a number of materials that tell us about the past.

The Social Sciences and Evolutionary Psychology

It is extremely difficult to precisely define the boundaries between sociocultural anthropology, sociology, and psychology. All of these fields study the minds and behaviors of people, have multiple subfields, and are directly relevant to understanding human behavior. All have a history of borrowing from each other. One facile and slightly sarcastic characterization of the difference between sociology and anthropology is that sociologists study people who wear clothes and anthropologists study people who do not. Sociocultural anthropologists have historically studied non-Western cultures, while sociologists have tended to study aspects of Western society. All social scientists, including psychologists, economists, historians, and political scientists, tend to emphasize learned behavior. The emphasis of sociology has been on societies that are at least somewhat familiar to Westerners, while anthropology has concentrated on the exotic (from a Western perspective).

More than any other organism, humans have evolved an extreme dependency on the learned, shared kind of behaviors and perspectives, which we refer to as **culture.** The main characteristic of culture that distinguishes it from any other activity is that it is strictly learned and shared with others. One of the fundamental challenges in trying to puzzle out the biological bases of human behavior is the separation of those things that are learned from those behaviors that are innate. At the same time, we must be interested in the kinds of things that are learned. It was an awkward scientist who said, "God is in the details." For students of human cultural behavior, "the details are in the gods." It is the comparison of broad classes of behavior that are needed to successfully define what it is that humans have in common.

One way of approaching this problem is through **comparative ethnography** (the documentation of how cultures and individuals behave), which isolates **cultural universals** or a **psychic unity** found in every culture, regardless of whether they have ever had a chance to share ideas and perspectives. The first step in isolating biologically based behaviors and thus understanding innate human behaviors is the construction of a **species-specific ethogram** from cultural universals. This concept was established by classical ethologists such as Konrad Lorenz (1903–1989) who popularized the idea of a species-specific ethogram, which is a picture of the typical behavior of a particular set of behaviors.

Quantification of behavior has been increasingly emphasized in studies of animal and human behavior. The mathematical operations involved in social science statistics are for the most part simple when viewed from the perspective of a mathematician. More important, most statistical results are easily manipulated or selectively cited. Like any other conclusion based on numerical trends, the conclusions drawn from them are only as reliable as the raw data. Unfortunately, the reliability of the data itself is filtered through the culture of the person recording the data. There is a "quantum effect" in the firsthand recording of human behavioral data in that the observation of the behavior is always altered by the presence of the observer. Good behavioral scientists take great pains to minimize this effect, but inevitably, an anthropologist with a notebook in the middle of a village influences the village itself.

Conclusions are held more likely to be true if the original results can be replicated in a number of independent instances. Conversely, there is an interesting trend in the social sciences (and other branches of observational science) to study anomaly in detail. In behavioral sciences (especially anthropology), there has been an interesting tendency to study **the exception that proves the rule.** This is also true in psychology where unusual behaviors receive much attention and publicity.

Many of the peoples and cultures that the general public is aware of have come to their attention because they are unusual when viewed against more usual human behavior. To paraphrase anthropologist Marvin Harris, the anthropologist makes the unusual usual and the usual unusual. The unusual naturally attracts attention among primate groups. Harris extends his observation one step further and suggests that human groups tend to take what is unusual or unique about themselves and define it as "good." Conversely, what is unusual or different about another "outgroup" is often classified as "bad." In attempting to understand the behavior of our species as a whole, "fascinating" information about other peoples and cultures can be a red herring that distracts us from the prevailing condition of humanity as a whole.

In anthropology, the study of now famous groups such as the Tasaday, Ik, Dogong, Trobriand Islanders, Tierra del Fuegans, and even Eskimos and Samoans have served to spotlight by contrast what is "normal" for most of the population of the planet. Anomalies are extremely useful in helping us to define what is "normal" for our species. However, regarding highly anomalous groups as indicative of potentially widespread normative behavior is misleading when it is used to suggest that these behaviors could easily come to characterize large segments of humanity.

On the other hand, the unusual can help us to define the extreme limits of human behavior. It is in this capacity that anomaly helps us to take the first steps in defining orthodox behavior. Perhaps the greatest difficulty emanates from the scientist's own ethnocentricity. Theoretically, the only way to avoid ethnocentric biases is to become a part of that culture. Cultural anthropologists are routinely told to **deconstruct** their own cultural biases. If one were truly able to totally abandon one's own culture, reporting back to the "home office" would be impossible.

Another perhaps even larger problem is that most people are not very familiar with a number of cultures. Anthropologists devote their scholarly activities to a handful of cultures at most. American students in general do not speak another language fluently and usually have impressions of other cultures that are based on brief vacations, readings, and the media. The United States presents a unique cultural situation in both its geographic and cultural isolation. Though composed of subgroups from around the planet, even ethnically distinct minorities become attenuated and "watered down" after only a few generations. For most Americans, foreign cultures are abstractions developed from television. "Common sense" requires common knowledge and experience. Even with the influence of communications, most of what Americans know about foreign cultures is the unusual. Even on scholarly television channels, it is much easier to find a program on head hunters than one dealing with the details of daily life of a rural village in Peru.

The concept of **predisposition** refers to the tendency of an organism to behave a certain way in response to a particular situation. In the same situation, behavioral responses will vary, but in each instance, the behavior is recognizable as essentially the same. For instance, if you put fifty people on a desert island, they will form smaller social units and subdivide the original population. If one could perform this experiment several times, after enough trials one population might fail to subdivide, but the vast majority of times the population would follow a predisposition for humans to form alliances and groups.

Predisposition can be strongly contrasted with the concept of **canalization.** Canalization refers to a predetermined unfolding or inevitable appearance of particular traits, be they behavioral or anatomical. The contrast between these two phenomena can be illustrated by pointing out that healthy humans inevitably develop five digits on each of their four appendages. These develop as a response to predetermined and highly canalized genetic instructions. In normal humans, the learning of a language is also highly canalized. From an evolutionary point of view, one would expect the canalized behavior to be very important either in the past or in the present. Human language ability is highly canalized. Learning to write is not canalized, but learning to communicate via a number of modes of expression is.

A Brief History of the Nature–Nurture Debate

The history of sociocultural anthropology and psychology in this century has behaved like a pendulum swinging back and forth between the nature–nurture question. This phenomenon can be briefly sketched by outlining the concerns and beliefs of leading thinkers in anthropology and psychology. In almost every case, those that had significant influence on thinking about human behavior were reacting to the social and political concerns of the eras in which they worked. Today, most reasonable researchers admit that both nature and nurture are important. However, the influences of the earlier part of the twentieth century and even those from the end of the nineteenth century are still with us. The swings in behavior seem to have proceeded almost at generational intervals. In the majority of instances, leading proponents of the day were reacting to antithetical social, political, and scientific doctrines, some of which were blatantly racist.

By the end of the nineteenth century, the dominant influence of scientific thinking about human behavior, cultures and individuals still centered on Darwinian evolution, especially as it was embodied (and often misunderstood) in natural selection theory. Natural selection became almost instantly both a blueprint for socioeconomic strategies and an apology for colonial rule. Darwinian fitness was mistranslated into "survival of the fittest." In this same doctrine, both communists and capitalists found predictive and explanatory power. Karl Marx (1818–1883) and his numerous disciples adopted the inevitable stages of social evolution that this doctrine seemed to imply. European colonialism found defense in "white man's burden." L. H. Morgan's (1818–1881) belief was that all societies pass through the same stages of evolutionary complexity. One clear implication of this theory was that some societies were more "advanced" than others. In Germany, anatomical and evolutionary studies were expanding at a phenomenal rate, as was German nationalism.

In North America in the 1920s and 1930s, the principles of genetics were being organized. The biological sciences in general were beginning to act like hard sciences. By the 1930s, Alfred Binet's (1857–1911) intelligence test had crossed the Atlantic where an idiosyncratic form of it was put to use by the U.S. government to evaluate army recruits and new immigrants. The result was an ongoing discussion about the "moronization" of America. The fusion between genetics and intelligence tests produced a particularly strong reaction in the United States. Previously, phrenology, the study of external features of the head (bumps on the braincase, prominence of the chin, shape of the face, and so on), had linked intelligence and morality. Genetics began to take on the character of a nomothetic pronouncement. In Nazi Germany, the Aryan myth not only had the public support of German scientists but also the tacit support of other European scientists.

Freud's contentious theory of the mind was highly influential and relied heavily on a view of the human mind as biologically dysfunctional. Maturation was the life-long process of reconciling the inescapable conflicts that one was born with. In parallel to Freud and his students were the behaviorists that supported the idea of the infinitely malleable mind.

It was out of a similar tradition of behaviorism that American anthropology evolved. **Franz Boas** (1858–1942), one of the founders of American cultural anthropology, reacted strongly to what he saw as a world heading toward reductionist and racist conclusions. Boas advocated the collection of facts in the field over philosophical theories developed in the armchair of the library. It was first necessary to develop a database of the characteristics of different groups before going on to generate "laws" about human behavior and culture. Though Boas became associated with **historical particularism,** the development of detailed case studies, the next generation of his students went on to classify cultures according to patterns (for example, Ruth Benedict, 1887–1948) or maintain that particular cultural manifestations had very little to do with underlying biology (for example, Margaret Mead, 1901–1978). The reaction to biological determinism was very American in that it placed an extreme emphasis on experience and environment as the major determinant of human behavior. Both Benedict and Mead saw vast differences between different cultures that could be accounted for only by environmental and idiosyncratic differences. Later, Julian Steward's (1902–1972) concept emphasis on **cultural ecology** and Leslie White's (1900–1975) emphasis on **cultural materialism** both heralded the path that American anthropology has only recently begun to depart from.

The collection of sociocultural "facts" that the Boasian school emphasized continues to be the source of a number of problems, not the least of which is the decision of which facts to collect. Today, few students would attempt to reach conclusions that are based on only a few years of fieldwork. The goals of any particular study are literally as varied as the number of researchers designing projects.

Today, there are virtually no anthropologists who doubt that the brain contains **"deep structures"** that are supported and made possible by the anatomy and physiology of the brain. However, as was true with Mead's work, questions of biologically determined categories are of little interest to most sociocultural anthropologists. Unlike psychology, which was virtually forced to abandon supraorganic explanations, anthropology still has not come to grips with the recent achievements of **biopsychology.** This tradition grew directly out of clinical studies that opened up a plethora of conditions that are simply inexplicable on the basis of experience alone. Modern sociocultural anthropology has continued on a trajectory that has narrowed the concerns of the discipline to a consideration of life experience only. Biological events in an individual's life or in a culture's accumulation of facts are treated only as far as they relate to the presumedly programmable parts of the mind. Even with the recent advent of medical anthropology and ethnopharmacology, two subjects that seem to demand dealing extensively with the biology of the brain, it is the learned social contexts that are emphasized.

A few important difficulties need to be underscored when assessing any reports on human behavior. One important point is what can be unfairly called the Margaret Mead principal. This refers to the fact that anthropologists can be misled into producing inaccurate reports for a number of reasons. One prevalent reason is that people often do not do what they say they do for a variety of reasons. Derek Freeman's follow-up work on Mead's fieldwork suggests that this is what happened when she studied the Samoans.

When Mead returned from her studies in Samoa, she decided that teenagers in that society were not subject to the same stresses as teenagers in the United States. She maintained that the frequency of sexual problems, intergenerational conflicts, and crime in general was much lower in Samoa because they grew up in a cultural context that essentially curtailed these kinds of behaviors. Decades later, and unfortunately after her death, Derek Freeman, who has spent much more time studying the Samoan culture, found that this culture exhibited all the social ills that are found in Western culture. Freeman argued that Mead got it wrong for a number of reasons, not the least of which was that she uncritically accepted most of what she was told. He also strongly implied that she did not speak the language very well and that she did not spend enough time with the people she was studying.

In fact, Freeman's field methods were exactly the kind of work that Boas had originally advocated. When Mead actually went into the field, the idea was so novel that no one had thought about how much time was required or how fluent one should be in the language. As a former physical chemist, Boas suspected that there must be laws that govern the structure of cultures. One of these laws, of course, was historical particularism. Differences in cultural histories were potentially and perhaps de facto unlimited; therefore the nature and variety of cultures must be unlimited. The belief that a real "Shangrila" is possible became very American.

A Methodology for Evolutionary Psychology

Most students of evolutionary psychology will be understandably challenged and at times frustrated by the diverse number of traditionally distinct disciplines distinctions that this new field must rely on. The integrating framework of evolutionary psychology as a whole is natural selection theory. Therefore, a detailed understanding of the development of Darwinian evolution is essential to an understanding of human behavior. Geology, biology, theology, and genetics contributed to the formative components of the modern synthetic theory of evolution. Although disagreement still exists about whether natural selection acts primarily at the genetic, individual, or species level, it is now universally accepted by all scientists that organic evolution is a fact.

The methodologies outlined below have as their objective the heuristic exploration of the relationship between evolution and human behavior. All of them no doubt will have to be corrected as this fledgling field expands. With this in mind, I suggest the following as the assumptions and approaches that evolutionary psychologists and students of human evolution in general bring to the field:

1. Humans and other organisms have innate behaviors and predispositions that are part of their species-specific ethogram evolved by means of natural selection. It is impossible to believe that humans have no innate biologically based behaviors. By definition, innate behaviors are genetically based, but some behaviors are predispositions that are modified by environment and experience. Some behaviors are all-or-nothing phenomena. Bipedalism, language, and tool dependency are ancient universal features of the human species. At the same time, reliance on these behaviors and many more behaviors are distributed along cultural and individual continua. Other features of human behavior are also universal, though they may be less ancient and less canalized.

2. Comparisons of interspecific behaviors become more or less valid depending on the phylogenetic and genetic relatedness of different species. For instance, chimpanzee behavior is the most relevant primate example with which to compare human behavior. At the same time, ecologically similar adaptations of less closely related animals are also relevant and always need to be considered, especially if they are terrestrial vertebrates from Africa. While cockroaches and starfish may tell us about the commonality of life, they offer little information about the details of higher primate behavior. Comparable **homoplasy** (Lat. *Homo*=same+*plasticus*=molding) is the basis of valid and useful interspecific comparisons. Homoplastic systems are homologous systems that change along the same parameters of selection and are the only meaningful means of reconstructing evolutionary histories. In other words, mating and other social systems should contain the same detailed elements of comparison.

3. The evolutionary process is both additive and transformational. Organisms are a collection and integration of both ancient and recent adaptations that influence and even circumscribe behaviors. Mosaic evolution is a key concept in understanding human behavior. All anatomical functions and behaviors are part of a feedback loop in which change in one system may influence another.

4. There is an anatomically based system of cultural and individual thoughts that can be characterized as cultural universals. The separation between mind

and brain is heuristically useless and historically troublesome. Humans have many types of thoughts, but they are all mediated by electrochemical processes housed in anatomical structures. The brain–body dichotomy is also increasingly harder to defend in light of the now overwhelming evidence that both are continually involved in constant interaction.

5. The brain has many stages or windows for the acquisition of new knowledge. Most of these windows are closely tied to the process of maturation, but cultural and individual experience can both reopen and close windows. In general, there are fewer windows after the attainment of adulthood. Brains begin as softwired hardware with redundant circuits that mature into hardwired mechanisms that are more resistant to change.

6. Exceptions prove rules. When a behavior is discovered that contrasts with most other categories of the same behavior, it should be taken as rare or possibly fraudulent. Unfortunately, much of the unusual human behavior that appears in popular literature is exaggerated or imprecisely reported.

Summary

The integration of historical sciences concerned with the past and paleoanthropology (archaeology and paleontology) with modern behavioral sciences (sociocultural anthropology, psychology, ethology, and sociology) allows us to assess the antiquity and nature of behaviors that characterize species. Natural selection theory allows us to understand the mechanisms by which certain behaviors have arisen. Genetics and sociobiology have brought our understanding of species-specific behavior to a molecular level. Sociobiology has advocated the idea that all behaviors can be best understood at the level of DNA. However, it is still difficult to decide how much of a particular behavior is canalized and how much of a behavior is simply the result of tendencies, predispositions, and experience.

If a behavior can be reasonably thought to be ancient in a particular species lineage, then logically there is a greater chance that it has been genetically reinforced through the selection of genotypes, which insure that the behavior is repeated in particular ecological contexts. Geologically recent behaviors may also be highly canalized, but these are logically expected to be far outnumbered by adaptive traits that have accumulated over millions or even billions of years. Nonetheless, certain mutations may rapidly fix themselves in the behavioral repertoires of a species, especially if the new behavior greatly increases an individual's inclusive or Darwinian fitness.

The new but rapidly emerging discipline of evolutionary psychology is tied directly to natural selection. The brains and nervous systems of organisms have evolved to deal with environmental factors that are crucial to their survival. Conversely, organisms do not pay attention to environmental influences and sensory inputs that are less important. Some selection pressures have been in effect for so long that organisms have canalized mechanisms to the point that they are what humans refer to as unconscious or autonomic. Over the billions of years of organic evolution on Earth, important and ancient behaviors have become genetically circumscribed. Other behaviors are relatively new but no less important in the context of natural selection. Organisms, especially animals, are a combination of ancient and recent behaviors that are supported and made possible by their anatomy. Determining the degree to which behaviors are supported and canalized in humans is the key to predicting human behavior.

One of the most important clues to predispositions in human beings is the determination of whether such behaviors are universal. Theoretically, certain universal behaviors may represent the development of similar cultural solutions to similar ecological problems. Indeed, the details of intercultural variation can and do differ tremendously. However, the function and broad structure of many human behaviors remain similar throughout the incredibly large structure of individual and social behavior. To understand modern human behavior, it is imperative to comprehend the evolutionary sequence and antiquity of behaviors as they can be discerned from the paleontological and archaeological record. These are the subjects of the next chapter.

QUESTIONS FOR REVIEW

1. What is the nature versus nurture debate?

2. How has thinking about human behavior been influenced by both biological and the social sciences?

3. What are the various components of the theory of natural selection?

4. What is the difference between canalization and predisposition?

5. How does sociobiological theory differ from classic Darwinian theory?

6. What are the basic patterns that scientists have discerned in the fossil record? What are the major controversies?

7. What is the difference between archaeology and paleontology? What is paleoanthropology?

8. Which of the traditional sciences are relevant to evolutionary psychology?

MIND AND BODY EXPERIMENTS

1. Make a list of selection pressures that are at work in your daily life.

2. Draw a diagram of the last three generations of your family. Make a note of nodes and radiations. Do some clades look more like their parents than others?

3. Ask your friends and family members what they think of evolution. Record their reactions.

SUGGESTED READINGS

Boas, F. 1966. *Race, Language, and Culture*. New York: The Free Press.

Darwin, C. 1936. *The Descent of Man and Selection in Relation to Sex*. New York: Random House. (Original work published 1871.)

Darwin, C. 1950. *On the Origin of Species by Means of Natural Selection*. London: Watts. (Original work published 1859.)

Dawkins, R. 1976. *The Selfish Gene*. Oxford: Oxford University Press.

Dawkins, R. 1982. *The Extended Phenotype: The Gene as the Unit of Selection*. Oxford and San Francisco: W. H. Freeman.

Eibl-Eibesfeldt, I. 1975. *Ethology: The Biology of Behavior*. (2nd ed.). New York: Holt, Rinehart and Winston.

Eiseley, L. 1958. *Darwin's Century: Evolution and the Men Who Discovered It*. New York: Doubleday.

Freeman, D. 1983. *Margaret Mead and Samoa: The Making and Unmaking of an Anthropological Myth*. Cambridge, MA: Harvard University Press.

Gould, S. J. 1980. Sociobiology and human nature: A postpanglossian vision. In *Sociobiology Examined*, A. Montagu (ed.) (pp. 283–290). New York and London: Oxford University Press.

Lorenz, K. 1965. *Evolution and Modification of Behavior*. Chicago: University of Chicago Press.

Lorenz, K. 1971. *Studies in Animal and Human Behavior* (Vol. II). Cambridge, MA: Harvard University Press.

Mayr, Ernst. 1982. *The Growth of Biological Thought: Diversity, Evolution and Inheritance*. Cambridge, MA: The Belknap Press of Harvard University Press.

Mead, Margaret. 1928. *Coming of Age in Samoa*. New York: Morrow.

Trigger, Bruce G. 1989. *A History of Archaeological Thought*. Cambridge: Cambridge University Press.

Wilson, E. O. 1975a. *Sociobiology: The New Synthesis*. Cambridge, MA: The Belknap Press of Harvard University Press.

Wilson, E. O. 1975b. Some central problems of sociobiology. *Social Science Information* 14: 5–18.

2 Mammals and Nonhuman Primates

Here in both space and time we seem to be brought somewhat nearer to that great fact—that mystery of mysteries—the first appearance of new beings.

—Charles Darwin

Paleontologists are scientists that try to apply modern biological concepts to fossil organisms. As noted in Chapter 1, uniformitarianism allows us to do this. At the same time, the concept of evolution instructs us that life is always changing, regardless of similarities between extant and extinct forms. There are no living fossils despite how much the popular press likes this simple concept. However, there are organisms that appear to have changed relatively little over the course of millions or even hundreds of millions of years. So-called lung fish and cockroaches are noted examples. Comparative anatomy convinces us that for whatever reason, these organisms have remained relatively stable in their morphology. Humans are primates, and by studying the fossil record and modern behavior of other primates, we gain significant insight into ourselves.

When trying to reconstruct paleobehavior, the problem is much more difficult. Usually, the only thing we have to go on is the identification of teleonomic morphologies, whose functions we know because of morphology or modern behavioral analogs. The problem is especially difficult with human ancestors. As we shall see, we know that our lineage arose from essentially apelike creatures. When we find a member of our family that is morphologically and temporarily between ourselves and fossil apes, do we apply human standards or ape standards and analogs of behaviors? Most would agree that if the specimen is closer to an ape in morphology, it may also be closer to an ape in behavior. In fact, at what stage we should refer to an ancestor as human is the subject of heated debate. Many times in the history of human paleontology, we have fallen into the trap of equating humanlike morphology with humanlike behavior.

Geology and Evolution

The history of life is one of both supplantation and colonization. Yet frequently, one class or organism must arrive first to prepare the way "for those who will come after." Bacteria are usually first with their ability to turn rock into soil, followed by plants and then animals. This is indeed the succession in which life evolved on Earth. Many of the great radiations of life have involved the colonization of new worlds. Because the continents are constantly being "recycled" through the actions of drift, collision, subduction, erosion, and deposition, as stipulated by our knowledge of **plate tectonics,** new environments are constantly being created and destroyed. As environments change, old organisms become extinct and new ones appear. On the bases of current understanding of geological history, it seems that there were distinct eras of extinctions and adaptive radiations.

The common pattern of adaptive radiations does not strictly adhere to human common sense. Organisms frequently appear and "hang around" for long periods before they radiate. This is probably because they require a declining ecosystem with sufficient vacant niches or because no unoccupied barren land is accessible. Examples of this process include island ecosystems such as Australia and Madagascar. On these islands, a few colonizing animals diversified into a number of species that filled empty niches. When species radiate into an empty land, they are unconstrained by the competition from indigenous forms. They are free to develop their own pyramid without reference to others. When interpreting the fossil evidence for such radiations, it is important to remember that when a form first appears in the fossil record, it must actually be older than its first appearance because the chances of finding the very first form to fossilize are extremely low. Similarly, the last appearance of a fossil is likely to reveal surviving or relict populations.

In addition to graphically representing adaptive radiations with phylograms, we can also represent them with histograms, which depict numbers of individuals or species with reference to time (Figure 2.1). When species are "doing well," their numbers multiply—the histograms are "fat." Many of the fat sections also represent large populations and widespread geographic distributions. When the histograms get thin and begin to "pinch out," they are representing times of decreased numbers and restricted distribution in space. These periods are referred to as **bottlenecks** for their obvious resemblance to a bottle. If the bottleneck pinches out altogether, extinction has occurred. If the bottle neck suddenly flattens out completely or becomes truncated, **mass extinction** has occurred. Bottlenecks must represent periods of increased selection pressures. Flattop bottles indicate that the selection pressure was so strong or so fast that the species had no time to evolve solutions. Histograms describe cultures and history just as well as organic evolution. After narrowing, if the bottleneck increases again and gets wider, it represents a new radiation in which one of the types of organisms "made it through" and then radiated.

Phylogenies constructed on paper are representations of fossils embedded in rock at scattered localities. Rarely is the record complete over any significant period of geologic time. In the field, there are no lines to connect the dots representing fossil assemblages, as they are more scientifically known. Furthermore, paleontologists frequently encounter the problem that first set Georges Cuvier and Jean Lamarck at each other. There are strata between fossil-bearing strata

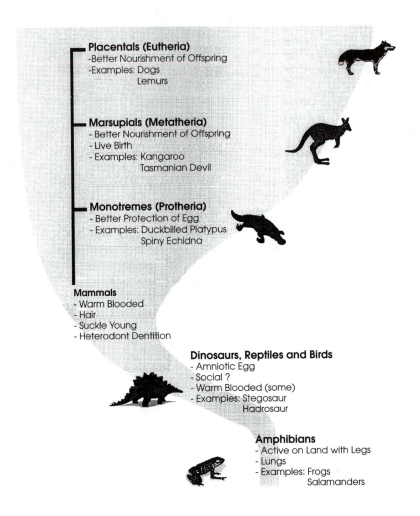

Placentals (Eutheria)
-Better Nourishment of Offspring
-Examples: Dogs
          Lemurs

Marsupials (Metatheria)
- Better Nourishment of Offspring
- Live Birth
- Examples: Kangaroo
          Tasmanian Devil

Monotremes (Protheria)
- Better Protection of Egg
- Examples: Duckbilled Platypus
          Spiny Echidna

Mammals
- Warm Blooded
- Hair
- Suckle Young
- Heterodont Dentition

Dinosaurs, Reptiles and Birds
- Amniotic Egg
- Social ?
- Warm Blooded (some)
- Examples: Stegosaur
          Hadrosaur

Amphibians
- Active on Land with Legs
- Lungs
- Examples: Frogs
          Salamanders

FIGURE 2.1   Histogram of Vertebrate Evolution in Which the Various Grades Are Represented

that contain few or no fossils. At one level, a geological formation is abundant with fossils, while two meters further up, there is nothing. The gradualists attribute the gap to the fortunes of climatic change or just plain luck of the draw. Sometimes climates change and animals move off only to live in environments that are not conducive to fossil formations or preservation. Hominid ancestors may have done exactly that (see below). Such a succession of local extinctions followed by re-population was in fact part of Cuvier's scheme of catastrophism.

The punctuationists maintain that what you see is what really happened, that the gaps are caused by bottlenecks in which the population numbers became so low that the chance of finding the few enduring survivors is terribly low. But the squeeze of the bottleneck is what makes new species spring forward in radiational bursts, represented by layers in which the fossil descendants become abundant once again. These abundant periods are periods of stasis in which little evolution is occurring. Inevitably, the climate or terrain will once again change rapidly and natural selection will once again wield its selective edge.

This argument has become even more heated because certain groups were put forward as the best evidence by each side. This is evolutionary biology in its most entertaining form; two sides looking at the same horse (whose evolution the gradualists like) and deciding whether it's a bird (an animal that the punctuationists favor) or not. The two groups that have been most debated are ones that are near and dear to ourselves: dinosaurs and hominids. The fate of both groups has been put forward as the *best* examples of the two diametrically opposed interpretations of the fossil record.

The Emergence of Mammals

By now even nonacademicians know about the **asteroid theory.** Also called the "Gunfight at the K/T Corral" or a "Border War" by some popular science writers, the controversy centers around what happened when the dinosaurs became extinct and the mammals took over. The **K/T boundary** marks the transition from the time of dinosaurs (**Cretaceous**) to the **Age of Mammals (Cenozoic)** (Gk. *Ceno* =recent+*zooic*=animals). Both sides of the argument agree that just below this border dinosaurs are found, and that just a few meters up, mammals can be found. That is about all the two sides agree on.

The asteroidists' scenario is that the Earth was hit by an asteroid, or possibly a comet, about 65 mya (million years ago). The site of the impact was near the present day Yucatan Peninsula in southern Mexico. Some researchers estimate the diameter of the meteor at about 300 kilometers. Others estimate that a meteorite only 19 kilometers across would release the equivalent energy of 100 million nuclear warheads. According to this theory, the impact raised enormous clouds of dust and ignited huge fires that burned for years pouring smoke and ash into the air. As the smoke rose into the atmosphere and was distributed around the Earth, it blocked sunlight, the primary source of energy for the planet's ecosystem. The effects have been compared to the hypothesized **nuclear winter** that would follow a thermonuclear war. Without sun, the plant life died and so on up the food pyramid until the dinosaurs were extinct. Proponents of the theory argue that many other groups, including marine microorganisms, higher plants, gastropods, and fish, also went extinct at this time. In fact, nearly every group of animals and plants shows decline across the K/T border.

The gradualists argue that all of these groups, including the dinosaurs, were already in decline before the impact. In fact, they believe there were perhaps only two species of dinosaurs in existence at the time of the impact. Some of the gradualists do not even agree that the worldwide occurrence of the extraterrestrially generated mineral iridium necessarily originated in outer space. However, it is true that a high concentration of iridium is characteristic of rocks straddling the K/T border. Iridium is also found in the products of volcanic rock. They suggest that volcanic activity may account for the iridium, but even massive volcanic activity need not be invoked for what are naturally occurring ecological processes. Most experts count at least five major extinctions over the last 450 million years in which from 50 to 85 percent of marine life went extinct. The more ecologically centered hypotheses suggest that massive adaptive radiations result from the creation of or accessibility to new land. These periods of adaptive radiation are then followed by extinctions, as ecosystems reach equilibrium and the "homeless" die off.

As usual, there is always a group of scholars that opts for a combination of uniformitarian causes, which included the drift of the continents into cooler latitudes. Perhaps a combination of an asteroid impact with drifting continents and a fluctuation of solar radiation due to a change in the earth's orbit may all be responsible. There is a cartoon from Gary Larsen's "Far Side" that shows the head dinosaur lecturing to an auditorium full of other dinosaurs. The lecturer says, "I'm afraid things are looking pretty bleak. There's an asteroid headed this way, the continents are drifting northward and we have a brain the size of a walnut." For the combination folks, that pretty well sums it up.

No matter which of the extinction theories one favors, they all have one thing in common: that extinction is somehow tied to changes in the natural environment. This is far different when compared to earlier theories of extinction that attributed extinctions to almost metaphysical instead of ecological causes. Such concepts as **racial senescence** suggest that all groups have a kind of built-in timer that inevitably causes a group to eventually "wind down."

One of the other groups that has been put forward as a good example of punctuated equilibrium is the Hominidae. It has been argued in fact that hominids are the best example in the fossil record of an animal that appeared rapidly. Hominids have also been implicated in the most recent period of mass extinctions of large mammals dating to between 10 to 25 kya (thousand years ago). We will examine these claims when we come to consider the hominid fossil record in detail.

Interpreting the Fossil Record

Some would argue that debates about the demise of the dinosaurs, or the details of evolution as a whole, are still too difficult to argue based on the fossil record as we understand it presently. Nonpaleontologists sometimes exhibit awe at just how much a "fossil hunter" can reconstruct from a fragment of jaw or a piece of a tooth. One answer is to be found in Cuvier's law of correlation, which says that certain kinds of body parts are inevitably found with certain other types of body parts, both of which can be associated with a certain adaptation. However, it is also true that tremendous fights have erupted over a handful of fossils of even a single fragment. Paleontologists do rely heavily on this wisdom, and this strategy makes even more sense in the contexts of ecology and evolution. Ecoevolutionary thinking has been around for nearly half a century now, even longer if one includes Charles Darwin and some of his contemporaries.

Even more recently, a new instrument has been added to the crime kit of the paleontologist. This is the study of **taphonomy** (Gk. *taphos*=entomb, bury+*onomy*=knowledge, laws). The artful science of taphonomy investigates the processes by which fossils are formed, deposited, and preserved. Fossils are almost always distorted when they are excavated, but the discipline of taphonomy not only helps us to understand a fossil's individual history but also to relate a fossil to its paleoecological community. Within physical anthropology, taphonomists usually deal with vertebrate fossils. The development of taphonomy has had a substantial impact on paleoanthropology, which has forced us to reconsider some of the human biases that we bring to our interpretations of the fossil record when we study our own ancestors. Previously most researchers assumed that hominid remains found with other animals were there because hominids had brought or killed them there for food. We now not only know that many of those interpretations were wrong but, in fact, many times the hominid was the dinner and not the diner. Furthermore, previous discoverers would often extract the hominid bones and ignore the nonhominid bones as largely irrelevant to understanding hominid evolution. The implications of these revelations for hominid paleobehavioral studies have been profound.

The study of hominid-associated paleontological sites has gone through a history that began first as an attempt to establish the association of hominids and extinct animals and then explain this correlation as the result of the **Deluge** or **Noah's flood.** As Shipman has noted, William Buckland (1784–1856), a staunch English antievolutionist, was perhaps the first earth scientist to conduct a taphonomic or **actualistic** experiment. From it he concluded that the bones from a nearby cave had been collected by hyenas. One of Buckland's contemporaries, Jacques Boucher de Perthes (1788–1868), managed to convince British colleagues (Charles Lyell among them) that he had discovered extinct mammals in association with stone tools. In the process, he helped to found the fledgling science of archaeology. Ironically, although Buckland was ahead of his time scientifically, it was Boucher de Perthes's less sophisticated and simpler argument that set the stage for what was to be the long-held assumption that the presence of artifacts or hominids with extinct animals signified an ancient home of "Man the Hunter." In the early part of the twentieth century, Raymond Dart (1893–1988), the Australian physician and discoverer of the early hominid species *Australopithecus africanus,* was to also conduct actualistic studies of the material from Makapan and other hominid sites in South Africa. However, Dart's study of the fossil fauna fragments supposedly illustrated how early hominids used bone tools. The assumption that hominids had manufactured them was based on his confidence that early hominids had in fact made stone tools. Modern taphonomy revealed that Dart was wrong, but this mistaken assumption was never convincingly attacked until the advent of modern taphonomy in the late 1960s.

Modern taphonomic studies are complex, careful, sophisticated, and increasingly reliant on technological innovations. Although taphonomists analyze fossil assemblages from a number of perspectives, some of the important parameters are:

1. **Taphonomic agents** (biological, geologic, and hominid): responsible for transport, interment, and preservation.
2. Analysis of population structure (sex, age categories, MNI (minimum number of individuals), seasonality, **death and life assemblages**).
3. Determination of ecological origin (**allocthonous, autochthonous**).
4. Condition of bones (weathering, gnaw marks, cut marks), location and quantity of bones.
5. Proportional representation of body parts (meat- and nonmeat-bearing parts).
6. Site layout, intrasite associations.
7. **Depositional environment** (high- or low-energy sediments).

These are only a few of the aspects of sites that are recorded, quantified, and analyzed. Perhaps more than any paleoanthropological and paleontological development in recent years, taphonomy has greatly expanded our knowledge of the paleobehavior of hominids in relation to their environment and ecology. Major questions such as hunting, scavenging, and procurement strategies have allowed us to more directly address larger questions about culture, diet, adaptation, and ultimately consciousness. In the chapters that follow, we will return repeatedly to taphonomic clues of behavior.

Vertebrates, Mammals, and Primates

Sun, Sea, and Land

The Greeks employed heat and water as a philosophical means of classifying animals. Animals could be arranged in a hierarchy going from cold and dry lower forms, such as insects, through cold and wet forms, such as fish, amphibians, and reptiles, to hot and wet higher forms, such as mammals and birds. The reason that this system works reasonably well is that terrestrial animals had to evolve ways of obtaining these essential catalysts for eating and reproducing. The original Greek grades of animals still reflects the general succession of adaptations developed to deal with selection pressures of life on the land.

The Conquest of the Land

A little less than 200 million years after their appearance, **vertebrates** (animals with backbones and an internal skeleton) began to colonize the land. Yet even before they arrived, the land had been colonized by plants and insects. The first animals to make the transition to land were the **amphibians,** who descended from **crossopterygian** (Gk. *crosso*=fringed+*pterygian*=wing or fin) or lobe-finned fishes. These fish possess limb bones attached directly to muscles rather than the unmuscled fins of **ray-finned fish.** The crossopterygian fin is equipped with tiny fringelike appendages, which eventually evolved into the digits of terrestrial vertebrates. An extant close relative of the lobe-finned fish known as the **lung fish** is so named because of a primitive simple lung that allows it to gulp air when surface water disappears. It is likely that the ability to breathe air and move across short land distances in search of water was the prototype of terrestrial locomotion. Being able to switch ponds in the search of food would also have conveyed a decided advantage over other waterbound species. This system of locomotion would eventually evolve into the limbs of amphibians, reptiles, and mammals and the wings of birds.

Although able to expand into the variety of empty terrestrial niches, the amphibians were and still are tied to water by the need to lay their eggs in water and the retention of gills in the immature form. Although they met with no competition for the insects and plants of the land, the land was for feeding and not for reproducing. The locomotion of the early amphibians was awkward and inefficient. Limbs that propelled them easily through water were splayed out to their sides and had to deal directly with gravity without the supporting buoyancy of water. To free themselves from the crush of gravity on their internal organs and to cushion themselves against the jarring crunch of walking, they evolved a stronger and more arched shaped spine from which to suspend the internal organs. They also evolved cushioning mechanisms in the form of pelvic and shoulder girdles. The latter adaptation also allowed them to more easily move the head independently of the body.

Although we cannot pinpoint any particular amphibian fossil as the direct ancestor of reptiles, we know that the next grade of locomotion and reproduction culminated in the radiation of **reptiles** and **dinosaurs.** Some authorities classify dinosaurs within the reptile group, but others have argued that they are more appropriately viewed as a higher grade that developed from the reptiles. Reptilian locomotion brought the legs more directly underneath the weight of the body. Some of the dinosaurs also became bipedal. Bipedalism developed many times among the vertebrates. Bipedalism, as we shall see, literally changes your outlook on the world. Whether you are a kangaroo or a bird looking for mates and watching for predators or a **Tyrannosaurus rex** (Gk. *turannos*=tyrant+*sauros*= lizard) looking for lunch, bipedalism not only drastically changes the way an animal gets around but the way it interacts with the environment.

While amphibians depend on water and a sticky gel to protect their eggs from the sun, reptiles developed the **amniotic egg** (Gk. *amnio*=lamb), which could be laid on dry land in a number of environments. The amniotic egg not only carried its own water supply but also had an extra layer of insulation called the *allantoid membrane* (Gk. *allan*=sausage+*oid*=shape), which puts cushioning water between the embryo and the external environment. The development of reptilian eggs also demands more oxygen, and the reptiles evolved a way to acquire oxygen directly from the atmosphere in the form of a leathery but semipermeable egg covering. From a behavioral standpoint, reptiles were almost certainly the first terrestrial grade of vertebrate to use internal fertilization. Unlike amphibians, fertilization must take place within the female. Many amphibians disperse their sperm directly into the water in an r-selected sociobiological mode. Sexual contact necessitated social contact.

Having "solved" the problem of more efficient locomotion, some of the dinosaurs known as **therapsids** (Gk. *thera*=heal, close+L. *apsid*=arch), or **mammal-like reptiles,** may also have taken the first steps toward solving the problem of thermoregulation. The beginnings of this experiment can be seen in a group of therapsids known as *pelycosaurs,* or sailback dinosaurs. They developed large dorsal fins that were supported by spines of spongy bone honeycombed with small tubules that may have functioned to carry small blood vessels like Haversian canals in mammals. It has been theorized that although they were **ectothermic** (Gk. *ecto*=outside) and relied on sunlight for warmth, they could behaviorally regulate their body temperature. The sailbacks could turn their fins parallel to sun rays to avoid overheating and radiate off some of their heat. To warm up, they could position their sails perpendicular to the sunlight to absorb heat. The microtubules help to more evenly distribute the heat to the body core. This adaptation was probably the first step in freeing the body from the need for external heat to power the biochemical processes of locomotion and digestion.

Therapsids may have developed complete **endothermy** (Gk. *endo*=within). In comparison with ectotherms, endotherms have more stamina and can be active for longer periods of time. The price that endotherms pay for a higher metabolism is that they must eat five to ten times more food than ectotherms. Greater activity also allows time for social behavior, which in turn encourages courtship, mating, and more intense parenting behavior. Evidence that supports the **social endothermic model** includes more medially placed limbs under rather than to the side of the body. This adaptation is seen in all extant endotherms. Also, the predator-to-prey ratio of about 3:100 (comparable to modern ecosystems) is characteristic of other ecosystems. Simple featherlike structures seen in some fossils originally may have been for insulation (Strickberger, 1996). It has also been argued, based on recent discoveries near the Arctic Circle, that dinosaurs lived in much cooler habitats than previously supposed.

Endothermy not only allows more time for feeding and mating, but it also allows more time for social behavior. Robert Bakker, Jack Horner, and John Ostrum have argued that nests of dinosaur eggs preserve the tracks of both adults and infants suggesting parenting behavior. The distribution of the eggs in concentric rows and a standardized spacing between nests suggest colonies of the kind seen in birds and mammals. Perhaps most important, analysis of dinosaur embryos indicates that some dinosaurs were born in a relatively helpless state that would have required parental investment.

Another development of the dinosaurs related to increased and more efficient metabolic activity is the development of a **thecodont** dentition (Gk. *theco*=

case, cover+*dont*=tooth). Thecodont dentitions display teeth that are set in jaw sockets. They are more resistant to pressure than teeth that are fused directly with the jaw as seen in most fish. They are also enervated and therefore more sensitive to the texture of the food being chewed. However, like amphibian and fish teeth, reptile and dinosaur teeth were **homodont** (L. *homo*=same+*dont*), that is, they all had the same shape. Carnivorous homodont teeth, like those of carnivorous dinosaurs, were dirk or blade shaped and functioned as tearing and ripping devices, but also as a "cage" to trap and hold smaller prey. They were very ineffective at reducing meat beyond the shape of large lumps or strips. One of the abilities of reptiles is the ability to swallow large lumps or whole vertebrate bodies. To do this, they have a very flexible set of jaws with a mandible composed of many bones instead of the **single dentary** of mammals. While this adaptation allows reptiles to eat larger pieces of food, it also means that the jaw is not well suited to side-to-side motion required for chewing. The importance of this will become apparent when we examine mammals below.

Using mammals as our guideline, most evolutionary ethologists believe that a higher and more efficient metabolism allows an animal to have a more dependent and consistent source of internal energy, which in turn allows it to be active longer. Longer activity allows for more time spent in foraging and feeding, but also for the social interaction of mating and the rearing of young. Increased parental investment, relatively undeveloped newborns, and social living are characteristic prerequisites of intelligence. On this planet, those animals that spend relatively great amounts of time engaged in such activities are also more intelligent. Though we have yet to define intelligence, these are some of the hallmarks that most scientists would agree on when comparing species.

The Rise of Mammals

Although we have previously reviewed some of the more discussed theories for the demise of the dinosaurs and in light of the punctuation-gradualism debate, we have not yet examined an equally fascinating and related event: the rise of the mammals. As mentioned in Chapter 1, genuinely useful theories are those that unite a number of seemingly disparate phenomena. In this case, it would be useful to know not only why the dinosaurs went extinct, but also how mammals and birds not only survived the mass extinctions but also went on to radiate and become the dominant vertebrate life forms on Earth. The Cenozoic is also the age of flowering plants or **angiosperms** (Gk. *angio*=vessel, shell, heart+*sperm*=seed), which produce fruit. Questions surrounding the relationship between plants and animals become even more intriguing in light of the fact that mammals, birds, and angiosperms coexisted with dinosaurs for millions of years. The early mammals and birds appeared between 150 to 200 mya and thus were synchronic and sympatric with dinosaurs.

One curious feature about the dinosaurs is that there are very few known adult dinosaurs that weighed less than 10 kilograms (about 22 lbs). Most (if not all) of the smallest carnivorous dinosaurs were well over this limit. On the other hand, the early mammals were so small that they could never have sustained dinosaurs as prey. It may have been that the dinosaur emphasis on size may have been so canalized that small niches never had enough time or sufficient available nutritive qualities to support small dog- and cat-sized carnivores with slow metabolisms. Yet another intriguing possibility is that birds and mammals occupied this sized niche.

Among theories that have tried to relate the extinction of the dinosaurs and the rise of mammals is the nocturnal predation of egg eating mammals. The sharp **apical** teeth of the early mammals would have been suitable for tearing open the leathery egg cases of reptiles. However, despite the fact that dinosaur nests have been intensely investigated, little evidence of mammalian poaching has been uncovered. If anything, the mammalian dentition with its emphasis of puncturing, shearing, and grinding seems most suited for an **insectivorous** diet.

It is possible to speculate that the insectivorous mammals fed for years or decades on dinosaur flesh and the insect populations that inhabited millions of rotting carcasses. Large carcasses, weighing up to many tons, may have attracted insects for as much as a decade. The mind boggles at the number of flies that an *Apatosaurus* could support. If the slow poleward drift of the continents and the gradual decline in dinosaur diversity and numbers was a contributing factor, mammals may not only have been able to adapt more quickly, but their endothermy and eventual **homeothermy** would have given them a decided advantage.

The Culinary Revolution

Although the extinction of the dinosaurs opened up new econiches, the mammals may have also benefited most from the evolution of angiosperms. Angiosperms, or flowering plants, developed a new reproductive strategy. Unlike the older **gymnosperms,** which depended on the wind for the dispersal of their seeds, angiosperms developed flowers, which allowed for sexual reproduction with the help of the insects that it attracted. Another innovation of the angiosperms was fruit. Edible fruit attracted vertebrates. The consumption of the fruit by mammals and birds allowed larger seeds to disperse much further. Although the period from 65 mya to the present is known as the Age of Mammals, it was in fact also the age of the "birds and the bees." The angiosperm radiation, which began in the Middle Cretaceous prior to the radiation of the mammals, would have created a variety of new vertebrate niches.

Mammals brought several new solutions or perfected old ones to the problems of reproduction, feeding, and locomotion. Today, only a few examples of the early prototypes are still alive. As a whole, the mammals developed constant body temperature, had hair, bore live young, and suckled their young with distinct milk-bearing organs. In fact, the word *mammal* comes from the Latin word *mamma* meaning breast. Mammalia is also the **Class** to which all primates belong. The **Order Primates** was one of the earliest, or perhaps the earliest, group of mammals to undergo an adaptive radiation in the Cenozoic Era.

From the fossil record we know that the early mammals had modified many features of the reptilian skeleton. The skull was more mobile and characterized by a **double occipital condyle** instead of the single condyle of reptiles. The once separate and distinct bones of the lower jaw were fused into a single dentary bone on each side, though the **mandible** still remained unfused at the mandibular symphysis. Two of the independent reptilian dentary bones developed into the delicate mammalian incus and malleus for improved hearing, which may have been selected for by nocturnal activity. The mammalian ear receives a wider frequency of air-born vibrations that do not depend on the ground vibrations on which reptiles rely for the perception of movement.

The early mammals also had a **bony palate** that separated the nasal passage from the mouth, which allowed them to more efficiently breathe while eating. The higher metabolism of mammals was selected for more efficient utilization of greater quantities of oxygen. Eventually, mammals developed to varying degrees flat, nasal **turbinate bones** in the nasal aperture, which as their names suggest are flat platelike structures that allow an enlarged mucous membrane to have more surface area for the detection of air-born molecules.

Much of what we know of early mammals is based on teeth. Instead of the continual replacement of homodont dentition in an ever-growing jaw, all mammals sported thecodont teeth, which were limited to only two successive sets of more stress resistant multirooted, deciduous, and permanent **heterodont** (Gk. *hetero*=other+*dont*=tooth) teeth. Unlike most reptiles that continue to grow throughout their lives, mammals cease growing relatively soon after birth. The mammalian adaptive strategy included a set of temporary "milk teeth" that were replaced with adult-sized permanent dentitions. The heterodont nature of mammalian teeth was a major adaptive advance over the reptilian dentition. The specialization of teeth into **incisors** for nipping; **canines** for ripping and puncturing; and **premolars** and **molars** for shredding, shearing, and grinding meant that each of the teeth could perform a specific task in the "disassembly line" leading to digestion in the stomach. Combined with side-to-side chewing and the addition of "smart" lingual muscles that could position and move the food along the rows of teeth, the increase of surface area to volume made for a much more uniform nutrient supply that could be broken down at a faster and more constant rate. In a very apt analogy, we can view reptiles as animals that put slow burning logs in the furnace and mammals as burners of saw dust.

To accomplish the more efficient breakdown of food, mammals evolved a more efficient use of chewing that combined crushing and shearing in **trituber-cular molars** that combined sharp crests, pulping cusps, and juice collecting basins in a single **tribosphenic molar** (Gk. *tribo*=three+*sphenic*=wing) arranged in a delta-shaped wing tooth that occluded with another delta wing tooth below it. All three actions could be accomplished as the result of the sequential movement of upper and lower teeth past each other in a single chewing motion. The genetic bases of the plesiomorphic pattern was diverse enough that some mammalian groups went on to emphasize puncturing and shearing (insectivores and carnivores), while others went on to emphasize pulping (primates), and still others specialized in grinding (ruminants). The exact details of mammalian occlusion and chewing are extremely complex, but even a rudimentary knowledge of the mechanics of mastication makes it clear that the early mammalian dentition was a significant improvement over the reptilian condition. Increased preprocessing of food before digestion was a major adaptational leap. We also know that as teeth became even more specialized and presumably efficient, most mammals reduced the number of teeth (the **dental formula**) from the original mammalian numbers. Although some groups lost all their teeth, no group has added to the number of teeth.

Over the years, there has been a great deal of speculation about the early mammalian and early primate diet. The procumbent (L. *pro*=forward+*cumbent*= leaning) nature of the anterior teeth, the incisors, has occasioned speculation that a significant amount of nonanimal food must have been part of the early mammalian diet. The best analogs among modern mammals seem to be gum eaters, who strip and score bark to obtain sweet resins. However, this arrangement is also seen in **prosimian** (L. *pro*=before+*simia*=monkey or ape) primates, which developed incisors that serve the entirely unrelated process of combing their fur with a **tooth comb.** Perhaps the most plausible reconstruction of the mammalian diet is that it was an omnivorous one, including both insects and fruit. It is further indicative of the fact that it is hard to feed on vegetation without inadvertantly including insects.

The Reproductive Revolution

All mammals are divided into three basic grades, largely on the bases of their reproductive systems. These grades include both extinct and extant animals. Members of the lowest grade are referred to as **prototheres** (Gk. *proto*=before+ *theria*=beast). These creatures are also known as **monotremes** (Gk. *mono*=one+ *tremes*=chamber) because the birth canal and waste canal are joined and undifferentiated. Although these animals used to be much more widespread, today there are only a few representatives of this **suborder.** These are the ant-eating echidna and the duck-billed platypus, which live in South America and Australia respectively. They are considered more "primitive" because, although they possess most of the other characteristics of mammals, they lay external eggs from which their young hatch.

The next highest grade of mammals, which are also more restricted than they were in the past, are the **metatheres** (Gk. *meta*=middle+*theria*=beast), or **marsupials.** They are considered in some ways to be intermediate in their biological organization and complexity between prototheres and **eutheres** (Gk. *eu*= true+*theria*=beast), or placental mammals. Today, marsupials are only found in South America, the southeastern United States (opossums) and Australia and Southeast Asia (kangaroos, wombats, the Tasmanian devil, and other beasts). Marsupials are animals that give birth to live young who then must "migrate" to the mother's pouch to suckle and continue their development. Although once widespread on the protocontinent of **Gondwana,** most species of these animals are now confined to Australia, where in their isolation and absence of competition from placental mammals, they underwent an adaptive radiation and diversified into a number of forms. The evolution of the various forms of Australian mammals into niches, which closely parallel those of placental mammals, are frequently cited as the classic example of convergent evolution.

Placental mammals represent the highest grade of mammals. These are mammals that spend a significant amount of time developing within an internal organ known as the **placenta.** The placenta both shields and nurtures the gestating organism in a way that is more efficient than that found in lower mammals. It acts as a kind of filter that selectively lets nutrients reach the fetus and at the same time screens out toxins. No filters are perfect, and many modern health problems in infants are caused by the inability of the placenta to filter out drugs and alcohol. But over the course of more than 100 million years, the placenta seems to have provided a decisive advantage for mammals that gave birth in this manner.

The Primates

Morphologically it is difficult to definitively separate early primates from early mammals in general. The only consistent way to do this has to do with an obscure character dealing with the construction of the bony primate ear know as the **petrosal bulla.** The earliest primates are about three times younger than the earliest mammals and date back to about 65 mya. The last known dinosaur lived at the same time as the earliest known primate. This first primate species is named *Purgatorius ceratops* because it was found at Purgatory Hill, Montana, in the same stratum that yielded the three-horned vegetarian dinosaur *Triceratops*. We only know of this earliest primate from fossil finds of some isolated teeth, but as Cuvier discovered, we can tell a great deal about animals from their teeth and claws. To make matters even more complicated, a number of scientists have suggested that this species was not a primate at all. If future discoveries support this interpretation, then we may have once again stumbled on a persistent problem of paleontology, which is "if this is not our ancestor, then the true ancestor was a creature that looked just like it and lived at the same time." Despite the lack of a "smoking gun," *Purgatorius ceratops* and its relatives help us to understand the evolutionary adaptations of primates as a whole.

Primates display a number of anatomical, physiological, and behavioral trends that as a whole distinguish them from other mammals. They also exhibit a number of traits that are plesiomorphic for vertebrates and mammals as a whole. It is the apomorphic traits that are most useful in distinguishing primates from other mammals. Just as we can view primates as the continuation and amplification of trends that first appear with the early mammals, we can view hominids as the amplification of behavioral and anatomical traits that characterize primates as a whole. Humans retain most of these traits.

Anatomy

1. Primates rely mostly on their sense of vision for survival. An increased reliance on vision and less reliance on olfaction (smell) is evident in the greatly reduced olfactory lobes of the brain. An emphasis on sight means that most primate communication must take place between individuals on a face-to-face or postural basis. However, it is also now apparent that primates retain the naso-vomero organ so important in sexual communication in other mammals. This organ is situated in the nasal area and has only been recently and incompletely studied in humans. Lower grades of primates scent-mark territories and each other. As part of an emphasis on vision, primates have evolved color and **stereoscopic vision** (3-D) resulting from the fact that they have more **rods and cones** in the eye than most mammals. Stereoscopic sight is achieved by overlapping fields of vision resulting from the forward-looking placement of eyes on the front instead of on the sides of the skull. Unlike most other mammals (including carnivores), primates do not require movement to perceive color. Early primates protected their eyes with an enlarged bony structure called the **postorbital bar,** which protects each eyeball. In higher primates, each eye is completely enclosed by a bony cup-shaped eye socket. Unlike mammalian carnivores, which have also evolved stereoscopic fields of vision, at least the higher primates, especially humans, are able to detect prey species in the absence of movement.

As part of their abandonment of smell as their primary sensory input, all but the lowest grade of primates, prosimians, have lost the continually wet, naked **rhinarium** (nose) and **vibrissae** (whiskers) possessed by other mammals. The lower primates still use scent glands located in their chest and anal areas to mark territories. Furthermore, sexual communication is still accomplished in the form of **pheromones.** Pheromones may also play a role in human sexual communication.

2. Primates are more **encephalized.** The size of their brain is larger in proportion to their body size and weight. As part of the need to pack more brain cells into relatively small volumes, in some primates, but especially in humans, the cortex of the brain is highly folded and convoluted. Among primates, modern humans are the most encephalized. However, for at least half of their evolutionary record, hominids maintained a brain size comparable to chimpanzees.

3. Primates are also **claviculate** and **digitgrade;** they have a **clavicle** (collar bone) that keeps the shoulder joints well separated and they retain the plesiomorphic condition of mammals in that they have five digits that allow them to grasp things in a precise manner. We will see in a later chapter that features of the hand and foot were highly modified in the course of hominid evolution. As a whole, primates are dependent on their ability to grasp, feed, and feel things with their hands through the use of digits. They possess **prehensile** hands. Primates retain five separate digits and lack claws; they have **fingernails** instead. This trait may or may not be a plesiomorphic condition for mammals as a whole. Fingernails may improve the tactile sense of primates. Some primates have secondarily developed special forms of nails called **grooming claws,** which they use to manicure their skin and hair. Such activities typically involve the removal of dead skin or parasites on themselves and others. Many modern humans engage in the same grooming activity on a daily basis.

4. Most primates are somewhat **omnivorous,** but their diets range from true omnivores (hominids) through highly insectivorous (prosimians) to nearly complete herbivores-frugivores (gorillas). **Follivores** (leaf eaters) tend to have body sizes in the midrange, probably because of the necessity of longer alimentary canals, which harbor bacteria capable of breaking down cellulose. Smaller sized primates make greater use of insects, and larger primates are much more dependent on the herbivorous component of their diet. Unlike most other mammals, primates usually use the digits of their front appendages (hands or paws) to bring food to their mouths. This kind of hand-to-mouth feeding is very rare among large vertebrates. Some of the few other mammals that also exhibit this kind of feeding behavior range from small to medium-sized animals, including rodents, raccoons, and opossums. Pandas and other bears also use their paws to bring food to their mouths. Pigs, elephants, and to some extent rhinos have developed a prehensile mouth, which manipulates food before it reaches the teeth. What all of these animals (except the rhino and panda) have in common is that are all **opportunistic omnivores.** They consume both vegetable and animal food when it is available. The front differentiated digits are also organs of locomotion and serve the functions of feeding, fighting, and fleeing.

5. Primates posses more **bunodont** (Gk. *buno*=round + *dont*=tooth) dentitions. Cusps are less sharp, and in comparison with insectivorous and strictly carnivorous animals, primates have rounder dental surfaces more suited to the crushing and pulping of fruits and other vegetable matter that they ingest. In the course of feeding, most primates inevitably ingest animal protein in the form of insects. Because of this, some primate teeth retain sharp cusps and ridges. Other more specialized primates are dependent on leaves as the major source of their nutrients and use these sharp structures for shredding leaves. Most primates derive their essential nutrients from vegetable food. Their teeth are shaped in a number of ways that allow them to consume both animal and vegetable foods. The width of the incisors is somewhat indicative of the frugivorous portion of their diet, with frugivores having wider upper medial incisors.

Most primates have large canines that are usually sexually dimorphic. Male canines are usually disproportionately larger than female canines. In primates, the canines serve the function of **predator defense** and **intraspecific competition.** Male canines are most sexually dimorphic in terrestrial species with a polygamous breeding system. Primate canines do not serve primarily as catching and holding devices for prey as they do in carnivores. Extant hominids and most fossil hominids are unique in having greatly reduced canines. In modern humans, they usually do not project above the occlusal surface of the rest of the dentition.

6. The body-plan of primates is **orthograde** (Gk *orthos*=straight). The organs and skeletal structures are organized perpendicular to the ground and not parallel

to the ground. Primates spend much more of their waking hours in a vertical, upright position. In other mammals, the body is organized parallel to the ground in a **plantigrade manner.** However, in terms of **locomotion,** all primates except humans are quadrupedal; they get around mostly on four appendages. Many primates can locomote in a bipedal fashion, but they can only do so at great cost of personal energy and only for short periods of time. Suspensory locomotion, using the front limbs and hands in some of the higher primates (gibbon, hominids), has resulted in a more dorsally placed scapula that allows for a more flexible and mobile shoulder joint.

Primates that spend more time in an orthograde, vertical, or upright sitting position also have a greater range of facial expression. In general, the higher primates exhibit much more complex facial expression than do lower grades of primates. The greatest range of facial expression occurs in hominids and the least in prosimians.

Behavioral Trends of Primates

Primates as a whole exhibit a number of behavioral trends that are interrelated to their anatomy. As one moves up in primate grade, each of these trends tend to become more emphasized, so that the higher grades accentuate particular behaviors in a stronger and more consistent manner.

1. In comparison with other mammals of similar body weights, all but one of the primates has reduced litter size to a single individual. One species of marmoset does retain a tendency toward twin births. Primates develop more slowly in comparison with most other animals of similar body size. Larger-bodied adult primates have greater gestation periods. Primates are more **altrical** than other mammals in that a much greater portion of their development takes place outside the womb. This slowing of the development process not only means that primates exhibit greater infant dependency, but also that there is a corresponding increase in **parental investment.** Simply put, parents must spend more energy and offspring must spend more time to reach adulthood. Why this trend was selected for over the millions of years of primate evolution is not obvious. Another feature of a prolonged childhood is that play lasts longer in primates. As we shall see later, play is not, biologically speaking, "a waste of time." Play in all mammals is the rehearsal of adult roles. Consider for instance what a cat does when it plays.

2. Although listed here as a separate primate behavioral trend, the great **socialness** of primates is almost certainly related to their slower maturational development. By socialness we do not mean simply that primates live in groups. Clams live in groups, but they are not (as far as we know) very social. Socialness implies the need for contact and interaction on a daily basis with others of one's own kind. Highly social animals require physical contact to develop into normal adults.

In a series of experiments, researchers showed that primates cannot develop normally in the absence of others of their own kind. In the 1970s, the husband

and wife team of Harry and Mary Harlow began a series of now classic experiments that demonstrated the importance of social interaction in normal primate development. What they showed was that monkeys (and by inference all primates) require both social and tactile communication as part of growing up. In other words, primates cannot develop normally without some form of social nurturing.

3. Primates are highly intelligent. It has been argued that this is a prejudiced observation made by primates who cannot unobjectively evaluate themselves in nature. Furthermore, it is becoming increasingly obvious that there are relatively advanced forms of nonprimate intelligence. It has been suggested that the determination of differences in intelligence is impossible and irrelevant to animals that are simply good at being good at their ecological jobs. As noted previously, this begs the question and does not deal with the obvious fact that we are more "intelligent" than an earthworm. This problem becomes much thornier when we ask the question, "Who is more intelligent, cats or dogs?" The subject of intelligence is so complex that chapter Eight is devoted to it.

Primate Grades

On the basis of fossil, biological, and behavioral evidence, living and extinct primates can be divided into a number of grades:

I. Prosimians (lemurs, lorises, and tarsiers)
II. Anthropoids (New and Old World monkeys)
III. Hominoids (the great apes and the lesser apes)
IV. Hominids (*Homo sapiens sapiens*)

The exact boundaries of these grades and even their actual existence has been the subject of decades of dispute. Some of the fossil species included in one grade or another show traits of both higher and lower grades. Indeed, the order primates is an excellent example of a case in which every authority has their own viewpoint. We use these grades here in a general way that not only represents the living groups of primates but also major episodes in primate evolution. Each of the grades is broadly representative of a period in our ancestry that produced particular adaptive shifts. Each of these grades seem to have arisen as the result of an adaptive shift involving the evolution of new physical and behavioral adaptations. These can be briefly reviewed in terms of scenarios that may have given rise to particular biological "innovations" or, in the words of the late paleontologist Alfred Romer, "new prototypes."

The Emergence of Primates

The earliest known primates appeared in the once tropical forests of North America where they radiated into a number of forms, which we refer to collectively as **Prosimians** and **Lemuriformes.** None of the many early fossil species currently recognized by paleontologists make suitable candidates for direct ancestors of the higher grades. In fact, due to their great similarity to other early mammals, some paleontologists have argued that many of them are "**paraprimates.**" Similarly, authorities have argued that tree shrews (*Tupiaidae*) should also be included in the order primates. In fact, tupiaids, with their high metabolism and **scansorial** (scurrying) locomotion across the leaf and branch litter of the forest floor, may make good analogous models for at least the earliest primates.

By the **Eocene,** prosimian-grade primates reached Asia, Europe, and Africa via land bridges and probably also by **rafting** on floating vegetation. Since no land bridges connect Eurasia and Africa, some sort of overwater dispersal must have been involved. Although tarsier-grade primates had appeared by the **Oligocene,** all the primates of North America were extinct by the end of the Oligocene. Although some of the prosimians may have been diurnal, with the exception of the lemurs of Madagascar, the remnants of the prosimian radiation are nocturnal and **crepuscular,** active at dusk or dawn. Wherever they have come in contact with higher grade primates, they have been outcompeted or adopted an arboreal (tree-dwelling) and nocturnal niche.

The early primates differed only slightly from their nonprimate mammalian ancestors and contemporaries in that the cusps of their teeth were rounder (more bunodont) and they probably had reduced litter sizes or even single births. Bunodonty has been used to suggest that there was an initial adaptive shift from a reliance on insect protein to fruit provided by the angiosperms. The relationship between primates and fruit-bearing plants is an excellent example of something evolving and something evolving to eat it.

It was at this time that we think most of the basic primate trends evolved. Most students of modern and extinct prosimian primates have related primate features to an **arboreal adaptation,** which best explains why primates have stereoscopic vision, excellent grasping ability, single births, and a highly frugivorous diet. Not surprisingly, this explanation is not without its critics.

Matthew Cartmill, a primatologist and student of the fossil record, thinks that the arboreal theory of primate characteristics and trends does not fully explain the uniqueness of primates. Cartmill, in a series of articles, basically posed the question, "Why don't squirrels also have primate characteristics?" Squirrels are not organized in an orthograde way. They come down trees head first, they lack stereoscopic vision and they give birth in litters that do not exhibit delayed maturation. They have some manual dexterity, but nothing as sophisticated as primates, who have fingers with nails and not digits with claws. He argues that arboreality does not explain the totality of primate traits.

Cartmill suggested that what had allowed primates to develop these traits was a specific adaptation for **visually directed predation** of insects and not an emphasis on fruit. In fact, both theories may be valid. The fact remains that among the innovations that primates developed were bunodont dentitions more suited for the kind of pulping and crushing action that would be expected of frugivores. The arboreal features of the primate skeleton would be suited to any kind of diet involving **suspensory feeding** from branches.

Modern Primates and Their Ancestors

Prosimians.   Today, prosimians have survived only in tropical Asia (India and Southeast Asia), Africa, and the island of Madagascar. On the island of Madagascar, the lemurs have undergone an adaptive radiation made possible by the island's long isolation and the fact that the island originally lacked mammalian predators until the arrival of humans. In part of the continental tropics, these creatures have remained nocturnal to avoid predators. Some, such as the slow lorises, have developed a creeping or **slow quadrupedal climbing** form of locomotion to avoid detection. On Madagascar, some of the lemurs (the **ring-tailed lemur**) have become diurnal and more terrestrial. Of all the extant primates, we think the lemurs are most representative of the original primate adaptation. Prosimians do not establish permanent pair bonds, but instead follow what is an essentially promiscuous pattern of mating. Lemur mating can be described as a "free-for-all."

Further complicating the picture that we once held is the observation that **dominance** of males is not obviously and always related to the access to mating partners of the opposite sex. Authorities have also pointed out that the contrast between arboreal nocturnal prosimians and the diurnal terrestrial dwelling lemurs of Madagascar may suggest that there is a tendency for terrestrial dwelling primates to be more aggressive. This assertion has important implications for hominid evolution and behavior.

The observations presented above concerning prosimian behavior also raise broader questions relevant to the study of primate behavior as a whole. The concept of **dominance** is sometimes difficult to define and objectively identify in the field. **Aggression** is easier to recognize and serves known functions in primate societies. Early primate field studies placed an emphasis on aggression and dominance, especially in relation to male behavior. It was and still is asserted that primate groups arrange themselves in **dominance hierarchies** that are **age-graded**. That is, there are different levels in a pecking order in which social positions are reinforced by daily social interactions including stereotypical or ritualized threats, gestures, vocalizations, postures, and physical force that reinforce the social structure of the group. The social structures are referred to as age-graded because the dominant individuals seem to be those that are strongest and most aggressive, which necessarily involves mature individuals at the peak of physical condition.

At least some human societies have a dominance hierarchy that is clearly similar to that seen in nonhuman primates. However, human dominance hierarchies also show some marked contrasts. First, nonhuman primate hierarchies must be defended on a daily basis, and dominance is very much tied to the physical ability of the participants to maintain or change their status. Humans have evolved a system where direct interpersonal physical aggression is not always involved. The human hierarchies, where they exist, are also age-graded, but age-graded in a uniquely human way. In agricultural societies, dominance is tied more to social possessions (for example, money, property, title), which usually (but not always) accumulates with age. It is possible to argue that modern human hierarchies come from recent sociotechnical developments. These points will be looked at in detail later, but for now it is possible to argue that dominance hierarchies are a plesiomorphic pattern for at least anthropoid and higher primates.

The flip-side of aggression can be observed in a behavior known as **grooming.** It appears to be just as important in maintaining relationships as is aggression. As the name implies, grooming is a form of physically caring for the skin by removing dead skin, parasites, and other debris. In primates, one individual grooms another. It appears, though we cannot ask them, to be pleasurable. Besides serving obvious hygienic functions, grooming also seems to be a powerful social mechanism for making and maintaining bonds. Like aggression, it is an integral part of the dominance hierarchy. One can also convincingly argue that it is common or even universal in humans. While we see indications of these kinds of behaviors, it is with the anthropoids that we clearly see dominance, aggression, and grooming as the glue of higher primate society.

Almost all primates are **sexually dimorphic** in that the males differ from the females in physical forms with males being stronger, bigger, and possibly more aggressive. The sexual dimorphism of this latter quality may or may not be a reality. This has been discussed by numerous researchers attempting to relate nonhuman behavior to hominid behavior. Later we will review the controversial subject of sexually dimorphic behavior in modern humans.

Anthropoids.   This second grade of primates includes **New and Old World monkeys.** We will not deal much with New World monkeys, not only for reasons of space, but also because they clearly represent a lower grade that displays a number of specializations that do not tell us much more about human behavior than that of the prosimians. Furthermore, among the higher primates, they are the most removed from humans in both space and time. This does not mean that they are not interesting in their own right. These more closely related and ecologically similar monkeys and apes allow us to make more direct inferences about the dawn of hominidlike behavior.

The primary features that set the off the lower prosimians from the higher primates are essentially differences in degree of the general primate trends, which first appear with the prosimians. New World monkeys occupy Central and South America and offer only distant models for human behavior. By 40 mya, anthropoids were present in Africa and possibly Asia. In comparison with prosimians, all monkeys, but especially Old World monkeys, are more encephalized, larger bodied, and for the most part more terrestrial. They occupy a wide variety of habitats ranging from the temperate zones of Asia to the tropics of Asia and Africa. They exhibit an equally wide range of social and reproductive organization. For the study of the biological bases of human behavior, they are of particular interest because they may occupy environments very similar to those in which hominids evolved. They are also very similar to humans in their anatomical organization.

Anthropoid groups occupying open savanna habitats have long been used for the construction of social and behavioral models that may have once applied to human ancestors. Terrestrial African monkeys, probably as the result of their more open surroundings, but probably also as the result of internal developments in the evolution of their social systems, have marked sexually dimorphic canines, which play key roles in both predator defense and social interactions. Large and very sharp canines, which hone on a **sectorial premolar,** are used in displays meant to threaten other animals, especially conspecific males. In fact, among both monkeys and apes, large canines serve a daily social function, and the display of teeth is always considered a threatening gesture.

Other physical adaptations have to do with a more intense and complex social life. The brain and body are larger; the eyes are fully protected by a bony socket, not just a postorbital bar, for more medially set (toward the vertical midline of the body) orbits; and there is an absence of a naked rhinarium. Anthropoids take comparatively longer to mature and consequentially demand more parental investment. They spend much more time in orthograde position, and some have developed **ischial callosities,** which are leathery pads on their buttocks that are adaptations for spending many hours a day sitting upright and looking around.

Adaptations for increased social communications are also apparent. Unlike prosimians, there is no frenulum to anchor the upper lip, which in monkeys frees the lips to increase the range of facial expressions and vocalizations. The muscle groups of the face are more diversified. Body posture and movement are even more expressive in comparison with prosimians. As mentioned above, large continuously sharpened canines are important not just as weapons against predators, but also in threat displays and threat follow up. The **threat yawn,** in which usually males expose canines, is a warning and not an indication that the animal is tired or bored. In baboons this can also be augmented by an **eyelid flash,** in which the animals scares other animals by inverting the eyelid to expose a white spot that terrifies others.

The range of anthropoid mating systems is nearly as diverse as those of human beings. The mating structure of Old World anthropoids ranges from the **promiscuous troops (polygamous)** of the common or savanna baboon (ME/ MF=*baboon*=gargoyle, simpleton) to the **harems (polygynous)** of the hamadryas baboon. Though they differ in social structure, all monkeys rely on **visually displayed estrus** (Gk. *estrus*=frenzy). This display involves a distinct and sometimes massive swelling around the female genital region accompanied by changes in female willingness to mate. At one time it was believed that the most dominant male received or took preferential access to estrous females. As mentioned previously for prosimians, it is now far from clear if this is the case.

Savanna baboons live in groups ranging from scores of individuals to under ten in number. They practice a means of splitting and coming together known as fission and fusion. The determinants of what causes the groups to aggregate or splinter is thought to be generally linked to the availability of resources. All the higher primates, including humans, employ this method of fine-tuning their population numbers.

In savanna baboons, mating is done in a **consort pair,** as mating couples are called, and is often openly and frequently harassed by other individuals (usually adolescents or young adults), who not only appear to be fascinated by the pair's attempts to mate, but also at times seem determined to prevent it. It is hard to relate this type of behavior directly to beneficial behavioral adaptations. At the very least, it gets subadult males up close and personal by giving them an opportunity to inspect adult skills.

Another form of mating group is that of the **hamadryas baboon,** which occupies the rocky, desert landscapes of Ethiopia. In this system, the male maintains a cohesive harem of females and their young by herding the females with the aid of threats and bites that prevent them from straying too far and, it is theorized, mating with other males. Females proceed across the landscape in a one adult male group that forages on a daily basis. In this case, the mating groups are also the foraging groups. In the savanna baboon, social structure foraging groups appear to have nothing to do with mating groups. Although the foraging and mating groups of the hamadryas baboons are the same, at night the separate harems aggregate into much larger sleeping groups, which occupy cliffs where they are relatively secure from predators. Neither kind of group seems particularly indicative of the way that human ancestors might have organized their sociosexual groupings.

When pioneering studies were first undertaken of baboons, the male observers emphasized aggression and mating relationships in the contexts of natural selection and reproduction. With the infusion of female researchers, initiated by paleoanthropologist Louis Leakey (1903–1972) and others, the emphasis shifted toward understanding **alliances,** mother–infant and female–female bonds. As one of my mentors once put it, "where there was once terror and rage, there is now sweetness and light." Current orthodoxy has it that the only enduringly stable bonds in higher monkey (and most ape) societies are mother-offspring (especially mother-daughter) bonds, which give stability to the group as a whole. Males more frequently move between troops, while females form the **stable core.** The accuracy and evolutionary significance of these observations is difficult to elucidate. This is true because of **paternal uncertainty.** In most primate societies, no male can know for certain that he is the parent of any particular offspring because pairing lasts only during estrus and mating. Because even so-called dominant males do not mate exclusively with estrous females, it is difficult to establish male lineages without taking blood or tissue samples. Every human society we know about has social mechanisms for solving exactly this problem. Thus, in relating hominid mating to natural selection, it would be extremely interesting to know how long ago and even how hominids first began tracking male lineages.

Other anthropoid groups—ranging from the extremely unusual multimale (**polyandrous**) groups of South American tamarind monkeys through the large troops of leaf-eating langur monkeys (polygamous) to the "distant male" polygynous structure of the open-dwelling patas monkey—also are probably far removed from social structures that we might reasonably postulate for early hominids. However, no final decision can be made on the basis of any of the anthropoid studies as to what structure may have characterized hominid ancestors. What anthropoid studies reliably indicate is the range of possible mating structures. Studies of open-dwelling savanna monkeys demonstrate the extreme danger of

PHOTO 2.1   *Orangutan, indigenous to Southeast Asia* (Tom McHugh, Photo Researchers)

living on the savanna. What they leave unanswered is how the more humanlike apes may have emerged from a monkeylike ancestor.

Hominoids (Apes and Hominids)

As with monkeys, apes further emphasize trends that first appeared with prosimian-grade primates. They are larger, more encephalized, take even longer to mature, and also appear to be even more intelligent than monkeys. They also exhibit a variety of social and mating structures, which because of the close genetic proximity and anatomical similarities, are of even more interest to students of human behavior. Anatomically and genetically, humans and apes are united by the synapomorphic character of lacking a tail. All other primates retain tails as part of the plesiomorphic mammalian condition. Within the superfamily Hominoidea, the Asian apes, gibbons, and siamangs (the **Hylo-batidae**), and orangutans (***Pongo pygmaeus***) (Photo 2.1) are most distantly related and most geographically removed from hominid origins. The African or great apes are very closely related to humans. DNA comparisons reveal that the only two African great apes, the **gorilla (*Gorilla gorilla*)** and the **chimpanzee (*Pan paniscus* and *Pan troglodytes*)**, are so closely related that 95 percent (perhaps as much as 99 percent) of their genetic material is identical to that of humans.

The fossil record of the living great apes is almost nonexistent. The orangutan does have a substantial fossil record if we are correct in deducing that they are a product of the **sivapithecine** radiation. We believe that all of the apes may have arisen out of a **dryopithecine adaptive radiation** that was underway by 20 mya in Africa. Although a number of these Miocene apes have been found in both Africa and Europe, none can be convincingly linked to any of the extant hominoids. Approximately 17 mya, some dryopithecines moved out of Africa into the broadleaf forests of Europe where they remained unchanged enough in their morphology that paleontologists still regard them as dryopithecines. Perhaps simultaneously or a little later, other dryopiths reached Asia where they have been recovered from the Siwalik Foothills of the Himalayas and coal deposits in southern China. The principal characteristics that differentiate the Euro-African fossil apes from the Asian group seems to have been the stockier, larger bodies and thicker-toothed enamel of the sivapiths. Some of the fossils from Turkey and even eastern Europe are so similar to modern orangutans that they make very plausible ancestors for extant orangutans.

In the first half of this century, fossils referred to as *Ramapithecus punjabicus* were thought to be the earliest hominids. This taxon was based on very incomplete fragments that were not only small in size but also had a relatively small canine. A similar form was discovered in Africa by Louis Leakey. Leakey named the fossils *Kenyapithecus wickeri* and further suggested that it had been a tool user. The decades of debate that followed not only saw intense arguments about the geographic origin of hominids (Africa or Asia), but also about whether reduced canines (in comparison with living apes), a *parabolic* or V-shaped jaw, and small body size were enough to identify early hominids at all. The hominid status of the ramapithecines was staunchly defended by Elwyn Simons and David Pilbeam of Yale University. In the 1960s and early 1970s, orthodoxy held that hominids dated back to at least 17 mya. With subsequent discoveries, this interpretation has been almost universally rejected.

In fact, many of the Miocene apes, especially the early Miocene forms, are now often referred to as only **dental apes** because it is only their dentition that is seemingly apelike. On the basis of much more complete knowledge stemming from decades of continued discoveries, few paleoanthropologists believe that Asia has yielded any hominoids, let alone early hominids, which are directly ancestral to ourselves. On the other hand, most are reasonably sure that sivapiths were the close ancestors of orangutans and also of the largest ape that ever lived, *Gigantopithecus blacki,* sometimes put forward as the "real" **Sasquatch** (also known as **Big Foot** or **Yeti**).

The reason for the complete lack of chimpanzee fossils has often been speculated to be because these animals occupied forest environments that are not conducive to the preservation of fossils. This may suggest that the common ancestor of African apes and humans occupied forest habitats.

Before proceeding to a detailed consideration of the behavior of the African apes, it is first useful to briefly mention a few aspects of the lesser apes that are exclusive forest dwellers. It was once theorized that gibbons might be the basal ancestors to humans to the exclusion of the African apes such as the chimpanzee. The reasons for this speculation were both behavioral and anatomical.

Asian Apes

Anatomically, gibbons are unique among primates in that they display no sexual dimorphism in body size. The males are the same size as the females. Although their legs, but especially their arms, have been modified for a special kind of arboreal locomotion known as **ricochetal brachiation,** which allows them to almost literally fly through the trees at great speeds, these animals tend to walk bipedally when they occasionally come to the ground. This observation led to the speculation that they might be good candidates for human ancestry because humans also walk bipedally. In fact, the gibbon walks bipedally because it is too specialized to proceed on all fours as the other apes do. Much was also made of the lack of sexual dimorphism because among the hominoids, humans exhibit the least sexual dimorphism. Human males are on average 10 to 12 percent larger than human females. Therefore, the apes with the least sexual dimorphism make the most logical human ancestor from the perspective of body size.

Behaviorally, the gibbon is unique among primates in living in what can be described in human terms as a **nuclear family** with a male and female mated for life and living with offspring, until they mature and leave the family group. However, this facet of behavior also seems to result from the fact that gibbons are by far the most arboreal of the apes and have specialized in an almost completely arboreal lifestyle that limits the number of individuals that can exploit a single tree at a given time. In spite of these speculations, it is now abundantly clear that something like or closely related to the gibbon was not a close human ancestor. The gibbon clade was in fact the first of the apes to split off on its own line about 17 mya. This is confirmed by both anatomical comparisons and biomolecular data.

While no one believes that the orangutans are much more closely related to hominids (in comparison with the African apes), orangutans are highly intelligent. They also exhibit a curious and difficult to understand social structure, which consists of solitary males that patrol large territories and mate with females seemingly whenever they encounter them. This mating pattern is possibly independent of estrus and seems to make little evolutionary sense. The orangutan mating pattern has been termed orangutan rape because human researchers have been unable to find an obvious connection between fertility and reproduction.

Just as curious is that orangutans live a solitary existence in the wild (females, however, raise the young) but are highly social when raised in captivity, where they seem to form permanent attachments and social alliances. However, there is a great deal about orangutan behavior that we simply do not understand. We do know that orangutans were much more widespread than their limited distribution on the islands of Sumatra and Java indicate. It may be that the orangutans that still survive are somewhat aberrant or at least atypical of a species that once extended from China to India.

The African Apes

Virtually all biologists agree that we are most closely related to the gorilla and the chimpanzee. In fact, we are so close that humans have been accurately referred to as "naked apes." Gorillas are as closely related to chimpanzees as they are to humans. Like all other nonhuman primates, the apes are quadrupedal and locomote in a manner known as **knuckle walking.** They are primarily vegetarian, though some fascinating instances of meat eating by chimpanzees are described below. Both creatures are forest-dwelling animals, but chimpanzees sometimes occupy more open habitats known as woodlands. The gorillas are exclusive tropical forest-dwelling animals regardless of whether they live in high mountain or lowland forests. Recently, **bonobos (*Pan paniscus*)** have been put forward as especially good nonhuman models of early hominids or protohominids because of their frequent bipedal locomotion and sexual behavior.

Chimpanzees

Chimpanzees consist of two varieties, the pygmy chimpanzee (bonobos) and the **common chimpanzee (*Pan troglodytes*).** The bonobos are poorly known in terms of their life patterns in comparison with the common chimpanzees, which have been closely studied for decades. By far, most of the behavioral data that we think is relevant to establishing the past lifestyles of our ancestors comes from the common chimpanzees. Primatologist Jane Goodall pioneered in the study of the common chimpanzee, and despite the fact that many have followed up on her work, hers are still the most comprehensive studies of chimpanzees. However, the bonobos have very recently provided surprising information, which we shall discuss below.

The common chimpanzee lives only in East Africa and occupies habitats that are generally referred to as woodland, which are both dense thickets of vegetation and more open glade areas. They live in groups whose sizes range from a few individuals to over thirty. There is no permanent pair bonding and little food sharing, and females raise the young without the assistance of males. Chimpanzees have excellent memories and are among the most intelligent of the primates. They make tools, but do not manufacture stone tools. However, they can be taught to make stone artifacts in captivity. In spite of these and other captive studies, it is what they do in the wild that we are most interested in. We can study chimpanzee behavior and biology from a number of perspectives that indicate why they are the best models for early hominid behavior.

Sexuality and Social Behavior.   Chimpanzee social organization and sexuality is similar to many of the lower anthropoids. Chimps live in promiscuously mating troops that occupy a particular home range through which they migrate on a daily basis. Mating depends on personal access to receptive females, who exhibit visually displayed estrus in the form of distinct and often enormous swelling in the genital region. As in baboons, a female will mate sequentially with several males in a series of consort pairs. Paternity is never known, and the female raises the offspring with the sporadic help of other females or immature males that may or may not be close relatives.

The pygmy chimpanzees have been the subject of recent studies, which have begun to overcome the difficulties in studying these forest-dwelling primates. Of particular interest is that bonobos engage in **ventral–ventral sex** (face-to-face sex). This seems to be unique among primates and has obvious implications for human sexual behavior. Furthermore, bonobos have been reported as spending relatively large blocks of time manipulating each other's genitals regardless of the sex of the partner. Frans de Waal, one of the few experts on wild bonobo behavior, has suggested that bonobos rely heavily on sex to mediate social interactions. He describes bonobo females as highly solicitous of sex in exchange for cooperation. His work strongly implies that human ancestors may have evolved from a very similar adaptation that emphasized social cooperation instead of dominance and confrontation.

Bonobo behavior is also of interest to students of human evolution because they seem to exhibit little sexual dimorphism with regard to body size. These observations raise the question about whether there is some relation between size, sexual dimorphism, social bonding, and sexual behavior. We shall return to this subject in one of the following chapters.

Sexual maturity is rapid in chimpanzees in comparison with most primates and other mammals in general. The gorilla and orangutan take longer than chimpanzees, but they reach a much greater adult body size. Chimpanzees, which reach an eventual adult height of approximately three-fifths to one-half of adult humans, mature in only six years. They exhibit a sexual dimorphic difference of about 10 to 12 percent, the same as that for prehistoric humans. There are very few reliable studies on the survivability of infants, but the figure may vary significantly from group to group.

After weaning, all chimpanzees must feed themselves. What constitutes food is learned from observation and other members of the troop. Food sharing does occur, but it is sporadic. The instances under which sharing occurs seems to be directly relevant to protohominid behavior because meat is the most-often shared food. This sharing occurs in the context of hunting or scavenging small mammals such as monkeys and immature bovids. De Waal reports that food sharing in bonobos occurs in the context of mating.

Tool Manufacture and Use.   Bonobos have not been observed to make and use tools in the wild. Common chimpanzees, however, do make and use tools. Their tools are simple and **nonlithic** and never manufactured or employed in the context of hunting vertebrates. One of the best-known chimpanzee tools is the **termite stick.** This is a twig that chimpanzees strip the branches off of to use to probe the inside of termite mounds. Individuals gather a few of the insects on the end of the stick and then lick them off. It appears to be a highly desirable chimpanzee food. These artifacts are often made well away from the site where they are used.

Another tool that common chimpanzees make is a **leaf sponge.** It is simply a crumpled up leaf that is used to absorb water from streams or tree hollows for drinking. These seem to be made in close proximity to the water source.

Chimpanzees learn to make these tools by observing other chimpanzees. From this perspective, this kind of process constitutes a simple form of culture because it is learned and shared. However, it is difficult to argue that the use of these tools is crucial to the survival of either individuals or groups. Indeed, though very subjective and therefore difficult to confirm or deny, it is hard to avoid the conclusion that chimpanzees practice these kinds of behaviors in an almost recreational way.

Chimpanzees have been taught to make stone tools in captivity. The most famous captive tool-maker is Kanzi, who learned to make sharp flakes by banging two rocks together or throwing stones against a hard floor.

Predator Defense.   A very significant aspect of chimpanzee tool use lies in what they do not do. Chimpanzees do not use tools to hunt or process meat. They do not use tools to defend themselves. This last aspect was made very clear by a piece of anecdotal evidence resulting from an experiment carried out and filmed by Adrian Kortland.

A stuffed leopard was put on a track and exposed to a group of chimpanzees as they walked by. The chimps perceived the dummy as real and became very agitated and frightened. Sticks and stones had also been left at the site of the encounter, and the chimpanzees did eventually use them to attack the leopard. Although it is interesting that members of the group had the foresight and intelligence to use naturally occurring implements to defend themselves, what is even more interesting is the level of skill and effectiveness. The use of the objects would have come too late for at least some of the chimpanzees had the leopard been real. Furthermore, attempts to strike the leopard were badly aimed and carried little force. This kind of response is probably much more similar to the displays that chimpanzees use to accomplish social intimidation. In these displays, any object such as a bush or a stone will be dragged, torn, thrown, or just generally moved in any fashion that attracts attention.

Although chimpanzees are perhaps twice as strong as most humans, the use of their strength is limited by the fact that they are very poor marksmen. This was evident in the leopard experiment. However, captive chimpanzees do become very accurate at throwing feces at zoo-goers. This type of behavior is probably not of much use in avoiding being eaten in the wild.

The accuracy and force of chimpanzees are also limited by the fact that they, like other nonhuman primates, are quadrupeds with a limited range of motion in the shoulder joint. In comparison with hominids, all other primates are limited by the fact that their arms are also organs of locomotion. Chimpanzees also lack a **precision grip,** which is the ability to oppose or touch the index finger to the thumb. This is why chimpanzees, in spite of their great dexterity, hold and pick up things differently than humans. They have problems picking up a dime. This seemingly small anatomical difference may have had a profound effect on the evolution of human behavior.

The most common form of defense against predators seems to be safety in numbers, their relatively large body size, large canines, aggressiveness, and vigilance. In these respects, they are similar to many of the large-bodied primates. The daily use of trees is also an important predator defense mechanism and depends on spending time off the ground.

Cannibalism and Aggression. When they were first studied in a systematic way by Jane Goodall, the chimpanzees of the **Gombe Stream, Tanzania,** provided most of the evidence for chimpanzee behavior. First reports indicated that chimpanzees were very aggressive. Comparisons were made to humans, which could be viewed as "killer apes" that had a "territorial imperative" for defending the areas that they occupied. Later it was realized that the **provisioning** of the chimpanzees was concentrating an unusually large number of individuals in a limited area. Goodall followed a procedure in which she would supply bananas to attract individuals for study. As individuals became crowded together, reports of aggressive behavior were emphasized. One of the important realizations that eventually came out of this early work is that virtually any primate can be made aggressive in a situation where desired resources are limited. This is also true of most, if not all, vertebrates.

An even more unusual, though perhaps questionable, illustration of chimpanzee aggressiveness stems from reports of murder and cannibalism, which were supposedly conducted in an organized way. The case involved a female and her adult offspring that supposedly ambushed other chimpanzees, especially those with infants, and killed them before eating them. In fact, when one checks the reports, infants sometimes just disappeared with no confirmation that they had been killed and eaten by other chimpanzees.

The careful study of chimpanzee behavior and anatomy is extremely important to the task of understanding the evolution of hominids. They are not only very closely related to us, but they also occupy the same kind of environments that have been proposed for early human ancestors. We can see in chimpanzees not an animal that we descended from, but one that must have shared a relatively recent common ancestor with ourselves. We see in their behavior what may be the glimmering of human culture. It is possible to theorize that such cultural tendencies would only have had to have been emphasized and selected for by the environment for millions of years to result in humanlike culture. Indeed, many of the hallmarks of humans that are subsumed under culture exist in chimpanzee society. Such behaviors might be termed as **protocultural.**

True cultural behavior has several qualities that help identify it. Culture should be natural, nonsomatically transmissible, arbitrary, idiosyncratic, and learned. By *natural,* we mean that it must occur in the wild as an integral part of common behavior. *Transmissible* means that it must be passed on between individual contemporaries and from generation to generation. Human managed colonies of Japanese snow monkeys demonstrate the rudiments of intergenerational transmission. After humans provided rice and sweet potatoes, snow monkeys learned to wash them. The introduction of rice and sweet potatoes were obviously not natural events. True culture is also *arbitrary* and specific to particular populations. Finally, culture must be *learned.* Nonhuman primates do learn to alter their behaviors in response to environmental stimuli. Modern humans meet all these requirements. Above all, modern humans are dependent on culture. It is not marginal or irrelevant to survival—it is absolutely essential. The same cannot be said of any of the putative cultural behavior of nonhuman primates.

A major objective in the study of human evolution is to develop an understanding of what circumstances and selection pressures could have resulted in the evolution of hominids. Chimpanzees provide us with a very plausible model for what our ancestors may have been like before these pressures began to transform an apelike animal into a large-brained, tool-dependent, and culture-bearing animal. It is with this in mind that we can look at the possible scenarios that have been put forward to account for the emergence of our own family, the Hominidae, in Chapter 3.

Summary

In this chapter, we examined the following three broad subjects: ways of conceptualizing evolution in space and time in light of natural selection and ecological theory; the rise of vertebrate adaptations in response to the basic selection pressures of locomotion, reproduction, and diet; and finally, the anatomical and behavioral adaptations of primates. Many of the principles that guide our interpretation of morphological traits are all useful for considering behavioral traits. Except in the special case of culture (see following chapters), morphology, by the logic of natural selection, can almost always be related to behavior. Behavior, along with geographic isolation, may be one of the principal mechanisms of speciation. Mutation may also initiate new behavior or reinforce previously existing behavior. Evolution probably proceeds in both ways.

Interpreting the fossil record not only requires that we make uniformitarian assumptions about behavior by extrapolating backward in time, but it also guides our taxonomic and phylogenetic assessments of paleospecies. Taphonomy lends some aid to this task, but it is our interpretation of modern analogs that provides the most effective means of interrelating paleobehavior, fossil morphology, and paleoenvironments. It is important to emphasize that anything said about the daily life or phylogenetic relations of the past is a matter of opinion. When opinion is involved, there is no ultimate criteria for settling scientific disputes. Consequently, heated debates about the tempo and mode of evolution, the causes of extinctions and radiations, or paleobehavior continue unabated.

It is possible to view vertebrate evolution as successive solutions to problems posed by the nature of life itself. Hundreds of millions of years have not only led to the occupation of every habitat by vertebrates, but also to the solutions of increasingly more fine-tuned adaptations to the limiting factors of temperature and water. A major selective factor in reproduction has been the dual need for adequate water. The invention of the egg followed by the amniotic egg and finally the placenta allowed for increasingly more efficient and competitive reproduction. The development of homeothermy, whether it began with mammal-like reptiles or not until the advent of the mammals, was made more efficient by changes in the dentition, which became most complex in the mammals. Along with the reproductive and dietary changes, we can infer enormous changes in behavior. Most controversy has centered around the evolution of socialness and an implied increase in behavioral repertoires. Such changes allowed an ever increasing range of behavior and expansions created by plate tectonics and the radiation of other organisms.

The early primates exhibited the basic ground plan of other early mammals. They were so plesiomorphic that scientists still argue about whether some of the early primates are not just generalized mammals. The reasons for the rise of the primates continues to be argued. Exactly what they were eating and how it influenced their behavior is still debated. Prominent explanations include a shift from insectivory to arboreal insectivory, a shift to a more frugivorous diet, or a shift to a more omnivorous diet. Details of the dentition can be used to argue all three scenarios. There is, however, general agreement that an arboreal life left its mark and continues to help explain many primate features. Studies of extant primates convince us that omnivory is much more common among primates than previously suspected. The trends, which continued to be emphasized throughout the last 65 million years of primate evolution, are easily related to an arboreal adaptation. The emphasis on vision, orthograde posture, the retention of grasping ability, and even a larger brain can easily be related to arboreality no matter what the details of the preferred scenario. The subsequent increase in body size seen in some anthropoids and most hominoids is also intertwined with a more terrestrial existence. Human ancestry, like all primates, went into the trees and, like certain monkeys and apes, came down onto the ground at some point, probably in the late Miocene between 5 to 8 mya.

An examination of extant primate societies and reproductive strategies clearly shows that there are certain primate commonalities in social structure, such as dominance hierarchies, alliance formations, the fission and fusion of groups, and an intense need for socialization and socializing. Relating these structures to reproductive success and then to natural selection is much more difficult.

Mating strategies are so varied in the monkeys and apes that it is difficult to select one as most likely for human ancestors. Considering our closest relatives, the hominoids, does not help to solve the problem of which is the best model for early hominids. The strategy that most closely resembles modern humans (at least superficially) is the alleged monogamous pair bond, which is found only in the Asian gibbons. Not only are they highly specialized tree dwellers, but they are in the wrong geographic region and were the first to split off from the other hominoids. The chimpanzee and the gorilla are our closest relatives. The gorilla is a specialized vegetarian and clearly, as we shall see in the next chapter, not a suitable model in light of what we know about our most likely hominid ancestors. The common chimpanzee is physically and genetically closely related, and tool using, hunting, and meat sharing models show at least the rudiments of human cultural behavior. It is not terribly difficult to imagine a chimplike animal evolving into us. The bonobos may be even more specifically like humans in some of their sociosexual strategies, but little is known about the details of bonobo adaptations. Furthermore, recent biochemical evidence suggests that they split off from the African hominoid line after hominids themselves had already emerged. Their humanlike behaviors may represent a good example of parallel evolution.

Finally, we may have to confront the fact that hominid behavior has no known counterpart in extant apes. Though our common ancestor probably resembled a chimpanzee more than ourselves, the behavioral differences that set us apart from the other African apes may have been marked from the beginning. In the chapter that follows, we will examine this and other hypotheses for the rise of bipedal apes that came to depend on the manufacture and use of tools. The origin and evolution of the hominids is the subject of Chapter 3.

QUESTIONS FOR REVIEW

1. How does the science of taphonomy help us to understand the evolution of life on Earth?

2. What were the basic innovations in dietary adaptations that characterize the difference between reptiles and mammals?

3. What reproductive differences characterize the difference between amphibians, reptiles, and mammals?

4. How do primates differ from other mammals?

5. What are the various primate mating groups?

MIND AND BODY EXPERIMENTS

1. Observe an awake reptile for thirty minutes and then observe a mammal for thirty minutes. What differences do you observe?

2. Besides size, what are the behavioral differences between a kitten and an adult cat or a puppy and an adult dog?

3. What is a cat's normal diet? What is a dog's normal diet? What strange things do either one eat?

4. How do you know when a dog or cat is angry or sick?

SUGGESTED READINGS

Campbell, B. G. 1983. *Human Ecology: The Story of Our Place in Nature from Prehistory to the Present*. Chicago: Aldine.

Cartmill, M. 1974. Rethinking Primate Origins. *Science* 184: 436–443.

Cartmill, M. 1975. *Primate Origins*. Minneapolis: Burgess.

Ciochon, R. L., and Fleagle, J. G. (eds.). 1987. *Primate Evolution and Human Origins*. Hawthorne, NY: Aldine de Gruyter.

DeVore, I. (ed.). 1965. *Primate Behavior: Field Studies of Monkeys and Apes*. New York: Holt, Rinehart and Winston.

Fleagle, J. G. 1988. *Primate Adaptation and Evolution*. New York: Academic Press.

Fossey, D. 1983. *Gorillas in the Mist*. Boston: Houghton Mifflin.

Goodall, J. 1986. *The Chimpanzees of Kombe: Patterns of Behavior*. Cambridge, MA: Belknap Press of Harvard University Press.

Goodall-Van Lawick, J. 1972. *In the Shadow of Man*. New York: Dell.

Hall, K. R. L., and DeVore, I. 1965. Baboon Social Behavior. In I. DeVore (ed.), *Primate Behavior*. New York: Holt, Rinehart and Winston.

Harlow, H. F. 1962. Social Deprivation in Monkeys. *Scientific American* 206: 1–10.

Kinzey, W. G. (Ed.). 1987. *The Evolution of Human Behavior: Primate Models*. Albany: State University of New York Press.

Kortlandt, A. 1980. How Might Early Hominids Have Defended Themselves Against Large Predators and Food Competition? *Journal of Human Evolution* 9: 79–112.

Kummer, H. 1971. *Primate Societies: Group Techniques of Ecological Adaptation*. Chicago: Aldine.

Romer, A. S. 1974. *The Vertebrate Story*. Chicago: University of Chicago Press.

Schaller, G. B. 1963. *The Mountain Gorilla*. Chicago: University of Chicago Press.

Schaller, G. B. 1971. *The Year of the Gorilla*. New York: Ballantine.

Shipman, P. 1997. Taphonomy. In F. Spencer (ed.), *History of Physical Anthropology*. Vol. 2, M-Z, pp. 1019–1022. New York: Garland.

Simons, E. L. 1989. Human Origins. *Science* 245: 1343–1350.

Simpson, G. G. 1949. *The Meaning of Evolution*. New Haven: Yale University Press.

Simpson, G. G. 1953. *The Major Features of Evolution*. New York: Columbia University Press.

Stanley, S. M. 1981. *The New Evolutionary Timetable*. New York: Basic.

Strickberger, M. W. 1996. *Evolution*. Sudbury, MA: Jones & Bartlett.

De Waal, F., and Lanting, F. 1997. *Bonobo, The Forgotten Ape*. Berkeley: The University of California Press.

Washburn, S. L., and Moore, R. 1980. *Ape into Human: A Study of Human Evolution* (2nd ed.). Boston: Little, Brown.

CHAPTER

3

Hominid Evolution

Prior to the discovery and description of ***Australopithecus afarensis*** (Photo 3.1, and Figures 3.1, 3.2) in 1974, there was no consensus about the anatomical definition and evolutionary origin of our own family, the Hominidae. However, there was widespread consensus that Asia and not Africa was the geographic "cradle of humankind." We now know that this is incorrect. Eventually, the number of

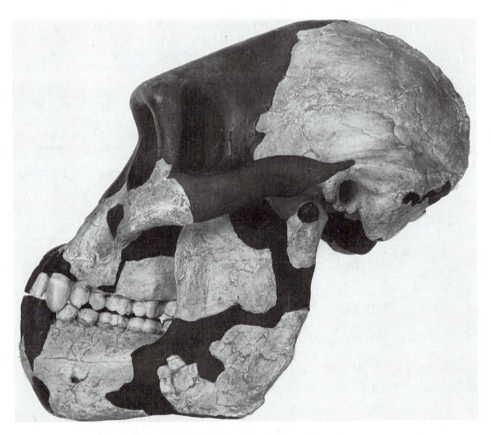

PHOTO 3.1   *Reconstruction of the Skull of Australopithecus afarensis*
(*Source:* Photo by L. Mecker and C. Tarka, courtesy of E. Delson.)

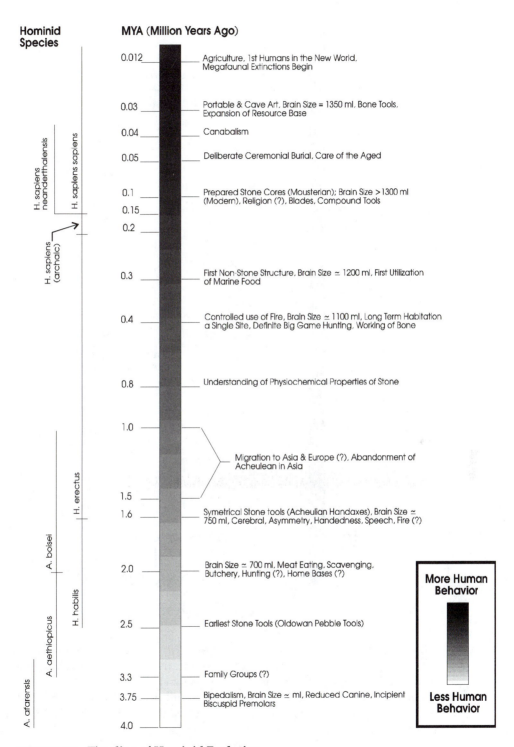

Hominid Species

MYA (Million Years Ago)

0.012 — Agriculture, 1st Humans in the New World, Megafaunal Extinctions Begin

0.03 — Portable & Cave Art, Brain Size = 1350 ml, Bone Tools, Expansion of Resource Base

0.04 — Canabalism

0.05 — Deliberate Ceremonial Burial, Care of the Aged

0.1 — Prepared Stone Cores (Mousterian); Brain Size >1300 ml (Modern), Religion (?), Blades, Compound Tools
0.15

0.2

0.3 — First Non-Stone Structure, Brain Size ≃ 1200 ml, First Utilization of Marine Food

0.4 — Controlled use of Fire, Brain Size ≃ 1100 ml, Long Term Habitation a Single Site, Definite Big Game Hunting, Working of Bone

0.8 — Understanding of Physiochemical Properties of Stone

1.0 — Migration to Asia & Europe (?), Abandonment of Acheulean in Asia

1.5

1.6 — Symetrical Stone tools (Acheulian Handaxes), Brain Size ≃ 750 ml, Cerebral, Asymmetry, Handedness, Speech, Fire (?)

2.0 — Brain Size ≃ 700 ml, Meat Eating, Scavenging, Butchery, Hunting (?), Home Bases (?)

2.5 — Earliest Stone Tools (Oldowan Pebble Tools)

3.3 — Family Groups (?)

3.75 — Bipedalism, Brain Size ≃ ml, Reduced Canine, Incipient Biscuspid Premolars

4.0

H. sapiens neanderthalensis
H. sapiens sapiens
H. sapiens (archaic)
H. erectus
A. boisei
H. habilis
A. aethlopicus
A. afarensis

More Human Behavior

Less Human Behavior

FIGURE 3.1   Timeline of Hominid Evolution

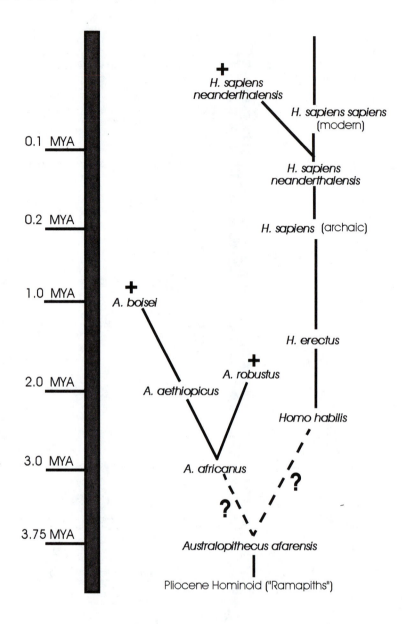

African finds and the invention of radiometric dating techniques made it clear that African hominids were far older than anyone had suspected. Today, the evidence is overwhelmingly in favor of the fact that Darwin was right: We are tropical animals from Africa. Also, as the result of the discovery and description of *A. afarensis*, there is common agreement that the fundamental anatomical definition of the Hominidae is **habitual bipedalism.**

At the beginning of the twentieth century, prominent European anatomists maintained that one of the most conspicuous unique traits of modern humans, a large brain, should also be characteristic in early hominids. A large brain was then believed to be the first step and the driving force of human evolution. This belief encouraged the uncritical acceptance of Piltdown Man (Photo 3.2), an alleged fossil hominid represented by fossil fragments discovered in a gravel pit in England by Charles Dawson from 1912 to 1915. This skull combined a large modern human cranial capacity with an apelike jaw. It was christened *Eoanthropus dawsoni* (*eo*=dawn+*anthropus*=man). The acceptance of the find as genuine convinced the leading anatomists of the day that hominids had originated in Europe. More important, most scholars became convinced that a large brain had preceded the appearance of a humanlike dentition. In fact, the perpetrator of the fraud had combined a cleverly stained modern human braincase with the broken jaw of an orangutan with a filed down canine. Whoever committed the fraud knew a sufficient amount about human evolution to modify the "fossils" in just the right

PHOTO 3.2   *"Fathers" of Piltdown Man*
Charles Dawson is seen standing in the back row, second from right.
(*Source:* Courtesy of the Natural History Museum, London.)

way. As had been prejudicially suspected, Piltdown Man "proved" that the earliest human ancestors not only derived from Europe but were also indigenous to the center of the British empire. For decades afterward, the acceptance of Piltdown hindered the recognition of real hominid ancestors in both Africa and Asia.

Before the Piltdown find, Eugène Dubois (1858–1940), a Dutch physician, had proposed that his 1891 find of *"Pithecanthropus erectus"* from the island of Java, Indonesia, was the earliest "apeman." *"Pithecanthropus,"* which is now labeled **Homo erectus** (L. *homo*=human+*erectus*=upright), had a small braincase that was only two-thirds the size of the modern human average (between 1,300–1,400 ml). Dubois's discovery was rejected by most anatomists as some form of ape that was far removed from human ancestry. The fact that it derived from the Asian tropics, an area supposedly populated by "degenerate races," further supported the scientists' contention. After his discovery, Dubois returned to Europe and spent the remainder of his life arguing bitterly that his find was a giant gibbonoid that was nonetheless directly ancestral to modern humans.

An even earlier find, that of the **Neanderthal** fossil in the Neander Valley in Germany in 1856, had also been widely rejected as a human ancestor. So called "primitive" traits such as a thick skull and pronounced brow ridges were denounced as pathological or as the result of a combination of disease and accident. After the Piltdown find, the cradle of humankind quite conveniently was fixed at the center of the British empire, where scholars had embraced social Darwinism as a welcome and scientifically supported justification for European colonialism.

Just over ten years after the Piltdown discovery, Raymond Dart had announced yet another fossil specimen as an "apeman" that was the "missing link" between apes and humans. Like Dubois's discovery, Dart's find in 1924 was also summarily dismissed as simply another ape or baboon. His find of an immature individual from a South African limestone quarry known as **Taung** is called *Australopithecus africanus*, literally "southern ape from Africa." The specimen was the antithesis of the Piltdown find because it exhibited a small cranium with a humanlike dentition. Even though Darwin had favored Africa as the geographic region where hominids had emerged, his contention that humans were closest to chimpanzees was rejected in favor of the hard evidence from Piltdown. It was not until the 1950s that a new dating technique (the fluorine method), developed by the British scientist Kenneth Oakley (1911–1981), exposed Piltdown as a fraud. This allowed scientists to conclusively state that the Piltdown jaw and cranial fragments were of different ages and geographic locations. Thus, they could not belong to the same individual. By the time of Oakley's findings, the evidence for early hominids in Africa and Asia was becoming overwhelming. Also very important to the rejection of Piltdown was the work of the physician and paleontologist Robert Broom (1866–1951) and the paleontologist J. T. Robinson (1923–1997), who for decades after Dart's announcement continued to turn up many more fossil finds, which made it clear that the Taung fossil was no freakish evolutionary development or misinterpreted ape.

Although the debate about the actual geographic origin gradually shifted in favor of the African supporters, all the participants of the debate shared two things. The first was that none of the participants understood the immense time periods they were dealing with. Some thought of human evolution in terms of tens of thousands or perhaps hundreds of thousands of years. The realization that hominid evolution had occurred over a period of millions of years would have to wait until the development of radiometric dating methods, which were first applied in the 1960s after Louis Leakey's (1903–1972) and Mary Leakey's (1913–1996) find of a fossil hominid at Olduvai Gorge in Tanzania.

The second thing that all the participants shared was the lack of an agreed-on anatomical definition of the Hominidae. Even after the Leakeys' discovery of *Australopithecus boisei* in 1959 (Photo 3.3), paleoanthropologists continued to argue about which fossil finds constituted early hominids. As mentioned in the previous chapter, one school led by the primate paleontologists Elwyn Simons and David Pilbeam argued that the earliest fossil hominids would show the marked reduced canine and V-shaped, or parabolic, dental arcade of modern humans. Others, of which Louis Leakey was one, held the belief that a relatively large brain would be a shared (apomorphic) feature of both ancient and modern hominids. Simons and Pilbeam pointed to the fossil jaw fragments of *Ramapithecus punjabicus*, which was discovered in the 1930s in what was then the Indian Siwalik Hills, as the earliest hominid. While this debate continued well into the 1970s, a behavioral component was added to the argument. S. L. Washburn, a physical anthropologist, Oakley, and others added a behavioral component to the definition of the Hominidae. They suggested that a small canine in conjunction with hands

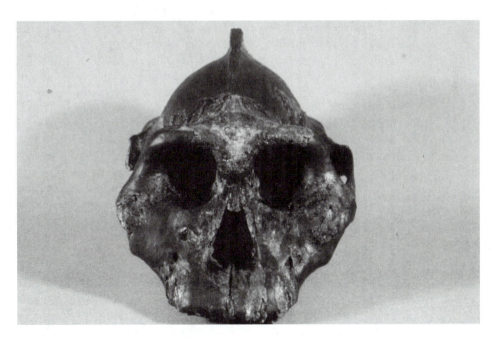

PHOTO 3.3   *Hyper-robust Australopithecine Found only in East Africa*

that had been freed by upright walking allowed the development of tool use. Louis Leakey's announcement of alleged tools from a fossil primate site at Fort Ternan, Kenya, and his announcement of tools from Olduvai Gorge further seemed to support that tool use was a very early characteristic of early hominids. The Washburn–Oakley–Leakey approach was well organized and very logical: free hands = tools = no need for a large canine = humanity. Dart had argued ever since his find of *A. africanus* that the associated faunal remains indicated an **osteodontokeratic "culture"** (Gk. *osteo*=bone+*donto*=tooth+*keratic*=horn). All of these early attempts missed the mark, and for years, there was no agreement about how to define a hominid. The final consensus as to the definition of the Hominidae and the age of the earliest members of the family eventually would be settled by two unrelated developments.

The first challenge to *Ramapithecus* came out of the University of California as the result of new biomolecular studies by Vincent Sarich and Alan Wilson. By comparing the blood proteins and DNA of chimpanzees, humans, and other mammals, Sarich and Wilson identified neutral mutations, which they argued acted like a **molecular clock** that could be used to accurately estimate the date of the ape/human divergence. They maintained that the earliest hominid was not 15 to 17 mya (the estimated age of the Ramapithecines) but 3 to 8 mya, an age that made the discussion of the meager jaw fragments moot. Sarich almost instantly became renown for his acerbic wit with pronouncements such as, "I don't care what it looks like, if it's older than eight million years it can't be a hominid." Some years later he quipped, "I know my molecules had ancestors, they [the paleontologists] can only hope that their fossils had descendants." The paleontologists resisted fiercely, but in the end it was not the molecular biology, but another fossil find that finally settled the questions of the age and defining anatomical characteristics of the human family.

The discovery and careful description of a new species of hominid, *Australopithecus afarensis*, which came to be known as Lucy (after the Beatles' song "Lucy in the Sky with Diamonds"), at Afar (also known as Hadar), a fluviolacustrine locality in Ethiopia, changed human origin studies forever. At first, working alone, the discoverer of Lucy, Donald Johanson, had relegated the new find to Dart's *A. africanus*. However, after beginning cooperation with Tim White, the two jointly authored a paper that proclaimed that Lucy represented a new species of *A. afarensis*. Key points that Johanson and White used to argue for the distinctiveness of the species emphasized that dentally *A. afarensis* was transitional in morphology between apes and humans. The canine, though large and projecting by human standards, was small when compared to apes. Second, the first lower premolar was incipiently bicuspid, unlike those of apes. Lucy's teeth had been caught in the act of evolving.

Even more important, Johanson and White argued that the **postcranial** (below the head) skeletal features, which distinguished *A. afarensis*, were all related to bipedalism, which also clearly separates modern humans from apes. Literally from head to toe, it was the distinctive skeletal features of bipedalism that were to become the defining criteria of the Hominidae. In fact, the skull of *A. afarensis* is so apelike that if it looked any more like an ape, it would be nearly impossible to distinguish it from presumed chimpanzeelike ancestors. The cranial capacity of *A. afarensis* was identical to that of living apes. Although even earlier specimens have now been reported and assigned to new taxa, they remain poorly known but apparently similar to *A. afarensis*.

Johanson and White based their descriptions on material from two sites. One site was Afar dating to about 3.3 mya; the other site was **Laetoli** (ca. 3.7 mya) in Tanzania, worked by archaeologist Mary Leakey. Hadar was remarkable in that it had not only yielded one of the most complete hominid fossils to date, but it would also give up the remains of at least twelve other individuals of both sexes and all age ranges, which would later come to be known popularly as the **"First Family."** Although the fossils from Laetoli were older, they were also much less spectacular as they consisted of fragmentary jaws and isolated teeth. Hobetweenwever, Laetoli, yielded another kind of evidence that was just as remarkable as Lucy or the First Family. Perfectly preserved in the hardened volcanic ash were the footprints of at least two hominids that had walked across the landscape nearly 4 mya (Photo 3.4). Nothing like it before or since has come to light at an early hominid site. These footprints are nearly identical to those of modern humans. They show that all the basic characteristics of the modern human foot had already evolved.

White, Johanson, and Mary Leakey combined the Afar and Laetoli fossils in one description. However, when Mary Leakey learned that White and Johanson proposed naming a new species, she withdrew her name from their planned joint article. She and others had decided that Lucy and her kind were not distinct enough from *A. africanus* to warrant a new species. For years after its announcement, *A. afarensis* came under various forms of attack. Some argued that the sexual dimorphism of the species was so great that at least one other species was also present in the so-called First Family. Instead of the 10 to 12 percent sexual dimorphism expected for a chimpanzeelike ancestor (and also found in modern humans), the *A. afarensis* sample exhibited a sexual dimorphism more characteristic of a gorilla, which is on the order of 80 to 100 percent. As will become apparent shortly, the question of sexual dimorphism continues to be a problem encountered in interpreting the fossil record. There are at least half a dozen views on where *A. afarensis* belongs in the hominid family tree. In fact, the identification of sex in early hominids is based largely on size. Lucy is designated a female because she is small, not because she shows the distinct skeletal traits of modern human females.

The notion that a large brain and human-sized canine are characteristics of the early hominids has now largely been abandoned. A relatively small canine (though not as small as that of modern humans) may also be correlated with bipedalism, but probably not for the reason that Washburn once put forward. Many of the often acrimonious debates about which fossils were human ancestors probably could have been avoided if past discoveries had allowed us to develop an agreed-on definition of our family.

It is important to emphasize that the earliest hominids were fully bipedal, though the details appeared to have differed slightly from later hominids. Even

PHOTO 3.4   *Footprint Trail Left by at Least Three Hominids, Dating to 3.7 mya.*

earlier hominids than Lucy—such as ***Ardipithecus ramidus*** (*Ethiopian ramidus*= root) (ca. 4.4 mya)—and ***Australopithecus anamensis*** (*Ethiopian anam*=lake) (ca. 4 mya)—were fully bipedal. We know of no transitional stages between quadru- pedalism and bipedalism. These earlier dates put us even closer to the split from apes so that there is less and less time for bipedalism to have evolved. It may eventually prove to be the case that bipedalism was a rather sudden event instead of a slow process. This very much favors a punctuated origin of bipedalism.

Hominid Bipedalism

Aristotle once defined humans as "featherless bipeds." (He did not know about kangaroos.) Although many primates including apes can walk bipedally, they can do so for only short periods. For nonhuman primates, this form of locomotion is both awkward and exhausting. Birds also locomote bipedally, but human walking involves a unique phase in which the upper and lower leg bones lock and the leg is fully extended at the knee. Hominids are habitually striding bipeds. During stride, the heel receives and supports the weight of the next step and the ball of the foot and big toe push off to begin the cycle all over again. Although we seldom think about these movements as adults, they are perfected through trial and error (and many falls) by little hominids. Because hominids became so committed to bipedalism, it is possible to observe a number of anatomical features, many of which also have behavioral implications and associations. The precise anatomical characteristics not only allow us to confidently identify fossil hominids, but they help us to understand how bipedalism changed our behavior forever. The hallmarks of bipedalism are so clear that even terribly preserved specimens are easily recognizable as hominids. These traits can be inventoried from the head down.

The Cranium

The position of our heads in relation to the rest of our bodies literally changes the way we look at the world. Among quadrupeds, the head precedes the rest of the body during locomotion. In hominids, the head basically arrives when the rest of the body does. Hominids differ from quadrupeds in the placement of the opening that admits the spinal cord to the brain, the **foramen magnum** (L. *foramen* = hole + *magnum* = large). In quadrupeds, the foramen magnum points posteriorly. In hominids, this large hole points directly downward because the head is balanced on top of the spinal column. We therefore survey the world from the top of a kind of moving tower. This produces other changes such as large bony attachments for the sternocleidomastoid **muscle** complex, which allow us to move our heads from side to side. Protrusions of bone located behind the ears and known as mastoids (breast-shaped) are poorly developed in both adult nonhuman primates and in immature hominids. After humans have learned to walk, these sites of muscle attachment become prominent and provide a site of attachment for the muscles that run to the sternum and clavicle. This complex allows us to move our heads rapidly from side to side, as when we watch a tennis match. They also support the side-to-side scanning motion of the environment that we frequently use when we walk or communicate with people. In animals with developed stereoscopic vision, such as carnivores and other primates, scanning vision is restricted, and more of the body must be moved to take in a scene.

Though humans are not known for their keen eyesight, they possess a unique ability related to vision. Most animals must wait for another animal to move to pick them out of the scene, which is why prey often freeze. Millions of years of mammalian evolution have relied on the fact that carnivores cannot lock onto prey without smell or movement. Humans, on the other hand, are very good at picking things out of the visual clutter. Where carnivores wait for movement, hominids create their own movement with side-to-side scanning. Some anthropoids also appear to employ a rudimentary form of this locating technique, but it is unclear what additional role scent plays in locating frozen prey.

The Spine

Nonhuman primates and other quadrupedal animals are built with their spine parallel to the ground, though primates in general are more orthograde in their body construction. As a result, they have more arched or bridge-shaped spines. In adult hominids, the spine is distinctly S-shaped. As with the mastoids, this shape does not manifest itself until little hominids begin to walk. The S-shape is a more efficient way of bearing vertically directed mass and weight. However, this adaptation is by no means completely efficient, and the number one medical complaint in Western societies is lower back pain. That pain is the price that hominids pay for bipedalism. The number of vertebrae have been reduced in hominids in comparison with apes, and the bodies of the vertebrae have also become shorter and wider. All of these traits result from the fact that humans must bear much more weight on the spine and two legs, while most other primates divide their weight between four limbs.

The Hip Joint

In hominids, the bones that make up the sides of the pelvic cavity have become shortened, flattened, and flared outward to form a sort of bony bowl that supports the upper body. In human females, the hips have been further modified for childbearing. This results in the obvious sexual dimorphism between the narrower hips of men and the wider hips of women. It is usually easy to dig up a hip bone of modern humans and tell if the individual is a male or female. However, it is important to emphasize that current sexual dimorphism in hip joints is an evolutionarily recent development related to giving birth to large-brained babies.

Although not preserved in the fossil record, the muscle structure of extinct hominids is also unique. Hominids are the only primates that have buttocks. More scientifically stated, our gluteus maximus is far larger than in any other primate. This muscle along with others allows us to bend at the waist and erect the upper portion of the body over the lower portion. It is extremely important in stabilizing the upper part of the body over the lower part when we walk. Bipedal walking also requires that all of the body weight be borne momentarily on one leg. At the same time, the hip muscles allow the off-ground leg to swing smoothly as the weight-bearing side shifts stress away from the movement side of the body.

The Knee Joint

The knee joint of hominids is equally distinct in its anatomy. In quadrupedal primates, the upper leg or thigh bone (the **femur**) meets the lower leg bone (the **tibia**) at an angle of 0 degrees. In hominids, the angle is always 11 degrees. It is literally possible to tell at thirty yards whether one is looking at the knee of a hominid or an ape. The increased angle of the hominid knee joint brings the center of gravity directly into the midline of the body. Like the adaptations of the spinal column, the knee joint is subject to so much stress that the ligaments, which tighten the knee joint, and cartilage, which cushions the knee joint, are often subject to extreme stress and frequent failure. Knee injury is the most common serious sports injury.

The Foot

The foot has also undergone a number of important evolutionary changes in response to the pressures of bipedalism. In contrast with other primates, the foot of hominids has become a strictly weight-bearing organ. Apes can turn the pages of a newspaper with their feet, whereas hominids find this difficult. In apes, the big toe is divergent, which means the big toe more closely resembles a thumb in its flexibility for grasping objects. In hominids, the big toe is enlarged and situated parallel to the other digits. The large size of the big toe is also a weight bearing adaptation that allows humans to push off with it during walking.

Hominid feet also have transverse and longitudinal arches, which support the weight of the body. That is, if the foot were cross-sectioned from the instep to the outer edge of the foot, the bones would be seen as an arch. If the foot were cut lengthwise, it would also be apparent that there is an arch beginning at the ball of the foot in the front and the heel in the back. Some people are born with poorly developed arches, which makes extended walking difficult and uncomfortable. The army tradionally rejected recruits for "flat feet."

Other Traits Related to Bipedalism

One of the other unusual anatomical traits of bipedalism in hominids is the very small human canine. In comparison with other primates, the human canine is greatly reduced in size and in effectiveness as a puncturing, ripping, and holding tooth. A number of paleoanthropologists have suggested that because of bipedalism, the canine lost its effectiveness as a threat and dangerous weapon. It can be argued that a canine is not of much use to humans because fighting is done with bare hands or weapons. We know from fossil records that even the earliest known bipedal hominids had greatly reduced canines that, though bigger than those found in modern humans, were distinctly different from the honing canine found in nonhuman primates. In nonhuman primates, the lower first premolar is sectorial and takes the form of a blade or bar that hones the large upper canine into a very sharp tooth that is sharpened every time the animal closes its jaws.

Most primate canines are formidable and intimidating weapons that are displayed and used with members of their own species and with other animals.

It is clear that early hominids contrasted with their ape ancestors in being fully committed bipeds and in the reduction of the canine. On the basis of our current knowledge, it seems that the earliest hominids did not make stone tools. From an ecological perspective, it is hard to imagine how a small chimpanzee-sized creature without weapons or large canines was able to survive in relatively open habitats (see below). It is also necessary to try to determine why striding bipedalism was so important that we still pay the evolutionary price for this unique mode of locomotion. Not only bad backs, but also weak knees and degenerated hip joints are the price we pay for a kind of locomotion that made us one of the slowest of the apes. It would seem that the earliest hominids had few obvious advantages going for them. In fact, human walking is so complicated that it has been described as a "controlled fall." No robotic device has come close to mimicking human walking, and it currently seems that biotechnology will allow us to grow new limbs before engineers can assemble them.

Theories for the Rise of Bipedalism

In puzzling out the "what and whys" of our evolutionary history, the theory that most precisely and simply explains the widest range of phenomena should be, and usually is, taken as the most likely and correct explanation. In discussing possible selective pressures for bipedalism, we need to explain observations such as why hominids are not only bipedal but also are essentially hairless, have small canines, depend on tool use, and have emphasized language and highly complex means of social communication.

Whether it is an artifact of sampling and luck or actually representative of a bottleneck in hominid evolution, hominids appear abruptly in the fossil record. By about 8 mya, the record of fossil African apes or dental apes essentially ceases. Just over 4 mya, hominids appear. The period in between has been christened by the paleoanthropologist F. Clark Howell as the "black hole." Some researchers have suggested that hominid ancestors underwent a period of intense selection pressure that greatly reduced population size. One theory suggests that tropical forests underwent an intense period of desiccation (the **Messinian salinity crisis**). At this time, the Mediterranean Sea appears to have become isolated from the Atlantic Ocean with the result that great deposits of salt precipitated out of solution in places like the island of Messina. Geological records from Asia suggest a similar climatic deterioration. During this period, it is also possible that terrestrial monkeys underwent an adaptive radiation, perhaps competing with and eventually relegating large Asian apes to isolated forest and woodland habitats.

One cannot be sure of the effect and severity of this climatic change. However, we do know that a quadrupedal ape walked on all fours into this time period and emerged as a bipedal hominoid, a kind of super ape that for whatever reason had become a fully habitual biped. The super ape retained an ape-sized brain on top of a fully bipedal skeleton. As noted above, its canine became reduced.

Alternatively or even synchronically, the apelike ancestor of the hominids may have occupied tropical forests. The perceived bottleneck has also been suggested to be the result of poor preservation. Tropical forests are terrible environments for the creation and preservation of fossils. Highly acidic soils, bacteria, and insects quickly reclaim the organic matter of dead organisms. One problem with this explanation is that we do have fairly good fossil records of orangutans and giant pandas, who are tropical and subtropical forest dwellers. In any case, what actually happened may never be known, but a number of theories and scenarios have been put forward to account for the advent of the super ape. Each has attempted to explain not only bipedalism, but also other aspects of early hominid evolution.

Tool Using

As mentioned previously, S. L. Washburn and others once argued that the main selection pressure that encouraged bipedalism was the advantage of having hands freed from locomotion by walking on two legs. The free hands theory is entirely logical and makes sense of what we see modern humans doing every day. Many other primates use their hands to manipulate the environment, but humans have their hands free all the time, unless they are holding something or clinging to something. Washburn argued that hands that were free all the time allowed the development of the skill needed for the manufacture and use of tools. The major problem with this explanation is that the first stone tools are only 2.5 million years younger than the earliest bipedal hominids, which date back to about 4.4 mya. In other words, there is an almost 2 million year gap between the time our earliest ancestors appeared and the time that they began to make stone tools. As part of this theory, it has also been suggested that functions such as cutting, ripping, and tearing that were carried out by the canine became replaced by more efficient stone tools. However, small canines also appear several million years before the earliest stone tools. Of course, it is possible to argue that hominids were using nonlithic (nonstone) tools instead of stone tools. From chimpanzee studies, we indeed think that early hominids must have used nonlithic tools, and most of tools made by hunters and gatherers today are nonlithic. Nonlithic tools are rarely preserved in the archaeological record. Therefore, even if a nonlithic explanation is correct, we have very little chance of testing this theory. Raymond Dart's osteodontokeratic culture has not held up to scrutiny. In fact, bone and dental tools appear to have been one of the last materials used by hominid tool makers.

Yet another tool-using theory remains highly plausible but little discussed. This is the rock throwing theory. Louis Leakey once performed an experiment in which he discarded his clothing and tried to survive on the African savanna using only what natural resources he could find. Together with a companion, Leakey found that by using stones he could drive off predators from their kills and obtain the meat for himself. Though originally viewed with some amusement, this experiment suggests an adaptive advantage that early hominids may have possessed. Leakey also once suggested that certain Miocene ape fossils, specifically

Kenyapithecus wickeri from Fort Ternan, which dates back to about 16 mya, were associated with stones that showed evidence of having been used or "bashed" as he put it. Though few scientists now put much credence in this observation, he may have inadvertently pointed to a unique characteristic of modern humans— that of accurate throwing.

In the description of chimpanzee tool use in the previous chapter, we saw that they were not very adept at killing or defending themselves from predators with either lithic or nonlithic tools. Though they are proportionately much stronger than modern humans, chimpanzees not only lack the mobile shoulder joint of humans, but also probably the mental architecture for precise and powerful throwing. Humans, on the other hand, are frightfully lethal with the simplest of tools, such as rocks. Professional baseball pitchers can throw a ball at more than 100 miles an hour. Even much lower velocities, of which any adolescent or adult human is capable, can easily injure or kill. Clubs are equally lethal in the hands of humans.

Temperature Regulation

The theory of temperature regulation is associated with the work of anthropologist Bernard Campbell. Campbell suggested that one of the main selective challenges in the African savanna is the need to stay cool. According to this theory, this was achieved by becoming bipedal. In comparison with quadrupedal animals, true bipeds have much less of their body surface area exposed to the direct rays of the sun. This is especially important, it is argued, during the hottest part of the day. Furthermore, the surface of a naked biped body presents maximum surface area to prevailing breezes. Much like the sailback dinosaurs, hominids can adjust the position of their cooling and warming surfaces. Unlike the sailbacks, the hominid body remained permanently adjusted to the sun without having to purposely reorient itself. Hominids cool themselves through surface evaporation or sweating. This in turn would select for hairlessness or nakedness. In fact, one of the unique characteristics of humans is that we sweat more than any other animal. Most mammals dissipate heat through respiration in the mouth. This is why dogs pant. Nakedness and sweating can also be related to the fact that, unlike most mammals, physically active hominids must drink water daily. Some groups of modern humans living in arid environments occasionally can go longer than a day or two without replenishing water, but other tropical mammals can go for several days without water.

It also has been suggested that because we sweat, we smell unappetizing to predators. This interpretation is more difficult to support. (Humans have been eaten by lions.) As part of his theory of homeothermy, Campbell suggested another benefit of naked sweating: that although the sweat of other individuals smells bad to us when we encounter it in the modern world, naked sweating attracts us to each other in the context of outdoor sunlight. Specifically, it has been suggested that sweat reacts to sunshine by being broken down into airborne hormones known as pheromones. Campbell argues that pubic and axillary (underarm) hair have been maintained in humans as mechanisms for broadcasting pheromones. Many pheromones in the animal kingdom are known to be extremely effective initiators of sexual behavior. What has been suggested for hominids is that increased sexiness may have given early hominids a reproductive incentive to mate more often. Increased attractiveness can be further theorized to have increased sociosexual cohesiveness.

Studies have shown that women are able to identify mates and family members by the smell of their clothing. Other studies suggest (though less strongly) that odor may also play a part in mate selection, especially as an avoidance device for genetically incompatible mates whose offspring may suffer from histological incompatibilities. Also supporting the possible importance of pheromones is the fact that cohabiting human females tend to have synchronized menstrual cycles. A distillate of the sweat of menstruating women applied under the nose of a nonmenstruating woman induces menstruation. Why this should be an adaptive advantage is frankly difficult to understand. The synchronization of cycles of fertility is common in animals that live in seasonal climates. The African savanna is subject to marked seasonality in the availability of food and water and does have a number of species with highly seasonal breeding cycles.

It is easy to see that offspring have the best chance of survival if they are born in the season with the most food. This is especially important in areas where there is very little food during some seasons. It is more difficult to relate this advantage to tropical forest adaptations, where food is more equitably distributed throughout the year.

As part of this theory, it is also possible to explain the unique reduction of the hominid canine. The possession of a large sharp canine would have been selected against because it could inflict too much damage on conspecifics that no longer possessed thick coats of hair and tough skin. All nonhuman primates can inflict serious and potentially lethal damage on naked humans. In short, settling fights by the traditional primate means of biting would have become a practice that early hominids could not afford in terms of the amount of blood spilled and the number of organs damaged.

Campbell's arguments and other similar scenarios have generated a lot of interest. The basic thrust of heat regulation theories is that bipedalism developed for physiological reasons. Such arguments deal directly with the fact that in terms of our physiological mechanisms, modern humans bear the characteristics of animals that adapted to a tropical environment. Physiologically for instance, that it is much easier for humans to stay cool than to stay warm. One of the major problems with Campbell's model is that many other terrestrial animals live on the savanna, and all of them are quadrupeds that retain hair or fur and do not sweat in the way that humans do. In fact, humans living in the tropics sweat so much that they require salt on a daily basis to maintain efficient physiological balance. For hominids, an important source of salt may have been the blood of other animals.

The Radiator Theory

Another anthropologist specializing in **paleoneurology** (the study of ancient brains), Dean Falk, has put forward a related theory emphasizing the need to keep the body from overheating. Falk's theory differs from Campbell's in that it more specifically emphasizes the need to keep the brain cool through radiational cooling. Falk's idea is concerned not so much with the advantages conferred by bipedalism as with why we were able to evolve a large brain. Simply put, she points out that the brain must remain cool in order to function. Her studies of the brains of modern humans and the endocasts (inner casts of the brain) of human ancestors suggest that hominids developed a special cooling system of veins in the head that lead to more efficient cooling of this important organ. This cooling system was so advantageous that even larger brains eventually evolved. What Campbell's and Falk's theories have in common is that they attribute the evolution of certain aspects of human behavior, such as intelligence and tool use, to factors stemming from another kind of selection pressure, namely heat regulation. In other words, the prime mover of human evolution had less to do with larger brains than with the past need to cope with physiological stress that our ancestors encountered in tropical Africa. It is also true that brains do not begin to enlarge until the appearance of stone tools.

The Arboreal Theory

Two scientists from the State University of New York at Stonybrook, Randall Sussman and Jack Stern, have suggested another explanation for bipedalism not unlike the gibbon theory of hominid origins mentioned in the previous chapter. These researchers believe that the morphology of the finger and limb bones of the earliest known australopithecines indicate that they spent much more time in trees than the savanna theories have recognized. They argue that the common primate manner in which hominids climb trees by always keeping the head above the trunk also would encourage adaptations that would constitute a suitable preadaptation for bipedal locomotion on the ground. It is relatively easy to tie this theory in with the apparent desiccation of Miocene forests by speculating that climatic change would have selected for life in the trees of the reduced forests.

Their basic anatomical argument rests on the fact that the early australopithecines have very curved digits, which are much more similar to chimpanzees than modern humans. Like extant arboreal primates adapted for grasping trunks and branches, Lucy and her kind may have also depended more on life in the trees than life on the ground.

Not surprisingly, this theory also has its flaws. The first is that curved digits are also characteristic of very strong muscle and ligament attachments and not necessarily associated only with arboreal living. A second criticism is that chimpanzees, to which the early hominid finger bones have been compared, do spend a lot of time in trees but are still not bipedal. Finally, we are still left with the problem of why other arboreal animals did not become bipedal. The arboreal theory of bipedalism is basically one of preadaptation, similar to theories that were once advanced to account for gibbon "bipedality" and the rise of primates as a whole. This theory, also espoused at one time by Washburn, pointed out that when gibbons do come to the ground for short periods of time, they walk bipedally. The problem with accepting this kind of locomotion as a precursor of bipedalism is that the extremely long and specialized arms of these primates allow the animal to balance in much the same way that a high wire walker does with a pole. This mechanism is in no way homologous to the downward and anteriorly directed center of gravity that aids the locomotion of hominids.

One advantage of this theory is that it may explain how a creature as small, slow, and defenseless as *A. afarensis* avoided being hunted into extinction. It is also important to remember that modern forest peoples also spend a lot of time in trees in the pursuit of resources. The harvesting of tropical coconuts is no easy task for city hominids from the West. Little hominids of many cultures also spend a relatively great amount of time in trees even when the acquisition of resources is not involved.

The Aquatic Theory

The aquatic theory is somewhat bizarre. It has not been, and in my opinion should not be, taken seriously by scientists. Yet it has enjoyed a wide audience in popular science. It receives mention here because it has been successfully popularized, and anthropologists are often asked to comment on it. Elaine Morgan (not a trained anthropologist) has contended that humans bear anatomical and behavioral characteristics that resemble marine mammals and that these characteristics are especially developed in human females. These include an extra layer of subcutaneous body fat in females; hair distribution patterns, which like marine mammals seem to be arranged for streamlining from front to back (in both sexes); and a general reduction in body hair (especially females). She also emphasizes the human infant's innate reaction of closing nostrils and mouth when submerged in water.

Her theory postulates that one of the primary adaptations of early hominids was the tendency to float in water to avoid predators. She maintains that because human females have more of the supposedly aquatic adaptations (subcutaneous body fat and "large breasts"), they spent more time floating than males. She deduces that males were spending much more time on land and hints that in addition to impregnating females, their other main evolutionary function was to serve as predator bait by diverting attention from females and their young. She further suggests that hair on the head serves as a means for allowing the infant to cling to the mother and this is why infants are born with a strong grasping reflex.

In fairness, some of her observations do demand systematic attention, or rather refutation. Females do have an extra layer of body fat, and most females, in contrast to males, are positively buoyant (they float rather than sink). Human infants do float and close up their nostrils and mouths when put into water. Finally, the reduction of body hair is in fact characteristic of marine mammals.

However, there are other more parsimonious ways to explain this constellation of traits without referring to an aquatic model. All of these sexually dimorphic traits are easily explainable in terms of the reproduction of a terrestrial mammal. Extra female body fat is probably an adaptation to the fact that females must nourish a fetus for many months. Whether they lived on land or water, they still need the extra margin of energy that extra subcutaneous body fat provides for the "little parasites" that they nurture before and after childbirth. There are other plausible reasons for the reduction of hair. Although it is characteristic of marine mammals, cooling would seem to be a much more parsimonious explanation for an obviously terrestrial mammal. The hair distribution and nostril closure reflex may be related to water, but the water is probably that of the womb and not that of a lake or ocean. This reflex is lost soon after birth. Perhaps more important, most humans on this planet are not very good swimmers. In fact, people must very carefully and consciously learn how to swim; it is not at all like learning to walk. Female human breasts are a subject that will be addressed later, but it is safe to say that not all of them are large. If human female breasts are somewhat larger than those of other primates, a simpler explanation is that there is a morphology that allows a mother to nurse while walking or standing and holding the infant on one hip or another.

The Grass Theory

The grass theory is a simple theory that says that hominids eventually developed the ability to be habitual bipeds so that they could spot predators (and perhaps prey) by seeing over tall savanna grass. The problem with this theory is that none of the numerous other savanna species became bipeds. All other African mammals do just fine as quadrupeds. Another theory related to life in an open grassland environment is that of Clifford Jolly, who suggests that the reduction of the canine was a response to the need to chew small and hard morsels of food such as seeds and tubers. This **graminivorous** interpretation was suggested primarily on his observations of the gelada baboon (*Theropithecus gelada*). The behaviors and anatomy associated with such an adaptation have been called the **T-complex** after *Theropithecus*. Jolly suggested that a grinding rotary motion of the jaws would have been much more effective in processing seed food. Such grinding cannot be carried out by animals with long canines because these large protruding teeth prevent rotary grinding. Seeing over the grass would have also been an advantage for such animals, and the reduction of the canine would have made the biting behavior of early bipeds less effective. One obvious problem with the T-complex is that even gelada baboons have very large canines, and, as mentioned above, all of the other savanna animals have failed to evolve habitually striding bipedalism.

Sociosexual Bonding Theory

With the exception of gibbons, no other primates form lifelong sociosexual pair bonds. Social carnivores and many birds do form such bonds. One nebulously discussed theory for the advent of bipedalism is based on the idea that stronger lifelong bonds between males and females would have conferred a reproductive advantage. With this in mind, workers such as the zoologist Desmond Morris have suggested that face-to-face sexual and social communication would have been a superior way of cementing permanent bonding. Ventral–ventral sex has been proposed as an adaptive innovation that has the advantage of involving facial expressions in the act of mating. The forward-facing position of the human female clitoris has also been implicated in such bonding. Bonobo sociosexual interaction seems to involve an unusually large component of face-to-face sex in social situations. The implication here is that more communication leads to greater intimacy and more stable sociosexual bonding. Morris has suggested a theory of self-mimicry, which maintains that hominids evolved to sexually signal in a face-to-face manner prior to ventral–ventral mating. As part of this system, human females supposedly developed large breasts that mimic female buttocks as viewed from the rear by males in nonhuman primates. It has also been conjectured that the gelada baboon has adopted a similar strategy with females developing a distinctly bright-colored patch of chest skin that is attractive to males. The red lips, which are accentuated with lipstick in our society, and the shape of the navel supposedly mimic the color and shape of the vaginal labia.

One of the major faults with this hypothesis is that ventral–ventral sex among humans was not the rule until the dissemination in recent history of the "missionary position." Furthermore, the attractiveness of enlarged female breasts cannot be shown to be a cultural universal, but instead a general characteristic of Western culture. It is important not to confuse anatomical indications of sex with indications of sexual attractiveness. We will deal with this in much more detail in the chapter on sexuality. Other sexual indicators of sex or attractiveness, such as hairstyle, body adornment, posture, and locomotion, are so variable as to be useless in determining what is "sexy" for any given cultural group. The main fault with Morris's theory is that it is extremely ethnocentric, which means it is based on the idiosyncratic characteristics of his own society.

While closer sociosexual communication is a popular idea in the late twentieth century of most Western cultures, it is hard to imagine that it would have been a driving force behind such a fundamental adaptive change as bipedalism. Other primates and other animals in general communicate perfectly well with one another. It is difficult to imagine that any of the vertebrate groups that have been studied would achieve a substantial evolutionary advantage from learning to carry out sexual communication in a "new and improved" way. Human sexual activity is different in that most of it does not result in reproduction. It is tempting to link our unusual sexual activity directly with increased reproduction, but in fact, human reproduction stands out for the comparatively low number of offspring.

The Provisioning Theory

Paleoanthropologist **C. Owen Lovejoy** proposed a very comprehensive theory of hominid origins and bipedalism that incorporates a number of the unique characters of hominids in a prime mover explanation. Reasoning from the standpoint of natural selection, animals that leave the most offspring are most fit and therefore will eventually outcompete those that leave fewer offspring. Because single births are plesiomorphic for primates as a whole, the number of offspring per female can be increased only by decreasing the time between births. Reduced birth spacing is in fact one of the apomorphic characters of modern humans. Other primates care for one offspring at a time and usually do not become pregnant again until the onset of the infant's adolescence. Human females, on the other hand, routinely raise several offspring and frequently several infants at one time. This is also unavoidable because of the extreme length of time required for human maturation. However, just as we pay an evolutionary price for bipedalism, multiple contemporary offspring also have a price. Lovejoy pointed out that that price was a decrease in female mobility. It is indeed difficult to travel across the landscape foraging with several "ectoparasites" in tow.

Bipedalism was the answer to the problem. Selection was not for a form of bipedalism that made early hominids faster, for as noted previously, we are the slowest of the higher primates. Instead, hominids evolved a form of bipedalism that allows them to cover a relatively great distance in a single day. No known primate covers as much territory in a single day as a hunter and gatherer. Thirty-five miles walking and as much as seventy miles running can be covered by a physically fit male. At the same time, the hands are freed, not just for tool use, but rather for carrying food. Specifically, Lovejoy suggested that there was intense selection for the provisioning of the female by the male. A very important point of the theory is that provisioning would not work if bulky low-protein foods were transported over long distances. The adaptation would only be advantageous if compact packages of easily transportable high-energy protein such as meat were the food being provisioned.

The theory is appealing because it seems to explain a number of other hominid oddities. The evolution of an advanced or radical system of cooling becomes almost a necessity, whether for the brain or the body as a whole. Water demand rises not only because of increased activity, but also for the digestion of raw meat. The theory also helps to explain the unique dentition of the earliest hominids, especially the appearance of a nonsectorial, bicuspid premolar. I believe that the anterior premolars of hominids began to function as a **neocarnassial.** Carnassial are the bladelike teeth found in carnivores that are used to slice meat. A simple home experiment demonstrates the function of the neocarnassial: Notice that a hamburger is eaten with the incisors, but a piece of steak is first bitten with the premolars. This agrees with Lovejoy's provisioning hypothesis that the shift to at least some meat eating took place early in the hominid clade. It is important to note that the provisioning theory does not distinguish between scavenging and hunting. The new resource could have been obtained in both ways.

Lovejoy's hypothesis also seemingly explains unique features of human sexuality. Basic textbooks on hominid evolution always note that human females are unique as having no visually displayed estrus and no distinctly circumscribed times when they will copulate. Furthermore, human sex is remarkable in that there is no synchronization between fertility and frequency of intercourse. Biologically, humans "waste" most of their sexual activity. This may also be explainable by the provisioning theory, and it has been suggested that these mechanisms help to increase the probability that the male will be rewarded sexually.

There are a number of criticisms that apply to the provisioning theory. First, the reduction in birth spacing supposedly results in more hominid offspring being produced in the same amount of time that an ape would produce less offspring. One problem is that apes become sexually mature much earlier and therefore can begin breeding earlier. If we conservatively take an average chimpanzee maturation age of eight years old, the chimpanzee can produce three offspring by the age of twenty-four. A similar number of offspring is highly reasonable for both early and extant hominids. However, twenty-four is a ripe age for a wild-dwelling chimpanzee, but might not have been for an early hominid. This question cannot be permanently settled because we do not know whether to apply apelike or humanlike maturation rates to our earliest ancestors.

Another limitation of Lovejoy's hypothesis is that it may not apply well to modern humans. Despite the burdens imposed by children, human hunter and gatherer mothers do manage to go about the countryside collecting most of the hunter and gatherer diet. After the age of four, children, especially little girls, can be a decided asset to collecting. As will become apparent in the next chapter, females become productive economic units much earlier than males. It is also possible to argue that even among adults, hunting is inefficient and undependable. In most hunter and gatherer groups, male economic productivity rarely equals that of females.

Although we have considered these theories separately, most of them are overlapping and many times mutually supportive. Lovejoy's theory seems to explain the greatest number of characteristics and becomes even more plausible in conjunction with Campbell's homeothermy model. What we cannot explain away is the fact that bipedalism initiated changes that would become profound. The shift to bipedalism may have been rapid and was undoubtedly the first major adaptive shift. Lucy and her kind were essentially bipedal apes who also had begun to change their diet to become more omnivorous through the addition of meat. Sometime before or after the time of Lucy, the Hominidae would develop two distinctly different dietary adaptations. One line, that of the robust australopithecines, would become specialized vegetarians who eventually became extinct approximately one million years ago. The other line, the so-called gracile australopithecines, would give rise to a new lineage or lineages that became sufficiently like ourselves that we now include them in our own genus *Homo*. The initial step in hominid evolution was just that—a step. The next would be the evolution of a "free brain" capable of putting free hands to work in the construction of culture.

The Australopithecines

The dating, classification, and behavior of these, the earliest hominids, remains hotly debated. Most of what we now know about the early australopithecines comes from discoveries made over the last seventy years, which showed that

Dart's *A. africanus* was preceded by an even earlier form. A series of new finds at Hadar and Laetoli have been especially enlightening. As mentioned above, these finds show that australopithecines date back to well over 4 mya. Together, these finds confirm that the earliest known hominids were fully bipedal, had small ape-sized brains, and did not make stone tools.

The australopithecines can be fairly characterized as "apemen." The anatomical characteristics that most closely approach modern humans are characteristics directly indicative of bipedalism. The dental anatomy, which link the australopithecines with modern humans, include an incipiently bicuspid premolar. In other aspects of their anatomy, the australopithecines were very apelike.

It is important to remember that australopithecine brains were no bigger than those of apes (about 450 ml), but that their brains may have been differently organized. The anatomical and behavioral characteristics that clearly set them apart from apes were their small canines and their habitual striding bipedalism. The ancestry and the eventual fate of these animals is still a matter of considerable debate. However, because the australopithecines were the only known bipedal primates dating to this time, most paleoanthropologists regard them as the undoubted progenitor of modern humans.

The Gracile Australopithecines

At Laetoli, geological conditions preserved the earliest known hominid footprints, which indicate that ancient hominids walked more like us than like apes. Here at least two individuals took a stroll across a field of recently erupted volcanic ash that through the fortunate circumstances of the local geology has been preserved for nearly 4 million years. Based on the size of the footprints, it has been suggested that these three were a female, a male, and an infant hominid. This combination is strongly suggestive of the nuclear family that we know today.

The small stature (less than four feet, six inches) of *A. afarensis* is similar to that of a chimpanzee. At a locality known by anthropologists as "Hominid Hill" at the Afar site, all ages and sizes of *A. afarensis* hominids are represented. In fact, the variation is so great that some scientists have suggested that more than one species is represented. On the other hand, it is entirely possible that these early hominids showed as much variation in size and stature as modern people. As a whole, the group is known informally as the First Family. Like the evidence from Laetoli, the Hadar evidence strongly suggests that the human family unit may be as old as bipedalism itself. No stronger statement about ancient sociosexual organization can be made at this time. Some of the continuing criticisms of this interpretation have argued that the roots of another clade are also present at Hadar.

Everyone agrees that *A. afarensis* was fully bipedal and was extremely apelike in portions of its anatomy. We do not know exactly what these hominids ate, but their incipiently bicuspid premolars and their reduced canines suggest that they may have had an essentially omnivorous diet. It is important to reemphasize that their brains were no bigger than modern apes and that, although bipedal (their gait probably being somewhat less efficient than modern humans), they were not much bigger than apes. It remains a great mystery as to how these slow locomoting ape-persons survived in relatively open terrestrial environments without the aid of great speed, large canines, large body size, stone tool technology, or other physical adaptations that most mammals possess. These questions remain unanswered but are the focus of intense and continuing research.

A. afarensis is generally accepted as the earliest well-known member of our family species. Some researchers believe that it does not deserve a separate species name because it is not distinct from A. africanus. However, most authorities believe that it is the basal hominid and that it gave rise to every other subsequent hominid species. Though the exact details have not been agreed on, almost every paleontologist agrees that A. afarensis gave rise to at least two different clades that had different ecological niches. One clade and niche is represented by what are referred to as **robust australopithecines.** The exact phylogeny and grade of these animals is still debated, but the ecological and anatomical adaptations of this clade are reasonably well known. The second line is the **gracile australopithecines,** which appeared between 2 to 3 mya. In this line, the canine was reduced nearly to the extent of modern humans, although the earliest members of the group had canines that still protruded beyond the tooth row. Our own genus *Homo* may have descended from A. africanus. Both A. africanus and Homo appear at between 2.3 to 2.5 mya. Although the australopithecines are known to have lived in the same places at approximately the same time, they probably followed very different ecological strategies. We assume that the gracile australopithecines were omnivorous.

The Robust Australopithecines

By at least 2.7 mya the robust australopithecines appear in the fossil record. The robust hominids are described as such because they show a number of dietary adaptations for the processing of tough vegetable materials. Their cranial capacities range in size from less than 400 ml to approximately 600 ml and fall within the range of all the known australopithecines. At their largest, they possessed cranial capacities less than half that of modern humans. Their massive jaws, teeth, and muscles of mastication were hypertrophied.

The robust australopithecines occupied both East and South Africa and are now known to have been evolutionary dead ends that left no living decedents. Known by a number of taxonomic names such as A. aethiopicus, A. boisei, A. robustus, or Paranthropus robustus, this part of the family diverged from more gracile forms and became specialized vegetarians. The robust australopithecines fall into two basic geographic variants. One group derives from the fossil karst caves of South Africa. These were recovered from a number of localities beginning with the work of J. T. Robinson, Robert Broom, and Raymond Dart. They are referred to as *Australopithecus robustus* or *Paranthropus robustus*, depending on which taxonomy one follows. Because all of these finds come from caves, they have been notoriously difficult to date precisely.

For decades it had been noticed that certain caves yielded only robust australopithecines, while other caves yielded more gracile specimens, which were classified as *A. africanus*. Specifically, the South African caves of Kromdraai and Swartkrans yielded the robust specimens, and the sites of Taung (now destroyed), Makapansgat, and Sterkfontein yielded the graciles. Until the results of new dating techniques of these complex deposits, it was believed that all the caves were approximately contemporaneous in age. One researcher explained this distribution of one-cave-one-species with the so-called **single species hypothesis.** The paleoanthropologist Milford Wolpoff argued that the more robust hominids were males and that the gracile hominids were females of the same species. New dating techniques now make it clear that the gracile australopithecines are all earlier than the robust specimens, and it now seems likely that at least some of the gracile species evolved into the robust species. However, the single species hypothesis is an excellent cautionary tale illustrating the importance of developing an evolutionary psychology securely founded in paleoanthropology and the fossil record. Simply put, separate male–female quarters are unknown among the primates and most mammals.

Though it is by no means a perfect explanation, it now seems that at least some of the robust species represent more specialized decedents of the graciles (some graciles may also have given rise to the *H. habilis* clade). The robust australopithecines show a number of masticatory adaptations for the processing of fibrous (vegetable) material. The top of the skull, at least in males, exhibits a **sagittal crest,** which is a thin plate of bone extending down the center of the top of the braincase. To compensate for the need for a big chewing muscle on a small skull, the sagittal crest greatly increased the area of attachment for the very large **temporalis muscle.** The temporalis muscle is so massive that the cheek bones through which it passes have been enlarged to form flaring **zygomatic arches** covering an enlarged **temporal fossa** for the belly of the muscle.

The dentition has also been modified. The incisors are greatly reduced and, like the other teeth, wear flat. The canines are also reduced and tend to wear flat as the result of repetitive grinding. The premolars were molarized (enlarged) to further increase the area of the grinding surfaces. We do not know exactly what these creatures were eating, but it does not appear to have included much meat. Taken as a whole, the anatomy of the robust australopithecines is very consistent with that of a specialized vegetarian. Diets that have been suggested included an emphasis on tubers, tough seeds, chutes, and even grasses. Detailed examination of pits and scratches on the dental surfaces suggest that grit was a regular part of the diet. The larger body size of at least some of the individuals strongly indicates that characterizing the robust australopithecine niche as a "hominid cow" would be accurate.

The other group of robust hominids are actually referred to as **hyper-robust hominids.** So far, these are only known from the fluvial lacustrine sites of East Africa, including Lake Turkana and Olduvai Gorge. They are referred to as *A. boisei,* or an earlier form, *Australopithecus aethiopicus.* These show an even more specialized form of the same dietary adaptations seen in the South African forms. The face was massive in relation to the very small braincase (approximately 510–530 ml). In superior view, this gives the impression of marked **postorbital**

constriction in which tiny frontal bones connect the massive face to the small braincase. The *A. boisei* specimen found by the Leakeys is so massive that it was nicknamed "Nutcracker Man."

The significance of the differences between the hyper-robust and the robust forms continues to be debated. They may be geographic variants adapting to slightly different habitats, or the South African forms may have evolved into the East African hyper-forms. Whether they are different enough to be included in separate genera continues to be contested. What is reasonably certain at this point is that both groups embarked on a specialized course of dietary adaptation that led to extinction. However, they were successful enough to have survived for nearly two million years.

One other circumstance that unites the robust groups is that they have both been found in association with species of early *Homo sapiens*. At Olduvai Gorge, Lake Turkana, and possibly Swartkrans, they also have been found in association with stone tools belonging to the **Oldowan** industry. This occasioned the speculation of a very few scientists that the robust hominids may also have made stone tools. In fact, when tools and hominid fossils are present, the genus *Homo* is also present. There is no site where only robust hominids are found with stone tools.

The Evolution of the Genus *Homo*

Sometime before 2.5 mya, hominids began to manufacture and use stone tools. It is also at this time that the brain began to enlarge in at least one clade. As emphasized previously, no evidence suggests that the australopithecines made or used stone tools. This period begins the **Lower Paleolithic** (Gk. *Paleo*=ancient, old+*lithic*=stone). The Lower Paleolithic begins (Figure 3.2) a unique process in the history of this planet, by which learned behavior began to outstrip instinctual behavior. It was also the time during which hominids came to occupy virtually all terrestrial habitats of the earth. The process is additive in that old developments are not discarded in favor of new ones, but instead appended and extended to preexisting technologies. Furthermore, the accumulation of complexity has not been simply arithmetic but also geometric. Tools became more numerous and more expertly manufactured over the course of the last few million years.

At first, the products of the new technology were simple. Without the benefit of formal archaeological training, artifacts appear crude and difficult to recognize. Later, the artifacts become more formalized and standardized. Their association with other artifacts and contexts became increasingly complex, especially in the last 100,000 years. Throughout this evolutionary process, the brain continued to enlarge and reorganize. At some point, hominids became not just tool makers and users but also and irrevocably **tool dependent.**

Among archaeologists and paleoanthropologists, the question of when we can apply the word *human* to our ancestors is a point of intense debate. Not surprisingly, opinions are highly polarized with one group maintaining that recognizable human behavior appears early on and the other extreme maintaining that human behavior only appears after the arrival of anatomically modern *Homo sapiens.*

In the context of laying a foundation for evolutionary psychology, the antiquity of a behavior is important. Old behaviors are more likely to become genetically reinforced. However, as the evolution of bipedalism may suggest, the rapid evolution of new behaviors is also likely. We have failed once again to escape from the debate of the punctuation versus gradualism polarities. One question of increasing importance and interest is whether particular behaviors can be correlated with particular species of hominids.

Homo habilis and the Advent of Technology

The habilines are the first hominids to show a significant and measurable increase in cranial capacity. At an average of approximately 700 ml, their brains reached a size approximately half that of modern humans. One principal area of growth was in the frontal lobes. *Homo habilis* (Photo 3.5) was the first hominid to have a truly vertical frontal bone, or forehead, as seen in such specimens as **KNM-ER 1470** and **KNM-ER 1813.** This is important because in modern humans the frontal lobes are involved with the so-called higher functions, including self-awareness and foresight. The braincase was rounder and more like that of modern humans, and in contrast with the australopithecines, the widest part of the skull was not at its base, but rather more superiorly situated. The geographic distribution of the habilines, like that of the australopithecines, seems to have been confined to Africa. (Various claims of a non-African range of *H. habilis* have sometimes surfaced only to be dismissed.)

The earliest artifacts known are **pebble tools.** These artifacts belong to the Oldowan industry (first recognized at Olduvai Gorge) and were manufactured and used by *H. habilis.* The term *habilis* (L. *habilis* = handy or adroit) refers to the fact that stone tools have been found with hominid bones of the same age. Pebble tools tended to be made from quartzite and local basalt, metamorphic and volcanic rocks that are not particularly tractable in comparison with rocks such as chert and flint. Although Oldowan tools were known long before their makers were ever discovered, opinions about their functions have fluctuated greatly. In the beginning, much of what archaeologists thought about the tools emphasized the probability that **core tools** (chunks of worked stone) were the object of manufacture and use. The advent of experimental manufacturing studies and electron microscopy altered this picture. It now seems that the amorphous but sharp flakes once regarded as **debitage,** or waste flakes, were the most used component of the tool kit.

The technology involved in the manufacture of Oldowan tools is basic. The primary manufacturing method is referred to as the direct hard hammer percussion technique. In this technique, a hammer stone is used to strike flakes off a stone core. The other technique is called bipolar reduction, where one stone was simply smashed between a "hammer" and an "anvil," effectively striking the core at both ends and producing sharp flakes. The archaeologist Glynn Isaac (1937–

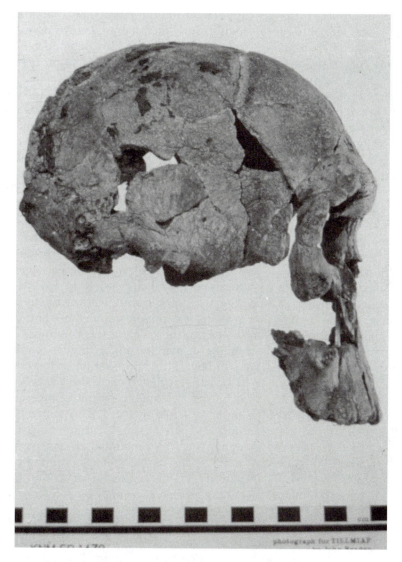

PHOTO 3.5   *Earliest Species of* **Homo, Homo Habilis**
Translated loosely by Mary Leakey as "Handy Man."

1985) referred to this technique more informally as "smash and grab," which aptly describes what the hominids were probably doing to obtain workable cutting edges. The resulting artifacts are so simple that they would be difficult to recognize if it were not for their distribution, taphonomic contexts, and geological setting. Specifically, a concentration of flakes found in association with the remains of an individual animal carcass in a geological setting where the stone material does not naturally occur strongly supports the interpretation that hominids were active at the site. Hominids also brought unworked stones known as **manuports** to serve as hammer stones for making other tools and breaking open bones for the marrow. Other artifacts show traces of having been used to process plants and meat. One of the principal lessons that the **industry** teaches us is that the artifacts required an absolute minimum level of skill to manufacture. Unlike successive tool industries, no arbitrary form, indicating a metal template, was imposed on the stone employed for making Oldowan tools. Stones transported across the landscape do suggest that at least a modicum of foresight was involved in the use and procurement of stone. However, such foresight can be accurately compared to the abilities implied by chimpanzee nonlithic tool manufacture and use. Nonetheless, the use of stone represents a strategy that apes have yet to take up in the wild.

Archaeologists have now demonstrated repeatedly that even small flakes are sharp enough to cut through the toughest hide. Cut marks have also been discovered on locations on fossil bones that indicate the removal of meat or disarticulation of joints. These would produce exactly the packages of protein predicted by Lovejoy's hypothesis. It is still impossible to always distinguish scavenged meat from hunted meat. Judging from the study of cut marks made by stone tools and gnaw marks made by carnivores, sometimes hominids arrived first and sometimes the carnivores got there before the hominids. As a whole, these studies indicate that the image of "man the mighty hunter" has been greatly overdrawn. Furthermore, we still have little appreciation of the importance of smaller vertebrate resources in the habiline diet. If early *Homo* was even remotely similar to recent hunters and gatherers, small vertebrates, invertebrates, and insects must have played a significant role in the diet. A general hunter and gatherer rule (with the exception of carnivores) is, "If it moves, we eat it." The reason for the carnivore exception may be illustrated by paleoanthropologist Alan Walker's discovery of a *H. erectus* femur that exhibits the condition of "hyper-vitamin A-osis." Carnivore livers store high levels of vitamin A in amounts that are toxic to humans consuming as little as a single large liver of a terrestrial carnivore.

The vegetable component of the habiline diet can only be guessed at. But once again, if modern hunters and gatherers are any guide, the proportion of vegetable material would have far exceeded the animal proportion of the diet (see Chapter 4). It is almost certain that unlike the synchronic and sympatric robust australopithecines, omnivory was a basic feature of the habiline adaptation. With the exception of certain foraging groups (for example, Eskimos), vegetable resources are more important and reliable. The vast majority of groups still value meat most. As will become apparent, the early shift to more meat may also be responsible in part for a number of the "civilized diseases" in which the modern diet is firmly implicated.

The habiline shift to omnivory was one that the robust australopithecines failed to make. In fact, it has often been suggested that the habilines and their descendants may have played a part in the extinction of the robust hominids through competitive exclusion or predation. The fact that *H. habilis* and robust australopithecines are found together strongly indicates interaction between the two species. Direct predation is not indicated by evidence of cannibalism, and tool inflicted wounds are unknown. Competition for the same resources seems much more likely. Extreme specialization of the kind seen in the robust australopithecines may have severely limited their range of foods. The omnivorous adaptation of the habilines may have conferred a distinct advantage, especially in response to dramatic climatic changes that, according to Elisabeth Vrba's theory of climatic oscillation, may have altered the African climate during glaciations. Omnivory combined with tool use and a larger brain may have resulted in an adaptational superiority to which the robust hominids eventually succumbed.

Unfortunately, it cannot be that simple. The fact that both clades were sympatric and synchronic for at least one million years suggests that some form of niche partition probably took place. The masticatory adaptations of the robust hominids strongly indicate that they were processing foods such as seeds and tough nuts that were out of the adaptive reach of the less specialized habiline dentitions. Grinding stones are unknown throughout the Paleolithic, and their presence in later sites is one of the hallmarks of the adaptive and behavioral explosion that took place in the terminal phases of the Stone Age. Other possible technological advantages have been detected in the archaeological record of the time.

One possible source of a competitive edge may rest in the social organization that has been postulated for *H. habilis*. Structures of stone and the evidence from **artifact and faunal scatters** have been used to support the picture of *H. habilis* as a creature of foresight. One structure is the **stone ring** at Olduvai Gorge excavated by Mary Leakey. Here a roughly circular scatter of stones, artifacts, and bones was discovered. The Leakeys speculated that the pattern of this accumulation may indicate an occupation site where hominids gathered and processed and consumed animal and other resources. They further speculated that this may represent a simple dwelling structure in which the larger stones were used to anchor thorn bushes to protect against predators, especially at night. A similar corral structure is built by modern African pastoralists in the Olduvai area. From this and other evidence, Glynn Isaac speculated about a **home base** and the social organization that such a camp might imply. In the original model, Isaac suggested that home bases provide a focus for food sharing, which is indicative of a **division of labor** along sexual lines. Isaac's model fits well with our knowledge of recent hunters and gatherers and also that of campers everywhere. Such behavior is recognizably human.

Other more recent assessments, especially those of Lewis Binford and Tim White, favor the idea that the stone ring was a natural accumulation caused perhaps by the actions of tree roots and natural drainage patterns. In assessing these criticisms, it should be remembered that the Binfordian "school of ex post facto reassessment" holds firmly to the belief that there is very little recognizably human behavior before the advent of anatomically modern humans. This extreme view is not shared with the majority of the paleoanthropological community.

However, the Binfordian conception of minimal culture for nonmoderns has been widely popularized. In its extreme form, it strongly implies that the modern capacity for complex culture is an evolutionarily recent development.

Other indications of recognizable sapient behavior at Olduvai Gorge have been unearthed. Large piles of unmodified stones referred to as **stone caches** have been found around an ancient lakeshore. Some archaeologists, such as Richard Potts, believe that hominids purposely stored these stones at various places on the landscape. Speculations about the functions of these accumulations range from "ammunition piles" to "hunting blinds." Potts has interpreted these structures as indicative of foresight and planning, though it is possible that these structures are natural.

Despite the Binfordian viewpoint, it does seem that the so-called living floors at Olduvai Gorge represent intentional hominid subsistence activity. A less pejorative description of the early *Homo* sites classifies them as activity sites instead of camp sites or home bases. One primary means of recognizing activity sites is that artifacts are concentrated as opposed to being randomly scattered across the landscape. Activity sites that have been recognized include **butchery sites, living floors** (multipurpose activity sites), and **quarry sites.** The propensity of humans to come together and share food is so ubiquitous that it is hard to believe that such behavior has a very recent evolutionary history.

As the name implies, butchery sites consist of relatively dense accumulations of artifacts in association with animal bones, many of which have been modified. Two of the better known sites contain an elephant and an extinct elephantid relative know as *Deinotherium*. Living floors may have been places where hominids gathered for what we would recognize as camp living and perhaps all the activities that the phrase *home base* implies. Quarry sites are places where hominids appear to have obtained the raw materials for stone tools. Animal fossils are usually absent or very infrequent at quarry sites. Also referred to as factory sites, some of these localities also appear to have been the focus of manufacture or at least initial modification of stone.

At Swartkrans and perhaps at Sterkfontein, A. Sillen and C. K. Brain reported bone artifacts that they concluded were used for digging and leather or hide working. Bones used for digging exhibit long scratch marks and a fine polish. Sillan's and Brain's own digging experiments failed to replicate either the polish or the scratch marks. Eventually, it was shown that carrying the tools in leather carrying cases did replicate the polish after several days of transport. The invention of carrying containers would have been a major feature of any kind of adaptation consistent with the provisioning adaptation postulated by Lovejoy. The digging hypothesis also receives support from Sillen's strontium–calcium study in which the St–Ca ratios of at least one of the Swartkrans specimens indicates that they were ingesting locally available tubers.

The earliest archaeological sites begin a process that was to continue for the next few million years. Although the broad category of sites will not change much and only a few new types of sites will be added to the archaeological record, it is nonetheless important to see the processes of intensification and **diversification.**

Activity becomes much more intense at butchery sites and much more diverse at multipurpose sites. Most significantly, stone tools are found increasingly further away from their quarry sources and they are **curated,** that is retouched, repaired, or resharpened. Identifying specific animal parts at sites makes it possible to hypothesize that hunting and not scavenging was involved. Much of the discussion of the archaeological assemblages are "low-range" discussions debating the reality of these activities.

Homo erectus—The Colonization of Eurasia

By at least 1.7 mya, a new hominid had appeared with a cranial capacity of at least 850 ml. Also known from much later finds are *"Sinanthropus pekinensis"* (China Man) from China and *"Pithecanthropus erectus"* from Java. Now jointly recognized as *Homo erectus* (Photo 3.6), this species of hominid endured for over 1.5 million years and become the first hominid to leave Africa and colonize the temperate regions of Eurasia. The cranial capacity of this hominid would eventually reach nearly 1,200 ml or nearly 85 percent the volume of modern humans. By the end of World War II, the taxon was so well known that a number of paleoanthropologists led especially by Wilfred Le Gros Clark (1895–1971) would conclude that it was sufficiently similar in morphology to be included in our own genus *Homo.* Superior technology developed by our own ancestors allowed them to expand their resource base as they became increasingly efficient at exploiting vegetable resources. All of these scenarios remain highly speculative. *Homo erectus* was essentially modern from the neck down, though a few postcranial differences distinguish it from ourselves. More important, at least from the perspective of evolutionary psychology, *H. erectus* developed a number of behavioral innovations in which modern complexity is firmly anchored. Though disputed by the Binfordians, the evidence for major behavioral changes leading to humanness is overwhelming. As will become apparent later in this chapter, the geological age and phylogenetic position of *H. erectus* play a crucial role in arguments concerning the origin of anatomically and behaviorally modern humans.

Cranial Anatomy.   The skull of *H. erectus* is notable for being extremely thick. Most of this "armor plating" results from the thickening of the outer layer (table) of bone. The function of thickened cranial bones is still poorly understood. Explanations have ranged from resistance through masticatory stress to interpersonal violence. None of these arguments have been particularly convincing. However, many of the crania from Asia appear to exhibit evidence of antemortem injury, but this is far from certain. One of the earliest members of the species is from Lake Turkana, Africa. This specimen, **KNM-ER 3733,** exhibits all the typical characteristics of *H. erectus* but does not show cranial bone thickening. One of the most obvious features of *H. erectus* is conjoined browridges. This continuous bar of bone above the eyes is known as a **supraorbital torus.** This, and the bar of bone known as a **sagittal keel,** a similar thickening of bone running along the sagittal suture of the top of the braincase, have also been interpreted as reinforce-

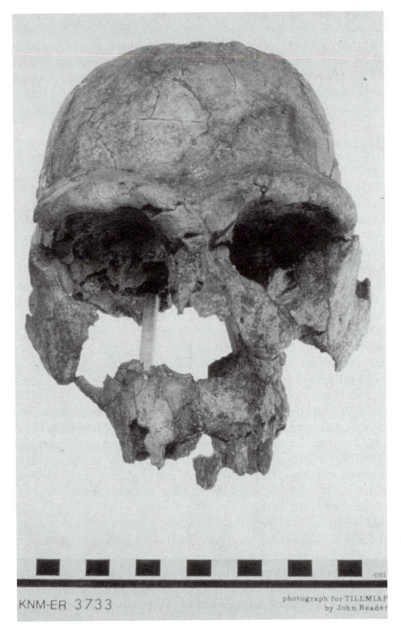

KNM-ER 3733

photograph for TILLMIAP
by John Reader

PHOTO 3.6   *Species of Hominid that First Appeared by 1.6 mya*
Characterized by a large supraorbital torus and usually (except in this
specimen) by thick cranial bones.

ment for resisting masticatory stress. Whatever its function (if any), a sagittal keel is in no way similar to the sagittal crest seen in robust australopithecines. The function of the sagittal keel is much more enigmatic. It is very tempting to conclude that the sagittal keel and supraorbital torus reinforce the skull as a whole, but no one has yet successfully demonstrated the particular stress that these ectocranial superstructures resisted.

A better-understood feature of the cranium is the **nuchal torus** and an angled occipital (in lateral view). These are probably related to large and well-developed nuchal muscles. Also apparent in lateral view are pronounced temporal lines, which mark the superior attachment of the temporalis muscle. The temporalis was well developed, suggesting the need for powerful mastication that was more forceful in comparison to modern humans. One kind of repetitive task that may account for all of these features is the use of the mouth as a vicelike "third hand" to pull on strips of some material such as meat, sinew, or hide. In general, the cranium of *H. erectus* is less prognathic in comparison with the australopithecines but displays marked alveolar prognathism in comparison with *H. habilis*. Viewed from above, *H. erectus* crania give the impression of postorbital constriction, which though more marked than in *H. habilis*, in no way approaches that seen in robust australopithecines. The upper incisors, especially the medial incisors, show a kind of scooplike shape known as shovel-shaped incisors. The feature is ubiquitous in the Asian members of the species. While a form of this is known in preserved African homologs and may be plesiomorphic for the genus *Homo*, the form that it takes in the Chinese specimens is different. Shovel shaping also occurs in high frequency in modern Asian and East Asian derived populations (for example, Native Americans). Internally, it is apparent from the surface of the braincase that there was an increased and more complicated system of arteries that nourished the cerebral cortex in *H. erectus* in comparison with the australopithecines. Their cerebellum also seems to increase its relative size in the brain of *H. erectus*. Viewed posteriorly, the widest part of the cranium is higher than in the australopithecines and similar to that seen in *H. habilis*. All of the lobes of the *H. erectus* brain show enlargement in comparison with the australopithecines and habilines.

Postcranial Skeleton.   There are some known differences in the postcranial skeleton based on the "Turkana teenager," **KNM-ER 15000** (Photo 3.7), in which the neural canals of the vertebrae were slightly narrower than in *H. sapiens*. Furthermore, the vertebral spines are more parallel to the ground than the more obliquely inclined spines in modern humans. Alan Walker has interpreted the narrower neural canals as indicative of a less than modern breath control of the kind required in fully articulate speech. He has also interpreted this narrowness as suggestive of less precise manual dexterity. The horizontal orientation of the spinous processes of the vertebrae may relate to repeated throwinglike motions of the arms.

In the pelvic region, a relatively narrower pelvis has been linked to the birth of small-brained hominids, indicating that the head size at birth was not similar to modern humans and not the approximately one-half adult size characteristic of apes. There are so few preserved pelvic fragments that it is not yet possible to say when the rotation of the fetus characteristic of large-brained human birth evolved.

Although we still do not know a lot about the functional morphology of the *H. erectus* skeleton, we know that some early African *H. erectus* individuals,

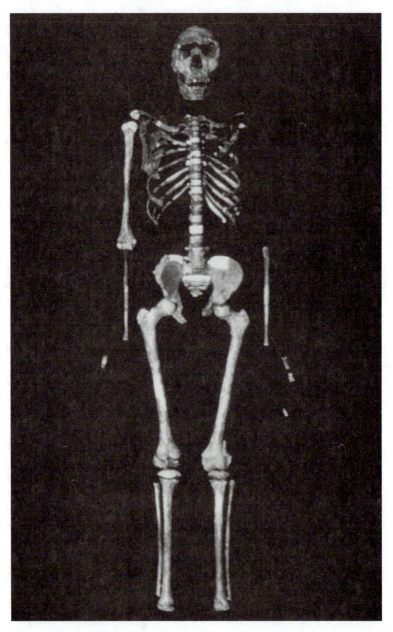

PHOTO 3.7   *Adolescent Hominid Dating to Approximately 1.6 mya from the Deposits of West Lake Turkana*

such as the Turkana teenager, approached and even exceeded the average of about 69 inches of modern human stature. The Turkana teenager may also have exhibited the tall slim body characteristic of humans adapted to the hot and arid environments.

Distribution and Dating.   *H. erectus* was the first hominid to leave Africa and spread into temperate latitudes as far north as present day Beijing, which lies at the same latitude as Chicago. *H. erectus* also may have been present in the temperate climates of South Africa (*Teleanthropus capensis* from Swartkrans).

The vast majority of *H. erectus* specimens have been recovered from the Far East in China and Java, Indonesia. Early discoveries at the end of the last century and in the first four decades of this century convinced contemporary students of hominid evolution that Asia was the ancestral hominid homeland. Recent claims have pushed the dates of the earliest Asian hominids back into the Pliocene era and contended that *H. erectus* may have been a contemporary of *H. habilis*. These dates from Java and southern China cannot be convincingly tied to the hominid fossils. It is much more reasonable to conclude that *H. erectus* reached Asia no earlier than about 1.3 mya. The earliest detectable presence of the species, dating to at least 1.4 mya, is claimed to be from the site of Ubeidiya, Israel. However, there are problems with this date because it is based primarily on faunal associations. A mandible from Dmanisi, Georgia (western Asia) has been accorded an even earlier date of 1.6 to 1.8 mya. This date is also based on faunal associations and cannot be substantiated by or tied into the radiometric and paleomagentic dates that have been reported from the site. The totality of the evidence from this locality does not suggest a Plio-Pleistocene age.

It is possible, but by no means certain, that *H. erectus* never penetrated into glacial Europe. No European fossil discovery can definitely be attributed to this species. Future research may alter this picture. The earliest fossils, all of which are imprecisely dated, have been attributed to a group usually referred to as **archaic *Homo sapiens*.** Although none of these individuals displays the characteristic morphologies of *H. erectus,* many do make excellent morphological candidates for transitional forms between *H. erectus* and later *H. sapiens*, including Neanderthals (see below). The recent discovery of numerous individuals from Atapuerca, Spain, is especially intriguing. Based on current evidence, they seem to represent a species other than *H. erectus*. Morphologically, they are suitable ancestors for the Neanderthals. One of the persistent problems of trying to understand this period in hominid evolution is what Glynn Isaac called "**the muddle in the middle.**" The muddle in the Middle Pleistocene (ca. 0.73–0125 mya) arises from the fact that absolute dating techniques are suitable for dating younger and older materials, but not those that fall between 0.05 to 0.8 mya. Another problem with ascertaining the antiquity of *H. erectus* is that the youngest specimens, especially those from **Ngandong (Solo)** in eastern Java, exhibit morphologies that diverge in the direction of modern humans to such an extent that there is debate about whether to place the specimens in *H. erectus* or *H. sapiens*. Unfortunately, some widely publicized workers have imperiously declared them *H. erectus,* as if most authorities agreed with such a designation. When such arbitrary designations are then included in phylogenetic arguments, the result is a false impression of unanimity that misleads both scientists and interested laypersons. The general consensus is that *H. erectus* was probably extinct by 0.2 mya.

Behavioral Adaptations.   *H. erectus* is associated with a number of archaeological developments that represent significant innovations in human behavior and technology. In comparison with the tool kit of the habilines, the tools of *H. erectus* were much more standardized. These tools are referred to as the **Acheulean industry** (Photo 3.8), named after the village of St. Acheul in France where they were first recognized by Jacques Boucher de Crèvecoeur Perthes more than two hundred years ago. Like the Oldowan, unstandardized flakes and cores were present, but a new element, the **hand axe,** which is a **bifacially flaked** artifact, had been added. Also frequently present are the wedgelike cleavers. Hand axes make their first appearance in the **developed Oldowan,** a tool industry that succeeded the Oldowan industry at around 1.5 mya. The advent of the hand axe marks a first in hominid behavioral evolution. For the first time, hominids are consistently producing **symmetrical** tools whoses final shapes are not determined by the natural shapes of the rocks that they are made from. This means that *H. erectus* had a **mental template** in mind of an arbitrary form that was imposed on the environment. The imposition of a standardized form on the natural world is very significant.

Making a hand axe took considerable skill while manufacturing an Oldowan chopper or flake took little. Making hand axes required practice and skill acquired over a period of years. Hand axes were also curated and retouched. Although retouching also occurred in the Oldowan, retouching became more frequent and consistent in the Acheulean, as is known from Africa, Europe, and western Asia. Hand axes came in all sizes, and it is believed that some of the smaller ones started out as larger ones that were gradually reduced in size with use. The distribution of artifacts found at *H. erectus* sites is more dense at localities postdating the Oldowan (including hundreds of hand axes at some localities), suggesting larger groups, more intense activity, or reoccupation.

The function of the hand axe has been debated for a long time. Some archaeologists argue that it was an all-purpose tool, the paleolithic "Boy Scout knife" that had many purposes ranging from the skinning or butchering of animals to digging. Some conjecture that hand axes were thrown, either after being hafted (as onto a spear) or with the hand. Others believe that the hand axe was not used at all but simply represents the remains of a core from which flakes were removed. On the basis of current evidence, the hand axe appears to have had many uses, most of them too carefully made to a standardized pattern to have simply been a throwaway component of tool manufacture.

Some of the African sites also show the exploitation of many individuals of a single species, such as baboons or large bovines. Whether these animals were hunted or scavenged remains the focus of debate. The presence of several animals of the same species suggests hunting. As will become apparent shortly, other sites in Eurasia strongly support the interpretation that hunting was a consistent part of the hominid behavioral repertoire, by at least the later phase of *H. erectus*.

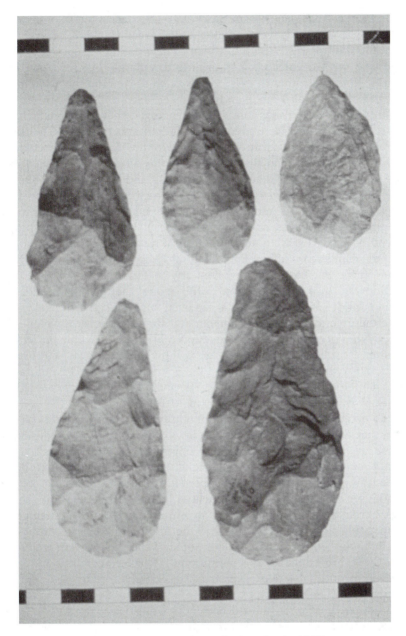

PHOTO 3.8   *Stone Hand Axes Traditionally Associated with* **Homo erectus,**
known from Africa, Asia, and Europe

Although introductory texts on human evolution routinely state that *H. erectus* made hand axes, not a single hand axe has ever been found in direct association with *H. erectus*. As if to increase the mystery of the hand axe, where *H. erectus* has been found in direct association with artifacts, the artifacts are decidedly non-Acheulean. Despite these facts, few researchers doubt that *H. erectus* made hand axes and cleavers; no other suitable candidates lived at the same time and in the right places. With the advent of new dating techniques, other possible authors of the Acheulean are beginning to emerge, but for now the mystery remains. Hominids other than *H. erectus*, such as Neanderthals and anatomically modern *H. sapiens*, also made and used hand axes.

In the Far East, it has long been recognized that the manufacture of hand axes ceased at the eastern edge of the Indian subcontinent. This boundary is referred to as the **Movius line** and is named for the Harvard archaeologist Hallam Movius (1907–1987), who first recognized the differences between Far Eastern stone artifact assemblages and other Eurasian and African assemblages. Instead of the formalized hand axes found farther to the west, the Far Eastern assemblages consist primarily of seemingly irregular-shaped flakes and so-called **chopper-chopping tools.** Movius, and many of those that came after him, proposed that this end of Eurasia was an area of "cultural retardation" that was somehow left out of the mainstream of hominid evolution. According to this scenario, *H. erectus* culture in the Far East never evolved any material culture more complex than the Oldowan. In a recent version of this model that accepts the Pliocene dates for the earliest Asian hominids, it has been suggested that *H. erectus* left Africa before the invention of the Acheulean and therefore never developed this technology. Not only does this interpretation rely on indefensible ancient dates, but it further assumes the cessation of gene flow, migration, and cultural diffusion. One is left with the absurd notion that *H. erectus* was capable of getting to the Far East but incapable of getting back. This model also cannot explain the presence of later *H. erectus* (ca. 1.4 to 1.7 mya) in Africa.

To accept the cultural retardation argument is to miss the behavioral revolution that was occurring with *H. erectus*. Although the Movius line is real, it is real for an entirely different reason: It emphasizes the behavioral sophistication and not retardation of the earliest Asians. The nonlithic model supported by all paleoanthropologists with actual experience in the region offers a much better explanation. Nonlithic resources such as bamboo were used to make artifacts ranging from a razor-sharp knife to an entire village. Far from being retarded in its capacity for culture, *H. erectus* was the first hominid to deemphasize the use of stone tools. This explanation does not sit well with Western-trained archaeologists, who are educated to "read stone." Furthermore, this model has been criticized as untestable. However, fossil wood can be recovered, and continuing research may increase our luck. Bamboo is so ubiquitous that it is hard to ignore as a resource that larger-brained hominids would have used.

Another adaptive shift that is impossible to ignore is that, prior to Asian *H. erectus*, there is no evidence for the occupation of tropical rainforests by early members of *Homo*. The geographic location of Java and southern China and the fossil mammals of the region leave no doubt that *H. erectus* penetrated the rainforest and eventually reached northern China. This fact is now indisputable.

Adding to this picture is the undeniable fact that the species occupied places with cold winters in spite of being biologically tropical animals. Hominids, like modern humans, had to use technology to deal with subfreezing temperatures. Even the Tierra del Fuegans that so impressed Darwin relied on furs and fire for survival. Though disputed by the Binfordian view, the earliest evidence that *H. erectus* acquired fire may date to between 1.0 to 1.4 mya from the sites of **Chesowanja, Kenya,** and Swartkrans, South Africa. At Chesowanja, reddened patches of earth suggest fires whose temperature exceeded natural bush fires caused by lightning or volcanic activity. Burnt bones from the later layers of Swartkrans are indisputable evidence of fire. The exact time when *H. erectus* first made and learned to control fire is still under discussion. It is essential to remember that bush fires caused by lightning strikes are an integral part of both temperate and tropical ecological zones. At the very least, hominids must have been familiar with the properties of fire.

The cave site of **Locality 1 at Zhoukoudian** near Beijing, China, contains burnt bone and stone and thick layers of ash, which strongly supports the interpretation that *H. erectus* used and maintained fire on a regular basis between 0.2 to 0.45 mya. Once again, the Binfordian "reappraisal" of the site has suggested that the fires were natural. Such a suggestion is patently absurd given the cave context of Zhoukoudian. Dated to about the same age, the Spanish sites of **Torralba** and **Ambron**a preserve the remains of butchered elephants in association with Acheulean tools and scatters of charcoal. This is currently the earliest direct evidence of **organized big game hunting** that employed a fire drive to stampede game into a swamp, where large animals were mired and killed. Binford has cast doubt on this interpretation.

Modern day Western temperate zone humans associate fire with warmth, light, and cooking, but fire did not develop in these contexts in Asia. In places like Southeast Asia, fire is used still to penetrate the jungle. Forests are burned yearly to clear undergrowth and natural litter that make the forest otherwise impenetrable for humans. Although speculative, it may be that fire brought from tropical Africa was the key to the first colonization of the Far East.

Skill and Speech. As noted above, making a hand axe takes training and practice. As remarkable as the development of bifacially worked tools was, the evolution of handedness was also a first. Nicholas Toth has shown that right-handers and left-handers leave discernibly different patterns on a stone that they work, in that they rotate the core in different directions. Handedness is unknown in other animals. In humans, 80 to 90 percent of the population is right-handed. Handedness is involved with **cerebral asymmetry,** which also appears for the first time with *H. erectus*. In humans, the left and right hands are controlled by the **contralateral hemispheres** of the brain. Taken as a whole, the evidence for *H. erectus* strongly suggests that the notion of symmetry may be associated with or made possible by an asymmetrically organized brain. Why this should be remains a mystery. Although highly speculative at this point, an asymmetrically organized brain may be associated with the concept of self-awareness. We will return to this in a later chapter dealing with the brain.

In addition to an asymmetrical brain, the study of *H. erectus* endocasts makes it clear that the **association areas** crucial to speech were also present on the cerebral cortex of *H. erectus*. Endocasts of the brain can inform us about the organization and development of higher brain functions. Noted paleoneurologists Ralph Holloway and Dean Falk both agree that by *H. erectus* times, **Broca's area,** which controls the production of speech, and **Wernicke's area,** which processes the comprehension of speech, were present. Holloway believes that this type of cerebral organization had occurred as early as *A. africanus*. Falk vehemently disagrees and argues that these features were not present until *H. erectus* or by early *Homo* times. Both agree that *H. erectus* probably had some form of language. This should be regarded as a certainty, even though some scientists still argue that the anatomical organs of speech, for example the larynx and tongue, were undeveloped. In fact, it is impossible to reconstruct the soft parts of the vocal apparatus from the fossilized, hard bony parts. The degree to which *H. erectus* used language is uncertain, but a minimum time frame of 1.5 mya is no longer debatable.

The cooccurrence of speech, cerebral asymmetry, handedness, and the manufacture of standardized symmetrical tools is surely not a coincidence. As we shall see in later chapters, handedness can influence language acquisition in modern humans. There appears to be no obvious solution as to why asymmetry evolved in the hominid brain. However, the asymmetric complex emphasizes that tool making and speech may be manifestations of the same process. Specifically, both behaviors involve the imposition of arbitrary forms and categories on the environment. The importance of this observation cannot be overstated. Languages are made up of arbitrary sounds and symbols that are only very rarely not onomonopoetic. Language is inescapably linked to complex culture. In fact, language only makes sense in the context of culture.

Decades ago, it was assumed that language must have something to do with "man the hunter." In fact, careful studies of hunting cultures emphasize that language is not essential to effective human predation. Successful hunters are quiet hunters. Hunting is opportunistic and more often than not unsuccessful. Hunters do not spot a target and then discuss how to kill it. A provisional plan must already be in place. Furthermore, communicating the site of a previous kill, whether it was yesterday or four months ago, is a poor way of locating new game. Similarly, art and a skill in stone tool making is not passed on primarily through language. Instead, it is passed on by visual example and trial and error. As with bipedalism, language also has an evolutionary price. Jeffrey Laitman, a paleoanthropologist, has pointed out that we are the only mammal that can drown while drinking if we don't close our respiratory tract.

In a subsequent chapter, we will see that the properties and neural mechanisms of the brain may suggest an essential function that had little to do with hunting but a great deal to do with gathering. The sexual dimorphism of language mechanisms is also a feature of modern humans that may have arisen in response to a hunting and gathering way of life. We also know that social contexts and perceptions are mediated by language. One of the properties of language is that it allows individuals who cannot see each other, or in fact never meet each other, to communicate. It also allows communication in real time. In a context of transcontinental migration, language will inevitably develop idiosyncratic features that become the hallmarks of ethnicity. To suggest that all the newly evolved behaviors of *H. erectus* were coincidental or unrelated is to ignore parsimony in the extreme. We must then realize and take as fact the observation that this species had already entered into an adaptation that exhibited the constellation of behavioral traits that we recognize as human.

Homo sapiens sapiens—The Behavioral Explosion and Eve

The fate of *H. erectus* is somehow inextricably tied in with the advent of *H. sapiens sapiens*. Currently, paleoanthropologists are engaged in a heated debate about the origin of anatomically modern humans, which recalls in intensity the debate that once raged over hominid origins. As with the hominid origin debate, this discussion has once again pitted the biochemical evidence against the fossil and archaeological evidence. In 1982, a group of University of California at Berkeley biochemists and molecular biologists led by Rebecca Cann and Alan Wilson announced on the basis of **mitochondrial DNA (mtDNA)** studies of different racial groups that modern humans all originated in Africa between 0.05–0.2 mya. According to this interpretation, all the known races of the world descended from a single female, which quickly acquired the nickname "Eve." The **Eve hypothesis** has also been termed the *recent African origin, out of Africa*, and the *Garden of Eden* hypotheses and especially the **replacement model.** Both the scientific and popular press have had and continue to have a field day with "Supermom."

The theory is directly at odds with an older interpretation referred to as the **regional continuity** or **multiregional hypothesis,** first put forward by Franz Weidenreich (1873–1948), the renowned anatomist who described the majority of the early *H. erectus* fossils from China and Java. The study of other hominid fossils known at that time, including those from Ngandong and the Upper Cave (a cave within the Zhoukoudian site complex), were crucial in Weidenreich's development of his hypothesis in the late 1930s and early 1940s. He believed that Chinese *H. erectus* developed directly into modern Chinese. He also implied that the descendants of nonmodern fossils of any geographical region had evolved into the modern local populations. The further implication of this model was that races were relatively old divisions created by the local adaptations of *H. erectus* to differing environments. As part of his model, Weidenreich also emphasized that reproductive isolation was repeatedly interrupted by migration and gene flow. Thus, isolation had never been complete enough to result in the production of synchronic species of *Homo*.

Like Weidenreich, modern supporters of regional continuity maintain that similar behavioral and anatomical continuities link the fossil and modern populations of any geographical region. According to this interpretation of the fossil and archaeological record, stone tools do not change much over long periods of time, and certain anatomical characteristics that appear first in regional fossil populations continue on into modern populations. This theory is being tested, especially in Europe and the Far East. The Eve theory logically predicts that innovative anatomical complexes and archaeological innovations should be associated with the complete replacement of indigenous populations.

Though the debate began as a disagreement between paleoanthropologists and molecular biologists, archaeologists were quickly and unavoidably drawn into the fray. The implication of the Eve model for archaeology is that some behavioral mechanism must have accounted for the complete replacement of *H. erectus* and its decedents. Therefore, the archaeological record outside of Africa was irrelevant to human evolution because *H. erectus* did not give rise to modern people.

At the crux of the biological part of the Eve hypothesis is the observation that the mtDNA of Africans is more diverse than that of other races. This supposedly means that it is also more ancient. The age of the "event" was determined by assuming that the mtDNA possessed many segments that were adaptively neutral. Therefore, mutations accumulated at a constant rate, which over generations acted like a molecular clock. Therefore, if the mtDNA of Africans was 2 percent more diverse than that of Eurasians, then African populations are more ancient. The accumulations of mutation in percent per time period was originally calculated by using archaeological age estimates for the populating of Australia. This date assumed that once Australia became populated, gene flow with the Eurasian mainland ceased. Finally, because mtDNA is only passed on by females, the original modern human must have been African and female.

The Eveists (as they do not like to be called) were immediately criticized not only for the assumption that mtDNA was neutral and therefore could not be treated as a clock, but also eventually for their use of a computer program that later turned out could "root" the tree of modern humans in any geographic region. The original estimates of the dating of Eve have also been altered many times and now range from 0.05 to 0.8 mya. The original studies were also criticized for using U.S. blacks to represent Africans. Curiously enough, when actual African data was included, the results were not altered, even though U.S. blacks have undergone centuries of admixture with non-African derived populations.

If the Eve debate touched off a dispute among molecular biologists and paleontologists, it also ignited a debate between laboratory and field people. At times, the paleontologists were accused of being a soft science tainted with cultural anthropology. Some theorists welcomed the Eve replacement model. The punctuationists saw themselves vindicated as did the Binfordians. The rejection of the model came from two camps. The first were students of Neanderthals who believed that Neanderthals had evolved into modern Europeans. The second group were scientists who had studied the fossil record in "outlying regions" like Australia and East and Southeast Asia. They believed that *H. erectus* evolved into modern Asians and Australians. Both groups of researchers have identified three basic areas of investigation for the replacement model:

1. There ought to be some evidence of such an enormous biological revolution. Because the event had to be rapid, it is logical to expect a marked morphological transition between indigenous fossil populations and the new invaders. The same

should be true of the archeological record, especially if it was technology that facilitated the replacement. In other words, new artifacts and fossils ought to make a dramatic stratigraphic entrance at about the time predicted by the Eveists.

2. If the replacement was documented in the geological record, then a mechanism must be identified that allowed replacement. Such a mechanism could be a combination of biological, behavioral, or even epidemiological evidence.

3. *Homo sapiens sapiens* ought to be oldest in Africa. Alternatively or conversely, radical new technologies ought to also be oldest in Africa.

Paleoanthropologists working at the eastern edges of Eurasia are unanimous in their opinion that such dramatic appearances are absent from the fossil and archaeological records. Just as the anatomical definition of the Hominidae was eventually defined by bipedalism, the definition of anatomically modern humans requires definition. This task has proved to be much more difficult than the first.

Archaic *Homo sapiens*

Many of the archaic *H. sapiens* have also been termed **ante-Neanderthals,** both because they predate Neanderthals and because they make good morphological ancestors. In archaic *H. sapiens*, brain size does not much exceed the brain volume of late *H. erectus*, and some are considerably smaller. There is no specific anatomical definition of archaic *H. sapiens*, but it is generally agreed that they look enough like modern people to be included in this species. Specimens of this category are recognized from Europe, Africa, and Asia. The African and Asian specimens are much more morphologically similar to each other than they are to any of the East Asian fossils. None of the finds from these three continents can be associated with distinctive archaeological assemblages. A plethora of species names have been proposed for archaic species of *Homo*. Currently the problem of what (and how many) scientific names are appropriate remains unresolved.

Neanderthals

Since the recognition three years before the publication of *The Origin of Species*, Europeans have been loathe to admit Neanderthals, *Homo sapiens neanderthalensis,* to the pantheon of modern people, especially modern Europeans. Every explanation from pathology to primitiveness has been invoked to exclude them. They have also received 130 years of bad press, and the term *Neanderthal* is not one of endearment in modern parlance. However, the Neanderthals developed cultural attributes that many modern cultures hold as sacred and admirable. The Binfordians and Eveists have systematically dehumanized the early ancestors of modern people, and almost all Eveists are adamant in their refusal to admit Neanderthals to the family phylogram. A few have held out the compromise of displacement instead of replacement, postulating that the demise of Neanderthals actually consisted of being marginalized and pushed into undesirable habitats, where they eventually went extinct with perhaps a little bit of inconsequential gene flow. One multiregional proponent, Milford Wolpoff, has pleaded for the acceptance of the Neanderthals as Ice Age "hillbillies."

Neanderthals are morphologically distinct in comparison with their contemporaries from Asia and Africa. The regional continuity people place Neanderthals squarely in our own species but warrant that Neanderthals were a morphologically distinct race or subspecies. Neanderthals are also divided into classic Neanderthals from Europe and progressive forms from the Middle East, also known as Levantine Neanderthals. The classic Neanderthals occupied glacial Europe from perhaps at least 0.2 mya until about 0.35 mya, while the Levantine Neanderthals appear to be younger than many of the European Neanderthals. A number of researchers have suggested that the Levantine populations were the decendents of European Neanderthals who moved south during periods of glacial maxima. One Neanderthal, the Teshik-Tash fossil, has been found as far east as Uzbekistan. Whatever the ultimate antiquity of Neanderthals is decided to be, they occupied an extremely inhospitable Europe for at least 100,000 years.

Anatomy

The distinctive anatomy of the Neanderthals has been viewed as an adaptation to a cold environment or one including a great amount of physical stress. Reproductive isolation has also been invoked as the cause of the distinct anatomy of the Neanderthal. Eveists believe that Neanderthals are distinctive enough to warrant their own separate species. Thus, they classify them as *Homo neanderthalensis*. Lately, this argument has been bolstered by the discovery of a Neanderthal pelvis from Kebara in Israel. Yoel Rak, a paleoanthropologist, maintains that the pubic bone of this fossil is too different to be included in our own species. However, there is no objective criterion that allows such a taxonomic separation. Those who argued that Neanderthal vocal tracts were also decidedly nonhuman were undoubtedly unhappy to find that the single Neanderthal hyoid, or throat bone, that provides attachment for the vocal apparatus is indistinguishable from modern humans. As mentioned previously, it is impossible to reconstruct the soft tissues of the vocal tract from the bony structures that support and underlie them.

Neanderthal skulls have long been a source of amazement and awe. Most of their features have been interpreted as adaptations to cold. The extremely large nasal aperture has been described as a "wonder to behold" and as an adaptation to the need to humidify cold dry glacial air. The large frontal sinuses (by modern standards) have also been interpreted as cold adaptations that helped to insulate the face and brain from cold air. (The smaller frontal sinuses of modern humans are the same ones that cause stabbing pain when one consumes a snow cone too quickly.) The large braincase may not have held a larger brain but instead a more insulated one surrounded by more meningeal fluid.

Other features are even less understood. Instead of the continuous supraorbital torus seen in *H. erectus*, Neanderthals usually have essentially separate and arching supraorbital tori. Neanderthals exhibit an **occipital bun** or chignon in association with a posteriorly flattened occipital bone. The face below the orbits exhibits **midfacial prognathism** in association with paranasal inflation. The faces of Levantine Neanderthals are less prognathic. The contour of the maxilla is long and sweeping, resulting in a tall face that contrasts markedly with contemporaries from the eastern edge of Eurasia. The midface looks as if someone had "pulled it forward" as if it was made out of plasticine. The teeth have "moved" anteriorly to create a **retromolar space** behind the third molar. Neanderthals thus did not have to suffer impacted wisdom teeth, which are the source of pain to numerous humans today. Yoel Rak and Eric Trinkaus, though they differ on the exact details, believe that this morphology may have evolved to resist stress resulting from using the teeth and jaws as a kind of "third hand" or vice to grasp objects in the mouth. The anterior dentition shows an unusual wear pattern, including beveled incisors, which is also consistent with the third hand hypothesis. One speculation is that Neanderthals held tough or frozen meat in their teeth while they cut it into more manageable pieces. All of these morphologies may result from **anterior tooth loading,** a term that describes an emphasis on powerful gripping and compression at the front of the mouth. The molars possessed large, hollowed pulp cavities, a condition known as **taurodontism** (L. *tauro*=bovine) because hollow teeth are also seen in cattle. This feature may have been an adaptation to a diet of cold or even frozen food. The feature is found in high frequencies in some apes and in modern Eskimos. The large face and some anatomical details of the cranium seem to link Neanderthals specifically with extant Europeans. Although most Neanderthals lacked a chin, some of the Levantine Neanderthals show traces of one. In general, the long faces and sweeping cheek lines of Neanderthals are most like modern Europeans. Neanderthal faces were very dissimilar to modern East Asians.

Based on the eruption time of teeth and the fusion of cranial and postcranial sutures, Neanderthals may have matured more quickly than modern humans. There has been some suggestion from Binfordians that Neanderthals experienced an unusually high incidence of infant death. It has been further suggested that this characteristic contributed to their extinction. According to this interpretation, they were eventually outcompeted by anatomically modern humans.

The postcranial skeleton was squat, barrel chested, and heavily muscled. Cortical bone is thick and dense. The forelimbs are relatively stocky and truncated, a characteristic that may relate to selection for a reduction in surface area to body volume predicted by **Bergman's and Allen's rules.** The morphology of the scapula suggests that muscles involved in a spear-throwing motion were especially hypertrophied. The distal phalanges of the hand are markedly flat and splayed, suggesting a powerful grip. In general, Trinkaus has characterized the Neanderthal body as adapted to life on a rugged landscape, which required a lot of travel over uneven ground.

The question of whether Neanderthal morphology represents an adaptation to the cold or is simply the result of isolation or genetic drift is a difficult one to answer. All of the Neanderthal characteristics have been related to an adaptation to a cold glacial climate, but many of them may simply result from the fact that classic Neanderthals were behaviorally or geographically isolated from other populations. However, Middle Eastern Neanderthals exhibit similar characteristics in what we believe were much warmer climates, although the same characteristics are less pronounced. Further complicating this picture is the fact that Neanderthals and anatomically modern humans can be shown to have existed side by side at the same time in both Europe and the Middle East.

A number of scenarios have been proposed to explain what happened to the Neanderthals. Proponents of the replacement model emphasize that Neanderthals overlap in time, or are synchronic, with anatomically modern *Homo sapiens (Homo sapiens sapiens)*. This overlap may have lasted at least 0.1 mya. The two groups are also sympatric. Eveists argue that being synchronic and sympatric rules out an ancestor–descendent relationship. One cannot be ancestral to one's contemporary. However, the contribution of earlier Neanderthal populations to the gene pool of moderns is very possible.

Regional continuity supporters point to a number of idiosyncratic features that cross the boundary between Neanderthals and moderns. These include features of the dentition, jaws, and skulls. Similar arguments for premodern Asians have been made for Australians and East Asians. In some cases, a particular feature decreases in frequency as it approaches the present, but is nonetheless shared by extinct and extant local populations. It is also apparent that traits that appear first in a given region have the highest frequency in populations occupying a particular region today. Thus, East Asians have the highest frequency of shovel shaping and Europeans have long (tall) faces. Many more such traits exist in various geographic regions. Although both groups have shovel-shaped incisors, the shoveling is different in its details. The shoveling of the premodern Chinese is identical to that seen in Chinese *H. erectus*.

The premodern hominids from the Far East (that is, China and Java) contrast markedly in their morphology from the Neanderthals. The putative glacial adaptations do not appear in Chinese crania, although the two groups occupied a similar latitude during glacial maxima. In fact, the Far East as a whole never underwent glaciations on an order of magnitude like those in Europe. However, some specimens do exhibit thick cranial bones, and one individual possesses large frontal sinuses. Other Chinese specimens exhibit extremely thin cranial bones. The biggest morphological contrast between the Chinese premoderns and the Neanderthals is seen in the small faces of the former and the contour of the cheekbones formed by a vertically short maxilla and horizontally oriented zygomatic bones, which contribute to the impression of "high cheekbones" in modern Asians.

Recent workers have begun to argue that evidence for the presence of anatomically modern humans may be as old in the Middle East as it is in Africa. A Mideastern origin for modern humans, instead of a strictly African continental origin, is consistent with the Eve hypothesis in general. The biogeography of the Middle East is consistent with the view that, in the past, places such as Israel were natural provinces of Africa. This area has also yielded behavioral evidence that suggests that Neanderthal behavior was much more modern than previously thought.

Neanderthal Behavior

Neanderthal culture has been the subject of much recent debate. At stake in the Eve–regional continuity debate is whether Neanderthal behavior was unsophisticated enough to facilitate their rapid replacement by moderns. Not surprisingly, the Binfordian and Eveist viewpoint has minimized the evidence for cultural complexity. The issues of foresight and planning and the "world view" have been much discussed in the scientific literature. Binfordians have contended that archaeological arguments for Neanderthal behavioral sophistication are based on poor evidence that does not indicate truly modern behavior. The technology of Neanderthals has also played a key role in arguments about their ecology and behavior.

Until recently, it was believed that Neanderthal archaeological assemblages largely could be classified as **Mousterian.** Named for the site of Le Moustier in France, the Mousterian culture exemplified a more sophisticated technique of stone tool manufacture. Recognizing the contrasts with the Lower Paleolithic, archaeologists refer to this period (between 0.125 and ca. 0.045 mya) as the **Middle Paleolithic** or **Middle Stone Age.** The new development of this age is the **prepared core technology.** As with the Acheulean and "developed Oldowan" industries, the Mousterian built on previous techniques that it retained by adding a new technique. It is also now apparent that the Mousterian varied geographically by cultural zones (western Asia, the Middle East, and eastern Europe). Furthermore, the Mousterian probably also extended to western Siberia.

Also known as the **Levallois technique,** prepared core technology allowed the more rapid production of more standardized flakes, which could be hafted on shafts of bone and wood. The selection of tractable raw materials was important enough that some were brought from great distances. Levallois core reduction was sequential and precise. In this technology, a piece of stone was first trimmed or prepared to manufacture a preplanned core, which was then struck to produce a single or multiple flakes. As Wolpoff has noted, the unfinished product did not look like the ultimate artifact until the last blow is struck. A sequence had to be carefully followed with an end form in mind, one that was not obvious from the core being worked at the time. In contrast with the manufacture of a hand axe or even a bird's nest, Mousterian tools did not look like the final product until the process was finished.

The marked geographic variation of Mousterian tool kits is indicative of subsistence strategies more finely attuned to local conditions. Regional differences also may reflect increasingly different ethnic identities. At the same time, it is clear that Mousterian technology was shared over long and short distances indicating that it was a culture in the modern sense of the word. There is some evidence that knowledge of the technique may have reached as far as southern China, but the possibility of independent invention cannot be ruled out. For whatever reason, Mousterian remains are rare in the Far East, which suggests that cultural and subsistence differences were already distinct in this part of the world. It is important to keep in mind that the succession of industries that have been described for Europe, western Asia and Africa are irrelevant to the Far East. The significance of this profound difference has been previously postulated to reflect an emphasis on nonlithic resources for tool manufacture in the Far East. It is entirely logical that the substantial modern-day cultural differences have roots that are decidedly older than civilization.

It is also clear from archaeological and taphonomic evidence that Neanderthals were successful hunters of large game, including rhinoceros, elephants, and bovids. Both their techniques of tool manufacture and their hunting success testify to foresight and planning.

Neanderthals are also the first hominids to have intentionally buried their dead. Intentional burial of the dead necessarily involves a belief in an afterlife. Some archaeologists have refuted the practice of intentional burial, arguing that it instead reflects the disposal of rotting bodies for reasons of comfort and health. It seems unlikely that, after millions of years, hominids suddenly would have decided that they could not tolerate the smell of death. For whatever reason, the burial of the dead appears in the fossil record about 50,000 years ago. Some sort of mortuary practice may be even older as indicated by the facial defleshing of a Middle Pleistocene archaic *H. sapiens* from **Bodo,** Africa. **Flexed burials** first appear with the Neanderthals. This position, which is found today in widely separated areas of the world, has been interpreted as a **prenatal position,** which perhaps reflects rebirth. The common experience with birth is the best way of accounting for the worldwide distribution of this orientation. Characteristically and very unconvincingly, Binfordians have argued that the flexed orientations are the result of postmortem rigor mortis. Such speculation is not convincing given the very different positions seen in cadavers.

Some of the most spectacular evidence for ritual burial comes from Shanidar Cave, Iraq. Dated at about 0.05 mya, at least nine individuals appear to have been intentionally interred. In one grave, a man is buried above two women, who are above an infant. Pollen in the grave has been used to suggest the inclusion of wild flowers in the burial. Intentional burials are also known from Neanderthal sites in Europe seen in the clearly intentional burials at La Chapelle and La Ferrassie in France. Other burials are also known from central and western Asia. The old man of Shanidar is an individual who had suffered extensive injuries to the head and body and yet had lived to an age of 40 to 45 years. His relative longevity has been attributed to the advent of "social security," in that other individuals would have had to help him survive. While other researchers have noted that the survival of crippled and maimed individuals also occurs in species that do not aid the impaired, it is hard to believe that people who ritually buried their dead did not also care for the sick and injured.

Perhaps the most spectacular evidence for belief in an afterlife comes from the cave site of **Krapina, Croatia,** where at least forty individuals were butchered and interred in what are perhaps secondary burials (reburials after a certain amount of time). It has also been suggested that cannibalism was practiced at Krapina. Cannibalism is significant because among modern people, with the exception of emergency cannibalism, the consumption of human flesh or organs always occurs in the context of ritual and spiritual belief. While the Western culture regards this practice as inhumane, quite the opposite may be indicated. The meanings may be different; in some cultures, you eat your enemy, and in others, you eat loved ones or relatives. We will probably never know the exact cultural context of the Krapina evidence, but it seems fairly certain that Neanderthals had developed some form of spiritual belief. There has also been some suggestion that Neanderthals practiced economic cannibalism, that is the consumption of other hominids as a regular food source. Specific taphonomic arguments supporting this claim have not been convincing, and in conjunction with the evidence for intentional burials and large game hunting, it seems unlikely that Neanderthals were dependent on human flesh for food.

Neanderthal sites have also revealed bones and teeth with artificial markings. The anthropologist Alexander Marshack has interpreted these objects as indicators of symbolic thinking. If these objects are an indication of art, they are few and far between. However, the fact that some of these are drilled does indicate **body adornment,** one of the cultural universals of modern humans. **Red ochre** has also been recovered from Neanderthal graves. Other indications of ritual and symbolism among Neanderthals, such as the offerings of a so-called **cave bear clan** and other grave offerings, have been disputed by Binfordians. Because much of the evidence was recovered prior to the utilization of modern archaeological techniques, original associations and site features make easy targets for critics. However, there is clear evidence supporting intentional burial. We would then have to suppose that Neanderthals buried their dead outside of a religious context, an interpretation which strains the limits of parsimony.

Language

In the last few decades, there has been a great deal of discussion about Neanderthal language. Some anatomists, such as Philip Lieberman and Jeffrey Laitman, have proposed that studies of the cranial base suggest that the soft tissue of the vocal track was different from speech-bearing modern humans. Specifically, they suggest that Neanderthals could not produce the full range of sounds found in modern humans. There are many problems with this interpretation. The first is that it is difficult (some would argue impossible) to accurately reconstruct the soft tissue anatomy of this region from fossil bones. As noted previously, the only known Neanderthal hyoid bone that has been recovered is completely modern in its anatomy. The absence of the full range of sound theory also neglects the fact that many languages (especially Asian languages) are tonal, meaning that the same sound can have completely different meanings depending on the tone of the word. Finally, it is difficult to imagine that a hominid with complex social features and the ability to produce highly standardized tools would have lacked language. This is true because there seems to be an intimate connection between language, handedness, and manual dexterity.

The origin and fate of the Neanderthals is as controversial today as when they were first discovered. Although we are now much more sure that they descend from *H. erectus*, we are not certain if they went extinct without descendants or if they evolved into modern humans. I strongly believe that at least some Neanderthal DNA is in modern populations, especially modern Europeans. This means that there is continuity in Europe and that the behavioral milestones of Neanderthals also represented many firsts in our own ancestry. Burial of the dead, spirituality, and a complex social organization involving care of both the young and old were probably present by Neanderthal times. In spite of the image in the popular literature of Neanderthals as crouching brutes, in fact many of the hallmarks of true humanity first appeared with this early form of *H. sapiens*. Language was probably also present among Neanderthals. No convincing evidence exists to suggest that it was not, and the brains of Neanderthals, so far as we can tell from endocasts, were no different from our own.

Anatomically Modern *Homo sapiens*

Anatomy

Unlike bipedalism, the anatomical definition of modern humans is based on very few objectively defined characters. Those that are considered reliable (though we shall see this is not always so) include the possession of a protruding chin, or **os mentum.** The mental bone is so named because the classical West considered a pronounced chin to be the mark of intelligence. The chin appears to be a response to selection pressure to reinforce the mandible without taking up space inside a smaller jaw with smaller teeth.

Related to the reduction in jaws and dentition is the common occurrence of an overbite. This feature occurs in 80 to 90 percent of modern humans. All earlier hominids exhibit **an edge-to-edge bite** of the kind that orthodontists are paid thousands of dollars to create. Generally, this complex has been related to the need for a highly mobile mandible required for the rapid articulate and spontaneous production of speech. The reduction of jaw size has also been related to **premasticatory food processing.** Just as the early vertebrates had begun the task of breaking down food before it reached the stomach, hominids take the task to its final step through cutting, cooking, and pounding food before it is eaten. As was evident from our discussion of *H. erectus*, less sophisticated versions of such techniques certainly antedate the appearance of modern humans. Some archaeologists argue that they were in place by at least 1 mya. Anatomically, modern humans are also recognized by their thinner cranial bones, rounder skulls, and more gracile skeletons in comparison with *H. erectus* and early *H. sapiens*.

Cranial capacity is perhaps the most unsatisfactory criterion for defining modern humans. Although an average of 1,350 to 1,450 ml is commonly used, in fact the sample of moderns is so great that the range of "normal" cranial capacity is from 800 to 2,200 ml. Neanderthals may have had an average cranial capacity larger than those of modern humans. There is no question that brain size begins to increase with the advent of culture. Beginning with the habilines, the brain reaches one-half the modern size. With late *H. erectus*, it eventually reaches just under three-fourths the size of moderns. It has often been erroneously concluded that cranial capacity changed little in *H. erectus*. Such is demonstrably not the case. The earlier specimens are smaller, and the latest specimens are larger. Furthermore, with the coming of moderns, cranial capacity essentially ceases to expand.

No one understands what gross brain size in hominids has to do with behavioral complexity, and many paleoanthropologists believe that reorganization has had much more profound effects on behavior. Within *H. sapiens* (including Neanderthals), behavioral complexity lags behind the attainment of modern cranial size. The surface convolutions of the human brain allow hominids to pack a maximum amount of neuronal material into a finite space, but other animals, such as cows, also have a convoluted cortex. Modern brain size is limited because it is curtailed by the size of the human female birth canal. In other words, human brain size has outstripped the ability of human females to bear larger-brained offspring. This is why human females are the only mammals to experience severe and sometimes mortal difficulties giving birth.

Behavior

It is now well established that Neanderthals overlapped in time with modern humans. Furthermore, it is also apparent that some of the more finely made paleolithic artifacts of the **Upper Paleolithic** were made by both Neanderthals and anatomically modern humans. Industries such as the **Aurignacian, Chatelperronian, Gravettian,** Solutrean, and **Magdalenian** were not only highly standardized and skillful assemblages, but for the first time in prehistory included a profusion of artifacts manufactured from the bone and teeth of animals. The two former industries once associated exclusively with anatomically modern humans are now known to have also been employed by Neanderthals. Among the bone artifacts are needles, harpoons for fishing, and jewelry. Jewelry not only denotes body adornment, but in foraging societies, it almost always indicates a belief in the supernatural. It is also during the Upper Paleolithic that art appears in the form of cave painting and small portable statuary. This period has been referred to as the Upper Paleolithic Revolution and more artistically by John Pfeiffer as the **creative explosion.** The archaeological record becomes so complex that descriptions and discussions of this last phase can and do fill hundreds of volumes.

A number of aspects of the Upper Paleolithic are still poorly understood. One of the most bothersome is not only the timing, but also the cause of the great surge in technology and culture. Although anatomically modern humans seemed to have emerged around about 0.1 mya, cultural complexity and ethnicity is not obviously apparent until about 0.045 mya. Mousterian tool technology is also a characteristic of early modern humans. The oldest modern human remains are from Skhul and Qafzeh, Israel, Omo (Kibbish), Ethiopia, and Klasies River Mouth, South Africa. All of these sites are problematical in terms of the morphology of the hominids and their dating. Other finds such as Liujiang, China, and Ngandong

(Solo), Indonesia, may be equally as old. The geochronology of these hominids does not afford an obvious solution to the problem of the geographic origins of our own species' cultural complexity.

Technology and Subsistence

A number of new artifacts and subsistence strategies appear to have either come into being or were greatly refined during the Upper Paleolithic. The production of highly formalized blades represents a great improvement. Blades are defined as narrow flakes (at least twice as long as they are wide) with parallel and straight edges. Not only do they maximize the ratio of cutting edge to volume, but they can also be produced in large numbers using a **soft punch technique** in which a number of blades can be quickly produced from a single core. The bow and arrow and the **atlatl** (spear thrower) also make their appearance during the Upper Paleolithic. Both of these devices extend the distance at which a hominid can be lethal, and the spear thrower greatly increases the force of a projectile. Some studies have suggested that it triples or quintuples the striking force of a projectile. This device easily helps a spear penetrate the hides of elephants. Bone was also used to manufacture entire huts made of mammoth skeletons.

Although there were previous indications of the utilization of aquatic resources from Terra Amata and Lazaret in France during Archaic *H. sapiens* (? or *H. erectus*) times, aquatic resources became common. Fowl is also added to the inventory. Burins and drills become significant components of the Upper Paleolithic tool kit, suggesting that the working of bone and wood were important. Lithic materials are transported from even more distant sources, and camps are occupied for longer periods of time by more people.

As J. Simek, J. Lindley, G. Clark, and others have emphasized, the transition to the Upper Paleolithic builds on the life ways of the Middle Paleolithic. It is a process of intensification not unlike the intensification of general primate trends that appeared with each new transition and grade. Another aspect of the Upper Paleolithic is that even within an area as small as Europe, there is **regional differentiation** in the makeup of artifact assemblages and the structure of sites. For instance, some occupation sites appear to have been cleaned, and hearths were the focus of activity other than cooking and keeping warm.

Art and Symbolic Behavior

It is highly likely that ethnic differentiation is also reflected in the Upper Paleolithic record. Not only do tools kits differ by region, but art is also restricted to specific areas. Most research on Upper Paleolithic art has been conducted on European sites and objects of art. However, it is also clear that art in the form of rock painting may be equally old in Australia. East Asia has so far failed to yield indications of paleolithic art, which may be because rock surfaces are relatively rare in the habitable coastal China plane and northern loess areas that have yielded most of the Chinese specimens.

Upper Paleolithic sites have also revealed objects made out of bone with engraved notations. Alexander Marshack has interpreted these objects as indicators of symbolic thinking or attempts to keep track of time (for example, the Abri Blanchard bone artifact from France). The inclusion of ornate grave goods suggests that special status was being recognized. Red ochre becomes a common component of burials during this time.

Cave Art. As mentioned previously, Upper Paleolithic art is classified into painted cave art (including some sculpted images), which was executed on cave walls, and portable (statuary) art. The subject of painted paleolithic art is almost exclusively the depiction of Ice Age mammals. Carnivores are rare, and horses and bovids are the most common. Geometrical figures in the form of angular and rounded "doodles" are also known. One other common motif is the tracing of a hand print (usually the left), a feature that can be observed all over the world today in modern graffiti. Some students of rock art have suggested that the small finger (digit 5) is depicted as truncated, suggesting that it was severed or that the finger was deliberately bent so as to preclude it being represented. Other symbols (if that is what they are) seem to be obvious depictions of projectile points piercing or at least aimed at the animals. Animal forms are often superimposed on each other, and occasionally, use of the natural contours of cave walls was made to accentuate animal forms. The human form is only very occasionally depicted and then only as stick figures. Most of the animals look pregnant or are at least fat, especially at such sites as **AltaMira**, Spain, and **Lascaux, France.**

Two fascinating facts have emerged about cave art. The first is that archaeologists have been unable to locate developmental stages in the skill of the artists. There are few, if any, relatively crude depictions indicating a lack of skill or familiarity with the subject matter. In the art of the last few thousand years, it is also difficult to demonstrate an increase in skill and sophistication, though conventions and styles have changed markedly. The artists who depicted these animals obviously knew them well. There is also no doubt that they attempted to represent the animals in motion. The noted expert on cave art, John Pfeiffer, has suggested that when viewed in the light of a flickering flame the animals give the appearance of motion. We also know that at least some of the animals were "sketched" with charcoal prior to the application of pigments.

The second peculiarity of cave art is its location. It is usually located in hard to reach subterranean places. In fact, many of the galleries require determined spelunking to reach. The paintings were not domestic decorations. Very few of them are placed near the mouths of caves where daylight could illuminate them. Neither are their locations associated with occupation sites. One of the most intriguing associations may be the footprints, including footprints of children, and carved stone oil lamps that have been found in the galleries.

Originally and quite logically, the purposes of the paintings have been interpreted as being manifestations of hunting magic. The depiction of obviously fertile or at least well-fed animals and pointy implements strongly supports this notion. This kind of magic is known as **sympathetic magic** and is widespread around the planet today. Depiction as a power is a common notion and ranges from voodoo dolls to a fear of photographs. However, cave art may have had an ancillary function.

In his book entitled *The Creative Explosion*, Pfeiffer suggests that Upper Paleolithic cave art functioned as a kind of training manual for instilling cultural knowledge in young members of the group. Pfeiffer notes that the flickering flames gave a lifelike quality of movement and life to the animals. He further speculates that the paintings were placed in deep, dark, and hard to reach places to influence the impressionable minds of little hominids. By bringing young hominids to the strange and underground world of a cave, they would perhaps be afraid and therefore alert. What Pfeiffer's theory describes is the psychological phenomenon of **imprinting.** The concept of imprinting refers to the fact that there are periods of life (usually before adulthood) when the mind is open to the development of permanent memories.

A similar technique is **brain washing,** which the U.S. army first learned of as the result of the Korean War. A similar and related phenomenon also received popular attention with Frank Sinatra's portrayal in *The Manchurian Candidate* and as the result of the Patty Hearst kidnapping case. After isolation and repeated mental and physical stress, the hostage finally joins the kidnappers. This phenomenon of isolation or of deprivation of self-awareness combined with constant company is also employed in religious cults. Pfeiffer's conjecture that cave painting was a kind of training device may have much merit. Though speculative, it is highly plausible. The discovery of juvenile-sized footprints in the caves also supports his interpretation. Furthermore, if drugs were involved, the experience might have been even more emotional.

It is likely that something as pervasive and important to us as art would have conferred an adaptive advantage on the Upper Paleolithic humans. Even those who argue that art has no evolutionary significance cannot argue that it does not strongly influence human experience and emotion. Pfeiffer explains that painting arose where and when it did because glacial Europe was cold, crowded, and competitive. Such an environment would have put increasing **population pressure** on humans as they encountered each other more and more frequently. There would have been increasing competition for the same resources. Populations that were more socially organized and cohesive may have obtained an advantage over less efficiently and complexly organized groups. In other words, the development of cultural identities would have helped to define and separate cultural groups who acted in their own best interests. This is a form of the ecological and sociocultural explanations discussed above. It is important to point out that this explanation does not involve a biological change in the brain but instead the development of new social techniques that utilize the already evolved propensities of the human mind.

Portable Art.   Upper Paleolithic portable art consisted of carved or molded clay figures and carved bone or antler. The subjects of portable art were both people and animals. Human figurines, much more common as the subjects, were depicted in what we believe is a realistic fashion. Most of these figures are female forms referred to as **Venuses.** These were thought to be symbols of human fertility. Many of them are plump with large breasts and buttocks. Some students have argued that they depict steatopygia, a form of female fat accumulation on the buttocks and lower torso observable in some hunters and gatherers such as Hottentots (indigenous people of Southern Africa). However, we know that both slender female and male figures were also made. Both male and female figures depict genitalia in detail with erect penises and clearly defined vulvae. The human figures do seem to emphasize sexuality, leading to one suggestion that they are the paleolithic equivalent of *Playboy* or *Hustler.* In addition to sexuality, at least one figure is the first depiction of "big hair" in the form of a paleolithic hairdo.

There is a tendency in archaeology to assign objects whose function is not obvious to the category of ritual paraphernalia. With Upper Paleolithic art, such a practice is probably justifiable. Perhaps even more important is the fact that thousands of years after their creation, these objects are still recognized by modern humans as art. Some of the figurine art that was fired has been speculated to be performance art. The archaeologist Olga Soffer argues that shattered figurines were purposely made from clay and silt that would explode when fired. A more likely explanation, apparent to anyone who has ever visited a kiln, is that final successful pottery is preceded by numerous failures.

One alternative but related explanation for the creation of portable carved or molded art can be termed the arctic hysteria theory. It could also be applied to cave art. This, in a mildly amusing way, refers to the fact that arctic people such as Eskimos pass long winter months indoors by creating portable art. It also refers to the fact that long months of confinement produce certain frustrations and psychological manifestations sometimes referred to as cabin fever. The implication is that for inhabitants of glacial Europe this kind of art may have represented both a symptom and a therapy for long months spent in a shelter.

In modern hunter and gatherers and many agriculturalists, art is emblematic of the group. Furthermore, until the advent of Western civilization, it was very hard to separate art from other important cultural features such as religion and music, which all modern cultures exhibit. Two of the most important of these features are religion and music. We shall explore the importance of this **cultural triad** (religion, art, and music) in the next chapter.

Geographic Expansion

The Upper Paleolithic is not only a time of cultural explosion but also a time of geographic expansion for *H. sapiens sapiens.* By 40,000 years ago, humans had reached Australia and by at least 20,000 years ago the **New World.** The colonization of Australia required some sort of water passage because even during times of low sea level, Australia was never connected to the Asian mainland. The colonization of the New World has long thought to have been across the Bering landbridge at a time of maximum glaciation. However, the curious distribution of the early dates for hominid arrival may suggest that the initial colonization of the

Americas was also accomplished with the aid of some form of water craft. The problem lies in the fact that the dates in South America are as old or older than those in North America, which is the presumed point of entry. There is no doubt that Amerinds (Native Americans) are of East Asian extraction. On the basis of dental evidence, the physical anthropologist Christy G. Turner II suggests at least two and possibly three waves of migration, one of Sundadonts from Southeast Asia and one from Northeast Asia of Sinodonts. Although highly speculative, I believe that it is possible that boats were involved in a coastal migration that allowed people to reach even the most distant parts of both continents in the New World very rapidly.

Tied to the question of dates, the great diversity of Amerind languages also poses a mystery. Depending on exactly how they are counted, Amerind languages number around two hundred. It is difficult to see how such diversity could arise in the one thousand years commonly accepted for the entry of humans into the New World.

At about the same time, North America and to some extent South America was the scene of **megafaunal extinctions.** Paul S. Martin has argued that early Americans may have been the cause or at least contributed to the disappearance of many of the animal species that had lived in North America for millions of years. Such creatures as mammoth, giant buffalo, camels, saber tooth cats, dire wolves, giant sloths, and even the horse disappear overnight in terms of the geological timescale. Arguments about the causes of the extinction recall those about the extinction of the dinosaurs (minus the asteroid of course). The disappearance of the horse is extremely puzzling because it had evolved for 60 million years and was perfectly suited for life in the Americas. In fact, when the Spanish reintroduced it in the 1500s, it immediately spread across the North American continent repopulating all of its former range. Similar extinctions occurred in the Old World at roughly the same time, but all of them, even in glacial Europe, were not as severe as those in North America. Conversely, extinctions were less dramatic in areas where hominids had been present the longest, that is they were least pronounced in Africa and Asia and most pronounced in Australia and the New World.

The Neolithic

Approximately 10,000 years ago, humans entered a stage in stone technology that led to the development of **agriculture**—the Neolithic (New Stone Age). For the first time, humans began to produce cutting implements with ground and polished stone edges. Ground and polished edges are not as sharp as flaked edges, but they hold a sharp edge longer when used in repetitive tasks, such as harvesting and timber cutting. **Grinding stones** for the processing of grains and seeds also became important for the processing of grains. Life became more sedentary. Another new phenomenon, which had first appeared in the Upper Paleolithic, would come to have a profound effect on the daily lives of humans. That new development was storage. Storage made agriculture possible, and most historians convincingly argue that storage inevitably led to **social stratification** and **craft specialization.** Social stratification means that societies began to be divided into classes in which certain levels of society had more access to desired goods and privileges than others.

Among mobile **hunters and gatherers,** storage is impractical because dwelling places are temporary and all possessions must be constantly transported from place to place. It is true that some storage, or at least curation, of possessions is known among hunter and gatherer groups, but it is not on a par with that of truly agricultural societies. Among hunters and gatherers, social stratification is also known in the forms of chiefs or big men, but in general, it is much less evident. Such societies are usually described as **egalitarian** because decisions and actions are carried out on the basis of group consensus.

Theories for the Rise of Agriculture

Why agriculture arose in the first place has been debated for centuries. It is clear that agriculture arose separately in several geographic places at different times. In most of these places, it was preceded by a Neolithic stage in which both wild and domesticated resources were used. Most of the explanations of the rise and invention of agriculture are ecological in nature. One theory postulates the depletion of wild game resources as a result of climatic changes at the end of the Pleistocene or human overhunting. As wild resources became scarcer, cultivated plants and domesticated animals eventually became the dominant food sources. Another climatic theory holds that as the last great glacial ice sheets melted and the sea level rose, humans became increasingly concentrated into smaller and smaller areas.

Yet another theory is one that has been called the **transhumance** theory. Transhumance refers to the fact that some groups move across the landscape in regular yearly cycles. It has usually been associated with nomadic herders or pastoralists, who must move their livestock according to the seasonal availability of fodder and water. Actually, nonpastoral people also have a seasonal cycle of movement. Regardless of whether the first proto-farmers were pastoralists or hunters and gatherers, both would have begun to notice that certain resources could be found in certain places at certain times. Encouraging the growth of certain desirable plants at regularly visited camps easily could have led to planned cultivation to the point where once marginal supplements of the diet could be counted on as stable and predictable resources.

A similar theory of seasonality is the **hydraulic hypothesis** of Robert Braidwood. The hydraulic hypothesis suggests that the seasonal flooding of the Nile River provided the impetus for human populations to organize the preparation of land for growing food. This preparation eventually required a strong social organization, that needed a centralized authority (initially priests and later pharaohs) to control it. There is also some suggestion that centralized religious organization arose out of these conditions. In fact, as we have seen, religion is far older than agriculture or civilization. Braidwood was especially concerned with the rise of agriculture and civilization in the Middle East, where evidence from the Fertile Crescent and the Nile River Valley still seems to be slightly older than in other areas of the Old World.

The Effects of Agriculture

The biobehavioral shifts in the human condition brought about by agriculture are profound. Many of the effects are negative enough that the invention of agriculture has also been called "the great mistake." Archaeological studies of populations undergoing the transition to agriculture reveal an increase in biological stress. The simple concentration of many people in a small space has a number of physiological and psychological health consequences. From a psychological perspective, the average city dweller probably encounters more people in a single week than a hunter and gatherer sees in an entire lifetime. It appears that the social conditions in which hominids evolved included the daily interaction with a few people for a prolonged period of time and not short interaction with a number of people on a daily basis. Furthermore, the number of years that an individual spends with a mate is double or triple that of the average fossil hominid. This surely has something to do with a divorce rate, which has reached epidemic proportions in the United States. These circumstances may, as we shall see later, be related to the most widespread psychological complaint of depression.

Another feature that the transition to agriculture reveals is that groups undergoing the transition show a marked increase in communicable diseases. This is easy to understand given the fact that the greater and more frequent contact increases the chances of contracting the diseases from other people. The change to a high-starch diet of a single staple also leads to dental caries (cavities). Prior to the advent of agriculture, caries was virtually unknown.

The Origins of Cultural Complexity

At the root of all discussions about the age of behavioral modernity is the basic question of when complex culture (including art and group idiosyncrasies) arose. The recognition of complex culture is itself a major focal point of debate. Most authorities would agree that the advent and propagation of nonutilitarian pursuits certainly constitutes complex culture. Some anthropologists have suggested that there is an inverse relationship between material complexity and mental complexity, as represented by cosmology and kinship. This viewpoint holds that peoples with complex tool kits have less complex social systems than people with simple tool kits. It is exceedingly difficult to apply this interpretation to the archaeological record of hominids, but it may be a valid, though general, characterization of some extant human populations.

The growth of human complexity began slowly and then accelerated in the most recent phases of human cultural evolution. The picture is neither one of gradualism nor punctuation, and overall, it is the textbook example of a geometric curve. All interpretations about when and why the cultural explosion happened must explain one difficult aspect of the emergence of modern humans: People of apparently modern anatomy are found in the archaeological record long before the Upper Paleolithic revolution begins at about 0.045 mya. Features such as art, complex tools, the expansion of resource bases, and indications of group idiosyncrasies (ethnicity) constitute a cultural explosion that waited at least one and probably two million years to happen.

Opinions about the reasons for the Upper Paleolithic explosion of culture can be divided into biological, ecological, and social explanations. The biological theory suggests that some fundamental change in the structure and functioning of the brain occurred. This could have been a sudden **mutation** that allowed for the production of truly modern language. This theory strongly implies that language or some other neurological mutation would have arisen in one place and quickly spread to other populations. Many proponents of the Eve theory are receptive to this idea. They argue that Africa has afforded the earliest evidence of both blades and anatomically modern humans, for example at Klasies River Mouth caves, which is considered to date to about 0.1 mya. The evidence for this theory, however, is strongly contested by opponents of the Eve theory. There is absolutely no good evidence for supposing that a genetic mutation was responsible for the complexification of human behavior.

Perhaps an even larger problem with the biological mutation theory is that there do not seem to be any fundamental changes in the brain either before or during the Upper Paleolithic. However, psychologist James Jaynes suggests just such a fundamental change in his theory of the **bicameral mind.** Jaynes suggests that the two hemispheres of the brain did not communicate with each other for most of the course of human evolution and that it was a very late mutation that allowed for the connection of the two brain hemispheres via the development of a dense connection of fibers known as the **corpus callosum.** He argues that the newly formed connection between the emotional right hemisphere and the more analytical left hemisphere led not only to a coordinated mind but also to such phenomena as dreaming and religion. Jaynes applied this idea as an explanation for the much later rise of Greek civilization. This idea is ludicrous because even the lowest vertebrates have such a connection. There is no question that nonhuman mammals dream. Birds and amphibians also exhibit something approximating dreaming. This explanation is equally unacceptable as a reason for the emergence of Upper Paleolithic complexity.

The ecological interpretation suggests that the severity of the glacial climate of Europe necessitated the development of complex forms of technology for survival. This kind of technology, including clothing, bone tools, and broadening of the resource base, would have been selected for by the harshness of glacial climates. Instead of expansion of the resource base, an alternative form of this explanation conjectures that glacial climates encouraged specialized dependence and exploitation of one particular kind of resource such as reindeer or sheep. Indeed, there is some evidence for this kind of specialization in the form of large kill sites. Although a particular group may have used many kinds of resources, one or two resources might have been more crucial. We see this kind of specialization among modern Eskimos and historically among the buffalo hunters of the North American plains.

The third type of explanation is sociocultural and simply posits that cultural complexity takes time to accumulate and diversify. Social systems tend to become increasingly complex, and the longer that social systems are maintained, the more knowledge they accumulate. There may be a trip point at which social systems pass a point in which complexity begins to accumulate at a geometric rate. None of these conjectural sociocultural explanations convincingly retrodicts the sudden complexity of the Upper Paleolithic.

There is no reason for assuming that Upper Paleolithic people and the Romans were anything but modern in their neural anatomy and physiology. Rather, archaeologists have discussed the differences between cultural capacity and performance. A facetious way of asking this question is, "Why didn't the Romans invent the telephone?" The answer involves the happenstance of history and ecology and not capacity.

Summary

Hominids arose more than about 4.5 mya in Africa. Bipedalism is the fundamental and earliest adaptation of our biological family. Exactly why early hominids evolved bipedalism is unknown, but theories that attempt to explain this rare form of locomotion tend to emphasize free hands as an adaptation for carrying things and as a preadaptation for stone tool making that would arise at approximately 2.5 mya. Bipedalism may have been a punctuated event as no intermediate stages are yet known. During the first 2 or 3 million years, hominids exhibited very few of the characteristics of modern humans apart from those related to bipedalism. Some dental changes in the direction of modern humans and a more omnivorous diet began to emerge in the early bipedal hominids. For the first 2 million years, the size of the brain remained the same as that of extant apes. With the appearance of our own genus *Homo*, the brain begins to enlarge and stone tools appear in the archaeological record. Whether these hominids hunted and had home bases with all the behavioral adaptations that these imply remains debatable. Scavenging and not hunting seems to have been the dominant mode of early hominid subsistence. Scholars agree that the brain had become reorganized in an asymmetrical way and that some form of language had developed by the time *H. erectus* appeared in Africa between 1.5 and 2.0 mya. Some feel that this reorganization actually dates back to the australopithecines.

H. erectus was the first hominid to leave Africa and colonize the temperate latitudes of Eurasia. Big game hunting, the use of fire, and the repeated occupation of sites over hundreds of thousands of years became common. The brain enlarged further. Although the Acheulean hand axe is supposedly characteristic of the species as a whole, in actuality, no hand axe has ever been found in direct association with the taxon. The Far East has yielded most of the anatomical and behavioral evidence for *H. erectus* lifestyles. Here it is associated only with amorphous flakes and so-called chopper-chopping tools. This seems to point to an emphasis on nonlithic adaptations first developed in response to Asian tropical forests.

The Eve hypothesis is based on the study of mtDNA and postulates that all modern humans descend from a single African female that existed between 0.05 and 0.2 mya. Also known as the replacement model, this interpretation holds that all decedents of *H. erectus*, including Neanderthals, were not ancestral to modern people. Neither the fossil nor archaeological record support this conclusion. Neanderthals share many behavioral traits with us. They developed a new and complex form of lithic technology requiring dexterity and planning. They were also the first hominids to bury their dead. There is evidence for religion in Neanderthal culture, but no convincing evidence for cannibalism. Although they exhibit idiosyncratic features that were once interpreted as "primitive," their Mousterian technology, ritual, and large brain confirms their humanness. The most parsimonious interpretation of the totality of the evidence is that Neanderthals contributed to the genetic makeup of modern Europeans.

Anatomically, modern *H. sapiens* developed a number of behavioral traits that link them with us, the extant cultures and races of the world. During the Upper Paleolithic explosion, the resource base expanded dramatically to incorporate all known forms of food, not just terrestrial mammals. Modern humans proceeded to colonize Australia and the New World and were possibly responsible for megafaunal extinctions that accompanied the withdrawal of the glaciers from Europe and North America. Ethnic diversity also became much more discernible in the archaeological record at this time.

Everywhere, the advent of distinct cultures resulted in a complex of behavioral and social traits that continue to distinguish mobile hunting and gathering bands from city dwelling agriculturally dependent states. Storage, which appears at least by Upper Paleolithic times, becomes emphasized. This results in social stratification, centralized authority, craft specialization, and eventually writing, which is the hallmark of civilization. Everywhere, the initial transition to agriculture was a time of increased stress as indicated by degenerative diseases resulting from crowding and repetitive tasks.

All of the behavioral traits discussed in this chapter are older than the earliest evidence for them; this is a given of prehistory and paleontology. New species and behaviors "linger" unobserved before they radiate. For traits to be detected in the prehistoric record, they must be successful. This is an important point, which underscores that many evolutionary failures go undetected. Even the extinct vegetarian robust australopithecines were at one time widespread, and they existed for at least 1 million years. Why some traits become successful is a much more difficult question.

It is imperative to emphasize that our modern way of life is at evolutionary odds with the lifestyle our ancestors followed for millions of years. The stresses that we now endure on a daily basis stem not from the natural environment, but largely from selection pressures of our own creation. We currently occupy an adaptive niche that is both recent and stressful. The underlying biology, which evolved first in Africa and later in Eurasia, has not kept pace with the rapid cultural developments of the last one thousand years. The specialization of civilized agricultural tasks often means that a great deal of the body that used to be exercised daily is neglected. Combined with a relative abundance of fat and meat, cholesterol is not used through physical activity but instead stored to the point where it promotes cardiovascular disease. For modern industrialized people, most sorts of stresses can only be solved in nonphysical ways. Many more agricultural and urban diseases could be listed. The fossil record of our ancestors indicates that we have evolved a kind of biology that does not suit the way we are living.

The few remaining groups of hunters and gatherers offer modern clues to our evolutionary legacy. In the next chapter, we study modern hunting and gathering people as a model for the way hominids probably have lived for most of their existence. The next chapter identifies traits that are found in all people regardless of how they live.

QUESTIONS FOR REVIEW

1. What is the chronological relationship between bipedalism, dental evolution, and the enlargement of the brain?

2. What are the major theories for the evolution of bipedalism? What are the criticisms of each theory?

3. What evidence exists for social organization in the austalopithecines?

4. What new behaviors appear with *Homo erectus?*

5. What human behaviors did Neanderthal exhibit?

6. What are the replacement and regional continuity arguments? How does the molecular evidence disagree or agree with the fossil record?

7. What is the Upper Paleolithic revolution?

8. How are modern humans defined?

MIND AND BODY EXPERIMENTS

1. Buy a leg or joint of some mammal (preferably with the bone and skin still attached) that modern humans consume. Butcher it with flakes of stone that you have manufactured from banging stones together. Leave a portion of the meat outside for twenty four hours. What happens to it? Use a stone to break open the bone and get the marrow. How does it taste?

2. Try to make a hand axe. Do you notice any difference in the "tractability" of different kinds of stone?

3. Try to make a fire using only sticks or stone. Try different rocks.

4. Place your index finger on the palm of a little hominid under six years old. What happens? Why?

5. Observe a little hominid learning to walk. What mistakes does he or she make?

6. Write a set of instructions for how to stand up and take a step.

SUGGESTED READINGS

Brace, C. Loring, and Ashley Montagu, M. F. 1977. *Human Evolution: An Introduction to Biological Anthropology* (2nd ed). New York: Macmillan.

Braidwood, R. J. 1960. The Agricultural Revolution. *Scientific American* 203: 130–141.

Brothwell, D., and Brothwell, P. 1969. *Food in Antiquity. A Survey of the Diet of Early Peoples.* London: Thames and Hudson.

Campbell, B. G. 1983. *Human Ecology: The Story of Our Place in Nature from Prehistory to the Present.* Chicago: Aldine.

Cann, R. 1987. In Search of Eve. *The Sciences* 27: 30–32.

Childe, V. G. 1936. *Man Makes Himself.* London: Watts.

Dart, R. 1925. *Australopithecus africanus*: The Man Ape of South Africa. *Nature* 155: 195–199.

Falk, D. 1975. Comparative Anatomy of the Larynx in Man and the Chimpanzee: Implications for Language in Neanderthal. *American Journal of Physical Anthropology* 43(1): 123–132.

Falk, D. 1987. Human Paleoneurology. *Annual Review of Anthropology* 16: 13–30.

Gowlett, J., Harris, J. W. K., Walton, D., and Wood, B. A. 1981. Early Archeological Sites, Hominid Remains and Traces of Fire from Chesowanja, Kenya. *Nature* 294: 125–129.

Holloway, R. L. 1983. Human paleontological evidence relevant to language behavior. *Human Neurobiology* 2: 105–114.

Howell, F. C. 1970. *Early Man.* New York: Time-Life.

Isaac, G. L. 1978a. The Archaeological Evidence for the Activities of Early Hominids. In *Early Hominids in Africa*, C. J. Jolly (ed.), pp. 219–254. New York: St. Martin's.

Isaac, G. L. 1978b. The Food-Sharing Behavior of Protohuman Hominids. *Scientific American* 238: 90–108.

Jaynes, J. 1978. *The Origin of Consciousness in the Breakdown of the Bicameral Brain*: Boston: Houghton Mifflin.

Johanson, D., White, T., and Coppens, Y. 1979. A New Species of the Genus *Australopithecus* (Primates: Hominidae). In *The Pliocene of Eastern Africa*. Kirtlandia 28: 1–14.

Jolly, C. J. 1970. The Seed Eaters: A New Model of Hominid Differentiation Based on a Baboon Analogy. *Man* 5: 5–26.

Leroi-Gourhan, A. 1968. The Evolution of Paleolithic Art. *Scientific American* 218: 58ff.

Lewin, R. 1986. Myths and Methods in Ice Age Art. *Science* 234: 938.

Lewin, R. 1987a. Four Legs Bad, Two Legs Good. *Science* 235: 969–971.

Lewin, R. 1987b. The Earliest Humans Were More Like Apes. *Science* 236: 106–163.

Lovejoy, C. O. 1981. Origin of Man. *Science* 211 (4480): 341–350.

Pfeiffer, J. 1982. *The Creative Explosion.* Ithaca: Cornell University Press.

Potts, R. 1984. Home Bases and Early Hominids. *American Scientist* 72(4): 338–347.

Prideaux, T., and the Editors of Time-Life. 1973. *Cro-Magnon Man.* New York: Time-Life.

Read-Martin, C. E., and Read, D. W. 1975. Australopithecine Scavenging and Human Evolution: An Approach from Faunal Analysis. *Current Anthropology* 16(3): 359–368.

Sarich, V., and Cronin, J. 1976. Molecular Systematics of the Primates. In M. Goodman and R. Tashian (eds.), *Molecular Anthropology: Genes and Proteins in the Evolutionary Ascent of Primates*, pp. 141–171. New York: Plenum.

Sillen, A., and Brain, C. 1990. Old Flame. *Natural History* 6–10.

Simons, E. L. 1989. Human Origins. *Science* 245: 1343–1350.

Spuhler, J. N. (ed.). 1959. *The Evolution of Man's Capacity for Culture*. Detroit: Wayne State University Press.

Stahl, A. Brower. 1984. Hominid Dietary Selection Before Fire. *Current Anthropology* 25: 151–168.

Stringer, C. B., and Andrews, P. 1988. Genetic and Fossil Evidence for the Origin of Modern Humans. *Science* 239: 1263–1268.

Toth, N. 1985. Archeological Evidence for Preferential Right-Handedness in the Lower and Middle Pleistocene, Its Possible Implications. *Journal of Human Evolution* 14: 607.

Washburn, S. L. 1960. Tools and Human Evolution. *Scientific American* 63: 413–419.

White, T. D. 1979. Evolutionary Implications of Pliocene Hominid Footprints. *Science* 208: 175–176.

Wilson, A. K., and Sarich, V. M. 1969. A Molecular Time Scale for Human Evolution. *Proceedings of the National Academy of Science* 63: 1089–1093.

4 Hunters and Gatherers and Cultural Universals

. . . [T]he universal thirst for a common communion not merely of the senses, but of our whole nature.

—Percy Bysshe Shelley

Nature hath made men so equal in the faculties of body and mind as that, though there be found one man sometimes maifetly stronger in body or of quicker mind than another, yet when all is reckoned together the difference between man and man is not so considerable as that one man can thereupon claim to himself any benefit to which another may not as well as he.

—Thomas Hobbes

Humans behave in ways that are both predictable and unreliable. In this chapter we examine what is known historically of **hunters and gatherers** and how these societies can be used as models of sociocultural evolution and organization shared by all human groups. These commonalities are referred to as cultural universals. Some of these universals must certainly stem from the psychic unity of our species, while others may represent similar universal responses to stimuli and problems that all human groups face. The human mind has deep structures that categorize the world in very similar ways, at least at a fundamental level. The use of modern hunters and gatherers as models for early hominid behavior is a highly contentious issue in anthropology and related social sciences. There is general agreement that it is unrealistic to simply project modern hunter and gatherer behavior back into our ancestral past. This is true not only because they are modern people with modern brains, but also because only the undiscovered groups have not been transformed by contact with agricultural communities. However, studying modern groups is still the best way we have of trying to appreciate a nonagricultural form of living.

Although the characteristics that we are studying are cultural and therefore by definition learned, the fact that they exist in every culture suggests that there are varying degrees of behavioral predispositions that are part of the biological makeup of humans. One of the reasons to emphasize hunters and gatherers in the search for cultural universals is that they are relatively easy to observe because of the simplicity of their material culture, small group size, and seemingly more finely tuned relationships between daily activities, subsistence, and the natural environment. This is not to say that such societies are any less complex in their thinking, social organization, or expressions than Westernized agricultural or industrialized societies. It is hard to prioritize the importance of cultural universals or definitely decide which arose first in the course of human evolution because each behavior supports the other. However, improved archaeological evidence one day may make it possible to identify learned behaviors that were as important to our family as innate bipedalism was.

It is important to emphasize that like human anatomical and behavioral traits, modern hunters and gatherers represent a mosaic of both evolutionary old and recent developments. Some of these behavioral traits are also shared with mammals in general and nonhuman primates, but they have become emphasized in hominids. Thus, in some cases there is a qualitative difference between humans and their immediate relatives, while in other cases, the difference is quantitative.

In the last decade or so, some archaeologists, especially Binford, have argued that surviving hunters and gatherers represent a recent behavioral development whose roots cannot be readily traced back to ancient Pleistocene hominids. These arguments maintain that nearly all modern groups represent recent adaptations to **marginal environments,** which came to be occupied as the result of the group's failed competition with agricultural populations. Put another way, the so-called hunter and gatherer groups that we see today are the result of competitive exclusion. Accordingly, these groups have for the most part come to occupy a **trading niche** that emphasizes the trade of forest resources or other products from marginal environments for agricultural products. This viewpoint also emphasizes the interpretation that a hunting and gathering way of life is an extremely recent adaptation that is confined only to late members of anatomically modern humans. According to this model, many of the universals considered below are very recent evolutionary developments. One point of contention has been the existence of and reliance on socially organized big game hunting. It is hard, for instance, to argue that Eskimo hunting was preceded by a period of failed agriculture. However, it can be argued that organized hunting was purely the domain of anatomically modern humans. The previous chapter has argued that this is demonstrably not the case.

There can be no doubt that some modern hunting and gathering adaptations may indeed be secondary adjustments to agriculturally based population pressures. However, some groups are engaged in a means of subsistence that is much more similar to the subsistence patterns of fossil *Homo* populations. The dichotomy between hunting and scavenging has probably been overemphasized. **Foragers** might be a better term for what it is that such people do for a living. Among mammalian carnivores and omnivores, hunters are always also scavengers. In terms of evolution, one means of subsistence is always found in association with the other. At the same time, opportunistic omnivory is an even better way of describing the subsistence base of nonagricultural humans.

It may be that the still surviving hunters and gatherers do occupy largely marginal environments that do not allow for agriculture. However, the reason for the occupation of dense forests and deserts is not necessarily failure. It is just as likely that an ancient way of life was left undisturbed by land that agriculturists either could not exploit or did not know about.

As with the dichotomy between hunting and gathering, the distinction between agriculture and horticulture has almost certainly been overemphasized. The hierarchically known range of Native American societies, for instance, frequently defies meaningful classification into most of these modes. It is also true that contact between hunters and gatherers and people practicing other means of subsistence has always resulted in the almost instantaneous modification of the hunters and gatherers. This, unfortunately, has frequently taken the form of the decimation and / or extinction of the former. Such extinction frequently comes as a result of disease and superior lethal technology. Until recently, hunters and gatherers existed on all continents except Antarctica. It may be true that there are virtually no such "untouched" cultures left. Regardless of what scientists actually decide to be the significance of the adaptive models that they suggest to anthropologists, it is clear that most of these isolated peoples will soon be gone. Contrary to the "recent culturalists," it is hard to believe that most of the cultural universals are largely of recent origin. The direct investigation of the behavioral and technological adaptations of people relying solely on nonmetallic tools is already relegated to visual images of film and historical accounts.

A Brief Survey of the Characteristics of Recent Hunters and Gatherers

Before proceeding to a consideration of cultural universals, it is useful to consider some of the widely agreed characteristics of hunters and gatherers that set them apart from agricultural and industrial cultures of the modern world.

Small Mobile Groups

Though hunter and gatherer groups change population size according to seasonal criteria (see below), the high mobility, small size, and the absence of beasts of burden do not allow for long-term storage and transport. The inability to accumulate large amounts of goods of any kind generally has been seen as the reason that hunter and gatherer groups are not socially stratified. The !Kung San Bushmen of southern Africa are among the most studied and discussed hunters and gatherers. They have universally been described as egalitarian. There is no chief or permanent leader. However, closer observation of the !Kung San and other groups suggests that some individuals more actively participate in and influence decisions than others.

The !Kung San occupy desert and subdesertic habitats, which are not desired by agriculturalists. Hunting territories and water holes are associated with certain groups and individuals, but access to these resources is usually granted to all.

Another reason they have been so closely studied is that they occupy open environments in Africa, the continent where our early ancestors evolved. One of the continuing controversies about their life has been the relative amount of time spent in obtaining food. Opinions have ranged from those who maintain that they spend most of their time searching for food to those who maintain that they have much more leisure time than agriculturalists. As with other hunters and gatherers, hunting is only successful about 20 percent of the time, and females' gathering is the most reliable source of food in all but arctic societies. In fact, hunters and gatherers are distributed along a **subsistence continuum** in which some groups rely much more extensively on hunting and others rely much more on gathering. Strategies also vary according to season. All of them are subject to the constraints of **optimal foraging theory,** which simply holds that a person or a group cannot expend more energy than they take in.

Examples of hunters include historical Plains Native Americans and Eskimos, who were and are largely dependent on hunting. Plains Native American adaptations were unusual to say the least, not only because they were essentially shaped by the introduction of the horse and gun, but also because they put an extreme emphasis on warfare, which intensified after the introduction of the horse and gun. The Northwest Coast Native American groups are also odd because of their emphasis on social stratification, which is as complicated and formalized as any agricultural population. Although these people practice little in the way of agriculture, their strong dependence on seasonal fish, especially salmon, represents a resource that mimics sedentary agriculture. This type of adaptation allows the aggregation of large communities whose existence is based on the storage of fish.

Little Task Specialization along Social Lines

Although there is a distinct sexual division of labor among hunters and gatherers, as there is in most agricultural communities, there is very little in the way of craft specialization. There are few if any inherited guilds or family specialization. However, certain individuals are almost always perceived as being better at certain behaviors (hunting, gathering, singing, **shamanism**) and the manufacture of certain goods. In general, each member must learn to manufacture and use a much wider range of the total artifact forms that are appropriate to their group and sex.

A Pervasive Belief in Shamanism, Animism, and Sympathetic Magic

Although not absolutely universal, there is a very widespread belief among hunters and gatherers that disease is usually not the result of natural processes. Shamanism, the use of a human mediator who specializes in bridging the gap between the seen and the unseen worlds, also characterizes most hunter and gatherer groups. The same is true of animism, the belief that animals, objects, and landmarks have spirits or spiritual connections. Such beliefs are also common in agricultural communities, but they are universal among hunters and gatherers.

Sympathetic magic is also widespread and can be very effective by employing psychophysiological pathways that scientists are just beginning to understand. All of the above features can also be found in both Western and non-Western societies, whether or not they are agriculturally based.

Cultural Universals and Alleged Exceptions

The Sexual Division of Labor and Diet

All known human societies divide tasks along sexual lines. Just as there is a distinct sexual dimorphism in physical makeup, there is also a difference in socioeconomic and sociocultural roles that males and females play in society. In terms of subsistence, there is female work and male work. In industrial agricultural societies, this division has become increasingly blurred, but in hunter and gatherer societies, traditional divisions of labor have only been significantly altered by the introduction of nonindigenous ideas and technology. With the exception of infant rearing, there is no true division of labor among chimpanzees or any other nonhuman primate. In almost all hunting and gathering societies, men do the majority of hunting, especially of larger animals. The majority of gathering and collecting of vegetable foods is done by females. Foraging almost always involves the collection of small vertebrates (rodents, reptiles, and amphibians) and invertebrates (mollusks, snails, insects). The importance of insects in the hunting and gathering diet (and in many agriculturalist diets) has been greatly underestimated by anthropologists, and yet it is ironic that insects are almost universally absent from the Western table.

As a very general rule, 20 percent of the diet of a group consists of animal protein and 80 percent of the diet consists of vegetable food. Women account for nearly 100 percent of the vegetable food and therefore supply most of the diet. Men account for nearly 100 percent of the meat. Variation in the diet is extreme and covers all possibilities. Eskimos are almost completely dependent on meat in the form of arctic mammals and fish.

In previous studies of hominid evolution, it was suggested that "man the hunter" was the most appropriate way of understanding the subsistence and social behavior of our species. Daily life was essentially conceived of as centered around the hunt, with such human features as foresight, planning, and even language arising out of a hunting adaptation. As more actualistic studies of hunters and gatherers were carried out, it became apparent that hunting was usually a haphazard activity that could not be relied on to provide food. In addition to skill and knowledge of the prey, hunting has always depended on luck. Much more recently in the history of anthropological studies, it has been suggested that "woman the gatherer" is a much more accurate way of understanding how it is that small groups of humans survive. In fact, gathered resources are much more predictable. A knowledge of their location in time and space serves as a more reliable means of repeatedly obtaining a recurring resource. As mentioned previously, female foraging also produces a great deal of protein in the form of invertebrates and small vertebrates.

Vegetable food does not run away, a fact that undoubtedly has always been important to slow-moving hominids such as ourselves. Although vegetable foods seem to be crucial to the survival of a group, meat is almost always regarded as more desirable. This may quite possibly relate to millions of years of using meat whenever it was available. We have been selected to have a natural desire for animal protein, and in most cultures, meat (and fat) is a prestigious food item. This may account for why it is that developed Western societies seem to eat too much meat (contributing to cardiovascular diseases) even though in places like the United States any kind of food is available. In terms of overall diet, the human species as a whole is probably best described as an opportunistic omnivorous forager.

Almost all cultures, even the few strictly vegetarian societies, desire oil or fat and sweet-tasting things. When cultures who have little in the way of these products are introduced to the more agricultural diet, the result is almost always a notable and quite often severe increase in health problems. Among Native Americans, diabetes is a major health problem associated with obesity and dental caries. One notable example is that of the desert-dwelling **Pima** peoples of southern Arizona. As the result of thousands of years of previous selection, the Pima developed the ability to quickly store energy in the form of fat when large quantities of meat became available for a short period of time. High-energy sugars were also rare and distributed only seasonally in the natural setting. Their recent Western diet with an emphasis on lard, flour, meat, and sugar has had disastrous effects. Recent experiments show that a return to the natural Pima diet of grains and seeds quickly resulted in a noticeable improvement.

From an evolutionary point of view, the desire for these things is not only understandable but inevitable. As mentioned in an earlier chapter, there also seems to be a sexual dimorphism in taste and smell among humans. Females are better at discriminating sweet scents. This may be a direct legacy of a division of labor that has been present for at least 2 million years.

One well-known exception to the rule of division of labor involving male hunting and female gathering are the **Agta** of the Philippines. These tropical forest people share equally in the hunting of large game (in this case, wild pigs), with females accompanying males on the hunt. Fishing is also an important part of their diet, and in general, the environment is very rich in terms of food and raw materials. One of the chief students of this group, Bion Giffin, has described the Agta as "the most laid-back people I have ever known." Indeed it may be that an "easy" environment relaxes selection pressures for maintaining a division of labor. The lack of division of labor is so rare that the Agta are well known to anthropologists as perhaps the only exception.

Some anthropologists have proposed a general rule of the relationship between male and female status and the division of labor needed for the procurement of resources. In groups that are more dependent on meat, females have less power and prestige. This largely predicts that women would have especially low status and authority in populations such as the Eskimo, where animal protein is virtually the only source of nourishment. Some have indeed argued that this is true. One would also predict that this would be true of the buffalo hunters of the North American Plains. It is true that the ephemeral plains cultures put an extreme emphasis on male virtues associated with warfare and hunting. However, plains cultures also provided for a great deal of latitude in female behavior with regard to sexuality and the division of labor. Berdaches, or "two spirits," could adopt any position along the gender continuum from male and female dressing and hunting to female dressing and not hunting.

Case studies of groups that spend long periods of time engaged in war where the males must be away from home have suggested that in these types of societies, women have much more authority and power and are more likely to be hunters. One famous example is that of the **Iroquois.** In this society, men were away frequently on war parties. The women exercised very great political authority and actually elected the candidates for chiefs. A parallel situation occurred during World War II, when the absence of men necessitated a dramatic change in the traditional role of U.S. women. Occupations that were previously reserved for males were quickly filled by women. "Rosie the Riveter" has become an icon of the kind of socioeconomic change that is possible when a group comes under stress. Today, however, jobs are still heavily skewed in terms of sex and compensation toward a traditional emphasis on males in Western society.

Conversely, we may predict that in largely or wholly vegetarian societies, women should have high social prestige. The ill treatment of women in places like China and India seems to utterly confound such a prediction. A further problem is that status is almost always connected with age and public expression of status, which often does not reflect domestic reality. For example, traditional Chinese culture has often been characterized as a largely male-dominated society. In fact, in many Chinese households, the man gradually loses the power to make economic decisions as his aging wife acquires more control of the finances and household. Although China is representative only of one generalized cultural milieu, it is the largest cultural area in the world.

One fairly consistent division of labor is the almost exclusive involvement of men in warfare (though women are highly involved as victims). This is supported by a number of physiological and sexually dimorphic anatomical features such as the hormonally mediated aggression and greater physical strength of males. Furthermore, many of the skills that are useful in hunting are the same as those that are useful in war. There also seems to be fairly consistent sexual dimorphism of childhood play behavior with more male play involving a greater use of space and the throwing of sticks and stones. Females, on the other hand, spend much more time in verbal, imaginative play including the enactment of domestic situations. This observation reinforces a stereotype, but few studies have concluded that such differences are purely the result of cultural training. Other studies are cross-cultural and suggest that the same types of socialization processes occur in widely disparate societies. Most studies indicate that differences between boys and girls are small. Most also concur in noting that there is good evidence for hormonal and genetic bases for sexual dimorphism in play and school.

Among hunters and gatherers and non-Western agricultural societies, it also appears that females become more economically important to the group at an earlier age. Girls often aid their mothers in the production of food at an age when boys are still playing. In pastoral societies, boys may tend domestic animals in the field at an early age and therefore serve an important economic function. However, there is considerable play included in such activities, much of it involving the use of sticks and stones. These observations seem to be true across cultures. There is no doubt that culture plays a tremendous part in gender differences and that the idea that there is a biological basis to these differences is unpopular in modern Western culture, especially in the United States. These behavioral differences cannot all be simply the result of learning because they occur in the vast majority of cultures.

Perhaps the most important aspect of the division of human labor is that it exists at all. It is so consistent that it is reasonable to suppose that it is a vital adaptation of our species. Much of the evolutionary reason for the division of labor certainly stems from the fact that it is females that, by definition, must bear the young. It often has been observed that the restrictions in mobility placed on the female by childbearing and childrearing inherently limit the kinds of economic activities in which a female can take part. Although the same is true for most vertebrates, a consistent division of labor that benefits other than the individual performing the labor is unknown among other primates. One of the unique attributes of the division of labor is that it benefits not just the individual but also the group, whether it is the family or the society as a whole. Among hominids, our omnivorous diet seems closely related to the division of labor. The two kinds of basic nutrients are divided between the two sexes. The division of labor is closely related to another unique feature of human behavior, food sharing.

Food Sharing

Food sharing is a behavior that makes the division of labor possible. This, almost uniquely humanlike bipedalism, seems to be one of the fundamental adaptations of hominids. Humans not only share between males and females and parents and infants, but also between designated members of society, whether or not they are kin. Most human social occasions are accompanied by some form of food sharing. Human food sharing is fundamentally different from the feeding behavior of nonhuman primates and other vertebrates in that it occurs on a daily basis throughout every season. Among some social carnivores, females will provision the young with hunted food. The same is true of many species of birds, but both males and females will take turns in guarding the nestlings or obtaining food for the relatively helpless infants.

For humans, food sharing with infants is absolutely critical to allowing the helpless ectoparasite to survive to the point where it can provide for itself. Once again, there is an important exception that proves this rule. The **I'k** of East Africa are a group that has found itself pushed into a marginal habitat that has almost no food. Their society is so stressed that it has broken down to the point where parents no longer feed their offspring. Infants as young as two are left to fend for themselves and sharing with other members of the family has broken down completely. Colin Turnbull who studied the I'k thinks that they will soon be extinct.

Lovejoy has postulated that food sharing began as a reciprocal relationship in which males traded high-protein animal food for sex. If this interpretation is valid, the trading of female collected food may also have been part of the "deal." But food sharing goes far beyond its nutritive aspects. It also has great symbolic significance in virtually all societies. Occasions such as marriages and quite frequently deaths almost always have specific consumables that are part of the ceremonies. The marriage feast is an extremely common form of public consumption around the world. The conspicuous consumption and distribution of food is an obvious part of every known human society.

Food taboos are also an integral part of every known social group. Such taboos range from cheese (in East Asia) through insects (in Western society) to human flesh (in most societies) to domestic carnivores (not in East Asia). Almost all food taboos involve animal protein. Why this should be true is hard to comprehend. All people also have certain psychological attributes and effects that they associate with food.

Although all societies share food, many have strict rules about how the food should be shared. Once again, the rules are applied most strictly to animal protein. A common phenomenon is that the preferred part of the animal should be given to the hunter, an elder, or a particular relative. The culturally determined "best" parts of an animal are often reserved for people of high status or guests, which by definition in many societies have the highest status. Assembling a number of people from both near and far is frequently occasioned by an abundance of food. Most vertebrates behave in a similar way with the formation of large groups in response to a seasonally plentiful resource. This of course is the same kind of fission and fusion seen in human societies.

Fast-food is a fact of modern industrial life and a number of studies have been conducted of fast-food customers. One observation is that those dining (if that's what one does at these places) alone often read while they are eating. It requires no stretch of the imagination to view reading as a substitute for human company. Dining from a communal plate is much more common than having individual servings, as is common practice in Western societies. Though specific research has yet to be conducted, it would be interesting to examine the relationship between the number of fast-food restaurants and the status of the family. Modern China would be an excellent place to start. In the Far East where fast-food growth has been exponential, the main motivation for local patrons is not the food itself, but rather the newness and the "Westerness" associated with the experience. In fact, cheeseburgers and pizza are some of the most despised foods in the East. On the other hand, french fries, some form of grain, and ice cream seem to be universal in their desirability. What originally evolved as an adaptation for making optimal use of opportunistic windfalls has evolved into an integral part of every society. Although Westerners divide food into meats, fruits and vegetables, and starches, Chinese divide food into hot and cold. Our ancestors may have perceived foods more precisely as sweet, fatty, and starchy. Fast (and dangerous!) food had a totally different meaning to our ancestors.

Tool Dependency

All human societies not only manufacture and use tools, but are also tool dependent. That is, they must use tools in order to extract a livelihood from their environment. There are no exceptions. Technology employs tools and one of the most important tools has been fire. It was once suggested that there were in fact some exceptions. The **Tasaday** of the Philippines, when first contacted, were thought to make only crude stone tools. Further investigation revealed that in all probability this and other characteristics once attributed to these people were fraudulent. The Tasaday were also said to lack a knowledge of how to manufacture or use fire. Again, the alleged isolation and primitiveness of this group could not be confirmed. The Tasaday would have been the exception that proves the ironclad rule that hominids have been relying on tools for more than 2.5 million years.

Another Southeast Asian group, the **Andaman Islanders**, may actually have lacked knowledge of fire. It has also been speculated that **Tasmanians** lacked a knowledge of fire. All these observations are hard to confirm or deny, but if true, they would represent the exceptions that once again confirm the rule.

Many cultures have strict divisions between male and female tools that are gender specific; some forbid the touching of male tools by females. Among Eskimos, a day of bad hunting is often blamed on female "pollution" of an important implement. In Western society, such distinctions have been relaxed, but it is still rare to see a female with a chainsaw. Western males and females are much more likely to have exclusive use of their individual towels, brushes, combs, and razors. The use of the barbecue is also a largely male prerogative. The analogy to "man the hunter" is obvious, but "man the barbecuer" is usually a weekend phenomenon not necessarily associated with "man the dishwasher."

Weapons form a category of tools whose functions range from defense through aggression and predation to warfare. One of the decided trends in the archaeological and historic record has been the development of weapons that allow humans to kill or injure at increasingly greater distances. Distance predation may have been a major advance in the procurement of resources, whether from enemies or the natural environment. As S. L. Washburn pointed out, the use of weapons is easily learned by young hominids. They find it enjoyable, and projectiles and clubs are a common part of human, especially male human, play. As noted previously, we are the only species that is lethal at a distance.

Tool possession also conveys socioeconomic status. Some tools also function as body adornment. Clothing is a tool, as are weapons, hats, purses, and cellular phones. The introduction of the symmetrical hand axe more than 1.5 mya began the blurring of the distinction between art and utilitarian objects. There are many social reasons for painting pots or manufacturing projectiles to certain specifications that have no obvious connection to utility. The important point to be made here is that humans do not usually separate form and function in artifacts. A socially acceptable harmonious blending of the two is common to every culture.

Fission and Fusion

Another feature of hunter–gatherer life is that group size, while always small by agricultural standards (from five to a few hundred), becomes larger or smaller according to the availability of resources. Group size increases when resources are abundant and smaller groups may fuse into larger groups. By the same token, groups tend to fission or split into smaller units when resources are scarce. As mentioned above, this feature of population distribution is in no way unique to humans but is part of the ecological strategy of many animals. It is frequently a seasonally formalized behavior in humans. Examples in the United States include activities ranging from having the extended family gatherings at Thanksgiving and Christmas to inaugural dinners. Like other animals, humans have a seasonal pattern of fission and fusion. Harvests are the most common type of group activity in agricultural societies. In the West, barbecues are also a seasonal manifestation of group formation that is closely tied to food sharing. One of the odd things about Christian-based societies is that formal fusion occurs most often in the winter months when resources are scarce. The "season," which runs from Thanksgiving to New Year's Eve, includes not only the lavish and formal celebration of cultural events, but also numerous other gatherings. It is interesting that there is also a marked rise in reported cases of depression and suicide during the same period. Some studies suggest that physiological effects are complicated by interaction with a large number of people in confined spaces. In all vertebrates, crowding causes an increase in intraspecific aggression.

Language

Like all mammals, human communication is **multimodal** in that it involves visual, auditory, and probably chemical olfactory interaction between individuals. All known primate and most of mammalian communication is **limbic** in that the communicators can only express their present state of emotional feeling. In humans, linguistic communication is characterized by the frequent expression of **nonlimbic** or nonemotional states of being. Language is so important that much of Chapter 6 is devoted solely to this subject. Its importance is also underscored by the fact that **linguistics** is one of the four fields of anthropology that is also studied by professional communicators (poets, novelists, salespeople, politicians), psychologists, and many other branches of the humanities and social sciences. Language sets us apart from all other terrestrial beings. Although some other vertebrates show glimmerings of linguistic ability, human language is so qualitatively distinct that it often vitiates comparisons of human and nonhuman behavior. Here we shall only outline its basic properties.

In the course of the nineteenth century, some scholars predicted that one day a group of humans would be discovered that were so "primitive" that they would lack language. According to the thinking at the time, the complexity of any particular language could supposedly be compared with others and correlated with the complexity of the speakers' social or moral system. Language is a fundamental part of the human condition. The only way to keep a normal human from learning language is isolation. On the other hand, scientists have spent millions of dollars trying to teach chimpanzees and even a gorilla to speak. They have attempted to teach language to apes by offering rewards of all kinds. An unbiased assessment of the results of these training programs makes it very clear that ape linguistic abilities are severely limited in comparison with humans. In contrast, little hominids not only require no reward but also regard language as its own reward, and it is frequently difficult to get them to stop enjoying the reward. When teaching chimpanzees to speak, the problem is getting them to do just that.

Although language is present in all normal humans and their societies, the way that its details are used and organized is highly variable. By definition, all languages have a **grammar**, a set of rules that is learned and is peculiar to that language. These rules dictate how it is that **nouns** are related (conjunctions, prepositions) to action (verbs) and description (adjectives, adverbs, prepositions). All languages share this. Some languages lack or only infrequently use articles or indications of plurality. Another universal feature of language is that it is an arbitrary system of learned vocal or visual symbols that does not have any necessary relation to the physical properties of the thing that it refers to. Some languages do label an object in a way that approximates the sound that an object makes. For instance, in Chinese a cat is "mao." In Indonesian, a certain kind of noisy lizard is called a "cicak" for the clicking sound it makes. Interestingly enough, domestic cats are recognized all over the world by a "mao" or "meow" sound. Observations such as this support the so-called **buzz-bowwow** theory for the origin of human languages, which supposes that the first human language arose out of the imitation of natural sounds. This theory seems unlikely given the arbitrary representation of natural sounds in human speech. For Chinese, dogs communicate vocally with a "gou, gou" sound. For Russians and many Americans, a dog responds with an "arf, arf" sound. Yet both cultures see it as a dog.

An extremely important point to reemphasize is that all mammals communicate with each other without the aid of language. Human language is different from other forms of mammalian (and probably all animal communication) in that it can be nonlimbic. Language is unlike other nonhuman primate communication in that its information content to listeners or readers is not limited to communicating the emotional state of the speaker. As a result, humans can communicate in an unemotional state, a feigned overemotional state (acting), and an unemotional state designed to fool those that they communicate with (lying). This suggests that it is the arbitrariness of language that is one of its main properties. Other theories for the evolution of this unique form of communication will be discussed later. While it is relatively easy to see the advantages of language, it is impossible to explain the evolutionary need for it. For now it is important to point out that no other animal possesses true language and that it plays an extremely important role in human adaptation.

Marriage

Marriage is an institution that in all societies is characterized by being both public and economic. Although it takes many forms, it also always involves some form of sanctioned new sexual access and restriction. The formal recognition of marriage is always associated with ceremony, ritual, and food sharing. **Polyandrous** (one female and more than one male) marriages are very rare, but **polygynous** (one male and more than one female) marriages were extremely common among many cultures until recently. Until the influence of Western Christianity, in most societies the number of wives a man could have was limited only by his economic circumstances. Normally, marriages are expected to produce offspring, which have inherited "rights." In many societies, marriage also has important social and political aspects that affect the culture and society of the group.

The circumstances and specific social rules of marriage are extremely varied. The exchange of wealth and services are almost always involved, as is a shift in residency of either the bride or groom. Other members of either of the spouses' family are also usually directly affected by the union. In many societies, there are such incitations as **bride price** (dowry given to the male's family) or **groom service** (tasks performed by the prospective husband for the prospective wife's family). It is very clear that nonhuman primates have no such social institutions.

Kinship Systems

Intimately tied in with marriage is a system of kinship that defines and often dictates the nature of human alliances and divisions with regard to social, economic, political, and many other relationships that give structure to the activities of human groups. Just as no one has ever discovered a society without language, there has also never been a human society without a system of kinship. For more than one hundred years, social scientists have attempted to relate kin systems to a variety of social and psychological phenomena.

Kin systems are as varied as types of marriages. Kinship ranges from being extremely important for making social decisions to being of only marginal importance. Like languages and social customs, the exact structures of kinship patterns change through time and space even within the same culture. Though the majority of kin systems emphasize the parent–offspring and sibling–sibling relationship, this emphasis is not universal. In a number of cultures, the relationship to one's parents may be just as important or even more important than the relationship to one's aunt, uncle, or grandparents. Because of the economic component of kinship systems, they are highly influenced by marriages.

Anthropologists have a long history of classifying cultures with regard to whether they are **patrifocal, matrifocal,** or **bilateral** in their emphasis. Recognized lines of descent have similarly been termed **matrilineal, patrilineal,** and bilateral. Whole theories of human behavior have been built around kinship. In the past, cultures have been held to represent different kinds of personalities depending on which sex was emphasized. The stereotype of the patrifocal society emphasizes male aggression and control of valued resources. Matrifocal societies have been stereotyped as emphasizing fertility, nurturing, and peacefulness. In fact, cultures exhibit any combination of emphasis and focus. Furthermore, female and male domains, where there can be said to be such divisions, depend on the particular aspect of the culture being studied. In our previous example of the Iroquois, there is great emphasis on male aggression, but females have enormous political power. In the Hopi of the Southwest United States, who are descended from thousands of years of Anasazi farmers, only males weave, while among their contiguous neighbors, the Navajos, who are descended from nomadic raiders, only females weave. Both are matrilineal.

Most cultures also have **fictive kin,** other individuals who are treated as close biological relations even though they are not closely related. The use of terms like *brother* or *sister* or *mother* or *father* is common. Adoption is one form of initiating fictive kin relationships in many societies. Most societies have some mechanism for adoption.

All societies have some sort of **incest taboo,** which specifies who can and cannot mate and produce offspring. The most common but by no means universal taboos are between parents and offspring and between siblings. In a number of societies, the usual mating taboos may be suspended in the case of certain situations. Especially common are the suspension of taboos in the case of royalty or the death of a relative's spouse. The general pattern is one of trying to insure **exogamous** relationships. These characterize most cultures, but the degree of exogamy required can vary greatly. Geneticists have often viewed exogamy as a beneficial adaptation that helps to limit inbreeding and thus the concentration of deleterious characteristics in particular lineages and families. The case of hemophilia in European royalty is a prominent example. One of the most widespread forms of adoption is induction into a group as a whole. Though not always formal, there are few anthropologists who have not been adopted by their study group.

Sociobiologists have a slightly different explanation of the universal existence of kinship systems. This has been referred to as kin recognition (see Chapter 1). Their reason for kin identification is that it is advantageous for related people to be able to recognize and therefore help each other. Accordingly, those individuals sharing a relatively large amount of DNA will know who to give the most help to. For the sociobiologists, this is the genetic principle that guides and explains important social alignments. This is the reason that all human groups have a formalized system of kinship, marriage, and recognition of common descent. Adoption is more difficult to explain in terms of sociobiological theory because one is in effect helping someone else's DNA. The fall-back explanation is that if the custom is practiced by the group as a whole (which it never is), then one's own DNA in the form of a relative may eventually benefit from this practice.

Infanticide and Geronticide

It appears that all societies have some form of **infanticide,** though this term is used here in its broadest sense and includes abortion. Contraception is not viewed here as infanticide, though it is also characteristic of most human societies. One of the commonalities of infanticide is that the decision of whether to bear children usually rests with females. Infanticide should not be confused with murder, as the decision not to bear an infant or raise a newborn is almost always based on the availability of resources for raising the offspring. However, physical deformity or mental defect is also a common reason. Yet another reason may be purely arbitrary or related to idiosyncratic features of a particular culture. One of the most prevalent and widespread forms of infanticide is the killing of females. This learned cultural characteristic has frequently focused on China, but this should not be taken as an indication that most cultures have a predilection toward female infanticide. **Geronticide**, the killing of old people, is also rare and its incidence among people living in harsh environments such as the Eskimo has often been noted.

Geronticide of the terminally ill and infanticide in the form of abortion are highly controversial in the United States. Moral outrage is apparent on both sides of these issues. In a society so concerned with individual rights, arguments for both sides can be persuasive. Basically stated, the issue is whether a mother's (or even a father's) right outweighs those of the unborn. In non-Western societies, economics is the overriding factor. Many times economics is also tied up with the issue of "legitimacy" as prescribed by cultural mores. What evolutionary psychology can add to this controversy is the observation that these forms of homicide are universal. However, infanticide and geronticide can also result from stress and mental illness.

Sociobiologists, not surprisingly, also have an opinion to add. It is now well known that some primates, social carnivores, birds, and almost every kind of social vertebrate commit infanticide. Male lions and langurs (leaf-eating monkeys) have been observed killing the offspring of other males that are absent or that have been displaced. Sociobiologists reason that this brings the females into estrus more quickly so that the new males can mate and pass on their own DNA. This does seem to occur from time to time, but it is certainly not a common feature of the species-specific ethogram practiced by most vertebrate males. Female social animals other than humans also practice infanticide and, as noted above, they are usually the final arbiters of the fate of newborns. Accidental or neglectful infanticide is also responsible for many of these deaths. Furthermore, in stressful conditions, infanticide increases in all mammals.

One final observation that is interesting is that most cultures have legends and tales about infanticide (and also about fratricide and patricide). They are always remarkable tales of the unusual that represent a violation of what everywhere is the cultural norm, the nurturing of children. Evidence of so-called Oedipal killing is extremely rare. Folktales concerned with infanticide and fratricide offer little support for Sigmund Freud's theory of innate parental conflicts that result in murder. Despite Margaret Mead's contention, generational tensions are universal.

Art

Art (together with music) poses the most overt challenge to sociobiological theory. Animals do not have it, and all humans do. In the Western sense, art includes all forms of public creative behavior, although many artists claim or may actually produce art for their own personal benefit. The fact is that art does not exist unless someone else sees it. It is, like it or not, the same as Bishop Berkeley's fallen tree. In the West, there has also been what I consider to be a rather silly discussion about what constitutes fine art and what constitutes utilitarian objects. All people, beginning in the Upper Paleolithic, possess both. "Art for art's sake" applies to the atlatl and the "Last Supper."

Some form of art is known among all people. We here include body adornment, clothing styles, and other artifactual forms of visual expression as art. Art also includes performance art such as music, dancing, and acting. However, to deal with the concept of art in a manageable way, we define it here in its narrowest sense by regarding it as a creative form of expression that uses shape and color as a form of expression and identification. A very important aspect of art is that it always has symbolic, social, and religious contexts.

Almost all forms of sociocultural groups and subgroups have a particular artistic symbol that identifies and differentiates their group from others. For instance, all clans, teams, schools, states, countries and even the United Nations have particular artistic expressions that symbolically represent them. Clothing and body adornment not only allow individuals to identify with a particular social subdivision of humanity, but they also allow members to recognize one another at a distance. This is entirely consistent with Pfeiffer's idea that art serves as a mechanism that promotes group cohesion. This statement is derived from evolutionary biology and does not attempt to deal with the more sublime aspects of a definition that has been speculated on for thousands of years. Any discussion of art deserves, at least, its own book, and hundreds of such volumes are available. It is not possible in a text of this length to even begin to deal with the importance of art. However, in a subsequent chapter on the brain, we deal with what seem to be universal aspects of color and form.

Music and Dancing

All cultures have music and dancing. The power of these forms of activity to both enthrall and enrage people is well known to the point where all of these activities have been actively suppressed or exalted by most cultures at one time or another. Music and dancing also function as a powerful form of group cohesion. All groups have their particular song, and most have their own particular dances and songs. All countries and many subgroups within a country or tribe have their own particular anthems. Such songs very frequently are correlated with visual details in the form of art and dancing.

One of the main characteristics of music and dancing among hunters and gatherers and also among many agriculturalists is that all members present participate. This is far different from Western cultures where performers have become specialized artisans who stage shows for an audience. Until very recently in human history, performance art was much more involved with audiences that were also participants. This is exemplified by the Barong dance of the Balinese. Strangely enough this "native dance" actually owes its current popularity to anthropologists who originally came to study and develop its native form.

Music and especially dance also showcase (a very appropriate Western term) aspects of sexuality. In the West, most dancers are under the age of thirty. I would wager that the tempo, rhythm, and volume of music played at parties is inversely proportional to the age of the listeners. In all cultures, music and dance often tell stories. They may range from ballads to group history, expression of thanks and hope, and just about any conceivable subject. An old saying from the 1960s, said in reference to the phrases of the Beatles' music, was "You change the music or the music changes you." Music is purely human despite snake charmers and the folk wisdom that "music soothes the savage beast." Music does not affect the limbic system in nonhumans in any way similar to the way it does in humans. The limbic system of songbirds is affected by "songs" of potential mates and rivals. However, the message of the song is invariable and finite. Different songs, though performed by the same individual, are essentially the same. Interestingly, songbirds are among the few organisms that also possess cerebral asymmetry, a trait that probably allows them to learn different geographically variable songs.

Humor and Storytelling

All groups tell jokes, but what is funny must be learned and varies considerably from culture to culture. However, no members of any culture have to learn how to laugh or smile. Though when to laugh is learned, the expressions themselves are universal and are not learned. On the basis of current evidence, it seems that all cultural groups have jokes that range from the scatological to the ironic. Some authors and researchers have contended that humor functions as a device for elevating the speaker's social position relative to the position of the listener or the butt of the joke. Richard Alexander has suggested that smiling and laughing constitute a "submissive grin," which may have evolved from the bearing of teeth seen in nonhuman mammals. According to this line of thinking, tickling may also be a way of inducing social submission. More certainly, laughing and smiling function prominently in social bonding. Humor is mediated to some degree by the neurotransmitter dopamine. People that have been laughing not only tend to laugh more, but they also have higher levels of dopamine. Whatever the social significance of humor and laughter, these behaviors do seem to be social mediators that can influence and intensify the feelings of others.

Storytelling includes the group of narratives referred to as folklore. All cultures have **creation myths** that explain, or at least recount, the origin of the storyteller's group and the world they occupy. Many anthropologists and students of myth have suggested that all myths and stories are binary in that they contrast opposites. The **structuralists** who hold this view believe that myth and other aspects of human behavior reflect the fundamental structure of the mind. For example, important components of U.S. political myths are free–not free, right–left, democracy–totalitarianism, honest–crooked, conservative–liberal, and so on. Stories and ideas do not have to be fictitious to be myth; they just have to be like culture in general—learned, believed, and shared. It has been repeatedly suggested that paleoanthropologists are very active generators of myth.

A common and perhaps universal feature of origin myths is that the world was different in the past or even removed from this world. For Westerners, it is the Garden of Eden, for Australian aborigines it is the Dreamtime. Flood myths are also common. It may be possible that these latter stories refer to the rising of sea level that occurred at the end of the last glaciation. This would mean that some subject matter may have been passed on from generation to generation for at least ten thousand years.

These components of culture are so pervasive that a separate subfield of anthropology (myth and folklore) is devoted solely to this aspect of human behavior. Sociobiologists have theorized that humor, storytelling, and myth allow the individual to deal with the world in a categorical way that reduces complexity and therefore lets the individual collection of DNA concentrate on reproduction. In fact, human beings "waste" so much time on these pursuits, it is hard to see how they function as other than group-binding fun.

Religion and Morality

All cultures have some kind of spiritual belief, and from this belief at least some of their rules about proper and acceptable behavior are generated and justified in the form of commonly held social mores. It is difficult to separate any of these aspects of human behavior myth. The difference between publicly condoned and sanctioned behavior and actual behavior is often great. Similarly, the differences between what people relate about how they behave and how they actually behave can be enormous. One feature of all spiritual beliefs is the conviction that there is a **supraorganic** quality of life that most people cannot ordinarily perceive. In most but not all spiritual beliefs, religious objects or ideas take on an animistic or anthropomorphic humanlike form when communicating with the believer. In most religions, dreams are accorded special significance. Like the subject of art, religion is too vast a subject for a single volume (though it is ironic that the principles and tenants of most religions are assembled in a single volume). One very important characteristic of religion is that it is almost always associated with some form of music or art.

Crime and Punishment

Laws are formally designated codes of behavior that in many cases are written down and always prescribe penalties for individuals who violate them. They are not only a hallmark of civilization but of any human group. Groups that do not use writing also have laws that are often codified with reference to religion and morality. In spite of laws and codes, all cultures have crime, which is the violation of these codes and laws. One of the greatest mistakes that anthropologists have ever made is to suppose that there were some societies that were free of crime.

The severest forms of punishment are death and banishment. Among hunters and gatherers, banishment is considered as tantamount to spiritual and often physical death. In Western society, solitary confinement is considered the only punishment short of execution, though torture is also common. In fact, execution is sometimes preferred by the convicted. About one hundred years ago, execution in the West ceased to be a public phenomenon. This is a worldwide trend, and even notorious violators of what the West calls human rights are most often executed in the presence of a minimum of witnesses. Previously, such public practices as crucifixion in Rome, beheading in China, hanging in the western United States, garroting in India, and many other forms of dispatching the condemned were the rule.

Aggression and Violence

Every vertebrate and possibly every animal exhibits some form of aggression under certain circumstances. It is unlikely that any life-form exists without exhibiting aggression at some time during its life because, by definition, all life-forms compete with others of their own kind. Competing with members of one's own species is referred to as **intraspecific aggression;** competing with other species is referred to as **interspecific aggression.** Sometimes both kinds of competition take the form of violence in which one individual or group attempts to competitively exclude another organism by immediately ending its existence. This is a somewhat arbitrary, but at least well thought-out, definition of what these terms mean. Aggression and violence are frequently confused with **predation.** Predation involves the killing of another organism for food. Rarely are any of these terms synonymous, but **economic cannibalism** may be just such a case. Economic cannibalism refers to eating other members of one's own species as a normal and usual part of the subsistence pattern. In the animal kingdom, most violence is nonlethal, though human tool use (ranging from spears to nuclear bombs) has undoubtedly departed from this pattern.

There are no studies that support the idea that interpersonal aggression between members of the same society takes place along racial lines. However, there is ample evidence that intergenerational conflict is a cultural universal. Intersocietal conflict (broadly defining a society) is also common. Warfare is not just an agricultural phenomenon. It occurs among hunters and gatherers as well. One of the common threads that unites agricultural and nonagricultural warfare is the contention that deadly force was unavoidable. This applies to clan vendettas as well as world wars. Tool dependency, social cohesion, and other uniquely human characteristics have resulted in a synergistic effect that makes us the most dangerous of vertebrates.

Ethnocentricity and Racism

Most group members tend to view their own culture as superior to that of others. As Marvin Harris has pointed out, cultural groups universally tend to identify unique characteristics of their own group as good and the unique characteristics of other groups as bad. **Racism** is a confused form of ethnocentrism that often blurs racial and cultural categories. All cultures seem to do this, but some do so much more than others. As mentioned above, there are a number of mechanisms such as art, music, and language that cultures use to identify their own members and exclude outsiders.

Play

Among humans, play in infants and children has the same function as it does among other mammals. It is a rehearsal of adult roles and activities. It is the enjoyable practice and honing of skills that will be useful in adult lives that occupies much of the time of children. In terms of evolutionary usefulness, there is no such thing as idle play. However, in humans, play continues well past adolescent years, and in most adult humans, play never ceases completely. Play also seems to be intimately linked with sexual behavior, again, especially in adult humans, but also in children. As we shall see in the chapter on language, play terms are often used to describe sexual activity. Conversely, terms that describe sexual activity are often used to describe other social interactions. Humans have evolved a lifelong fusion of sex and play.

All over the world, child's play is extremely similar. There is also cross-cultural sexual dimorphism in play. As mentioned above, male play tends to be more physical and involves more emphasis on the long-distance manipulation of objects (throwing) and the use of more space. In females, play tends to be more verbal and involves the manipulation of objects close at hand. The particular game being played by children in any culture varies tremendously, yet the rules of any game are almost intuitive to any adult from any culture after only a few moments of observation. There seem to be good evolutionary reasons for this, which we shall discuss in a later chapter.

Imprintability

All individuals in all cultures have a time at which they are particularly susceptible to accepting new information. In most groups, this occurs before adulthood. Infancy, childhood, and puberty seem to be particularly intense periods of imprinting. In these periods of the life cycle, humans seem to permanently acquire basic attitudes and ways of doing things either through planned instruction and exposure or accidental experience that is remembered throughout life. Behavioral psychologist Conrad Lorenz (1903–1989) dramatically demonstrated this by convincing goslings that he was their mother simply by being present during their first days after birth. It is important to remember that periods of imprintability do not determine the details of what we will learn, but they do seem to determine when and what we learn. Some examples are given below.

The subject of sexual attractiveness is dealt with in detail in a later chapter. Here we simply introduce it. All cultures have certain male or female character-istics that influence standards of sexual attractiveness. The range of what is con-sidered sexy varies considerably not only between individuals, but also between cultures. The range between cultures is staggering. In South Pacific Samoa, the exposed female navel is considered sexy. In the nineteenth century United States, it was female ankles. The gluteus maximus in females was further enhanced by a bustle in the early part of this century. The U.S. preoccupation with breasts is also most assuredly learned. Freudians maintain that there is great connection between sexual attraction and breast feeding. Cross-cultural comparisons do not support this interpretation. Many cultures, however, equate breast development with simple femaleness or child bearing.

With regard to personal space, all vertebrates have a limit to which they will tolerate the presence and proximity of others of their own species. This limit of "personal space" can vary according to sex, season, or the availability of resources. The thing that unites all the species is that personal space is species specific. This means that each species has an identifiable pattern of spatial tolerance of other conspecifics that is usually maintained through various forms of aggression.

Human personal space varies according to culture and is usually a subdivision of an arm's length. In Western cultures, personal space is comparatively large, perhaps being equal on an average to a full arm's length. However, personal space collapses in certain situations. Friends and especially lovers are permitted to shrink the space (in the former case) and sometimes do away with it all together (in the latter case). Asian cultures are well known for having very small personal space requirements. The obvious ecological explanation might be that this is an adaptation to crowding. However, hunters and gatherers generally have a great tolerance for interpersonal closeness. Australian aborigines who occupy extremely large areas of the landscape have similarly great tolerances for interpersonal closeness. Therefore, simply the availability of space is not an adequate explanation of cultural differences in individual spacing.

What these great intercultural contrasts probably illustrate is that interpersonal space requirement is extremely flexible. However, there is no doubt that what one is comfortable with is almost certainly determined by upbringing. In U.S. culture, the extremely close approach of strangers is considered either aggressive or sexual, depending on the sex of the interacting individuals. Touching, the elimination of interpersonal space, also has very specific meanings in all cultures.

"Edibility" is a fascinating aspect of humans in that they are capable of eating a wider variety of foods than any other animals (with the possible exceptions of pigs and bears). However, human groups have very specific definitions of what is edible. Food taboos and preferences have often been established by influential individuals. In every culture, foods have not only been given desirability ratings, but in many cases spiritual or sociocultural meaning. Though repugnant in our society, we have already seen that cannibalism is practiced in some societies.

We know of no society that does not have food taboos. Certain segments of Hindus and Buddhists, adherents of two of the world's great religions, have a number of taboos, as do the followers of Islam and Judaism. Most of their taboos do not make obvious ecological sense, though abstinence from alcohol and pork are medically sound. Although hunters and gatherers also have taboos, they eat a much wider range of animal protein occurring in their environments. Almost all of these groups make important use of invertebrates (insects). In U.S. cultures, these are almost always considered inedible, though if it is a marine invertebrate (lobster, shrimp, and other shellfish), high prices are charged for these items. There is also, not surprisingly, great individual variation. Most of our preferences and avoidances are learned in childhood. The compliment, "just like Mom used to make," has the same meaning in many cultures. By being imprintable, especially with regard to food preferences, immature hominids can adjust more easily to ecologically changing environments.

There are many more examples of universal categories that vary tremendously in their specific individual and cultural details. The student is encouraged to help discover them through a knowledge of the differences between individuals, sexes, and different cultural and subcultural groups.

Summary

In the real evolutionary world, the cultural universals outlined in this chapter are so interconnected and interdependent that in the end they can only be categorized arbitrarily. Different aspects of all cultures contrast greatly in the elaboration of any of these aspects. Most (if not all) cultures recognize the same categories but see them as interconnected in fundamentally different ways. We have tried to outline a kind of panterrestrial viewpoint that recognizes categories of primate–hominid behavior and thought that already exists in the minds of all humans. Such a task is as impossible as selecting an "average American."

By maintaining that such cultural universals do exist in the minds of people, I am assuming that while envoys from two different cultures may not like the other's music or art, they could mutually agree that both of these phenomena and classes of behavior exist in each of their respective cultures. A stranger at first may not recognize a marriage ceremony as such, but when the visitor does eventually recognize it as such, there will already be a shelf on which to put the information. One might not recognize a screwdriver, but one would very shortly recognize it as a tool.

Western art critiques form a long and endless discussion about what constitutes art. Similarly, there has been a more recent but equally unresolved question among scholars about whether the hand-held objects of Native Americans constitute art or artifacts. The difficulty of resolving such questions points to the structure of the brain itself. Both answers will eternally be relegated to the confines of cultural experience and evolutionary psychology. The really significant thing is that such conversations can take place at all between different individuals and perhaps even more interestingly between different cultures. That the argument ever took place is evolutionarily significant.

The fundamental assumption of cultural universals represents categories of learned behavior that were important enough to the origin of humans that all human beings have them. The more fascinating argument concerns the question of why we have these categories. Some of the categories of universals were maintained even though they possess the potential for a number of disasters. Combining tool use and aggression has produced both individual and genocidal devastation. Yet the same combination of categories feeds billions of people. Language allows a kind of complex communication that is without precedent on this planet. It is the prime means of motivating others to actions ranging from the sublime and ridiculous to the horrendous and terrifying. A number of human behaviors can be meaningfully compared with the behaviors of other vertebrates, but human language is unique.

Other broad categories of human behavior are so similar across cultures in their details that there must be a strong biological predisposition for them. These include a division of labor, food sharing, marriage, kinship, tool use, art, music, and religion. There are also other highly canalized behaviors that may be more subtle, but whose details differ so much that one suspects that there is a less strong canalization for the behavior. These include social organization, sexual attractiveness, food preferences, ethnicity, and probably dozens of other behaviors that cannot be neatly categorized as to how much they are supported by biological substrates. Many of these latter behaviors are mediated by the predisposition for mammals to imprint with regard to basic behaviors. This process is certainly a biosocial one that involves both the physiology of the body as a whole and the brain specifically. It is the structure and function of the brain that we examine in the next chapter.

QUESTIONS FOR REVIEW

1. What are the fundamental differences between hunters and gatherers and agriculturalists? What happens when these two lifestyles come in contact with each other?

2. Why have surviving hunters and gatherers been traditionally used as the bases for hominid social evolution? What is the Binfordian criticism of this practice?

3. How does growing up in their respective societies differ between chimpanzees and humans?

4. What evidence is there for sexually dimorphic behavior in modern humans?

5. What alleged exceptions to cultural universals have been claimed in the observation of modern human societies?

6. What social activities occur just before, during and after marriage ceremonies? How do they compare and contrast with funerals?

7. Which of the cultural universals appear to be less flexible? Which appear to be more flexible?

MIND AND BODY EXPERIMENTS

1. Go camping for a week or two. What do you notice about the way camp chores are divided up? Give examples.

2. For as long as possible, study the "singles meet" advertisements in the media. What do you notice about the kinds and qualities that people are looking for in

potential mates? How many are physical and how many are behavioral? Make a list with a rough calculation of percentages.

3. What are the foods you liked and disliked as a child? Have your food likes and dislikes changed?

4. See if there is a sexual dimorphism between people that like chocolates and people that like anchovies on their pizza. How many people like Chinese food in comparison with Japanese food? Theorize on the reason for any observed differences.

5. How does music in your place of worship differ from the popular music experience? How did the emotional and intellectual content of music change over the last fifty years? Briefly characterize it decade by decade.

6. Borrow one of your classmate's lecture notes (with permission). In addition to notes, what else do you find in them?

7. Make a list of jokes that you remember from before you were eighteen years of age. Do they have anything in common?

8. Where would you go to meet new potential mates in a public place in which male–female space is reduced to a minimum? What are the most interesting (or ridiculous or effective) lies you have heard in such places?

SUGGESTED READINGS

Aberle, David F., Bronfenbrenner, U., Hess, E. H., Miller, D. R., Schneider, D. H., and Spuhler, J. N. 1963. The Incest Taboo and the Mating Patterns of Animals. *American Anthropologist* 65: 253–265.

Barkow, J. H. 1973. Darwinian Psychological Anthropology: A Biosocial Approach. *Current Anthropology* 14: 373–388.

Binford, L. 1981. *Bones: Ancient Men and Modern Myths.* New York: Academic Press.

Chagnon, N. A., and Irons, W. (eds.). 1979. *Evolutionary Biology and Human Social Behavior.* North Scituate, MA: Duxbury Press.

Freedman, D. G. 1979. *Human Sociobiology: A Holistic Approach.* New York: The Free Press.

Giffon, B. 1984. *The Ethnography of Southeastern Cagayan Agta Hunting.* Masters thesis, University of the Philippines.

Goody, J. 1983. *The Development of the Family and Marriage in Europe.* Cambridge: Cambridge University Press.

Harris, M. 1965. The Cultural Ecology of India's Sacred Cattle. *Current Anthropology* 7: 51–66.

Lee, R.B. 1969. !Kung Bushman Subsistence: An Input-Output Analysis. In A. P. Vayda (ed.), *Environment and Cultural Behavior.* pp. 47–49. Garden City, NY: Natural History Press.

Lee, R. B. 1984. *The Dobe !Kung: Foragers in a Changing World.* New York: Holt, Rinehart and Winston.

Lewontin, R. C., Rose, S. P. R., and Kamin, L. J. 1984. *Not in Our Genes.* New York: Pantheon.

Low, B. S., Alexander, R. D., and Noonan, K. M. 1987. Human Hips, Breasts, and Buttocks: Is Fat Deceptive? *Ethology and Sociobiology* 8: 249–257.

Middleton, J. (ed.). 1970. *From Child to Adult: Studies in the Anthropology of Education.* Garden City, NY: Natural History Press (American Museum Source Books in Anthropology).

Morbeck, M. E., Galloway, A., and Zihlman A. (eds.). 1997. *The Evolving Female.* Princeton: Princeton University Press.

5 The Triune and Bicameral Brain

I put my hat upon my head,
I walked into the strand.
And there I met another man
Whose hat was in his hand

—Samuel Johnson

After each evolutionary step, the older portions of the brain still exist and must still be accommodated. But a new layer with new functions has been added.

—Carl Sagan

With the possible exception of the heart, no organ of the body has been contemplated more than the brain. Most of us have heard the popular folk wisdom that "we only use 10 percent of our brain." Natural selection makes this possibility extremely unlikely because, as mentioned before, environments tend not to tolerate organs that use energy and yet have no function. This is especially true of an organ like the brain, which uses an extraordinary amount of the body's energy. The 10 percent analogy (more recently cited as more than 30 percent in scientific literature) more accurately describes what we know about the brain and not what the brain does not do. Natural selection and our evolutionary history are reflected in the gross structure of the brain. The evolution of the brain parallels the evolution of culture itself in that it has been an additive and transformational process. Furthermore, although it is possible to localize many functional areas of the brain, the voluminous amount of data that has accumulated in the past few years is constantly revealing interconnections between areas once thought to be essentially independent of each other. One indication of this complexity is that, although known "control centers" govern certain functions located at rather specific places, global damage (damage at several sites in the brain) has a greater effect than localized damage (damage to a limited area). What this indicates is that although the brain is composed of both separate and overlapping units, the organ functions best as a whole.

A volume such as this cannot do more than summarize some of the basic features of the human brain, but from an evolutionary perspective that makes sense in terms of the fossil and archaeological record, we can learn how it is that we think. As neuroscience has progressed, it has become clear that there is an electrochemical basis to everything the brain does that is housed in and made possible by neuroanatomical structures, whose morphology is plastic in many cases. It also has become clear that the brain–mind dichotomy and the brain–body dichotomy are artificial divisions that do not reflect the complete evolutionary unit of the organism that we call "self."

The duality of the **materialist** versus **non-materialist,** or **emergent,** schools is also outdated. Nonmaterialists support concepts such as the mind or even the soul; nonmaterialists believe that the mind is best understood as a physical device. I fall into the materialist camp and believe that human thought ultimately will be understood in terms of physical entities that are so complex that even the most sophisticated means of investigation cannot adequately explain the details of thought, perception, action, and consciousness. However, in the course of scientific investigations, complex mysteries have never turned out to be unknowable. Enlightened speculations about the nature of the brain, thought, and consciousness, even when aided by **actualistic** investigation, has a long history of eventually wandering into philosophy. This is still the case today, but more and more of the new neurophilosophies are grounding their discoveries in clinical, anatomical, and computer studies.

Major Debates in Attempts to Understand the Brain

A number of new megatrends are emerging in attempts to understand the brain and how it works. Although they do not necessarily provide mutually exclusive and competing hypotheses about how the brain works, they are different in their emphasis. They can be listed according to what they emphasize.

1. The structure of the brain directly reflects stages of evolution. This is best seen in the triune brain theory discussed below. At another level, but in the same vein, Terrence Deacon has suggested that the human brain has evolved to pay attention to what is important to it and to filter out what is unimportant to it. He views the brain as a number of competing systems that reflect evolutionary history in the number of neurons that are devoted to particular functions. Noam Chomsky, and more recently Stephen Pinker have argued that human language must have evolved as the result of natural selection because for some reason language was important to early hominids. Human linguistic ability has much been discussed and increasingly has been linked to explorations of symbolic behavior and consciousness itself.

2. Another emerging venue of debate in the neurosciences has been the discussion between the **connectionists** and researchers who emphasize the importance

of **association areas** in the brain. The concept of association areas dates back more than two centuries and emphasizes the importance of particular areas of the brain, especially the cortex (see below), in the performance of various functions. The connectionists emphasize the importance of the connections between several parts of the brain in normally functioning brains. The connectionist school of neurocontemplators believes that behavioral and conceptual repertoire are stored as patterns of widely dispersed neurons that store mental states as distinct patterns of activity. The pattern of brain activity, and not necessarily the anatomically localized focal points (for example, association areas, nuclei), is emphasized in this model. While the model argues for analogies between computerized circuitry and the brain, as yet it offers few suggestions about the evolutionary development of the brain. Both schools concede that their respective competing models are ones of emphasis and not mutually exclusive interpretations.

3. A third prominent way of modeling the human brain has come from computer simulations. As one who has served for years on the Artificial Intelligence Committee at a major university, I remained convinced that computer simulations are so far the least useful way of developing accurate pictures of how the brain functions. The brain is not digital, and it is not composed of clusters of microprocessors. Neurons are transducers in that they transform one kind of energy into another in electrochemical, but also anatomical, interactions. Neurons and the synaptic clefts through which they communicate with each other also change size, shape, and structure in accordance with their functions. Thus the possible permutations of neurons, multiplied by their sheer number, mediated by changing brain environments, then influenced by the outside environment in the form of resource and activity at the organismal level, far exceed the capabilities of the most powerful artificial device. Although the organic systems that we call brains can create computers, it is highly unlikely that computers will ever create brains.

4. Another area of dispute and contention about the human brain involves a concerted emphasis on the origin and nature of consciousness. From my perspective, these discussions, which often involve ancillary topics such as virtue and morality, have not been very productive. Furthermore, they have tended to treat these brain activities as emergent, nonphysical, or even metaphysical entities, which are not subject to neuroanatomical and clinical investigation. Opinions in the plethora of works that have appeared in the last few years range from regarding consciousness as a fundamental, indivisible property of the universe (like subatomic particles or gravity) to a "process" (and not a thing) that, as usually described, has all the qualities of a soul. These arguments have not wandered very far from classical Western philosophy.

Until recently, most of what we knew about the brain came from clinical evidence. That is, much of our evidence results from the study of accidents that impair normal function, behavior, or activity. Certain areas can be impaired or destroyed because of trauma (blows, wounds), vascular accidents (strokes, aneurism), or tumors. Both conventional and chemical surgery have also afforded a somewhat more controlled form of data collection. Electrical mapping, carried out by stimulating parts of the brain, has also allowed us to understand what particular parts of the cortex and other areas of the brain do. We cannot only locate the area of anatomical damage, but also observe associated behaviors, which take the form of negative or positive symptoms. Negative symptoms are those in which portions of normally observed behavioral sequences fail to appear in response to a particular stimulus. Positive symptoms are those that were not present before a particular biological event. These are somewhat arbitrary definitions. In fact, certain so-called positive events may actually result from the brain's failure to normally suppress a certain behavior or electrochemical process. Anger seems to be a good example of a state that the brain normally tries to suppress. Until recently, the basic approach to brain research was to see what happened when a particular part of the brain was destroyed or impaired.

The new techniques, which allow us to both visualize the anatomy of the brain and monitor its activity, have been summarized by Raichle. CT (computerized tomography) scanning is an x-ray technique that allows the production of computer-generated cross-sections of the soft tissue that comprises the brain. PET (positron emission tomography) allows us to monitor the uptake (and therefore the activity) of a radioactive substance by different parts of the functioning brain. PET relies on the observation of glucose and oxygen utilization and blood flow to certain parts of the brain while the subject is engaged in perception, thought, or physical tasks.

Another method of brain imaging is MRI (magnetic resonance imaging). This technique measures the brain's differential utilization (and nonutilization) of oxygen in the course of performing certain functions. It is more sensitive than PET scans because it does not just measure blood flow, but instead the actual utilization of the oxygen that the blood's hemoglobin carries. This is important because some functions in the brain are anaerobic. Thus, the presence of unutilized oxygen in an active area can also be recorded. MRI can track activity in real time and can thus allow for an instantaneous recording of external stimulus and response of brain activity. One limitation in studying the brain with PET is that electrical activity is much faster than oxygen utilization and blood flow. The best way of understanding the functioning brain is achieved by the integration of all of these techniques. The invention of old techniques and the invention of new ones continues to expand at a staggering rate. One of the greatest achievements of the neurotech revolution is that we can study live brains in real and increasingly "natural" time. However, one of the still unattained objectives of the next few decades will be the ability to understand the brain in contexts outside the laboratory or clinic.

In normally functioning brains, various areas function best when they are integrated with each other. It is possible to raise an obvious analogy: When researchers mimic the brain itself by organizing massive conference calls and exchanging information, they are in many respects behaving like a functioning brain.

The Triune Brain

The neuroanatomist, Paul MacLean, after years of research and thinking about the human brain, proposed a theory known as the triune brain (Figure 5.1), which seems to make evolutionary sense of the gross "vertical" organization of the brain and explains several intuitive and scientific aspects of everyday life that bring such diverse fields as psychology and paleontology together. The word *triune* comes from Greek meaning "three levels." It refers to the fact that the brain seems to be organized on three levels, each having its own types of functions. These levels are also broadly equivalent with general grades through which human ancestors passed in the course of their evolutionary history. In fact, it is becoming increasingly difficult to demarcate discrete systems in the brain as research reveals more and more connections and interactions. As we shall see shortly, the totality of the brain is much more complicated than this, but the concept is useful as an introduction to one of the universe's unique achievements.

The Paleoreptile Brain. The lowest organizational level of the brain is referred to by MacLean as the paleoreptile brain. This includes the brain stem, which lies between the spinal cord and the rest of the brain and part of the cerebellum (literally "small brain"), which is connected to the posterior part of the brain stem. In this, the most central and the anatomically lowest part of the brain mediates such functions as body temperature regulation, respiration, reflexes, and generally those functions that are involuntary and autonomic ("automatic"). The cerebellum traditionally has been associated with the coordination and control of motor activities. Indeed, a reptile or amphibian is a good example of an animal with only this part of the human brain. One thinks of reptiles as perhaps only

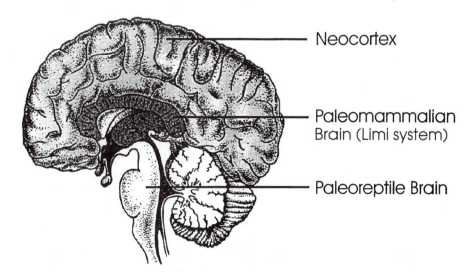

FIGURE 5.1   **The Triune Brain**

acting in involuntary, but constant, ways to a particular stimulus. Such a stimulus might be a potential food or interaction with others of its own kind. If humans possessed only this part of the brain, they would probably be as interesting as a lizard. Dangling a fly in front of a frog produces a paleoreptile response even though frogs are amphibians. However, it is important to emphasize that even with the paleoreptile brain, learning and memory are present. Frogs repeatedly presented with a poisonous insect soon learn to ignore it. Invertebrates, especially cephalopods (squids and octopi), are also capable of learning. In fact, certain worms also appear to learn. One quality that may set animal life apart from plant life is the ability to learn. However, it still appears that most of the functions of the paleoreptile brain are innate, though subject to internal changes as the result of environmental changes.

The Neocerebellum.   The neocerebellum of humans has also been implicated in the processing of conceptual and linguistic categories. The cerebellum contains more neurons than any other part of the brain and is connected to the neocortex by some 40 million nerve fibers. Connections are not just to the motor cortex, but also extend to other parts of the cortex. It does not fit neatly into the triune brain model, but rather seems to bridge these gross divisions. In comparison with other vertebrates, one part of the cerebellum, the dentate nucleus, is uniquely large in humans. This area has been implicated in linguistic and "mental dexterity." Damage to this area does not result in motor impairment. A number of researchers have implicated this area as part of a cerebellar complex that fine-tunes linguistic and symbolic thinking. PET scan data reveals that the dentate nucleus is active during linguistic activity. Clinical studies indicate that patients with damage to this area of the neocerebellum develop a form of paralexia (Gr. *para*=on the side+*lexia*=word) in which they associate related but inappropriate noun and verb categories. Furthermore, such patients apparently fail to learn to pick up on clues to appropriate responses to perceptual, linguistic, and symbolic problems. From an evolutionary perspective, the cerebellum may have begun as a center for the coordination of physical movement and evolved into a center for also coordinating and analyzing at least some linguistic and symbolic thought. It thus seems to also be involved in planning and foresight—activities traditionally associated with the frontal lobe.

The Paleomammalian Brain.   As its name implies, the paleomammalian brain is a generalized mammalian brain that possesses all the attributes that we associate with nonhuman mammalian behavior. Here, behaviors such as rage, aggression, thirst, hunger, sexual drive, and fear (and love?) are situated. It may be associated with perceptions of pain and pleasure. This middle level of the brain is composed of what we generally refer to as the limbic system (Figure 5.1). For our purposes, the limbic system can be thought of as the emotional part of the brain, although we now know that it is not limited to the anatomical structures for which it was originally named. There is also no doubt that what we think of as emotion is mediated by the limbic system.

Like other mammals, nonhuman primate communication is always limbic in that it only conveys the current emotional state of the speaker. An important mammalian response, the fight or flight response, is also located primarily in the limbic system. This is the seemingly instantaneous decision that animals make as whether to fight or flee. This response has been classically understood as a relay of sensory information to the cortex, then to the amygdala (Gk.=almond), followed by the relay of input to the hippocampus (L.=seahorse) and a subsequent arousal of physiological components of the organism's stress and emotional responses. Some stimuli may pass directly from the thalamus to the amygdala, allowing an even faster response time. There is now evidence that some responses take place "without thinking," that is before they are perceived by the cortex. Loud sounds and quick movements are examples of sensory input information that reach the amygdala before they are perceived by the cortex. This is an obviously important asset for survival and predation in the wild. Recent research has also suggested that, along with parts of the cerebellum, the limbic system is important in learning or memory. Both human and nonhuman primates quickly learn an aversion to snakes. This suggests that emotion and feeling play an important part in learning and memory.

An example of what a mammal with this kind of brain is like is your dog or cat. None of us doubt that these animals have emotions or that they can learn and retain new behaviors. Once again, it is important to emphasize that whatever your cat or dog is "thinking," it is emotional. One of the main behaviors that nonhuman mammals seem to lack is planning and foresight. Although animals seem to have strategies for such actions as obtaining food or social interaction, it is hard to show that these can be projected very far into the future. It is unlikely that cats or dogs get up in the morning and think about what they are going to do later that day. Some primatologists have indeed argued this is exactly what some primate species do because they seem to behave in optimal ways when searching for and obtaining food. However, their arguments are unconvincing because many animals behave in seemingly optimal ways simply as the result of reflexes. Primate studies have indicated that some species have stereotyped vocalizations for specific predators and resources. Others have interpreted laboratory experiments as indicating an ability to deceive. Such conclusions, respectively, attribute linguistic ability and planning to nonhumans. Such abilities do not, however, provide convincing evidence for nonlimbic (unemotional) states. Specific responses to vocalizations and carrying out sequential actions do not by themselves indicate nonemotional thinking.

The Neocortex. The third and "highest" level of the human brain is the neocortex (Figure 5.1). It is referred to as *neo* because it was the last part of the brain to appear in the course of human evolution. The term *cortex* refers to the fact that it is the part that we can see when we look at the external surface of a brain. It is important to emphasize that all mammals have a cortex. The human cortex differs from other animals in being an extremely thick structure that covers most of the underlying structures. It is also remarkable in the development and depth of the "wrinkles" or crenulations that cover the surface. These wrinkles are called gyri (the plural form of gyrus). A gyrus is actually the ridge formed between the valleylike crenulations. The valleys in between these ridges are referred to as sulci (the plural form of sulcus). Neither are random in their form and distribution in the brain. In fact, they are so standardized that certain functions of the brain usually can be related to certain gyri and sulci. The evolutionary reason for the convoluted surface of the brain traditionally has been explained by the need to pack a very large number of brain cells into a relatively small space, but there are a few problems with this explanation.

The first is that Neanderthals actually had a larger brain size than modern humans. They solved the "packing problem" by having larger braincases. If more space was required, then there seems little reason for the decrease (small though it is) in braincase size with modern humans. Furthermore, even early species of *Homo*, such as *Homo habilis* dating back to more than 2.5 mya, had a convoluted cortex. There is also the very strange observation that cows have very convoluted, though very thin, cortices. Chimpanzees and dolphins in comparison with other nonhuman mammals are also relatively convoluted, but neither of them approach the convolutional complexity of the human neocortex. The spiny anteater or echidna, a marsupial, has also been suggested to have proportionately the largest frontal cortex of any known animal. On the other hand, it has also been claimed that the human brain in the course of evolution has not seen a disproportionate increase in the size of the frontal lobe. Size does not seem to offer any obvious clues or insights into the mechanics of behavioral differences, at least at this point in our understanding of the evolution of the brain.

The functions of the neocortex are complex and sometimes hard to categorize. In general, the cortex is thought of as the seat of the so-called higher functions. Most of the higher functions of humans, identified by philosophers for thousands of years, seem to be mediated here on the outer surface of the brain. Among these are foresight, personality, language, sequential logic, mathematics, art, and music. However, the picture is much more complicated, and we shall look at the question of which areas of the cortex are associated with certain functions in more detail.

The triune model of the human brain is very useful because it mirrors what we know about the order of appearance of grades in vertebrate evolution. It is logical (at least to the human brain) that the earliest structures to evolve are also the lowest in the brain. It is consistent with the Western perception that logical analysis is different from emotional feeling. After all, they are mediated by different levels of the brain. However, there is another aspect of the brain that makes this picture much more complicated. This is the fact that one level of the brain can influence other levels, and the levels do so all the time. For instance, one can begin by coolly and logically thinking about something and then become emotionally agitated to the point where one becomes emotional. It is well known that emotional states have profound effects on paleoreptile behaviors such as breathing, sweating, blood pressure, and the elimination of body waste. Polygraph examinations utilize this interaction between brain and body. At the same time, polygraph results are inadmissible in most courts of law because they are not consistently reliable. Conversely, there are many well-known cases of people being able to control both paleomammalian and paleoreptile functions of the brain by simply wanting to. The possible combinations of input from any level are staggering. Add to this our still imperfect understanding of the brain at the cellular and biochemical level, and it is easy to see why the human brain is far more complex than the fastest and most sophisticated computer.

Bicameral Organization of the Brain

The human brain is also grossly organized into two distinct but interconnected right and left hemispheres (Figure 5.2). Judging from clinical and experimental data, these hemispheres specialize in different functions. A more accurate statement is that the same functions are represented in both hemispheres, but one or the other of the hemispheres is dominant with regard to certain abilities. Because certain functions appear to be more common in one hemisphere than in the other, we recognize the principle of cerebral asymmetry. Both hemispheres communicate

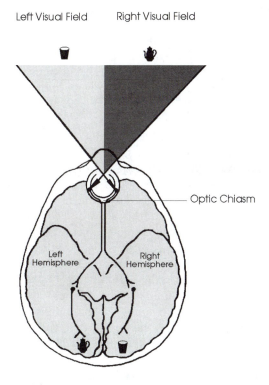

FIGURE 5.2 Left and Right Hemispheres of the Human Brain

with each other primarily through a thick bundle of fibers known as the **corpus callosum** (L. *corpus*=body+*callosum*=large). There are also other connections through the optic nerves and the cerebellum. Most of the recent PET and CT data indicate that there are verifiable differences between the right and left hemispheres, but much of what we know about hemispheric differences still derives from split-brain studies. In the past, a common treatment for epilepsy was the surgical disconnection of the corpus callosum. Why this disconnection alleviates and sometimes eliminates the common symptoms of seizures and unusual sensations characteristic of epilepsy is poorly understood. What these studies indicated was that the two hemispheres have different properties that are somehow integrated in normal humans.

All mammals and most vertebrates possess a corpus callosum, but only a few seem to exhibit cerebral asymmetry. Songbirds are one of the most notable examples of vertebrates to exhibit cerebral asymmetry. Songbirds (who do not really sing in the human sense of the word) must learn the song that is appropriate to their species and location and store their repertoire on one side of the brain, usually the left. At least one study has also indicated that chimpanzees may exhibit cerebral asymmetry in the form of larger portions of the left hemisphere associated with language in humans. In all higher vertebrates, the corpus callosum allows both hemispheres of the brain to communicate. However, the way in which the two hemispheres are integrated in a single individual is somewhat more complex. A system of contralateral control exists in which the right hemisphere is "in charge" of the left side of the body and vice versa. Each hemisphere has association areas on the cortex that specialize in particular functions. The left visual field is composed of visual input from both eyes, but information is processed more thoroughly on the right. The information from both fields of vision crosses at the optic chiasma, where the right and left optic nerves cross on the way to their respective control hemispheres.

Humans and other animals that have their corpus callosum cut develop a condition known as disconnection syndrome. A number of bizarre behaviors are seen in these individuals. One syndrome is neglect syndrome, in which the subject fails to identify one side of the body as their own. They may forget to wash it, forget to dress it, and largely deny that it has anything to do with their own existence. Stimulus presented to one side of the body may be consciously ignored but responded to. In short, disconnection syndrome subjects behave almost as if there are two people inhabiting the same skull. It is also now clear that disconnected hemispheres can "reeducate" each other and interpret external cues in a more global framework characteristic of intact brains.

Before examining the cerebral asymmetry of the different association areas of each hemisphere, it is also necessary to point out a fundamental feature of association areas. These areas are areas on the cortex that are associated with certain perceptions or reactions. First of all, they are variable in location and extent between individuals. Although most humans have particular functions in a particular area, the individual variation that Darwin emphasized is also apparent in the brain. Association areas are actually slightly more complicated and are divided according to the magnitude and nature of symptoms that are effected by stimulation or destruction.

The destruction of a primary association area causes a complete loss of the function. The destruction or removal of the occipital visual association area on one hemisphere causes loss of vision on the contralateral visual field. Damage to a secondary association area usually results in the impairment of a function. Secondary areas are usually peripheral to primary areas. In the case of the visual cortex, blindness would not be complete, but details may be lost. Damage to a tertiary association area results in the impairment of the primary function and also in the impairment of an unrelated function. This arrangement strongly suggests that association areas of the cortex overlap. The simple organization presented here is in reality much more complicated, but an understanding even at this level will allow us to place brain and behavior in an evolutionary context. It also explains why the different locations and the extent of injuries to the brain can produce a variety of effects. With this in mind (literally!), it is possible to examine some important functional areas of the cortex.

The Frontal Lobe. Each cortex is divided into large anatomical areas known as lobes (Figure 5.3), which are located on each of the two hemispheres. The most anterior of the lobes is the frontal lobe, so named because it is covered by the frontal bone. It is delimited posteriorly by the central gyrus. It is divided into the

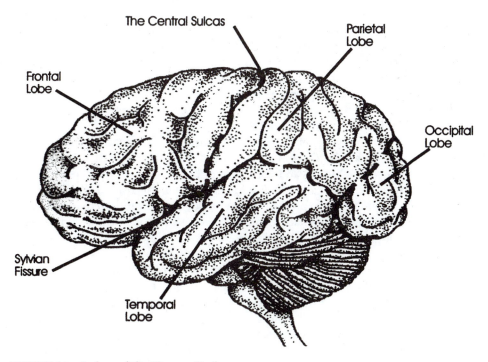

FIGURE 5.3   Lobes of the Human Brain

prefrontal cortex and the posterior frontal cortex. The posterior frontal cortex manages and controls motor activity of the various parts of the body. The fine motor activity of the body is located here. The hands (especially the thumb and forefinger) and the face (especially the tongue and lips) have much greater and a disproportionately large amount of cortex devoted to them than other parts of the body. This correlates well with the precision grip of hominids and the complex signaling apparatus of facial communication. It is also not surprising to find that a great deal of cortex is devoted to management of the complex movements of the tongue and lips required for speech. The areas of the *somatomotor* (body movement and body sense) *cortex,* which are responsible for the control of move- ment, are mirrored by the areas of the somatosensory cortex situated on the posterior edge of the central gyrus. Thus, input and output of information centers are closely approximated on the cortex.

The prefrontal cortex is involved with the management of the so-called higher functions. In fact, conscious management itself appears to be situated here. The prefrontal receives sensory input from all areas of the body. In human evo- lution, this part of the brain expanded most dramatically during the course of the last 2 million years. Although at least one recent study has denied a dispro- portionate expansion, on the basis of the fossil evidence, I remain unconvinced. The exact functions of this lobe are poorly understood but are undoubtedly com- plex. It has been suggested that the frontal lobe is the seat of planning, foresight, control, and personality. It also seems that what we mean by *rationality* (a very philosophical concept) is "located" in the frontal lobe. In the earlier days of clinical psychology, it was believed that a malfunction in the frontal lobe caused aggressive and violent behavior. This was the basic rationale for frontal lobotomies, which involved the insertion of needles through the orbits and the destruction of frontal lobe tissue. The results of such "treatments" were highly unpredictable, producing a reduction of aggressive behavior in some patients and no discernible change in others. Though this surgical procedure is now rarely carried out, the equivalent is still accomplished chemically.

One piece of anecdotal but meaningful information comes from the famous case of Phineas Gage. Gage was a dynamite specialist who worked with high explosives. One day in the process of tamping down black powder in a drill hole, an accident blew a 1 $\frac{1}{4}$ inch-wide bar through his frontal lobe (Figure 5.3). Though he survived the explosion, his behavior underwent a remarkable change. Before the accident, Gage had been described as a reasonable and civil person of average intelligence. After the accident, he became childlike, impetuous, and often quar- relsome. In contrast with his former self, he now drank heavily and swore. He was unable to hold a job or carry out many of the schemes that he was constantly formulating. As a whole, this case is similar to others in which planned behavior disappeared and was replaced by highly emotional and volatile childlike behavior.

The emotional state of Gage is especially interesting because it has been used to suggest a suppression theory for one of the basic functions of the frontal lobe. This interpretation proposes that one of the general functions of the frontal lobe is to actively and continuously suppress the limbic system. In the case of

Gage, this control was removed resulting in the essentially irrational behavior that he exhibited after the accident. In fact, the frontal lobe may mediate the action and influence of many of the association areas and lobes of the brain. A reasonable analogy might be a picture of the frontal lobe as kind of "central government."

Once again, this is a simplification, but it is one that may give us an important evolutionary insight into human behavior. One of the major cranial differences between the australopithecines and the first members of our own genus was the enlargement of the frontal lobe. This enlargement continued in the species that followed early *Homo*. The fossil evidence strongly indicates that there was marked selection pressure for space in the skull for the part of the brain in charge of sequential, organizational behaviors. Specifically, the prefrontal lobe is concerned with the planning of strategies and other nonlimbic behaviors. As the frontal enlarged through time, the evidence for the consistent procurement of large game also increased. It is hard to believe that this is a coincidence. More recently it has become apparent that the ability to contemplate and plan contingencies is an important part of truly complex social behavior.

The frontal also contains an association vital to the production of speech, the "social glue" of human social organization. This portion of the prefrontal cortex also seems to have expanded as the frontal enlarged. This area, **Broca's area** (Figure 5.4), is named for the neuroanatomist Paul Broca (1824–1880), one of the researchers who discovered it in the nineteenth century. This early work also produced some of the first indications of cerebral asymmetry. Damage to Broca's area, which is situated on the left frontal and parietal lobe, is most consistently associated with difficulties in the production of speech. Its importance is discussed in the next chapter. The fossil endocast evidence indicates that this association area is present at least as early as 1.5 mya. Ralph Holloway suggests that the equivalent of Broca's area is present in the earlier australopithecines. Dean Falk vehemently disagrees with Holloway and believes that this feature does not appear until the arrival of the genus *Homo*. The fact that the related function of handedness and the appearance of symmetrical stone tools are also associated with the appearance of our own genus tend to support Falk's conclusion.

As mentioned previously, the frontal also has been implicated in the voluntary control of fine motor movements. Lesions in the frontal cortex produce impairments of body, limb, and finger movements. This is especially true when a task involves sequential movements. Damage to the frontal lobe also produces difficulties in changing strategies of sequential movement in response to new stimuli. The formulation of sequential strategy in general is very affected by frontal lesions. The frontal seems to have a general ability to order movement in space and time. Lesions in the frontal lobe also reduce the ability to use voluntary gaze to examine a set of objects and discern matching sets or oddness. Although nonhuman primates can also perform these tasks, humans are much better at it.

If one examines the abilities of the frontal lobe in light of human evolutionary history, it is easy to see how enhancing the basic primate abilities of the frontal lobe might confer a distinct advantage. Fine motor movements are particularly required for tool manufacture. Indeed, humans excel at such movements and

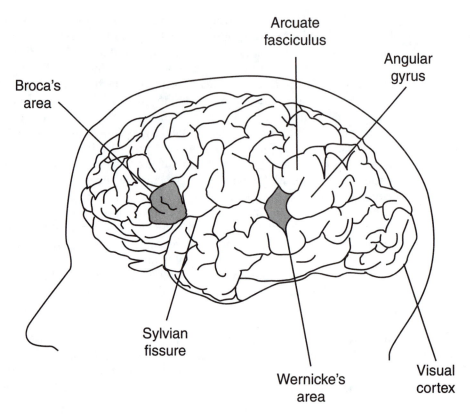

FIGURE 5.4 **Broca's Area**

possess a precision grip of the thumb and forefinger not seen in other primates. This is true despite the fact that many nonhuman primates are anatomically equipped for such tasks. The ability to develop strategies of movement also has obvious uses in hunter and gatherer groups, which move across the landscape seeking food and other resources. The ability to pick out stationary objects is of great utility whether searching for fruit or looking for small prey that tend to freeze as a means of avoiding detection. Most predators depend primarily on smell and movement for detecting prey, and when potential prey freeze, it is very difficult for them to detect their presence with the aid of vision alone.

In general, the frontal lobe seems to be a kind of "clearing house" and coordinating center for other parts of the brain. Lesions to this lobe appear to impair almost all known voluntary functions. Once again, in terms of the brain, it is the constant enlargement of the frontal lobe that stands out as the hallmark of the last 2 million years of human neural evolution. It is an oversimplification, but in general the frontal lobe seems to have evolved as the part of the brain that is most involved with voluntary motor activity requiring temporal ordering. The fact that this lobe enlarged so much in the last half of human evolution suggests that there was very strong selection pressure for a number of the specific activities that this general ability allows.

The Parietal Lobe.   The *parietal lobe* is located beneath and is protected by the parietal bone of the braincase. These two bones are so named because, unlike the frontal bone, they occur as a pair (one on either side of the cranium). If the frontal lobe can be simplistically thought of as concerned with action involving its somatomotor cortex, the parietal lobe can in an equally oversimplified way be thought of as concerned with the general perception and integration of sensory stimulus. The perception of sensory stimulus is located in the anterior part of the lobe, and the integrating functions are located in the posterior part of the lobe.

One of the most conspicuous features of the somatosensory tract is the disproportionate space devoted to certain parts of the body. If one constructs a homunculus, which is a model of a "little man," in which the amount of cortex devoted to certain body parts and functions is scaled, the hands and face would be grotesquely enormous. The area devoted to the hands (especially the fingers) and face in general (but especially the lips and tongue) are much more extensive than for other parts of the body. The amount of area devoted to a particular part of the body is a good indication of what is ecologically and behaviorally important to the organism. Animals with vibrissae (whiskers), such as cats and mice, have large areas of the cortex devoted to sensory input from these sensory organs.

In light of what we have already learned about the archaeological and anatomical contexts of human evolution, it is easy to understand why a tool-dependent animal that possesses speech would possess extensive sensory areas for the processing of input from relevant parts of the body. The two fastest reflex arcs in humans are the ability to withdraw the finger and tongue from an undesirable stimulus. This latter feature probably partially explains why most people do not find visits to the dentist enjoyable. For ourselves and our ancestors, the ability to withdraw the tongue quickly, or at least quickly analyze something that was about to be ingested, may have been and in many cases still is critical to survival. Probably of equal importance is the use of the tongue and lips in speech.

The posterior parietal lobe is concerned primarily with the integration of sensory information, especially that concerned with language (left parietal lobe in most people) and spatial relationships (right parietal lobe). It is for this reason that the left and right parietal lobes are treated separately. At the same time, it is important to emphasize that in normal individuals, both hemispheres function together in an integrated way under most circumstances.

The left parietal lobe has been studied more than any other part of the brain. Wernicke's area (after the neurologist Carl Wernicke, 1848–1904) (Figure 5.4) is responsible for the comprehension of speech. It is connected to Broca's area by a bundle of fibers known as the arcuate fasiculus ("arch-shaped bundle"). Wernicke's area is also connected posteriorly to the visual cortex of the occipital lobe by another bundle of fibers known as the angular gyrus. The ability to recognize words and objects and to formulate grammar and syntax are mediated by these verbal association areas. A great number of language disorders known as aphasias can be produced by lesions to these areas. Many of the various aphasias have very specific symptoms. Wernicke's aphasia manifests itself in the inability to comprehend speech and the inability to formulate sentences that make grammatical sense. Anomia (L. *a*=non+*nomia*=knowledge) and agnosia (L. *a*=non+*gnosia*=recognition), respectively, refer to the inability to recognize words and objects. In some cases, a patient may recognize an object but not be able to name it (anomia). In one interesting case, a subject was shown a picture of a boat at anchor and asked to name the anchor. The subject could not think of the name of the anchor, but finally said that he knew it was used to "anchor" the ship. In other words, he was perfectly aware of the function of the anchor, but still could not name it. Using it as a verb apparently posed little problem, but for the subject it had ceased to be a noun. Another case of anomia involves a similar situation in which a subject could recognize and name vegetables and fruits, but could not recall the word for carrot when a picture was placed in front of him. He was perfectly aware of all the properties and uses of a carrot, but of all the fruits and vegetables, it was carrot only that he could not name. From the perspective of human evolution, this observation offers the suggestion that certain memories are very specifically stored. We shall return to this aspect of language in the next chapter. Most normally functioning people have had similar experiences. In the case of agnosia, a subject faced with a similar situation might be able to name anchor and carrot, but have little or no idea of their uses.

The right parietal lobe is generally associated with functions involving space, form, and the general gestalt (overall position and situation) of the body in any given situation. There is also good evidence that the recognition of familiar faces is localized in the right parietal lobe, while the analysis of unfamiliar faces is dominated by the left hemisphere activity. Lesions to the right parietal lobe result in a condition known as apraxia, which is the inability to carry out purposeful movements. Another symptom of right-side lesions is contralateral neglect syndrome, in which the subject is unaware of or unconcerned with the left side of the body and has trouble representing the left side of objects. The right parietal lobe seems to be involved with constructing concepts of wholeness in both the perception of the body and the external world. From an evolutionary perspective, it is easy to see how this ability would be important to any animal. However, in humans there is evidence that the spatial abilities of the right parietal lobe are sexually dimorphic. Specifically, most males do better than most females at spatial analysis tasks.

The Temporal Lobe.   The *temporal lobe* is in contact with the frontal and parietal lobe as well as the hippocampus of the limbic system. As such, it has secondary and tertiary connections with all of these regions. The temporal lobe with its proximity to the auditory region is also not surprisingly the seat of the primary auditory cortex. It serves a role that is analogous to the parietal lobe in that it is also the primary lobe concerned with the spatial location of sound.

The special kind of sound known as music is also processed primarily by the right temporal lobe. The temporal lobe is also involved with the storage of long-term sensory memories. The precise location of a music association on the right hemisphere remains elusive. A few scholars have suggested that music is somehow intimately involved with the cadence of language.

With the exception of a few functions, such as the processing of music, the temporal lobe of humans is very similar to that of nonhuman primates. The temporal lobe is sometimes the site of temporal lobe epilepsy, which in the past has been treated by the removal of part or all of the lobe with the result that it is then possible to study right and left differences.

The right temporal lobe is more active in the recognition and processing of music and musical components such as pitch, tone, and timbre. Interestingly enough, in contrast with amateurs, professional musicians process music with their left temporal lobes. This may be because trained practitioners of music perceive music in a much more systematic and mathematical way. The right temporal lobe, like the right parietal lobe, also seems to process the appreciation of art and the recognition of faces.

Right temporal lobe lesions have also been implicated in obsessive behavioral changes. The constellation of changes in affected individuals includes hypergraphia (the tendency to produce numerous pictures and written documents); hyperreligiosity (an extreme concern with religion); viscosity (the reluctance to end conversations); and impulsive, unpredictable aggression. Bilateral lesions have also been strongly indicated in a change in sexuality. Such changes may take the form of a change in sexual preference or an increase in or the loss of sexual interest. This set of symptoms has been nicknamed *Van Gogh's syndrome* because the famous artist may have manifested many of these symptoms in his final years.

The *left temporal lobe* is similar to the right in that it seems to be involved with the processing of many of the same phenomena as the left parietal lobe. Lesions in the left temporal lobe are much more likely to cause deficits in linguistic abilities and can result in word deafness or the inability to recognize written words. Verbal memory is also impaired, and subjects often lose the ability to form word associations such as black and white and up and down. Speech in general is located on the left cerebral cortex in most people. In left-handed people, speech is twice as likely to be represented bilaterally.

The Occipital Lobes. Although cerebral asymmetries exist in the temporal lobes, in comparison with the frontal and parietal lobes, the temporal lobes are much more similar to those of the higher nonhuman primates. The same is true of the *occipital lobes*, which contain the visual cortex. There is little to be said in an evolutionary context for important evolutionary changes in the occipital cortex in humans, except that it makes the unique aspect of language known as reading possible.

Bicameral Behavior in Evolutionary Perspectives

As we have seen, the lobes of the brain are cerebrally asymmetrical with regard to functional and perceptual dominance. The only exception seems to be the occipital lobe. In the popular press, it has become normal to describe the two hemispheres of the brain as having essentially different properties. In fact, when lesions occur that affect a function that is characteristic of either the right or left side of the brain, the dysfunction is usually much more severe if the damage is bilateral or global. However, each hemisphere can be said to be dominant with regard to a particular function. It is possible to think of the two hemispheres as having general themes of expertise or dominance. Before examining humans, it is useful to briefly survey the evidence for cerebral asymmetry in other species.

Handedness.   Most mammals and some birds have a corpus callosum or similar structures that link the two hemispheres. A few marsupial mammals lack this structure. Among songbirds, who must learn their particular songs after birth, there also seems to be evidence for cerebral asymmetry. Although they do not exhibit a consistent asymmetry for certain functions, many animals, including chimpanzees, exhibit limb preference for certain tasks. The preference for right or left limb among chimpanzees is roughly 50 percent.

This is far different from humans in which an average of 80 to 90 percent are right-handed. Culture undoubtedly influences handedness, and the prejudice against using the left hand for certain tasks in the Middle East is well known (the word *sinister* derives from the Greek word meaning "left"). It also seems that the retraining of left-handers to use their right hands has detrimental effects on linguistic abilities. Retrained individuals are much more likely to exhibit increased incidences of dyslexia (reading–writing difficulties and disorders). Ambidextrous (L. *ambi*=both+*dexterous*=hand) individuals are much more likely to be women, but left-handed men outnumber women. Typically, ambidextrous people use one hand for certain tasks (writing) and the other for another task (eating). One conclusion of split-brain studies is that the left hand, which is controlled by the right hemisphere, is much better at recognizing objects through tactile stimulation. The left hand also seems to be much better at positioning objects. This is very consistent with the superior spatial abilities noted for the right hemisphere. The right hand seems to be better at the precise direction of force. This of course is entirely consistent of hominid tool manufacture and use. No such handedness bias has been observed in nonhuman primates. Such consistent differences in hemispheric controls strongly suggest that there are other differences between the two hemispheres.

The Left Hemisphere.   As mentioned previously, the popular press and literature have tended to characterize the left hemisphere in certain simplistic ways. It has been repeatedly reported that the left hemisphere is analytical and logical. There is a good deal of evidence that such functions as mathematical thinking and sequential operations are dominant for the left hemisphere. This is also consistent with the evidence that professional musicians have more active left hemispheres when listening to, composing, or playing music. The analytical superiority of the left hemisphere may also be evident from studies that suggest that when we meet new faces, we process them with our left hemisphere. Meeting familiar faces activates portions of the right hemisphere. Sadness involves increased activity of the left frontal lobe, and happiness is associated with a dampening of left frontal lobe activity.

One of the few anatomical differences between the left and right hemisphere is that the temporal planum, involved in speech processing in the left hemisphere, is slightly larger than the corresponding area of the right hemisphere. This is consistent with left hemisphere superiority in language. One other noticeable difference is that the left hemisphere possesses a greater amount of gray matter. *Gray matter* is an informal term for unmyelinated neuronal fibers. Myelin can be thought of, for our purposes, as performing the same insulating function as insulation does in an electrical cord. It can be reasoned that unmyelinated fibers allow for a greater number of faster connections. In fact, the situation is much more complicated because the distribution of myelin also influences connections between neurons, but the basic argument is that unmyelinated fibers allow for more rapid connections, which are perhaps associated with behaviors such as speech and rapid sequential analytical behavior.

As the result of a series of split-brained experiments, another facet of the left hemisphere has also emerged. Researchers presented a picture to the left visual field (right hemisphere) of a split-brained subject and asked the subject to match it with a related picture by selecting from a group of pictures. The left hemisphere was presented with a different set of pictures and given the same task. After the left hemisphere's attention was directed to what the right hemisphere's hand was pointing at, it was asked why it had chosen a picture that had nothing to do with the task. What emerged was a common tendency for the left hemisphere to rationalize about why the right hemisphere had chosen the picture that it did. It therefore seems that the left hemisphere is not only the most verbal hemisphere, but that it is the "explaining" hemisphere. It seems to be very good, in comparison with the right hemisphere, at creating or attempting to create a cohesive reality. It makes intuitive sense that the verbal part of our brain should be the portion that is charged with "making sense of things." However, as mentioned previously, the right hemisphere is also somewhat linguistic.

The Right Hemisphere. The popular literature states that the right hemisphere has been characterized as emotional, creative, and holistic. This is not a terribly inaccurate way to characterize the specializations of the right hemisphere. Just as there are many kinds of intelligence (to be examined in a later chapter), there are also many kinds of creativity. The right hemisphere has 20 percent more myelinated fibers than the left hemisphere. It has therefore been hypothesized that the right hemisphere is more concerned with the transmission of "long-distance" signals, which allow it to conduct parallel processing. This last term refers to the idea that stimuli are not processed in a linear sequential way, but rather simultaneously.

There is also evidence that the right hemisphere has some linguistic ability, but almost all studies agree that it is significantly reduced in comparison with the left hemisphere. The right hemisphere can read and comprehend language.

It deals readily with nouns and not quite as well with verbs. It has very little reading ability and a very poor understanding of grammar and syntax. Most of these findings come from split-brain studies and the study of people who have had the right hemisphere traumatized or removed. As is the case with many injuries that occur early in life, if a left hemisphere disability occurs at an early age, the maturing right hemisphere can assume many of the linguistic processes that would have normally been processed by the left hemisphere in normal individuals. However, adult speech in these subjects is never completely normal. The right hemisphere is also involved in understanding tonal qualities of voices. There is some evidence that speakers of tonal languages (for example, Chinese, Native American languages) have much more involvement of the right hemisphere in written language.

An interesting phenomenon can be observed that differentiates users of alphabetic (a phonetic system in which symbols represent sounds) and ideographic (a system in which symbols represent ideas) writing systems. If one asks users of an alphabetic language whether they can read in their dreams, the answer is overwhelmingly no. If the same question is asked of Chinese, the opposite result is obtained with the vast majority of people responding positively. Written Chinese depends on what are essentially picture symbols that also have meaning. The ideograms (characters) that children first learn are simple pictorial representations of everyday forms. For instance, the ideogram for big is a person with outstretched arms and small is represented by a person with their arms together. Even the more complicated characters are combinations of simpler pictures. Results of a study on Japanese, who use a combination of ideograms and a phonetic alphabet, indicates that like Chinese, they read in their dreams. All of this suggests that the right hemisphere does have substantial linguistic capabilities. The right hemisphere is capable of recognizing nouns, but does poorly at linguistic tasks that require an understanding of verbs and prepositions.

Sexual Dimorphism in the Brain

Although there is substantial disagreement about the extent and significance of male and female differences in the brain, the evidence overwhelmingly indicates that there are differences between male and female behavior that are mediated by different linguistic and nonlinguistic organizations in the brain. Anatomically male brains are absolutely larger on average. However, females have 10 percent more neurons concentrated in the layers of the cortex. They also have a relatively larger corpus callosum and thus, it is assumed, more complete communication between the two hemispheres. The anterior part of the corpus callosum is also more active in most perceptual and thought processes in females. In general, females seem to use more of their brains to perform a given mental task than males. Especially noticeable is the fact that females show activity in the anterior limbic system almost twice as much as males. Females are also twice as likely to suffer from depression than males.

Prenatal and postnatal exposure to male hormones (especially testosterone) presently seems to be the chief determinant of sexually dimorphic behavioral differences. Females normally learn a more diverse and extensive vocabulary at an earlier age and routinely construct more complex sentences at an earlier age. Female play also tends to be much more verbal than that of males of the same age. In short, females have superior linguistic abilities at an earlier age in comparison with males. Males perform better on tests that emphasize spatial abilities. Males exceed at computing trajectories of objects and correctly identifying what the same solid or shape looks like from different angles. These differences have held up cross-culturally, creating little doubt that they have a biological basis. The differences manifest themselves strongly in early adolescence, but are already observable in early childhood.

Males also seem to be superior at mathematical and computational skills. However, males are also much more likely to take more mathematics classes than females as the result of cultural influences. At least some biological basis for a mathematical superiority is indicated by studies that show that mathematics scores of both sexes increase if they are given the male hormone testosterone. Norman Geschwind (1926–1984) and Albert Galaburda have suggested that testosterone, which occurs in higher levels in males, delays the growth of the left hemisphere. This allows male spatial processing areas to grow more rapidly in comparison with the analytical skills of the left hemisphere. The immune system is also theorized to be influenced by the male hormone testosterone. A higher proportion of allergies and myopia occurs in nonright-handed males. In relation to mathematical tests, several researchers have found that females with high levels of male hormones (especially testosterone) test higher than females with low levels of these hormones. Counterintuitively, males with low levels of testosterone tested higher in mathematical tests than males with high levels of testosterone. Doreen Kimura has suggested that there may be an optimal level for both sexes that falls between the high and low extremes

Kimura, a long-time student of mental sexual dimorphisms, also reports that males are better at long-distance spatial tasks and that females are better at fine motor movements involving objects in close proximity to the body. Females are also superior at distinguishing emotions expressed by faces. Both sexes identify happiness equally well, but males are much worse at identifying female sadness.

It is well known that females mature faster than males, and many researchers have suggested this is why they show greater linguistic ability at an early age. In addition to a greater preference for more localized play, female children also show a preference for traditional female toys (for example, dolls, tea cups, table settings). Girls exposed to male hormones in early development showed a preference for more male gender toys (for example, trucks and guns). One possible explanation is that angularity and roundness may play a role in toy selection. Most of these studies have been based on Western cultural data, but the few cross-cultural studies and observations available support the reality of such differences.

One interpretation is that male spatial functions are more localized in a smaller area and that the more slowly an ability develops the more localized it will be. Female linguistic and interpersonal perceptual abilities may be more diffuse or widely scattered. This may be why females in general seem to suffer less damage as the result of left hemisphere lesions. In general, damage to the posterior left hemisphere is much less likely to affect female linguistic ability. Most clinical evidence derives from subjects with lesions to the posterior portion of the frontal lobe. Females utilize more of the prefrontal region in speech production and in the perception and interpretation of interpersonal communication. Much of this evidence is disputed, and only more research will allow us to develop a more exact picture of male and female differences.

Kimura has also suggested that there are substantial differences in the way in which males and females navigate across a landscape. Such findings are directly relevant to the division of labor and the reconstruction of hominid evolution. Furthermore, Kimura has shown that these differences are cross-cultural. Males tend to navigate by direction and distance, using more of a coordinatelike system. Females tend to rely more on landmarks. The best way to make adaptive sense of these differences is with reference to the evolutionary record, which indicates differences between woman the gatherer and man the hunter.

Consciousness

Contemplating consciousness probably dates back to the origin of consciousness itself, and almost all philosophers have offered opinions on the subject. Understanding consciousness is perhaps the most difficult challenge to our understanding of human behavior and almost unavoidably leads directly into the realm of philosophy. As is the case with language, there are as many theories of the nature of consciousness as there are about language. Like language, perception, and thought, consciousness must have a physical basis to its reality. Once again, the notion of emergent properties (the soul) does not help us to understand the phenomenon of consciousness. Questions about consciousness meld into questions about perception, unconsciousness, language, and categories of thinking that can only be artificially separated for the purposes of discussion. It is useful and necessary to maintain these overdrawn distinctions in order to consider what may be the most unique facet of human existence. One of the most perplexing dualities of human consciousness is that unconsciousness (reflexes and "behavioral macros," in computer parlance) is normally embedded in consciousness and vice versa, and consciousness (lucid dreaming) is nightly embedded in unconsciousness (sleep).

One of the founders of American psychology, William James, defined consciousness not as a thing but as a process. Recent theories of the definition and reality of consciousness have suggested that some kind of synchronization of neuronal activity and/or electromagnetic waves may account for consciousness. Such synchronization of the firing rate of neurons in different perceptual systems of the brain may form a single conscious experience according to Francis Crick (of DNA fame) and Christopher Koch.

David Chalmers suggests that this theory begs the question and does not address why consciousness should exist at all. In evolutionary terms, it is necessary to answer the question of what adaptive advantage consciousness provides. Alternatively, consciousness may be a telenomic phenomenon that arose as the result of the needed interaction between a number of brain systems. Chalmers admits that there are neuroanatomical correlates to consciousness, but goes on to suggest that consciousness should be treated as one of the fundamental irreducible phenomena of the universe. I cannot agree with this, and the history of science and knowledge is replete with so-called fundamental phenomena that are now cogently understood in terms of individual and interactive components. According to this view, consciousness is like gravity in that it is an irreducible and unfathomable fundamental fact of the universe. I cannot agree with the well-known opinion that the "universe is stranger than we can know."

In an evolutionary vein, Adam Carley proposes that consciousness is an adaptive mechanism by which the brain lies to the mind. Consciousness incorporates memories that are subjective because reality is too complicated to be dealt with in detail. This approach agrees well with what we know about the sensory systems of the brain. Specifically, one of the chief functions of the various sensory processing systems is to filter out irrelevant or at least useless information. Paying attention to every sound or sight or smell is logistically impossible. Humans and other animals therefore emphasize what is most adaptively useful. Carley suggests that even a false memory is evolutionarily useful if it works. Selection therefore would act on the efficacy of consciousness and not necessarily on the reality of consciousness and memory. It is difficult to conceive of a decision-making process that would act otherwise. Irrationally disliking or adoring another individual may be adaptive in many situations.

However, an accurate representation of reality logically seems adaptive, as long as reality does not contain details of information that cannot be acted on. To paraphrase Carley, memories can be false but simultaneously useful. The self in Carley's model is a cartoon, a fairy tale, or, in the model proposed here, an icon. As an icon, the concept of self allows more concerted interaction with the environment.

One problem with Carley's highly appealing explanation is that we intuitively know that we spend a great deal of energy and time on things that seem to have no evolutionary usefulness. On the other hand, contemplating angels on the head of pin, one's navel, or non-Euclidean universes may serve the function of keeping the brain active for dealing with proximate and "important" situations. I also suspect that consciousness is crucial to planning. Some higher vertebrates do seem to plan activities, but no one has yet argued successfully that dogs plan their day. As with so many behaviors, we can see the glimmerings of consciousness in hominoids (and arguably in some monkeys) who recognize themselves in the mirror. The intersection and interaction between symbolism, language, memory, and learning is so intertwined that the why of the evolution of consciousness continues to elude us. I believe that when we meet extraterrestrial consciousness, we will recognize it as just that.

Summary

As of yet there is no consensual, unified theory of the brain. From an evolutionary perspective, the brain–mind dichotomy is fruitless. As Deacon and others have pointed out, the brain evolved to pay attention to things that were important for survival. At any level of biological organization, brains that did not pay attention to environmentally important things are no longer with us. For reasons that we still fail to comprehend completely, language and tool use became extremely important to the survival of our ancestors, and, as their descendants, our brains pay an extraordinary attention to these things. The triune brain model is extremely consistent with the paleontological record of vertebrates. The evolution of the brain was an additive process in which new levels of organization were built on top of and integrated with earlier systems that emerged as animals moved from the sea to the various environments of the land. Earlier systems were not replaced but instead were augmented and transformed. Although the highest level of the brain, the neocortex, is present in most vertebrates, the anatomical thickness and complexity of the human neocortex is without equal on this planet. It is important to emphasize that although each level of the brain is organized for different kinds of tasks, all levels interact with each other and any level is capable of significantly influencing the functioning of another level. The paleontological and archaeological records are intricately reflected in the structure of the modern human brain, which places a concerted emphasis on socialness and communications. This is one of the most fundamental founding principles and lessons of evolutionary psychology. The evidence for why we do what we do comes from the living and the dead.

The divisions of the neocortex are basically the same in humans as they are in other mammals. The differences in humans are once again a matter of degree. In hominids, the importance of the frontal lobe is reflected in its persistent and constant enlargement over the course of the last 2 to 3 million years. Although there is an evolutionary correlation between brain size and behavioral complexity, we still do not understand the details of that correlation. The functions of the frontal are numerous and complex. The frontal seems to be involved in the control of many forms of voluntary behavior. It may be the overriding control mechanism for the brain as a whole. It certainly plays a vital role in the production of the uniquely human form of communication known as language. If there is a "theme" to the frontal lobe, it is one of initiating and planning actions. If there is a theme to the parietal lobes, it is one of sensory perception, processing, and integration. In both the frontal and the parietal lobes, the motor and sensory cortices have disproportionately large areas devoted to tool use (and manufacturing) and linguistic communication, which are hallmarks of the uniquely human brain and mind. This is highly consistent with the fossil and archaeological records of a tool-dependent and linguistic animal. Interestingly, although bipedalism is also one of the unique features of hominids, there is not a large area of the brain devoted to the hips, knees, or feet. Bipedalism is not represented by any extensive association area on the cortex and may suggest that bipedalism is old and that the brain has no need to consciously monitor these parts of the body because the behavior has become more or less automatic.

This may indicate a nomothetic deduction about the evolution of the brain: The older and more established a biological function is, the less space is devoted to it on the cortex. The special areas devoted to spatial processing and language, but especially language, suggest that these abilities are, evolutionarily speaking, new in comparison with autonomic and emotional processing systems. If the theory is correct, and if language arose less than 100,000 years ago, then spatial abilities would also have a similar antiquity. Because we are descended from arboreal primates, which appeared at least 65 mya, this is unlikely. It seems more logical to date improved manual dexterity and language to the time when the brain of *Homo habilis* began to enlarge or to the time when *Homo erectus* left Africa, spread into Eurasia, and took up more systematic foraging strategies including hunting. The modern brain then fits well with the fossil and archaeological records. However, there are those who now believe these developments to be of approximately equal antiquity. My own years of research convince me that such conclusions are wrong and are based on faulty dates. The enlargement of the brain from the time of *H. habilis* to the spread of *H. erectus* can best be understood as a continuous process of a lineage that had somehow embarked on a course of unprecedented resource expansion that made it more "competent" to occupy all of the climatic and geographic diversity of the Old World.

There is no obvious logical reason for the development of either a bicameral brain or cerebral asymmetry. It is safe to say that if one sat down to design a brain, these aspects would not be part of the fundamental design. One could argue that, as in a spacecraft, the two-hemisphere brain would represent a redundant backup system in case one side failed. Redundancy is much more pronounced in immature hominids, and contralateral hemispheres can more adequately assume functions of the other hemisphere before maturity is reached. Multiple neural pathways connecting different areas decrease as we age. The brain goes from becoming soft wired to hard wired as we age.

Deacon's model of sending more neurons to a function of evolutionary importance and then pairing them down as perceptions, responses, and actions become more focused makes a great deal of evolutionary sense and implies that there is a correlation between environment stimulation (adaptational need) and the function that initially gets the most neurons. Needing to send more neurons to particular areas may account for why bigger brains are smarter brains. More is better because it provides more clay to model and whittle into a final form arrived at through behavioral "mistakes and adjustments." The plasticity of this model is also evolutionarily appealing and suggests how it is that animals adapt to changing environments: Each generation gets a chance to vary the intensity of neural adjustment according to the current selection pressures in which it is maturing. This is Darwinian thinking at its most concise. It fits well with what we know about learning without being Lamarckian because neural emphases are maintained through cultures and similar environments and not passed on through genes.

Speculations as to why the left hemisphere should be dominant have ranged from the placement of the aorta on the left to the spin of the earth. A general, though speculative, explanation of cerebral asymmetry and lateralization may be that rapidly performed and "important" functions are more efficient when they are physically close together or connected by unmyelinated fibers. Other features of the brain, like superior mathematical performance by males, may simply be teleomatic in that they result from the fact that males normally have higher levels of testosterone than females. On the other hand, the connectionist school has emphasized that the anatomical seat of what we have called functions is much more global than has been previously supposed.

Even if this is true, one very important aspect of the study of human behavior that the brain illustrates is that specific behaviors have specific anatomical correlates, meaning that for every behavior there is a specific place or constellation of places and neurons that allow and facilitate a behavior or thought. At the same time, it is imperative to realize that association areas and nuclei of the brain are interconnected in complex ways that currently defy detailed description.

In an evolutionary framework, the sexually dimorphic human brain makes logical sense. The division of labor that we see in hunters and gatherers is reflected in the structure of male and female brains. The superior spatial abilities of males, their ability to understand objects viewed from different angles, and their ability to compute trajectories makes perfect sense for a hunter.

The superior linguistic abilities of females also make evolutionary sense, though a number of evolutionary reasons have been suggested. One possibility is that superior linguistic abilities were selected for because females do more of the socializing of the very young. The trouble with this explanation is that it does not explain why female linguistic superiority appears early on in childhood. Another problem with this interpretation is that the degree to which males also participate in infant socialization varies tremendously from culture to culture, with some males spending a substantial amount of time caring for children. Females become economically important persons at a much earlier age than boys. Siblings also play a significant role in the socialization process, but it is unclear whether this difference is innately sexually dimorphic.

A more direct explanation of female linguistic abilities, and even the way in which they navigate, may relate directly to the female role in gathering. In contrast to the object of the hunt, which will probably have a different location every day, the objects of gathering tend to be stationary. Landmarks thus always become useful reference points. Animals may move out of the range of usefulness for a fixed reference point; plants do not. Plants, however, are seasonally variable. Information about the suitability of plants for harvesting must contain more information than simply location. Information must be provided on abundance and ripeness. In short, they must be labeled in more detail to be useful. With animals, hunters need only know if they are there, and this usually cannot be determined without direct observation. It is interesting that it was once widely accepted that language probably evolved as the result of "planning the hunt." In fact, hunters may go out to hunt with only a very general plan: "If it moves, kill it." There is no sense in developing detailed verbal plans that will have to be altered or abandoned when faced with the actual situation. Furthermore, conversation during the course of a hunt is a disastrous strategy. Female gathering is quite different in that plans must be made for how the resource will be brought back to camp. This involves bringing the right procuring equipment and containers. What will be true about a fruit tree this May will be true about it next May. The division of labor not only helps to explain many aspects of the brain, its influence on the development of language also seems to help us understand language itself. This is the subject of the next chapter.

QUESTIONS FOR REVIEW

1. How do new techniques for studying the brain differ from those used before the application of electronic technology?

2. How does the triune brain model reflect evolutionary history?

3. What are association areas? How do connectionists differ in their interpretations of association areas?

4. What are the differences between functional and anatomical asymmetries?

5. How is the course of hominid evolution reflected in brain sexual dimorphism?

6. What is meant by "higher" and "lower" brain functions?

MIND AND BODY EXPERIMENTS

1. Record two conversations and play them simultaneous to males and females. Test their comprehension of the subjects of the conversation.

2. Watch the eye movements of a person presented with a complex problem to solve. Where does the gaze point? Are there differences between individuals?

3. What are your first memories? How old were you?

4. Place spheroidal, cubic, and pyramidal solids on a table in a room with equal numbers of boys and girls. Invite them to examine the objects. Does any sexual dimorphism in activity become apparent?

5. Ask males and females for directions to their residence (or other place). Is there any sexual dimorphism in responses?

SUGGESTED READINGS

Bridgeman, B. 1988. *The Biology of Behavior and Mind.* New York: John Wiley & Sons.
Brown, R., and McNeill, D. 1966. The "Tip of the Tongue" Phenomenon. *Journal of Verbal Learning and Verbal Behavior* 5: 325–337.
Chalmers, D. 1996. *The Conscious Mind: In Search of a Fundamental Theory.* Oxford: Oxford University Press.

Chomsky, N. 1972. *Reflections on Language*. New York: Pantheon.

Chomsky, N. 1988. *Language and Problems of Knowledge: The Managua Lectures*. Cambridge, MA: MIT Press.

Crick, F., and Koch, C. 1990. Towards a Neurobiological Theory of Consciousness. *Seminars in the Neurosciences* 2: 263–275.

Deacon, T. 1997. *The Symbolic Species: The Co-evolution of Language and the Brain*. New York: W. W. Norton.

Falk, D. 1987. Human Paleoneurology, *Annual Review of Anthropology* 16: 13–30.

Fuster, J. M. 1980. *The Prefrontal Cortex*. New York: Raven Press.

Gazzaniga, M. 1970. *The Bisected Brain*. New York: Appleton-Century-Crofts.

Gazzaniga, M. 1983. Right Hemisphere Language Following Brain Bisection: A 20-Year Perspective. *American Psychologist* 38: 525–537.

Gazzaniga, M. S. 1985. *The Social Brain*. New York: Basic Books.

Geschwind, N. 1965. Disconnection Syndromes in Animals and Man. *Brain* 88: 237–294, 585–644.

Geschwind, N. 1970. The Organization of Language and the Brain. *Science* 170: 940–944.

Holloway, R. L. 1980. The O. H. 7 (Olduvai Gorge, Tanzania) Hominid Partial Brain Endocast Revisited. *American Journal of Physical Anthropology* 53: 267–274.

Holloway, R. L. 1981a. Volumetric and Asymmetry Determinations on Recent Hominid Endocasts: Spy I and II, Djebel Jhroud 1, and the Salb *Homo erectus* Specimens, with Some Notes on Neanderthal Brain Size. *American Journal of Physical Anthropology* 55: 385–393.

Holloway, R. L. 1981b. The Indonesian *Homo erectus* Brain Endocast Revisited. *American Journal of Physical Anthropology* 55: 503–521.

Holloway, R. L. 1983. Human Paleontological Evidence Relevant to Language Behavior. *Human Neurobiology* 2: 105–114.

Jerison, H. 1973. *Evolution of the Brain and Behavior*. New York: Academic Press.

Kimura, D. 1973. The Asymmetry of the Human Brain. *Scientific American* 228: 70–78.

Luria, A. R. 1966. *Higher Cortical Functions in Man*. London: Tavistock.

Luria, A. R. 1970. The Functional Organization of the Brain. *Scientific American*: 66–79.

MacLean, P. D. 1958. Contrasting Functions of Limbic and Neocortical Systems of the Brain and Their Relevance to Psychophysiological Aspects of Medicine." *American Journal of Medicine* 25: 611–626.

MacLean, P. D. 1973. *A Triune Concept of the Brain and Behaviour*. Toronto: University of Toronto Press.

MacLean, P. D. 1978. The Evolution of Three Mentalities. In S. L. Washburn and E. R. McCown (eds.), *Human Evolution, Biosocial Perspectives*, pp. 3–57. Menlo Park, CA: Benjamin/Cummings.

Penfield, W., and Rasmussen, T. 1950. *The Cerebral Cortex of Man: A Clinical Study of Localization of Function*. New York: Macmillan.

Penfield, W., and Roberts, L. 1959. *Speech and Brain Mechanisms*. Princeton, NJ: Princeton University Press.

Pinker, S. 1994. *The Language Instinct: How the Mind Creates Language*. New York: William Morrow.

Popper, K. R., and Eccles, J. C. 1977. *The Self and Its Brain*. Berlin: Springer-Verlag.

Sperry, R. 1974. Lateral Specialization in the Surgically Separated Hemispheres." In F. O. Schmitt and F. G. Worden (eds.), *The Neurosciences: Third Study Program*. Cambridge, MA: MIT Press.

Sperry, R., Gazzaniga, M., and Bogen, J. 1969. Interhemispheric Relationships: The Neocortical Commisures—Syndromes of Hemisphere Disconnection. In P. Vinken and G. Bruyn (eds.), *Handbook of Clinical Neurology* (vol 4). Amsterdam: North-Holland.

Sternberg, R. 1985. Beyond I.Q.: A Triarchic Theory of Human Intelligence. *Behavior and Brain Sciences*. New York: Cambridge University Press.

Wada, J., and Rasmussen, T. 1960. "Intracarotid Injection of Sodium Amytal for the Lateralization of Cerebral Speech Dominance: Experimental and Clinical Observations. *Journal of Neurosurgery* 17: 266–282.

6

Language and Communication

Truth is the most valuable commodity we have, let us economize it.
—Mark Twain

Man is the only animal that blushes and the only one that needs to.
—Mark Twain

If we could study children "in the wild" to discover their natural tendencies, we could then design the perfect language that took advantage of what kids do spontaneously.
—Terrence Deacon

From any perspective, language is the most unusual characteristic of humanity. It is difficult to comprehend the need for or adaptive advantage of human language. All other species communicate perfectly well without it. However, because it is unique and universal to humans, there is good reason to believe that it somehow conveys on our species an innately based competitive advantage. Language— whether spoken, written, gestured, or signed—is largely symbolic, but the referent of each symbol must be learned. In this aspect, it differs from the so-called dance of a honey bee or the threat yawn of primates, though these also have learned components. Human language also allows us to undercommunicate, overcommunicate, or mislead members of our own species. Other organisms mislead, but deception is usually practiced on species other than their own.

If more detailed and intricate communication among organisms is adaptive, why do all other species (most of whom are more ancient than humans) reproduce and endure perfectly well without it? Language also seems to be tied up with consciousness or, more succinctly, with awareness of the self in the past, present, and future. One of the nagging linguistic questions, and one that is perhaps unanswerable, is the question of whether linguistic categories form mental categories or whether innate brain categories form linguistic categories. The position favored in this text is that language allows us to accumulate and access much more information than other species. Language seems to represent a means of storing a great deal of information without being conscious of it from second to second. At the same time, most linguistic information is usually accessible at a moment's notice. Language is the primary social medium of modern humans, but it is difficult to imagine how this could have played a pivotal role in the transformation of apes into hominids. Like bipedalism, human linguistic ability comes attached with disadvantages, ranging from suffocation while eating or drinking to violence generated by written or spoken words. It conveys its Pandora's box of treasures between individuals and across the centuries.

That language is biologically and genetically based is now indisputable. Language is such an important form of communication that many parts of the brain are devoted to it. There are almost as many definitions of language as there are people who have thought about it. Linguist Noam Chomsky has argued that there is a "language organ" in the brain that mediates an innate grammar. Though at first dismissed, Chomsky's idea that there was a strong biological basis to language is now accepted as fact. For decades, some researchers argued that other animals also possess language. We shall examine this and other questions in an evolutionary perspective, which will allow us to develop an understanding of the possible functions of language and how they may have evolved. We shall also address the more philosophical question of how we use language to perceive and order the world. Symbolic communication is at the heart of language.

More controversial is the proposition that sexual dimorphism in human language is not wholly learned. Specifically, human females differ from males in a number of linguistic features. These differences are explainable with reference to the cultural universal of the division of labor on the basis of sex.

Communication

By definition, no form of social behavior works without communication. Like most mammals, humans communicate in a number of ways using a multimodal system of senses. In addition to language, humans also utilize other forms of communication such as postural (body language), gestural (an emphasis on the limbs and fingers), and facial expressions. These modes are normally integrated in often complex and sometimes contradictory messages. Olfaction is also a means of immediate or delayed communication between organisms. In many animals, olfactory communication can span miles. When organisms scent-mark a home territory or range, they are communicating with others that do not have to be present at the same time. Humans also communicate with olfaction, but such interaction is comparatively reduced in higher primates and greatly reduced in humans. Human females appear to be better at olfactory communication than males and possess a superior ability to identify relatives and loved ones by smell. Linguistic communication, in humans can span continents even without technological devices by "word of mouth." In humans, delayed communication occurs primarily through spoken language, books, and works of art and architecture that can communicate "from the grave." Human females are better at facial communication than human males.

Although there are commonalities to all cultural behavior, there are also idiosyncratic features that are arbitrary. In addition to language, visual art, music, and dance are also important forms of human communication. All of these forms of communication can be limbic or nonlimbic. This is a unique feature of human communication. We will present a brief survey of some of these forms of communication drawn from both our own culture and that of others.

A Definition of Language

The connection between handedness, the archaeological record, fossil endocasts, and modern human neuroanatomy is no coincidence. Handedness, symmetrical stone tools, asymmetric brains, and the first evidence of early *Homo* all occur sometime before 1.5 mya and as early as 2.5 mya. As mentioned previously, the connection between the production of symmetrical or formalized stone tools and language is the quality of arbitrariness in which the final form of the artifact is not determined by the medium but by a preconceived mental template. The notion of an arbitrary and preconceived form also applies very well to language. Language can be defined as a learned system of communication that relies on arbitrary sounds and symbols understood and shared by a group. Just as all cultures have a commonly understood system of kinship, all languages have a commonly understood syntax (rules) and grammar (structure). As mentioned previously, language is multimodal (visual, auditory, tactile). It is both limbic and nonlimbic. The acquisition of fluent language is decidedly easier for children than for adults, and it proceeds in regular stages or windows of biological development.

There has been a continuing suggestion that some animals also have language. This text takes the position that with the possible exception of cetaceans (dolphins and whales), no other animals use language in the wild. Even some of the studied cetaceans may show only a rudimentary or precursive form of language. When animals supposedly learn language in the laboratory, it is as the result of many hours of training involving rewards.

Nonhuman Primate Experiments

Serious attempts to investigate the linguistic abilities of nonhuman primates quite logically first turned to the apes, specifically chimpanzees. About four decades ago, a chimpanzee named Vicki was raised in a household by a couple named Hayes and instructed in speaking. After years of training, Vicki could say a few words such as "papa" and "cup," which could be understood only if one listened carefully. This project demonstrated that chimpanzees lack the physical vocal apparatus for human speech. Vicki was very good at imitating everyday human activities ranging from putting on makeup to doing housework, but never progressed linguistically beyond a few spoken words.

To overcome this problem, other chimpanzees were taught ASL (American sign language) or instructed in the manipulation of plastic symbols or computer symbols. One of the best-known ASL experiments involved a chimpanzee named Washoe, who was raised by Allan and Beatrice Gardener in their home. After more than four years, Washoe not only learned more than 130 of the signs that she was purposely taught, but also those used by humans conversing with each other in sign language. Washoe was best at stringing nouns together and seemed to be able to apply labels to objects. She was reported by her trainers as being able to use verbs, but most of her communication seemed to be limbic in that it expressed personal desires or emotional states. As a whole, Washoe produced many more words than Vicki. Washoe also supposedly taught other chimpanzees to sign. Washoe learned to express the limbic concepts of *sorry* and *please.* When someone stepped on her doll, Washoe was quoted as saying, "Up Susan: Susan mine please up; gimme baby; please shoe; more mine; up please; please up; more up; baby down; shoe up; please move up."

Another couple, Anne and David Premack, used plastic symbols to obtain very similar results and claimed that Sarah, the chimpanzee that they trained, produced sophisticated "sentences." The Premacks credited Sarah with a number of complex linguistic constructions including *if–then* propositions, *same and different*, and the ability to ask the name of objects. Like all other chimpanzee projects, it is hard to argue that Sarah's statements were anything more than limbic.

An even more sophisticated approach was that of teaching a chimpanzee named Lana to communicate using a special computer keyboard and an artificial language called Yerkish, named for the Yerkes Primate Center where the experiments were conducted. Lana not only constructed fairly complex sentences but also carried on conversations with humans.

Some very interesting commonalities have arisen from these studies. First, to get the chimpanzee to cooperate in learning, a system of rewards needs to be used (for example; food, tickling, play). This contrasts markedly with the language acquisition process in humans. Little humans do not have to be rewarded to speak. In fact, they must frequently be rewarded or trained not to interrupt the conversations of others. In humans, speech does not have to be rewarded because speech is its own reward. Anyone that has been around infant hominids for any period of time has heard periods of what seems to be highly enjoyable babbling. Speech among humans is "limbically" rewarding, but as it matures, it is not limited to limbic subjects. The babbling of human infants eventually comes to mimic the rhythm and cadence of language long before it incorporates the intellectual content of a language. The babbling stage has not been reported in infant apes. One scholar, C. Hasty, has suggested that the sequence of rhythm and cadence of language are intimately bound up with music (see below).

Second, almost all the subject matter of the chimpanzee sentences involves what the chimpanzee feels or desires. It is easy to argue that what is being communicated is limbic information about the state of the communicator. There is nothing special about this in mammals. Once again, it is nonlimbic communication that sets humans apart from apes. One experiment was set up to see if Lana could lie. It involved Lana misleading her trainer about the whereabouts of a snack. After having the snack taken away from her every time she identified its true location, she learned to say that it was somewhere else. If this is really nonlimbic communication, it still involves reward. Humans can mislead for many more reasons than immediate gain. Additionally, they have many more uses for nonlimbic communication. It is also difficult to know if Lana thought she was lying or thought she was playing a new game.

A third commonality that characterizes chimpanzee language acquisition is that sentences become longer, but only slightly more complex as training progresses. This is true only to a certain extent. One example is a sentence that progressed from something like "Gimme apple" to "Gimme, gimme sweet, sweet apple now, now." The sentence did indeed get longer, but the information content increased only minimally. Indeed all the chimpanzees reached a point at which the information content ceased to increase. Again, the sentences remain very limbic and self-centered.

Like chimpanzees, little hominids are also self-centered with initial communication limited to what they want or their emotional state. Their sentences get longer, but they also get more complex. They differ from chimpanzees in that their sentences do not reach a threshold where length and complexity cease to increase. The information content of little hominid sentences also increases at an almost geometric rate. Chimpanzees do not seem to progress beyond the linguistic competence of a three-year-old hominid. Furthermore, little hominids use what they have learned with other little hominids. It has been claimed that chimps use sign language with other chimps, but the evidence is minimal and confined to artificial contexts.

Further casting doubt on claims that chimpanzees have sophisticated language abilities is the Clever Hans phenomenon. Clever Hans was a horse that supposedly could do arithmetic and communicate the right answer to a problem through the number of times he raked the ground with his hoof. In fact, careful analysis of the phenomenon showed that the animal was taking subtle, and perhaps, subconscious clues from his trainer. The psychologist H. Terrace has suggested that the same phenomenon is going on with many of the primate language experiments. We know that many animals can be trained to look as if they are responding intelligently to verbal commands, and of course there is no argument about the large number of behaviors a dog will perform on the basis of verbal or gestural commands. But it is very difficult to combine these commands in complex sequences that lead to a new behavior. The meaning of "Lassie, go warn gramps that the bridge is out!" introduces philosophical problems for philosophers of language, but probably produces no deep meaning for Lassie. The Lassie phenomenon is the product of script writers imposing human thoughts on non-human minds.

A kind of Clever Hans phenomenon seems to be involved in Penny Patterson's claims for the extensive development of language in the gorillas Koko and Michael. In a film used widely in anthropology classes, Patterson is seen interpreting subtle hand movements made by Koko in the story of the animal's capture in Africa, the killing of her mother, and her boat trip to the United States. To an observer, the claims look very overdrawn. If anything, it appears that it is Patterson that has been trained in a way that might be termed the "clever Penny" phenomenon. If Koko really possesses this kind of fluency, then she should be able to communicate the same story to any other person conversant in ASL. When such an experiment was suggested, Patterson would not allow it. When funding for the project was discontinued, Patterson locked herself in a trailer with Koko and refused to come out unless funding for more research was found. Funding was found, and more recently, Patterson has displayed the paintings of Koko and Michael as gorilla "art." Although comprehensible as art to twentieth-century humans, they would not have been interpreted as fine works of art two hundred years ago, originating from either humans or gorillas. The ultimate defense of these outlandish claims resides securely (at least for now) in the fact that we cannot know what it is that nonhuman animals think they are doing.

One of the problems that Patterson's and many other studies illustrates is the personal attachment that researchers and trainers develop for the subjects of their study. One prominent researcher is on record as saying that chimpanzees should be placed in colonies where they can be taught to farm. Such a plan not only shows an ignorance of chimpanzee manipulative abilities, but also an ignorance of the anatomy of the brain. The same researcher in a film is seen explaining on camera that one of the young chimpanzees learned sign language from one of the older chimpanzees without ever having seen it used by humans. As the researcher is talking, the young chimpanzee can be seen in the background intensely watching the researcher's hands as he uses ASL while he is speaking. Thus it is wise to be skeptical about sweeping claims for the advanced linguistic skill of chimpanzees.

What chimpanzees seem to exhibit is perhaps protolinguistic abilities, which one can imagine as being transformed into true language if the right selection pressures continued long enough. There is no doubt that apes are highly intelligent animals that have long memories and the ability to devise new strategies in the face of new problems. They are especially good at mimicking human behaviors. Humans are equally as good or better at mimicking apes.

Cetaceans Studies

Cetaceans studies will be dealt with only briefly. The difference between chimpanzee and dolphin studies is that when we study dolphin communication we are studying a system that is used naturally in the wild by the animals to communicate with others of their own kind. We are not imposing a human communication system on them, though we often get them to perform actions that we order. We know that at least some dolphin sounds are learned because they differ from group to group. At least one dolphin call is a self-identification signal. On the basis of this observation, it is tempting to speculate that self-identification may have been a first step in the development of a conscious concept of self in hominids, which in turn laid the basis for a grammar and syntax. However, there is as yet no objective way of determining if a self-signal is voluntary or nonlimbic.

More artificial studies, which induce dolphins to change the order in which they perform various acts, may also suggest that dolphins have a grammar or are at least capable of learning a grammar. We still do not know to what extent dolphin communications are limbic or whether the dolphins regard performing for humans as enjoyable. In any case, it would be hard to argue that the evolution of dolphin language has had much to do with the evolution of human language. An extensive and complicated system of learned arbitrary symbols with contextually variable meanings is absent in all nonhuman protolinguistic systems.

The Origin of Language

As with theories for the origin of bipedalism, theories for the origin of language range from the extremely plausible to the laughable. In all these theories, it is assumed that language probably provided some adaptive advantage involving improved communication and social organization. Once again, the mystery of human language is found in the fact that other animals communicate perfectly well without it. Language must surely provide some enormous advantage that we have perhaps overlooked because we take it for granted. Many theories have been advanced to account for the origin of language, but few have convincingly provided a compelling explanation of exactly what evolutionary advantage was obtained as the result of language. Some theories of language origins follow.

Buzz-Bow-wow Theory

This has been mentioned previously as an unlikely origin for language. One of the outstanding qualities of language is that it is arbitrary, with most words having little to do with an object's natural sound. In fact, many objects do not make any sound at all. However, all languages contain onomatopoeic words, which are words that imitate a natural sound. Among modern people, few animal sounds sound the same across cultures. Dogs make many sounds in Western cultures: "bow-wow, arf, ruff, grrr, yip-yip," and so on. Chinese do not usually recognize these sounds as those of dogs. Chinese dogs bark "gou-gou" or "gun-gun." Cats, however, make similar sounds across cultures: "meow" or "mao." Interestingly, many bird songs can be identified cross-culturally when reproduced by skilled human imitators.

The advantage that natural imitation would have given Paleolithic humans is hard to imagine, though the obvious one is the ability to decoy. Communication about the availability of certain species or predators may also have played a role in hunting. Skillful hunters and some pastoralists can call or attract animals by mimicking calls. However, these abilities do not seem great enough to have required the massive reorganization and augmentation of the cortex, which is one of the chief characteristics setting humans apart from other organisms. The number of sounds that we imitate are woefully few in comparison with the vast majority of words that do not have an obvious similarity to the object being described or talked about. Buzz-bow-wow theory was initially closely tied to the "man the hunter" theory, whose importance in human evolution has probably been over-emphasized.

One might suggest that a visual form of the buzz-bow-wow theory is appropriate for the origin of some written languages in that they were originally based on the recombination of pictures as in Chinese and Egyptian hieroglyphics. Similarly, Chinese characters, or ideograms (Figure 6.1) represent stylized pictures of various objects. Although young students of this system of writing begin learning them with reference to the physical forms that they depict, the graphic qualities are much less apparent in the more complicated forms, which adults use for reading and writing. Nonetheless, it is clear that beginning language learning as a system of picture writing produces differences that remain in the adult brain. Specifically, literate Chinese use the right hemisphere of the brain much more when engaged in linguistic tasks.

The Gestural Theory

The gestural theory suggests that language arose out of a previous system of gestures, which as hominids became bipedal allowed them to use their hands more. This theory is consistent with the archaeological and fossil records and is also in accord with evidence that handedness and language are intimately connected. Furthermore, it is well known that members of every culture use their hands in conjunction with speech, but paradoxically, most humans find it difficult

FIGURE 6.1   Chinese Ideograms

to simultaneously concentrate on speaking and on unrelated manual tasks. However, practiced jugglers can become quite good at this.

Some cultures and individuals use gestures more than others. In the West, we are familiar with the Italian cultural stereotype of a speaker whose motions and gestures are very animated. In fact in most cultures, few speakers make dramatic or important points without the use of gestures. Gestural features like tones (in nontonal languages) and inflection change the intensity of the message. These are termed *paralanguage*. If the gestural theory of human languages is at least partially correct, then gestures are probably an integral component of language and not merely a superfluous enhancement. Native, deaf speakers of ASL store their language in the same areas as vocal speakers.

All cultures also have greeting gestures and obscene or derisive gestures. Greeting gestures always involve the hands. The positioning and stance of the body are also usually involved. The open-hand greeting is seen in chimpanzees, Western humans (the handshake), Chinese traditional greeting (bowing and shaking one's own hand), Southeast and South Asia ("praying" hands), and Native Americans (raised hands). Other gestures for basic meaning are much less standardized. For instance, the Western waving hand for "good-bye" is interpreted in parts of the Far East as "come here" and in other parts as "go away." Gestures conveying obscenity, insanity, stupidity, and other qualities also vary greatly.

Widely spread negative or aggressive gestures include pointing the index finger at people or revered objects, the clenched fist, or pounding of the fist. In Thailand, using feet to point is highly offensive. White Australians use their lips to point. Although gestures are used in conjunction with verbal communication, they augment speech rather than change the meaning of speech. There is currently no convincing evidence that a gestural language proceeded spoken language. Indeed, the fossil and archaeological records strongly support the interpretation that gestural communication accompanied rather than proceeded spoken language. Moreover, it is now apparent that even the acquisition of sign language in speaking subjects is accomplished by first learning the sound or tactile form (ASL, Braille) of a word.

The Social Organization Theory

One highly plausible idea is that language evolved as a device for social organization and mediation, which gave early hominids an adaptive advantage over other primates. The ability to subdivide social members into subgroups with various relationships and duties may have allowed the more efficient exploitation of resources. It can be argued that assigning individuals to a subgroup within a society may inevitably lead to assignment of rank. The problem with this is that hunters and gatherers in general are known for their lack of social stratification. Furthermore, nonhuman primates and other animals can have fairly well-established social structures without language. Once again, the exploitation of resources, mating and reproduction, and defense from predators has been carried out successfully for millions of years in millions of vertebrate species without the use of language.

Although language is a powerful tool for social mediation, it is also frequently the instigator of physical aggression. Homer's *Apple of Discord* would have had little effect if it had not been labeled "To the Fairest." In human history and myth, language seems to have an equal ability to bring about reconciliation or create havoc. From Rush Limbaugh to Howard Stern, language has the power to simultaneously enrage and assuage. One of the first "privileges" that tyrants remove is the right of free speech. It is an amazing fact of human existence that people can forfeit their life because of what they say.

Proponents of the social theory of language also suggest that speech functions as a replacement for physical violence and therefore helps to maintain group harmony. Thus, lying can smooth over potentially dangerous confrontations, but also has the opposite potential. Like a great idea, language has the capacity to facilitate great good or great evil. Once again, all other social mammals usually avoid lethal social interaction without the use of language. Potentially lethal interactions among nonhuman conspecifics are usually resolved through ritual competition or confrontation. Human language is also used in ritual, but these account for a very small proportion of the multitude of uses to which language is put.

The Rape Theory

Richard Wrangham has proposed what can only be described as an odd and implausible theory that purports to explain female linguistic superiority and human speech in general. Wrangham suggests that speech first evolved among females so that females could identify rapists to other members of the group who would either avoid such individuals or punish them. Of course, males would have been required to have the capacity for understanding such accusations. This theory should be taken about as seriously as the aquatic theory for hominid origins. It is hard to imagine that rape prevention would be a prime mover in the evolution of our own species, especially because rape is still present in all known human societies. Furthermore, although socially unacceptable, rape leads to reproduction. Sociobiologists (Wrangham included) can argue that the identification of rapists would keep males from raising the offspring of others. One final objection to this theory is that such emotional acts as rape, and even mating in general, do not result in an increase in the articulate skills of people, but instead the opposite condition of increased "limbicness," which is characteristic of highly emotional states.

The Icon, Long-Distance Resource Theory

Here I propose a new theory of language evolution that is part of a larger long-distance theory, which also draws on what others have suggested about the origins of symbolism and resource procurement. The models of Deacon (symbolism), Lovejoy (bipedalism), and others can be integrated into a model that explains not only linguistic origins but also other aspects of the uniqueness of hominids.

It now seems evident that hominids stand out from other animals in the number and range of resources that they utilize for survival. No other vertebrate is even close to us in the number of things that they will eat in the wild. Our domesticated omnivores the dog, pig, and "picnicized" bears are also like us in their dietary habits. One of the things that higher primates, but especially humans, have evolved is a markedly decreased ability to chemically discriminate between useful and nonuseful or dangerous foods. Some basic tastes and smells, such as sweet, sour, bitter and salty, remain crudely developed but do not approach the acuity of mammals with a naked rhinarium. Hominids have carried the general primate trend of reduced olfaction to extreme form. Hominids have essentially cut themselves off from a mode of sensory input that most other vertebrates find crucial. Similarly, hominid hearing is also reduced in the range of frequencies that it can perceive.

The highly developed sense that hominids were left with as the result of 65 million years of evolutionary emphasis was vision. Like other primates, humans are very good at color perception. This is a notable plesiomorphic feature of primates. Unlike other mammals, all primate vision, but especially hominid vision, does not rely on movement for detection of form and color. This is no doubt true because fruit does not run away. Hominids are very good at solving static visual problems like jigsaw puzzles and discovering "Where's Waldo?" Among the vertebrates, hominids excel at this ability and use it daily to locate resources.

Additionally, we have the ability to draw fine distinctions between non-dietary resources such as stone and wood, to name but a few examples. In other words, humans search for and utilize a huge number and classes of raw materials that other animals ignore. As mentioned previously, the idea that brains evolve to pay attention to what is important to them makes sense with our current understanding of brain architecture. Therefore, the question arises, "What selection pressures act on a brain that has to pay attention to everything and has essentially only sight to rely on?"

As part of this adaptation or because of it, hominids evolved the ability to cover long distances through bipedalism. Lovejoy's model emphasized the need for the long-distance foraging of food. In fact at some point, which I believe to be early on, materials for tools also became essential to hominid survival. Furthermore, the need to avoid predation was and is also crucial. One also has to look for potential mates, identify potential friends or foes at a distance, and generally remember where all these things are more or less likely to occur. In a more facetiously but not inaccurate way, we have the evolutionary problem of a sensory impaired animal covering long distances everyday to placate a ravenous hunger for resources. Such an animal also has an enormous information management problem. Ecce *Homo*!

At some point, human ancestors embarked on an adaptation that selected for the utilization of the maximum amount of resources, which led to an adaptational flexibility that came to greatly outstrip other mammalian competitors. Dogs can make much more subtle distinctions between resources based only on smell, but the resources they are paying attention to are much more circumscribed.

In all but emergency times, carnivores are looking only for animal protein. As such, they became very good at discriminating between kinds of protein.

I believe that the primary impetus for language was a mental mechanism that allowed us to use icons and labels. Deacon has referred to us as the "symbolic species." As primates, hominids were always denied acute senses of smell and hearing but not sight. When sight became the most important sense in combination with a remarkably diverse diet and adaptation to long-distance travel, sensory processing mechanisms, and not the senses themselves, were selected for. In a very real sense, there was no evolutionary alternative to survival. For humans it is not the mind's eye that is important, it is the eye's mind.

This theory emphasizes the ability of language to "chunk" a lot of information under a single linguistic symbol, which preserves the multisensory nature of experiences. The phenomenon of chunking has been noted in many psychology texts, but its importance in humans has never been sufficiently emphasized in my opinion. One of the things that language allows humans to do is to carry around a huge amount of accessible information without having to constantly inventory and be aware of it. This works somewhat like the icons on computers in that we are aware that the information is there to be called up whenever we need it. This may indeed be what we mean by consciousness. A single word or phrase can affect humans at all three levels of the triune brain. A symbol can do the same thing. Consider the information stored under the linguistic icons *mom*, *motel*, *Thanksgiving*, or *God*. These nouns activate a number of areas in the brain. The arguably concrete noun *God* is especially effective in activating the posterior temporal lobe. One researcher has even suggested that there is a "God organ" or lobe of the brain.

On a more speculative note, it can be suggested that nouns have a greater emotional impact than verbs. This would be in keeping with the suggestion that most people's right hemispheres deal with nouns, especially concrete nouns, much better than they do with verbs. Despite the use of nouns like *freedom, slavery, love* and *hate*, concrete nouns like *handcuffs, whip, Marilyn Monroe*, and *Hitler* seem to elicit greater emotional responses. The more specific the icon, the easier it is to recall information. There has been considerable debate about where linguistic memories are stored. The most recent research indicates that memories are much more global than previously suspected. I suspect that words are more effective for chunking than visual forms, but there is no consensus about this opinion. There is, however, a good consensus that the learning of written word proceeds more effectively when the words are pronounced or at least mentally pronounced as they are read. There is also no psychological consensus about whether we think in words, symbols, or both. ASL signers report thinking in forms and "thoughts." In our quest to understand language, we inevitably stray very close to metaphysics, a cultural universal that takes the form of religion.

Following this interpretation, the patient who no longer recognized the word for carrot may have simply lost the icon or "control" button for carrot. Thus, he could remember the tactile, visual, and taste characters of a carrot, but not its name. In support of this interpretation are recent studies that suggest that a second language learned after childhood is not stored in the same area as a native language. Conversely, two first languages learned simultaneously are stored in the same areas.

From an evolutionary perspective, the icon theory may also explain female superiority in terms of the need to label a number of qualities of gatherable resources. It may also explain why even young females show superior linguistic ability. This is tied to human ecology by the fact that females in hunter and gatherer societies typically become productive economic members of a group at an earlier age than males. Boys require years of development of strength and coordination to become effective hunters. The unfair biological fact is that while little girls are busy helping their mothers, little boys are playing. This is of course a broad generalization, but one that most anthropologists can confirm. Successful and efficient gathering requires a long-term knowledge of the location, suitability (ripeness, quantity), and reliability of a particular resource. While such information is also useful in hunting, it depends to a great extent on the chance that this kind of past information about a particular animal resource is still consistently useful. Returning over and over again to the location of a previous kill is an ineffective hunting strategy, but it is a valuable gathering strategy.

Hunters must contend with an unknown distance, direction, and location. Preparations for a hunting party require a calculus into which supplies (tools, water, food) must be factored. The supplies for a female harvesting trip can be determined much more precisely. The fact that such sex differences are present before puberty suggests that they are not just hormonally mediated. Given the difference in economic productivity between boys and girls, the human hunter and gatherer past is highly consistent with such differences.

Linguistically, these differences are less apparent in the modern world where most destinations are fixed. However, women are better at remembering the location of objects, while males are better at learning routes. In Western society, most of us have heard of or experienced a male asking, "Where is my shirt?" Usually the stereotypical answer from the female is something like, "Wherever you left it." In a similar anecdotal vein, most females will have noticed the tendency of lost males to refuse to stop and ask for directions. Finally, it seems that Western females "go shopping" while males "go out to buy something."

Of importance in the long-distance-wide resource-based adaptation would be the ability to remember sporadically used minutiae that could be quickly recalled, but that did not have to be considered again until they were needed. As with any adaptation, details that were once trivial and irrelevant can suddenly become important in a new environment. This might be at least part of what we mean by "learning." Sharing of the details through language would provide access to even more potential resources.

At some point, travel distance, memory, and categorical organization reached a critical mass. I believe that point was reached with the appearance of our own genus *Homo*. The ability to label and remember things as classes of phenomena, for instance the properties of fruit or edible animals, would have become even more crucial as hominids made the transition from a home-range way of foraging to a migratory way of making a living. This transition had certainly occurred by the time *Homo erectus* left Africa and almost instantly (on the geopaleontological scale) colonized the various environments of Eurasia.

The stages of language acquisition are artificially distinct, though I believe the general order of appearance of these features to be highly probable. Emphatically, feedback between these artificially segregated categories must have been important in early *Homo* as it is today in modern humans. It is almost certain that bipedalism preceded the other adaptations. If Holloway is right, language would have preceded stone tool use, but necessarily for dietary resource expansion. Icon thinking, or chunking, would logically have accompanied tool use, but a more formalized kind of icon thinking would not have appeared until the Acheulean. Following the journey out of Africa, I hypothesize that categorical thinking had evolved and that it facilitated the exploitation of environment encountered in an even more mobile migratory phase. At every stage, language would have increasingly intensified social communication.

None of these postulated stages should be taken as "gospel," but they currently represent best guesses that are consistent with the fossil and archaeological records. Given an evolutionary context, the sequential development from labeling to icon to categorical thinking is in my interpretation also mirrored in the individual language acquisition of children considered below. One aspect of linguistic evolution, which this interpretation is strongly at odds with, is the notion of many linguists that language is of comparably recent origin.

The Antiquity of Languages

Knowledge of our hunter and gatherer past also suggests an age for the emergence of at least some fundamental linguistic abilities. Once again, all the archaeological and behavioral features that first appear in the hominid record by at least 1.5 mya suggests that it is also at this time that language arises. This does not support the much more recent age favored by some archaeologists and many linguists.

Glottochronology (the study of the age of "tongues") attempts to establish the age of languages by comparing the similarities and differences between them and developing estimates of the rates at which linguistic features evolve. This approach assumes that all languages have a common origin or at least a few common origins. As in mitochondrial DNA studies, glottochronologists must also assume something approaching a constant rate of change in languages. One estimate is that about 15 percent of words are replaced every one thousand years. Using this or similar "clocks," most glottochronologists have arrived at a date of between 0.1 to 0.2 mya for the origin of language. As is obvious from our discussion of the origin of modern humans, proponents of the Eve theory welcome this conclusion. Once again, the anatomical and archaeological evidence does not support a recent origin for language. It is difficult to believe that the appearance of cerebral asymmetry, symmetrical stone tools, the use of fire, and the initial migration of hominids out of Africa was not accompanied by the development of at least some form of language.

Some archaeologists have suggested that modern language is tied to the Upper Paleolithic appearance of stone tools such as blades. The argument basically equates finely made and highly standardized blades with sophisticated categories of thought. In fact, among modern people, anthropologists have suggested that there is, in fact, an inverse correlation between technological complexity and cosmological complexity. Put another way, more intricate and diverse material culture is associated with simpler worldviews. While no scholars suggest this relationship as a cultural universal, it can be defended in a number of examples from around the world.

In reference to the fossil record, the argument can also be made for *Homo erectus* and the invention of symmetrical tools. Early *Homo* also shows increased cranial capacity and more modern cerebral reorganization in comparison with earlier hominids. Anatomically modern humans show no such anatomical differences in their neuroanatomy in comparison with their immediate predecessors. In other words, the brains of Upper Paleolithic humans and the brains of ancient Greeks do not differ anatomically from the brains of modern people. However, it is easy to argue that modern sociotechnological day-to-day existence is much more complex and that monotheistic religions are simpler than those associated with hunters and gatherers. However, it is difficult to defend the idea that some languages are more complex or difficult than others. Therefore, it seems highly unlikely in the absence of a gradation of complexity of extant languages that there was a past gradation of diachronic languages in the past. The fact that there are no "primitive" languages may argue that there never were and that language has, at least over the course of at least one million years, been an all-or-nothing phenomena. The archaeological record does indicate that complex behavior takes time to accumulate regardless of the anatomical equivalency of modern human brains.

Individual Language Acquisition

I believe that human language acquisition broadly follows the stages at which our species acquired language. This is a highly controversial hypothesis but, like other good hypotheses, is highly consistent with the paleoanthropological evidence. All individuals in all cultures develop language in a sequential and predictable way, which has a biological basis. The psychologist Jean Piaget (1896–1980) suggested that linguistic development is intimately linked with the development of such concepts as self and other. Children seem to organize the linguistic and perceptual world first into labeling and then into basic classes or categories, which they later increasingly subdivide into more precise and intricate categories. The first stage of babbling interestingly enough functions as a very precise (and obviously limbic) self-identification signal for adults. If music is not perceived at this stage, a response to it follows soon after. *Ma* quickly transforms itself from a label for a single individual into a class of humans known as *mommies*. In the United States, all nonhuman mammals are likely to first be referred to as *cat* or *dog* depending on the household. Thus, the first encounter with a bear is likely to be filed under cat, which signifies all animals. In Sequoia National Park, I once had to prevent my little brother from going out to play with a 600-pound bear, which he labeled *kitty*. Children's abilities to formulate categories, whether they are verbal or conceptual (and there is probably very little difference), is one of the many current mysteries of the universe. According to a recent study, a dog is still a dog if you shave it, and is probably still a dog if you remove its skin, but not a dog if you keep the coverings and take out the insides. Somehow, little hominids evolved to classify, name, and communicate their world.

The acquisition of a second language is well known to be much easier for children. If begun at an early enough date, children grow up to be equally fluent in more than one language. It is also true that a foreign language learned after the age of twelve can seldom be learned without an accent. (There is of course individual variation in linguistic skills at any age.) Why adults should be less plastic may be at least partially explainable on a neuronal level. The neurons (brain cells) develop a number of interconnections before the age of two. After this age, most of them are progressively lost as the brain matures. It is now known that in young brains there are a number of alternate pathways leading to the same location. In this state, the brain can be referred to as "soft wired" because alternate paths are available for signals. If one is destroyed, others already exist that can be activated or emphasized. As the number of connections are reduced, fewer and fewer paths are available for signals. When the number of paths are reduced to a minimum, we can think of the neuronal connections as "hard wired." All brain injuries, when received early on in an individual's development, have a much better chance of exhibiting normal function than if they are received as adults. This process is almost certainly not limited to linguistic skills and probably applies to the acquisition and retention of many kinds of knowledge and skills. Language, however, may be one of the best examples. Two native tongues learned at an early age are located in the same portion of the brain. However, a language (or languages) learned after puberty is stored in a different (though usually adjacent) part of the cortex than the native language. Thus, certain kinds of trauma are now known to affect one of a multilingual individual's language but not the other.

Though it is not clear why, females are more likely to show less initial brain damage and recover more normal functions than males. It is quite likely that testosterone in some way mediates the loss of alternate connections. Note that this interpretation does seem to be consistent with the idea that testosterone suppresses the maturation of the left side of the brain in most males. It is also now clear that in comparison with males, females use more of their brain in a number of tasks. Logically, any localized lesion would be less likely to alter the female neural system as a whole.

I contend that this approach to the world is also reflected in many language structures across the planet. Chinese language speakers and many other Asian languages divide much of the world into basic nouns, which are then modified by descriptive terms. In Thai, the word for water is augmented by other words to produce the name for any kind of liquid. English does the same thing when naming kinds of cats and sciences ("ologies"). This kind of organization reflects a filing system that has obvious uses for hunters and gatherers. It describes the noun and its attributes.

With the globalization of the world village, language acquisition has entered a new phase in which new nouns and to a lesser extent verbs are assimilated phonetically. However, languages (to greatly varying extents) preserve or abandon native words. Thai, for instance, adopted the English words for *ham* and *bacon* as *mu (pork) ham* and *mu bacon*. The extent to which modern Japanese phoneticizes Western words is legendary. Ten to twenty percent (or more) of modern Japanese is of Western origin. Chinese, on the other hand, has a long history of resisting the assimilation of foreign words but not foreign concepts. As a fluent speaker of Mandarin, I can think of few borrowed words that have not been rendered into Chinese concepts. Although educated Chinese now readily recognize *komputa* for *computer,* for years *computer* was referred to in Chinese as *electric brains,* and calculators are still *hit the calculating device. Hamburger,* however, did enter the language as *hambobo.* I believe that the willingness and tendency to adopt new words may reflect cultural flexibility and ethnocentricity. This is not a politically correct opinion, but it is not at all at odds with history. I further believe that languages like English, which are simultaneously known for the ease with which they assimilate new words and yet preserve their ethnicity, may indicate an adaptability that needs to be studied to aid the preservation of the cultural diversity of the planet.

Language and Society

Claude Lévi-Strauss, the French structuralist (a school of anthropologists that investigates the mental structures underlying human thought and language), was interested in how people use language to organize their thoughts and their world in general. Lévi-Strauss believed that all people organized their thoughts not only in words but also in terms of opposites. We saw previously that some aphasias support this notion. There are certain obvious exceptions; one of these is colors. Most cultures generally agree on the classification of the primary colors red, blue, and yellow. However, there is little agreement on further subdivisions of these colors or on colors that are perceived as related. Gradations of colors may depend heavily on the idiosyncratic experience and cultural environment.

Other notable examples of perceptual differences can also be found, such as the Eskimos' classification of kinds of snow (for example, color) or the classification of the intensity of pain. However, as the widespread use of computers demonstrates, almost any phenomenon, including graded phenomena, can be described in a digital binary way, that is, most phenomena can be crudely classified as closer or farther from any point of reference. It is unlikely that the brain works in such a simple way. However, in terms of social relationships, all societies seem to have terms that rank people as socially closer or farther from themselves. We generally refer to the system of these terms as kinship. People also have social terms for denoting social rank, though these may be minimal in many hunter and gatherer groups. As noted previously, terms denoting rank and kinship of individuals that in fact have no close genetic relationship are termed **fictive kin.** These are those individuals who have been accorded the status usually reserved for true consanguineous (related by blood) relatives. They may include "brother" or "sister," denoting equality, or "mother" or "father" or "aunt" and "uncle." These terms denote social ranking and proximity. This type of naming is extremely common throughout the world. Together they illustrate the importance that humans put on establishing and publicly identifying social relationships with language. This perspective lends support to the idea that language evolved, at least in part, as a device for efficiently organizing human society.

Sex and Gender in Language

Much has been written about sex and gender (social qualities pertaining to a particular sex), especially in modern U.S. society. In general, it has been pointed out that in the United States and many other non-Western societies that males are generally given titles or referred to by terms that connote superiority to females. Females are often assigned a diminutive title. The terms *sir* or *madam* appear to denote social equality, and in fact many times they are used this way in public and somewhat impersonal situations. The terms *man* and *wife,* which commonly appear in tandem in Western society, differ in that man denotes sex, but wife denotes a sociosexual function. This stems directly from the fact that until recently most important public social roles were those of men. Furthermore, in many societies females are still effectively and sometimes quite literally male property. From a more biological point of view, there is an interesting linguistic patterning to language having to do with sex, reproduction, and social position. Sociobiologists have offered a biological explanation for this phenomenon. We shall use examples from our own society while noting that, although widespread, the way in which gender and sex is reflected in language varies greatly from society to society.

Names and Derogatory Slang

In our society, at least until recently, the married female took the last name of the male. In English, many last names referred originally to an occupation. Obvious examples include Miller, Clark (British for clerk), Carpenter, Cooper, Mason, Shepherd, and so on. Last names are also used to denote ancestry or place of origin (for example, Jacobson, Bengurion, MacDuff, De Chardin, and de Tocqueville). A comparison of male and female first names, with the exception of those derived from the Bible, exhibit an interesting pattern in English. Men are seldom named after months, while woman frequently are. These include March, April, May, June, Julie (July), Augusta (August), Spring, and Autumn. The few male month names originate from individuals who had months named after them: July (Julius) and August (Augustus). What is apparent is that no fall (with the exception of autumn) or winter months are represented. Few people name their daughters after any months from September through February. A similar emphasis on fertility appears in another group of female names: Daisy, Rose, Iris, Violet, Petunia, Laurel, Heather, and others. Although culturally unrelated, this pattern also appears in Chinese male and female names, with females being named for flowers and seasons and males being named for public accomplishments and virtues that the family hopes for. However, English Christians also name females for publicly recognized virtues: Hope, Faith, Charity, and Chastity.

Yet another group of female names can be found in gems: Ruby, Sapphire, Opal, Pearl, and Jade. The pattern that emerges for male and female names in English is that males tend to be named by occupation and ancestry, while females are named for objects of value and fertility.

The use of nonanatomical insulting slang terms reveals a similar pattern for females, but a more diffuse pattern for males. In English there are over two hundred slang terms for females but only perhaps as many as fifty for males. Female terms include *tomato* (in a previous generation), *peach, doll, babe, baby-doll, chick,* and *bird* (in England). Although in recent generations some of these terms have been extended to both sexes, their origin, like the seasonal first names of females, derives from female referents connoting fertility. *Gal* is simply a corruption of *girl,* and *chick* probably derives from the Spanish *chica* (girl). However, *chic* may be perceived in English as representing a baby chicken (chickadee). Male slang names are much more neutral, usually connoting only maleness. These include *bud, buddy, chap, bloke, fellow, guy, mac, dude, boy,* and *man.* Although there is a female equivalent of these last two terms (*girl* and *woman*), they are limited largely to ethnic subcultures. What is interesting is that not only do English speakers feel a need to identify the sex of people, but also that there are so many more pronouns for females than for males. Many languages do not formally differentiate between males and females in everyday speech. None of them seem to have as many slang terms as English. At least part of this diversity comes from the fact that English speech has absorbed the terms of many other languages. One suspects that whatever the origin of the words, there is some reason for identifying sex when possible.

Derogatory Female and Male Terms

Derogatory female and male terms also exhibit a concern with fertility and ancestry. (Note: Both sexes can be referred to using reproductive and scatological anatomy.) For females, an obvious concern with sexual activity is evident in derogatory terms, which include *bitch, slut, strumpet, trollop, tramp, whore, chippy, witch, spinster, old maid,* and *biddy.* All of these terms have implications of fertility and sexual activity. It is interesting that females are ridiculed for (1) not having sex, (2) giving sex away for free, and (3) charging for sex. The last four terms refer to females that are past the point of fertility or who refuse sex probably for assumed reasons of infertility.

Male insults are also related to sex and fertility, but in a different way. Male insults include *son of a bitch, bastard, motherfucker* (originally male, but now used by both sexes), and *yo'mama* (implying your mother is described by one of the female derogatory terms). In contrast with females, males are rarely criticized for giving away sex, refusing it, or charging for it. They are criticized with reference to their ancestry. In Chinese, one of the worst things you can call a man is *son of a sea-turtle* because the laying female turtle makes a sound that is disgusting to Chinese speakers. Once again, there are far fewer derogatory terms for males than for females. *Liar, thief,* and *coward* can be applied to both sexes, but in English, they are much more frequently associated with the actions of males. As with English male surnames, it is their occupation or ancestry and not their sexual activity that is the subject of social criticism.

Terms of Endearment

When males and females become intimate with each other, especially when they are "falling in love" (see Chapter 7), there is a transformation in verbal behavior. The terms of endearment are usually the same for both sexes. These include *honey, sugar, cup-cake, sweety-pie, dumpling, butter-cup,* and not infrequently nonsense names in English. These are truly "sugary" terms. Other terms include *baby, pet,* and *dear.* The only other context in which these terms typically occur is during childhood. Also returning from the childhood years is the tendency to use diminutive forms of words often used by adults to talk to infants and small children. During intimacy, especially while one is falling in love, speech becomes more paedogenic (childlike). As we shall see in the next chapter, there are probably good biological reasons for this that relate to the fact that humans undergo periods of their life during which they are highly susceptible to both linguistic and conceptual imprinting.

Other Forms of Communication

As mentioned previously, humans also communicate in a multimodal manner in the same way as other primates through gesture, posture, and especially facial expression. As with most types of human behavior, there is substantial variation between cultures. However, there are not surprisingly certain universal forms of communication found in all cultures. Although most higher primates are capable of the same range of gestures as humans, human cultures have a far greater range with specific meanings. Posture is also influenced by culture, but once again, certain postures have the same meaning in all cultures. The most visually complicated signaling system is the face. It is this part of the body that we gaze on first when interacting with other people.

Facial Expression

One of Darwin's other works was his book on *The Expression of Emotion in Man and Animals.* Darwin's baseline of comparison was as its title implies—other animals. In humans, the face is an extremely important "organ of communication." It is therefore hard to see why the males of many human groups retain so much facial hair. One could argue that male whiskers developed only after humans moved into cold climates, but many African groups also have whiskers, while other people living in cold climates lack facial hair. Facial hair may simply be a teleomatic factor resulting from the fact that males have more testosterone, which stimulates the growth of body hair in general. However, a well-known experiment may indicate otherwise. When the same lecture was given to two different audiences by the same man who was not an expert on the subject, the lecturer was more likely to be believed if he wore a false beard. In most cultures, a beard is associated with adulthood, and a gray beard is associated, for obvious reasons, with wisdom and experience. Some experiments have also suggested that bearded men win more arguments and are perceived of as more aggressive. In our culture, beards can also convey a lack of "normalcy" and conformity often associated with qualities ranging from wisdom to drug use.

Covering the face does mask much of facial expression, which may perhaps aid those who are trying to hide emotions. On the other hand, it can also be argued that beards interfere with those trying to establish rapport and empathy with another person. In other cultures, such as those of Native Americans and of some Asians, the facial hair is plucked out as it grows in. The mustache may be thought of as a partial beard. Its form and presence in various cultures has many different connotations. It is interesting that the meaning of facial hair not only varies greatly from culture to culture, but that it has varied greatly in our own culture. In the United States, beards were the rule for men until shortly after the turn of the century. Perhaps the invention of the cheap safety razor, but more likely the various wars of the twentieth century and the perceived need for orderliness, made a clean-shaven face the often required rule. In the 1950s and 1960s, those that disapproved of normalcy adopted beards once again. Long hair in males also returned. Although it is difficult to link male facial hair to any definite biological function, the fact that it must be consciously cared for in order not to interfere with eating suggests that it may have an important evolutionary function.

Excessive female facial hair development is considered unattractive in our society. Female axillary and pubic hair is considered acceptable in some Western societies and undesirable in others. In most of the subcultures of Western society, the shaping of eyebrows receives considerable attention to the point that females will endure unpleasant modifications such as plucking and electrolysis. The same is true for the removal of female "mustaches."

The primary functions of eyebrows and eyelashes are probably to protect the eyes. However, as mentioned previously, all cultures recognize the eye flash as a sign of greeting or recognition. In our culture, females often try to make their eyebrows more aesthetic. Eye contact is a very important part of nonverbal communication. Among many, if not all, mammals, direct gaze into another's eyes is a signal of aggression. It also functions this way in humans, but it can also signal encouragement or sexual attraction. Most cultures have explicit or implicit rules for situations in which this behavior is permissible. Studies have also shown that dilated pupils are sexually attractive. As Desmond Morris has pointed out, many photographs used in advertisements have been retouched with this in mind. In all cultures, there is a tremendous emphasis on communication that is carried out with the eyes. The importance of eye communication to humans is represented in a number of phrases in many cultures.

The smile is a unique form of human signaling. It occurs in the same kinds of contexts in all societies. As mentioned in the chapter on nonhuman primates, it is difficult to see how this behavior may have evolved and been transformed from its original plesiomorphic mammalian meaning. There is no doubt that the smiling reflex is not learned because it is present very soon after birth. The grimace is the counterpart to the smile, but may have a number of meanings, none of which connote pleasure and most of which connote disgust, fear, and aggression. Cross-cultural investigations indicate that all cultures agree on the facial recognition of fear and disgust. Furthermore, cultures everywhere also differentiate between these two expressions.

Happiness and sadness and their visual and auditory correlates, laughter and crying, are equally human forms of communication. Deacon has speculated that they have their roots in selection pressures for social cohesiveness. He also points out that these modes of communication are the first to appear in infants. There can be no doubt that they convey important information to parental caretakers, especially mothers. Other mammals have equivalent signaling systems in the form of squealing and tail wagging. It is not surprising that as higher primates, humans also involve facial expressions in these emotions, but the nonlinguistic sounds that accompany these expressions are still a mystery. They may result from the physical alteration of the breathing apparatus for speech. The smile may result from an emotional-limbic override of the normally highly monitored, controlled, and "supervised" muscles of speech. Weeping may be subject to a similar override that results in a cessation of controlled rhythmic breathing necessary for speech. It is possible to speculate that fast-acting neurotransmitters related to endorphins may eventually prove to be mediators in these phenomena.

Although this is a very brief and simplistic survey of the main forms of facial communication, it is clear that none of these signaling mechanisms function alone, and it is the total constellation of all these features working together with facial muscles that convey various emotions. People from any culture can be shown facial pictures of happiness, rage, surprise, fear, disgust, and friendliness and agree on their meaning. Looks alone are seldom enough in human communication, and language always enhances the precision and meaning of this form of human interaction.

Postural Signals

The meaning of the attitude and orientation of the body and its various parts differs from culture to culture. However, there are a few generalities that seem to hold up. Bowing and kneeling, though not used in every culture, are almost always understood as deference or submission. Crossing the legs while sitting is considered to be rude or a self-isolating mechanism in a number of cultures. Though not consciously considered as such in the West, it has been suggested that open legs signal openness. Though anyone that has seen the film *Basic Instinct* may understand why a sexual motive may underlie this interpretation, in our culture this phenomenon is further confused by the premium we put on female legs. Sitting or standing rigidly seems to connote formal attention or vigilance in most cultures, but this is once again variable. Many cultures also interpret one's own hands on one's own hips as disapproval. It certainly functions this way in many Western contexts.

There is also no doubt that the way we walk is a cultural phenomenon. People of different ethnic groups or races acquire the walk of the people in the environment in which they are raised. Walks can and frequently are exaggerated to emphasize male and femaleness. These are learned qualities. The same is true of aggressiveness, alertness, or relaxation. All of these can be communicated through the way one walks.

One of the evolutionarily important aspects of human communication is probably the ability to identify the composition of human groups from a distance. This is consistent with the uniquely large foraging range of hunters and gatherers. Determining the sexual composition of a group would have been very important. A group of hunting males will react to an all-female or all-male group in very different ways. Group composition is signaled at a distance by body shape and size, age, gate, hair, and implements. Body adornment is also an effective means of communicating and identifying strangers. The nature of such long-distance signals vary greatly, but they are always present in some form.

Gestural signals are also variable, but seem much more universal. One of the most common if not universal gestures involves either the exposure of an open empty hand or handshake seen in Western cultures. A very similar greeting is also seen when chimpanzees greet each other. In a number of cultures, one's own hands are pressed together either in the form of homage or as a kind of self-greeting gesture. The degree to which the near universality of the handshake is a diffusion of Western culture is probably substantial. The main significance of all the greeting rituals is that they involve the hands. Not only does an empty hand signify the absence of weapons, but the hand and fingers are one of the most sensitive parts of the body. On the other hand, Nuguini (New Guinea) men greet by grabbing each other's penis.

The opposite of an open hand is a closed fist, which for obvious reasons is nowhere taken as a sign of greeting. Desmond Morris has pointed out that a further elaboration of the closed fist is the baton in which the closed fist is raised, shaken, or pounded on a surface. Modified batons also occur in the form of a pointed finger. In very few cultures is pointing at people or sacred objects considered other than rude. In general, the baton is always aggressive or at least assertive. Morris further pointed out that this gesture is very common among dominant males.

Other gestures involving the fingers take an almost infinite number of meanings. Despite the intuitive feeling that the communication of numbers under ten and such basic acts as drinking water and eating food would be fairly uniform, in fact their signals vary tremendously. Chinese, for instance, indicate six by holding up the thumb and little finger of one hand. Ten is a clenched fist. Most gestures for the intake of food and water do motion toward the mouth, but the form that the hands take can be very different. To indicate a desire for water, Westerners form a cup with two hands, !Kung San Bushmen form a cup with one hand, and Chinese and other Asians form a sort of teapot with their thumb and little finger.

Similarly, the gesture for insanity involves the head, but many different gestures are made with the hand in the direction of the head. Even *yes* and *no* is not standardized. In India, moving the head from side to side means *yes*. In China and Thailand, nonmovement of the head means *yes*. It is be interesting that neither of these languages has a single word for "no." A shrug of the shoulders may mean *yes, no,* or *I don't know* depending on the culture and the social context. The lesson to be drawn here is that with a few exceptions, human gestural language is as varied as spoken language. The same neural substrates may underlie each type of communication, but the details differ greatly. People who have impaired or lost their spoken linguistic abilities can frequently be retaught to communicate through alternative gestural or symbolic means.

Music, Dancing, and Art

We have mentioned previously that music, dancing, and art are present as cultural universals. At the risk of venturing into the realm of philosophy and aesthetics, we will say only a few words about art (form and color) and music in general. As John Pfeiffer has speculated, these two forms of human expression have a great deal of power to promote group cohesiveness and cultural identity both between and within cultures. Like sex, eating, or play, these have a tremendous potential to be pleasurable or unpleasant. The common feature of visual art and music is that they are meant to have an audience. In modern Western society, these works are usually performed by specialists, but in hunter and gatherer societies, they involve the execution and the enjoyment by and for the audience. One is very tempted to conclude that singing songs around campfires is quite possibly universal. The same may also be true of storytelling. The effect of these activities is one of group cohesion through entertainment.

Music and Dancing

Music has been briefly explored previously as a cultural universal. Despite our propensities to describe certain behaviors of other species in other terms, only humans behave in these manners. Dancing does not require music, but it almost always is associated with it. Music and dancing are unique to humans as a species. In some cultures, dancers create the music, while in others, dancers follow the music. Both forms of expression are emotional and usually public. The many kinds of music and dance are communal and are also powerful mechanisms of fusion and fission. As mentioned previously, music may be intimately connected to the rhythm and cadence of speech. Also like language, music and dance can both facilitate social cohesiveness or social divisiveness. Both are also their own personal reward. In seeming contrast to mathematics, music and melodies are learned spontaneously. Like language, which is also its own reward, music and dance probably fulfill some adaptive function. Organizations that forbid music and dance are going against human nature.

Ballet and rock 'n' roll combine fundamental human propensities for public expression that engage both the mind and the body. Like marriage, kinship, or language, they function as social glues that are public celebrations of emotions and group belonging. All these behaviors must have an important evolutionary function, and it is hard to imagine language and gestures without poetry and music. It is unlikely that any of these behaviors evolved separately or at different times. Humans appear to have an innate intellectual need to be limbic at times. The vast majority of this need is expressed publicly in front of or as part of a cohesive group.

Visual Art

Our examination of the brain convinces us that there are specific association areas that are critical to the appreciation of visual and tactile forms related to color (for example, golden eagle, red apple, scarlet pimpernel). Color and form are extremely important to all humans and primates in general. In fact, in comparison with other animals, humans excel in identifying phenomena on the basis of these two qualities. Lesions to the area where the temporal lobe joins the occipital lobe produce symptoms in which a subject is not able to associate a particular color with a particular form or shape. Although on dangerous empirical grounds, it also seems that there is a certain universality to the effect but not the perception or cultural meaning of colors. The large body of anthropological literature on cultural contrasts and classifications of color between societies makes it clear that some cultures subdivide certain colors to the point where a great deal of confusion can occur in intercultural communication. These differences are almost certainly cultural in origin. There has even been some suggestion of sexual dimorphism in color perception. There may be more of a biological bases for these differences, and male color blindness is a well-known genetic phenomenon.

Setting these problems aside for the sake of discussion, it is possible to examine the psychological effects that colors seem to have on at least some societies as a whole. We can at least do so within our own culture. What we intend to examine is not the cultural, moral, or cosmological meanings that colors have, for these vary tremendously between cultures. Instead, we are interested in the effect on our species that color seems to have.

Black and white are not really colors at all; their association with different moral and physical attributes such as good and bad, death and life, pure or virginal varies tremendously from culture to culture. Their association with dark and light is obvious. In many societies, white is the color of death and evil, and black is the color of nobility and goodness. In any case, these shades produce no consistent reactions in humans. In U.S. society, we are well aware of the connotations of these colors. What is interesting is that we tend to view black and white as opposites. There is some physical reality to this because white light occurs as the result of the combination of all the primary colors, while black represents the absence of any colors or light. It is also interesting that comparatively few national flags emphasize black or white.

Red is very different. In all cultures, red attracts attention. The color red is not surprisingly associated with blood. Red is the most common color in the flags of the world's countries. It is used in separately evolved bureaucracies in both the West and the Far East to call attention to important matters. It is also the most common color used for body adornment of the skin in largely naked people. Sources of red color are very common on the surface of the earth (for example, the iron oxide, ochre), and one might argue that this is why it is so prevalent in hunter and gatherer cultures. More interesting is the fact that all over the world in both prehistoric and historic times, it has been associated with funeral rituals. In Western culture, red connotes warning. In East Asia, it connotes good luck and prosperity.

The reason for the importance of red and the reason that it so readily gets our attention seems intuitively obvious. Human ancestors that did not pay attention to this color may have been selected out of the population millions of generations ago. In addition to being the color of blood, red is also the color of heat (embers) and freshly killed and butchered animals. It is also fairly obvious that shades of red play a part in social and sexual communication. Depending on the situation, blushing can signal anger, excitement, exhaustion, frustration, or embarrassment. Language clarifies the exact meaning of these visual signals.

A lighter shade of red that has been diluted with white (pink) in our culture seems to have a calming and pacifying effect. One example is the case of a police holding tank that was the scene of repeated violent encounters between prisoners. Though the reasons are obscure, the holding tank was repainted pink. Violent interactions between prisoners decreased markedly after it was painted. The reason for this may have to do with the possibility that pinkness connotes sexual activity, which usually does not involve violence. There is no obvious answer to why it had this effect, but after a while, violence once again increased in the tank. This is anecdotal information, but it is very easy to argue that, at least in our culture, pink does not seem to lead to violent emotional states.

Quite the opposite result was obtained when a classroom of mixed blind and sighted students was painted in black and orange stripes. In this experiment, all the children, whether blind or not, became noticeably more agitated and unruly in the striped classroom. As a whole, this observation tends to argue that both color and form have marked emotional effects in humans.

The colors blue and green also have intrinsic effects on the behavior of people. It is no coincidence that all sorts of public institutions are painted "institutional blue" or "institutional green." Surgical rooms and gowns are usually this color to avoid eye strain. Blues and greens relax people. The most prevalent combination of colors on world flags is green and red or blue and red. Although speculative, the psychological message of such emblems may be a simultaneous command to attention and a promise of restful tranquility. More literary minds might term it "War and Peace."

The reason that blues and greens might have such a relaxing effect on people may once again be intuitively obvious. Blues and greens were the most common colors of our surroundings for millions of years. When we go camping for recreation, it is these colors that we generally seek to surround ourselves with. Cities and city dwellers value the greenery of parks and gardens as precious commodities of fecundity and fertility, which as noted above are also reflected in language. It is hard to believe that our evolutionary past has not had a major role in shaping these preferences. Organizations such as Green Peace, which are advocates of ecological preservation, have chosen their name wisely. In our culture, blues have also come to be associated with depression or sadness. "The blues" and "blue funk" are two examples that are associated with a down but contemplative emotional state. Blue is also cool, glacial, and still.

Yellow and orange seem to have yet another kind of psychological effect on us. These colors make us happy and hungry respectively. Again, there is an evolutionary explanation deriving from the natural world. Most ripe vegetable foods are yellow and orange. It is also true that meat that has been lying around in the sun quickly turns to shades of these colors. As mentioned in a previous chapter, it is scavenging (rather than hunting) that probably characterized the early stages of hominid evolution. Even after meat was killed, hunters probably did not refuse to eat meat that had turned brown. Most scavengers are not this picky. With the exception of raw meat, very little of what we put in our mouths is red or blue. By the same token, there is no coincidence about the color of the "golden arches" at McDonald's or the orange interiors of Howard Johnson's and most other coffee shops. Denny's is yellow and Wendy's is yellow and red. Taco Bell is yellow, red, and brown. This is in contrast to Kentucky Fried Chicken's red and white motif and Popeye's largely red colors.

Madison Avenue and You

Advertising for everything from politicians to soap powder attempts to manipulate people on a daily basis. Sometimes they have discovered powerful techniques for attracting your attention and persuading you to do what they want. The technique of subliminal advertising was found to be effective enough that it was banned several decades ago. This technique flashed a brief almost imperceptible visual message to the brain that is long enough to be remembered, but not long enough to be consciously perceived. Advertising companies know that jingles are learned much more easily than mathematical theorems—at least in Western cultures. Every American can repeat the McDonald's theme, but far less can write a Euclidean proof. Music is innate. Counting and manipulating large numbers is not. Goods in the United States still sell for $19.95, and a number of people hum advertising jingles to themselves during each day. Many languages have a word for amounts over 3 or 10 or 20 that translates as *a lot*. English has equally vague phrases such as *a few, a bunch* (a fascinating term given our foraging past), *a passel* and many others. This makes perfect sense because one does not have to count bananas to know that there are enough or more than enough. The concept of much or few is embedded in every language. Precise counting and the complex manipulation of numbers is not a legacy of our evolutionary past but is an outcome of our agricultural and industrial history.

Advertisers have stumbled on to these shopping windows of opportunity, but they do not know from whence they came. The origin of the effectiveness of any campaign strategy that is used to sell anything is our innate willingness to be social and acquire resources in social contexts. The structure of the brain makes possible and ensures that we will participate in groups. Music and a fondness for colorful forms as symbols of well-being are the evolutionary bases of always fluid social convictions.

Other manipulations are almost as subtle. It should never be forgotten that primates are color-perceiving animals and that humans not only perceive color but also attach moral significance to them. Red, white, and blue appears to be no coincidence and, as mentioned previously, includes the two most common colors found in the world's flags. Holidays also have specific color combinations. In the United States, Halloween is orange and black (fall ripeness and the darkness of night, but now also disturbing) and Christmas is red and green and white (the hearth, and rebirth in the middle of snow). Easter is yellow and pink (fertile). Red is the most expensive color for new cars. Almost every formal organization has distinctive colors that identify it to other groups and philosophies.

Physical Touch

Physical touch is an important part of human communication. Interestingly, physical touch divides largely into acts of intimacy or acts of aggression; in between are greetings (a handshake or a threatening baton). The amount of interpersonal physical contact and interpersonal space varies tremendously with emotional state and culture. The Harlows' experiments demonstrated that all primates require interpersonal physical contact for normal maturation; they cannot mature normally without it.

Almost all specific modes of physical touch are employed in private and public communication. Who we allow to touch, where and when are culturally determined but universal categories of social communication. Some of these tendencies have obvious roots in our primate heritage; others are specifically programmed by the cultural environment. Humans emphasize gestures and facial expressions more than other primates, not only because of their freed limbs and hands, but also because so much of the brain is devoted to the hands and face. Those that wish to manipulate people know that many standard signals work, but most do not know why they work. It is this perspective that an evolutionary viewpoint provides. Like all human propensities, the potential for good and evil is manifold.

Summary

As with other animals, human communication is multimodal. It is also limbic and nonlimbic. Humans differ from other primates in their natural use of language. Despite years of intense research and experiments, chimpanzees cannot be shown to possess linguistic abilities beyond those of a three-year-old human. Claims of humanlike linguistic capabilities put forward by some researchers cannot be substantiated. Ape communications are limbic in nature in that they convey only the current feeling or desire of the communicator.

The origin of human language is still debated, and a number of theories have been proposed, most of which do not fit well with either the paleoanthropological evidence or the observation of modern humans. Glottochronologists have greatly underestimated the antiquity of languages, and no rates of language evolution can be reliably estimated. In this chapter, I have proposed that language was the solution to an information management problem resulting from a reliance on vision and bipedalism of expanding foraging ranges that concentrated on an enormously wide range of dietary and nondietary resources. The brain developed the ability to store large amounts of information as rapidly retrievable information. The notion of self and consciousness is probably also intertwined with the evolution of language and helps to account for the selection of an innate language "organ" in the brain.

Humans use language to denote and organize almost all parts of their existence. There are distinct social components to language as well as sexual dimorphism. Sex and gender are strongly reflected in some languages, as examples from our own and other cultures show. In other cultures, it is impossible to discern the sex or even number of individuals being discussed without specifically asking. Concepts of time, space, and numbers, as represented in language and art, differ greatly from culture to culture. Regardless of the differences, the categories of different language are essentially identical. There are nouns, verbs, subjects, and objects and rules for relating parts of the world to each other. The existence of grammar and syntax may derive from and be based on the concept of self. This is the reference point from which all language is comprehended.

Humans also communicate visually using posture, gesture, color, and form. Music and dance are also a form of communication that is more than just auditory or kinetic. All of these modes of communication can be used to influence the emotions and actions of humans. Such influences range from group cohesion to advertising. Another important form of signaling involves sexual signaling. Once again, this kind of communication is shared with other primates, but the way in which it is carried out is uniquely human. This is examined in the next chapter.

QUESTIONS FOR REVIEW

1. What are the possible evolutionary functions of language?
2. What does Chomsky mean by the term *language organ?*

3. What is meant by *hard wired* and *soft wired* in regard to brain architecture?

4. How would sociobiologists explain a sexual dimorphism in words of males and females?

5. What are the linguistic differences between Broca's area and Wernicke's area? What are the apparent differences between the left and right hemispheres of the brain?

6. How are gestures used in common ways in different cultures? Are there any universals?

7. What are the commonalities of visual art, music, and dancing? How could they have been selected for in the course of human evolution?

8. How do colors influence the human mind? Why?

9. What devices are used in advertising to get you to buy things?

10. How does ape language and communication differ from human language?

11. What is the icon theory of human language?

MIND AND BODY EXPERIMENTS

1. Compile a list of female and male names from your class (first names and surnames). Is there any pattern to their meanings or origins?

2. Ask a little girl and a little boy, "What are you going to do today?" Compare the details of the replies.

3. Make a list over the course of a few days of the context and ways in which *yes* or *no* are conveyed. Are they associated with any particular body language or gestures?

4. Find a two-year-old and show him or her pictures of animals. Ask the child to name the animals.

5. Ask people to imitate the sound of a dog barking and a cat vocalizing. Record and compare the answers, paying attention to sex, ethnicity, and education.

6. Compare and contrast the flags of various countries. Calculate the percentage of space devoted to each color and the geometric shapes or other symbols used in each flag. What are the commonalities and differences?

7. At a social function, how do you know when someone is "coming on to you"?

8. List all the deductions you can make from simply looking at someone. After that, talk to them. How has your information changed?

9. Compare the popular music of the last five decades (decade by decade). How does it differ in theme, form, and content?

10. List the symbols that you wear on your body. What do you think they convey? Or get a temporary tattoo and tell people it's permanent. How do they react?

11. Stare at a dog. What happens?

SUGGESTED READINGS

Barrow, J., Commies, L., and Toby, J. 1995. *The Adapted Mind, Evolutionary Psychology and the Generation of Culture.* (2nd ed.) New York: Oxford University Press.

Berlin, B, and Kay, P. 1969. *Basic Color Terms: Their Universality and Evolution.* Berkeley: University of California Press.

Bickerton, D. 1984. The Language Bioprogram Hypothesis. *Behavioral & Brain Sciences* 7: 173–221.

Boas, F. 1966. *Race, Language and Culture.* New York: The Free Press.

Brown, R. 1973. *A First Language: The Early Stages.* Cambridge, MA: Harvard University Press.

Brown, R., and McNeill, D. 1966. The "Tip of the Tongue" Phenomenon. *Journal of Verbal Learning & Verbal Behavior* 5: 325–337.

Chomsky, N. 1972. *Language and Mind.* New York: Harcourt, Brace, Jovanovich.

Chomsky, N. 1980. *Rules and Representations.* New York: Columbia University Press.

Deacon, T. 1997. *The Symbolic Species, The Co-evolution of Language and the Brain.* New York: W. W. Norton.

Falk, D. 1975. Comparative Anatomy of the Larynx in Man and the Chimpanzee: Implications for Language in Neanderthal. *American Journal of Physical Anthropology* 43(1): 123–132.

Falk, D. 1987. Human Paleoneurology. *Annual Review of Anthropology* 16: 13–30.

Fouts, R. 1985. Friends of Washoe. *Central Washington University*: Winter.

Fouts, R., Fouts, D., and van Cantfort, T. 1989. The Infant Louis Learns Signs from Cross-Fostered Chimpanzees. In R. Gardner, B. Gardner, and T. van Cantfort (eds.), *Teaching Sign Language to Chimpanzees.* Albany: State University of New York Press.

Gardner, B. T., and Gardner, R. A. 1975. Evidence for Sentence Constituents in the Early Utterances of Child and Chimpanzee. *Journal of Experimental Psychology: General* 104: 244–267.

Gardner, H. 1983. *Frames of Mind: The Theory of Multiple Intelligences.* New York: Basic Books.

Gardner, R. A., and Gardner, B. T. 1969. Teaching Sign Language to a Chimpanzee. *Science* 165: 664–672.

Gazzaniga, M. 1970. *The Bisected Brain.* New York: Appleton-Century-Crofts.

Gazzaniga, M. 1983. Right Hemisphere Language Following Brain Bisection: A 20-Year Perspective. *American Psychologist* 38: 525–537.

Gazzaniga, M. S. 1985. *The Social Brain.* New York: Basic Books.

Geschwind, N. 1970. The Organization of Language and the Brain. *Science* 170: 940–944.

Hewes, G. W. 1973. Primate Communication and the Gestural Origin of Language. *Current Anthropology* 14: 5–24.

Hickerson, N. P. 1980. *Linguistic Anthropology.* New York: Holt, Rinehart and Winston.

Leroi-Gourhan, A. 1968. The Evolution of Paleolithic Art. *Scientific American,* 218: 58ff.

Levine, S. 1966. Sex Differences in the Brain. *Scientific American*: 84–90.

Liberman, A. M. 1974. The Specialization of the Language Hemisphere. In F. O. Schmitt and F. G. Worden (eds.), *The Neurosciences: Third Study Program.* Cambridge, MA: MIT Press.

Liberman, A. M. 1982. "On Finding That Speech Is Special. *American Psychologist* 37:148–167.

Lieberman, P. 1975. *On the Origins of Language: An Introduction to the Evolution of Human Speech.* New York: Macmillan.

Lieberman, P. 1979. Hominid Evolution, Supralaryngeal Vocal-Tract Physiology and the Fossil Evidence for Reconstructions. *Brain & Language* 7: 101–126.

Lieberman, P. 1984. *The Biology and Evolution of Language.* Cambridge, MA: Harvard University Press.

Lieberman, P., Crelin, E. S., and Klatt, D. H. 1972. Phonetic Ability and the Related Anatomy of the Newborn, Adult Human, Neanderthal Man, and the Chimpanzee. *American Anthropologist* 74: 287–307.

Luria, A. R. 1964. Factors and Forms of Aphasia. In A. V. S. de Reuch and M. O'Connor (eds.), *Disorders of Language.* Boston: Little, Brown.

Luria, A. R. 1966. *Higher Cortical Functions in Man.* London: Tavistock.

Luria, A. R. 1970. The Functional Organization of the Brain. *Scientific American*:66–79.

Needham, R. 1972. *Belief, Language and Experience.* Chicago: University of Chicago Press.

Parker, S. T., and Gibson, K. R. 1979. A Developmental Model for the Evolution of Language and Intelligence in Early Hominids. *Behavioral & Brain Sciences* 2: 367–408.

Patterson, F. 1983. Why Koko (and Michael) Can Talk Gorilla. 6: 2.

Patterson, F., and Linden, E. 1981. *The Education of Koko*. New York: Holt, Rinehart and Winston.

Pavlov, I. 1927. *Conditioned Reflexes*. New York: Oxford University Press.

Penfield, W., and Rasmussen, T. 1950. *The Cerebral Cortex of Man: A Clinical Study of Localization of Function*. New York: Macmillan.

Penfield, W., and Roberts, L. 1959. *Speech and Brain Mechanisms*. Princeton, NJ: Princeton University Press.

Piaget, J. 1924. *The Language and Thought of a Child*. New York: Harcourt, Brace and World.

Piaget, J. 1954. *The Construction of Reality in the Child*. New York: Basic Books.

Piaget, J. 1973. *The Child and Reality*. New York: Penguin Books.

Premack, A. J., and Premack, D. 1972. Teaching Language to an Ape. *Scientific American* 277(4): 92–99.

Pribram, K. H. 1971. *Languages of the Brain*. Englewood Cliffs, NJ: Prentice-Hall.

Rozin, P., Poritsky, S., and Sotski, R. 1971. American Children with Reading Problems Can Easily Learn to Read English Represented by Chinese Characters. *Science* 171: 1264–1267.

Rumbaugh, D. (ed.). 1977. *Language Learning by a Chimpanzee: The Lana Project*. New York: Academic Press.

Rumbaugh, D., Savage-Rumbaugh, S., and Scanlons, S. 1982. The Relationship between Language in Apes and Human Beings. In I. King and J. Forbes (eds.), *The Lance Project*. 361–385. New York: Academic Press.

Skinner, B. F. 1957. *Verbal Behavior*. New York: Appleton-Century-Crofts.

Slobin, D. I. 1971. *Psycholinguistics*. Glenview, IL.: Scott, Foresman.

Swadesh, M. 1959. Linguistics as an Instrument of Prehistory. *Southwestern Journal of Anthropology* 15: 20–35.

Wada, J., and Rasmussen, T. 1960. Intracarotid Injection of Sodium Amytal for the Lateralization of Cerebral Speech Dominance: Experimental and Clinical Observations. *Journal of Neurosurgery* 17: 266–282.

Zaidel, A. 1983. A Response to Gazzaniga: Language in the Right Hemisphere, Convergent Perspectives. *American Psychologist* 38: 542–546.

Zivin, G. (ed.). 1985. *The Development of Expressive Behavior. Biology-Environment Interaction*. Orlando, FL: Academic Press.

CHAPTER

7 Sex, Reproduction, and Love

Of all the causes which have led to the differences in external appearance between the races of man, and to a certain extent between man and the lower animals, sexual selection has been the most efficient.

—Charles Darwin

Pushkin, the poet of women's feet, sung of their feet in his verse. Others don't sing their praises, but they can't look at their feet without a thrill—and it's not only their feet.

—Fyodor Dostoevsky

If then you make the function of reproduction the kernel of sexuality you run the risk of excluding from it a whole host of things like masturbation, or even kissing which are not directed toward reproduction, but which nonetheless are undoubtedly sexual.

—Sigmund Freud

A hard man is good to find.

—Mae West

Most people who examine this text read this chapter first. There is a good reason for this kind of behavior. Whether in the form of regulation or participation, human primates take an extraordinary interest in sex. It is difficult to relate most human sexuality directly to reproduction because mating usually occurs when the female is not fertile. In fact, well over 90 percent of human mating has no direct connection to reproduction. Attempts to explain this discrepancy have often invoked the theory of permanent pair bonding as the feature that accounts for the seemingly unique system of love and reproduction that characterizes the human primate. In this chapter, we consider human sexuality and reproduction from the perspective of sociobiology and natural selection, which suggests that differences in male and female sexuality result from the inherently different stakes that either sex must invest in reproduction. Like other mammals and most vertebrates, human females must devote a substantial amount of their energy to bringing to term and bearing little hominids. Human females appear to be unique among primates in convincing males to also contribute a substantial amount of time and energy toward the rearing of offspring.

Human Reproductive Strategy

More than any other primate, humans have developed a reproductive strategy that emphasizes great **parental investment** and slow maturation. The term *reproduction,* as used here, does not just refer to mating and giving birth. Instead, it is the Darwinian sense of the word that is emphasized, in that it is **viable offspring** that matter in the context of evolution. Human reproductive strategy is an extreme form of the rifle or blue chip approach. Part of Lovejoy's provisioning theory emphasized the close connection between birth spacing, parental investment, and intelligence (see Chapter 8). Humans, although very slow reproducers in comparison with nonhuman primates, arguably raise a greater percentage of their offspring to adulthood. However, there are no firm figures on whether earlier maturing chimpanzees produce a greater total number of offspring. As mentioned previously, the human growth curve is highly **altrical**, meaning that a great deal of development occurs after birth and not in the womb. This altricality is also the key to understanding human intelligence, and it is therefore useful for understanding human reproduction before attempting to comprehend intelligence.

One of the unique aspects of human sexuality is that human females spend more time mating than they do getting pregnant. They do not have distinct seasonal patterns, though there is some seasonality in temperate climates of birth (in North America, most births are in April and May). By far, the most outstanding characteristic of the human mating pattern is not only that it occurs most frequently when the female is not fertile, but also that mating persists long after the production of viable offspring is likely. This has often been interpreted as related to permanent pair bonding. Just as Lovejoy suggested that early hominid females traded sex for food and other forms of long-term male energy input, modern theorists have pointed to the social bond that sex helps create and maintain among humans. An often heard psychological platitude is that females trade sex for intimacy and males trade intimacy for sex. Among humans, sex also bears a great deal of similarity to play in that it persists well after midlife when both play and sexual behavior become greatly reduced in most mammals. It is very hard to see how these types of behavior contribute directly to either Darwinian or inclusive fitness. It may be that postreproductive sexuality is a teleomatic character resulting from the advantage of intense bonding that takes place during the younger child-bearing years. Furthermore, because humans take so long to mature, prolonged sexual bonding may help to provide a more stable family environment for raising adolescents. It is also important to note that humans in healthy environments live far longer than their ancestors of only a few thousand years ago. Theories seeking to explain the evolutionary significance of menopause or prostrate disorders are actually dealing with gerontology and not evolutionary biology. Most people have sex because it is fun.

Sex and Play

In humans, sex and play seem to be closely related. Previously we discussed the infantile behaviors that humans display when engaging in courtship or falling in love and how it is reflected in language and other behaviors. In effect, humans preserve aspects of preadult behavior well into adulthood. In general, prolonged paedogenic behavior in most behavioral aspects is characteristic of humans. This is especially true of sex.

Allan Dundes, an anthropologist and student of folklore, has suggested that some human games and sports reflect human sexuality. Dundes maintains that American football is an acted-out metaphor for sexual activity. Baseball can be subjected to a similar scrutiny. It is possible that common football terms such as *end zone, penetration, thrust, reception, sack, tight end,* and *split end* are really Freudian in nature. He has pointed out that the way the quarterback lines up with his hands in the center's crotch and the frequently seen "fanny pat" may further indicate a homosexual metaphor. In fact, the similarity to sex and football probably derive from the aggressive territorial (and therefore warlike) nature of the game on the one hand and the fact that football padding leaves very few places on the body exposed that are capable of sensing touch. Touch is frequently necessary for communication in a loud and often chaotic situation where time is of the essence.

The analogy between baseball and sex is something that is learned from late childhood onward. Most young teenagers know what "getting to first base" and the bases that follow means in sexual terms. Although adults frequently drop the base analogy, the term *score* is clearly understood in sexual contexts. The same is true of *strike out*. In fact, sports analogies are by no means restricted to informal descriptions of sexual activity. We use sports terminology to describe a variety of activities from presenting reports at meetings to making money. As human beings, we tend to describe the world as a game and a game as the world. All of this reflects the human predisposition toward prolonging childhood. The childlike behavior and emotional state of premating behavior strongly supports this contention. Although all cultures have ways of recognizing boundaries between maturity and immaturity, in comparison with other mammals, we remain childlike longer. Even if Dundes's appraisal of sex and sports is somewhat facetious, the fact that the comparison is interesting and entertaining to most people is telling in itself.

Sexual Attraction

An understanding of human and vertebrate sexuality is further complicated by what has been called the *Coolidge effect*. This refers to a story concerning President Calvin Coolidge's visit to a farm where the farmer proudly pointed out a single rooster that routinely mated several times a day with the farmer's hens. Mrs. Coolidge, who accompanied the president, sarcastically suggested that the president could learn from the rooster, to which the president retorted that many different hens gave the rooster a distinctly greater incentive. Studies of bulls also demonstrate the Coolidge effect: A bull will mate many more times if new cows are continually presented to him.

Novelty in both partners and circumstances enhances sexual attractiveness. In U.S. culture, this seems to be especially true for men. For U.S. females, social position is more important. Many sexual encounters occur in close association with unusual or infrequent life experiences. In U.S. culture, such social functions may include proms, the Christmas office party, an encounter with somebody of higher socioeconomic status, or vacations. A cross-cultural phenomenon is that females usually seem to "marry up" in society, taking mates that are older and more established in the social group. A seemingly valid aphorism is that "power is the greatest aphrodisiac." But so are new surroundings. Both males and females seem to become more sexually excited in new surroundings. I term this the *motel effect*, as couples report a higher level of sexual desire when sleeping in motels or other comfortable lodging outside of the home. I suggest that novelty in partners is much more important for males and that novelty in circumstances is much more exciting to females, at least in U.S. culture.

Conversely (and despite Freudian theory), most siblings are not sexually attracted to each other. The prolonged contact of growing up together insures that sexual novelty is minimal. This has often been confused, in my view, with the *incest taboo*, which adults impose during upbringing to prevent mating within the nuclear family. In fact, sexual exploration among siblings (as opposed to just mating) seems to be common among children of most cultures. What would be regarded by some as homosexual activity in humans occurs regularly in nonhuman primates, where it not only serves the function of play, but also the practice of gestures and postures that are important in the adult dominance hierarchy.

Studies of carnivores report what may be an inverse corollary of the motel effect phenomenon in which carnivores returning to the area in which they were raised show a reluctance to mate. This inhibition may be a natural form of the incest taboo, which decreases the chances of an animal mating with close relatives. Closely inbred groups show a higher frequency of birth defects and deleterious genes. In humans, well-known examples include hemophilia, cleft palate and lip, and lower intelligence test scores. Others have argued that the deleterious effects of incest have been exaggerated and that numerous cultures permit and even encourage unions between relatively closely related relatives. This is especially true in the case of royalty, though the reason behind such arrangements are overtly political and not biological.

Sociobiology can explain a sexual dimorphism in novelty preference as the result of the difference between male and female reproductive potentials. A male attraction to partner novelty reflexes the male attempt to maximize the number of impregnations. Females are programmed to maximize the quality of pregnancies and subsequent parental investment. Males therefore lower the standards to novelty, while females regard novel circumstances as an indication of the male willingness to commit resources. In fact, both sexes seem to like both kinds of novelty, and both will lower their respective standards in the absence of both quantity and quality. Of course, the local cultural upbringing also has a strong influence on mating patterns.

Human sexual behavior differs from all other primates in that it is private. Although consort pairs are formed for mating in nonhuman primates, copulation nonetheless occurs in full view of other primates. Gorillas may be a notable exception because recent studies have maintained that most matings occur in the relative privacy of the nightly nest. However, in most other primates, nonmating individuals are not only interested in the copulation, but in the case of adolescents, they frequently seek to interfere with or participate in it. Despite the general human prohibition against public sexual activity, it is apparent that both humans and nonhuman primates learn a great deal about sexual behavior from observation. Among human societies, despite the strong public prohibition against public sexual activity, pornography is an extremely lucrative industry. The intense primate interest in observing sex suggests that pornography can be extremely effective in shaping sexual attitudes. It is thus potentially both dangerous and beneficial. Among nonhuman primates, the example of a captive gorilla that did not know how to mate until he was shown films of other gorillas mating indicates the importance of observation in the acquisition of effective mating behavior in primates. Another captive gorilla study shows that maternal behavior must also be learned from observation. Among humans and other primates, sex and gender behavior must be learned through observation.

Visual sex is important to humans, but the attractiveness of nakedness varies tremendously between cultures. The definition of nakedness itself varies greatly. Most individuals of either sex like to see the naked parts of the body that they consider attractive. However, no culture reports the naked penis as being attractive, but the males of most cultures report an uncovered vagina as being attractive. In fact, there are very few cultures (perhaps none) that are completely naked. In most cases, covering of adult genitals is usual. It has been suggested that this practice serves the strictly utilitarian practice of protection from injury, but in fact, most covering affords only minimal protection.

Certain males of some cultures of New Guinea not only cover their penises, but also enhance their size with penis sheaths made from gourds. Codpieces, which became popular a few hundred years ago, specifically enlarged the appearance of the penis. High heels and wigs were also invented in France for use by men. The enhancement of sexually dimorphic characters seems to run throughout the animal kingdom. Among deer, it is antlers. Among human males, the emphasis is frequently on muscle size and definition, height, and square body features.

Human females tend to emphasize roundness, but their adoption of high heels in Western culture suggests that height is also an important cultural consideration. It is important that so far most of these emphases seem to be found primarily in Western cultures, but they have quickly spread to non-Western cultures. It has also been suggested that female attractiveness is in fact more universal than previously thought. The ratio of hip-to-waist size has been suggested as being fairly constant in young Western movie stars. In other words, the classic hour glass figure seems to be considered as highly desirable.

The obvious explanation for a universal attractiveness in males and females is that humans seek reproductively superior mates. Both sexes seek reproductively fit mates. Men seek women with "good hips," and females seek men with strength. Some researchers have suggested that men are especially attracted to nubile females. Nubility supposedly indicates fecundity. Conversely, it has also been suggested that females have selected "demonic males" capable of protecting and providing for them and their offspring. Once again, the true evolutionary significance is confounded by the fact that most human mating has nothing to do with reproduction. The temporal oscillation of what is attractive makes the importance of sexual signaling an even more complex subject. Currently, there is no consensus about whether there is a universal formula for sexual attractiveness. In cultures where food is scarce, fat is considered attractive. In most Western cultures, where food is abundant, thin or at least not fat is the preferred morphotype. However, within cultures (especially Western ones), what is attractive has a long history of change. Because humans are uniquely dependent on culture and language, body adornment, speech, and social position also play an immeasurable part in sexual attraction.

The Mystery of the Orgasm

All mammals appear to be capable of orgasm. The evolutionary function of this pleasurable sensation seems to be to maintain the species interest in following the steps necessary for reproduction. (As noted above, most humans have sex because sex is fun.) Among humans, however, while male orgasm is necessary for reproduction, female orgasm is not. Most reports also find that human females do not have orgasms most of the times that they copulate. At the same time, human females are clearly capable of multiple orgasms during a single mating. Most do, however, report that mating with established partners is pleasurable even in the absence of orgasm. Some studies have suggested that female orgasm decreases the acidity of the vagina and uterus and therefore encourages the survival of sperm. Some researchers have also suggested that a female's clitoris may be teleomatic and the result of the fact that in a system requiring male ejaculation, the simplest biological means of achieving this is to insure that both sexes are capable of orgasm. Observation of pygmy chimpanzee mating behavior suggests that female chimpanzees derive pleasure from copulation, though it is difficult to confirm orgasm. As mentioned previously, it has been suggested that orgasm in both sexes encourages long-term bonding, but it may just be that the existence of orgasm in both sexes simply encourages interest in copulation.

In modern societies, especially industrialized ones, unwanted pregnancies remain a widespread problem. This fact presents a dilemma to sociobiological theory. If females are not mating to reproduce, how can they be mating to please the male in order to gain support for the rearing of offspring? If females are simply copulating to gain support for themselves, then such behavior seems to have little to do with inclusive fitness. Socially conditioned aspects of values and biological attraction seem to have much more to do with such situations than inclusive fitness.

Pair Bonding and Pair Breaking

The importance of pair bonding in humans has been strongly emphasized in anthropological literature. In fact, lifelong pair bonding is typical in some cultures and atypical in others. Among nonhuman primates, only gibbons truly mate for life. Although there is no systematic body of data, gibbons who lose their mates or even lifelong companions from another species (humans, for instance) usually suffer deteriorating health and, in many cases, death. Gibbon pair bonding is strongly physiological in nature.

In the Western world, marriage is almost always entered into because of love. Yet in many other societies, love is a consideration secondary to socioeconomic factors. Most of the marriages in the world occur because people want to reproduce with the approval of their society. Economic and utilitarian partnership is also part of this package, but love is something that is expected to occur (if at all) after marriage. In cultures with a long history, infidelity, especially male infidelity, is tolerated if a few basic rules are adhered to. Perhaps the two most basic rules are that extramarital unions should not substantially drain the economic resources of the marriage and that the extramarital partner is not publicly acknowledged, especially in the presence of the spouse. In many Eastern societies, these rules have been formalized in the form of "tea money" for the man. This is a sum that the wife gives back to the man from the resources of the marriage. The sum is negotiated between the couple, and the purpose of the sum is understood and not much discussed unless the amounts become excessive. Although this practice is still widespread, it is becoming less common as the entire globe Westernizes. As birth rate falls in proportion to the education of women, so does the practice of having separate sexual partners in a marriage. I believe that what all this underscores is the economic nature of the unique practice that human primates call marriage.

Among humans, divorce or separation is widespread, especially in industrialized societies. Divorce or loss of a spouse is also a leading social factor associated with a deterioration of physical health. Interestingly, marriage is the second leading cause of physical and mental deterioration in humans. Divorce is also demonstrably on the rise in so-called developed countries. Reasons for divorce rarely include "sexual incompatibility," but often include infidelity. One reason is almost certainly the fact that the people of developed countries routinely outlive the mechanisms that were selected for in individuals, who died much earlier in the evolutionary past. These mechanisms must certainly apply to emotional, physiological, and social bonding mechanisms, which are often difficult to separate from sexual mechanisms. In human societies, all are intimately intertwined with the vast social changes of the modern world. Marriage, though universal, is becoming destabilized in the modern world.

Sociosexual Regulation of Copulation

In addition to marriage, societies also regulate sexual behavior in the form of laws or common codes of morality. Few societies place a great deal of value on male virginity. In fact, the opposite is often the case, with male sexual experience being valued over male virginity and presumed incompetence. Female virginity as a rule is valued in human societies, so much so that a public disclosure of the premarital nonvirginity of a female can make marriage socially difficult or impossible. Such rules rarely apply to males in any known society. As the previous chapter pointed out, these differences are consistently reflected in language. Extramarital or premarital sex is publicly prohibited in about 75 percent of societies, but tolerated in 50 percent or more of those same societies. There have been various explanations for the double standards. Almost all of them eventually make reference to innate biological differences between males and females. The sociobiological explanation is no exception and holds that males have been selected to leave as many offspring as possible, and that females have been selected to maximize parental investment in offspring.

Females

Much evolutionary attention has been paid to female sexuality. Nonhuman and human female primates share certain commonalities. The sexual maturity of both kinds of primates is influenced by the availability of resources. Menarche (first menstruation) in human females can be delayed several years as the result of a poor diet. The general rule is that most girls undergo menarche at about the time they reach just over one hundred pounds or about 95 percent of their adult weight. Shorter adult females as girls may reach puberty under this weight; taller girls tend to reach puberty later. Over the last one hundred years, females in the West have reached menarche earlier and earlier, probably as the result of a diet that includes more animal protein. This makes good evolutionary sense because it seems adaptive to delay fertility in environments that do not have adequate nutrients for the individuals that are already living there. For at least 2 million years, animal protein has been one of the extra competitive edges that hominids have relied on.

Although most females can bear children at about thirteen years of age, most societies do not permit them to do so. Prohibition against early reproduction may be explicit or implicit in cultural rules. This prohibition also makes evolutionary sense because young teenagers rarely have the resources or the accumulated knowledge necessary for nurturing infants. In comparison with Western agricultural societies, reproduction occurs much earlier in hunting and gathering societies. In all societies, there is a direct correlation between industrialization and female education and a delay or decline in reproduction.

Human females use a number of signals and rituals to communicate their ability to reproduce and their willingness to copulate or at least be courted. Very specific secondary sex characteristics in humans begin to emerge during puberty. In females, these include the enlargement of breasts, the development of distinctly female hips, and growth of pubic and axillary hair. These indicate to other members of the society that the female is sexually mature. However, females also retain infant characteristics into adulthood. The pedogenesis of the human female has been mentioned previously in relation to attracting males. Female skin remains soft, and the extra layer of subcutaneous fat ("baby fat") and a higher pitched voice normally persists into adulthood. Facial features, such as the angle of the nose and the prominence of the brow ridges and chin, remain reduced in comparison with adult males. In Western society, females are also encouraged or at least permitted to retain more childlike behaviors, such as the public display of emotion. These features have been likened to the evolution of the cartoon character Mickey Mouse, which started with acute angles more reminiscent of a rat than the cute little squeaky voiced, small-nosed mouse that is now recognized today all over the world.

By far, most female signaling of willingness to copulate is learned. In all societies, it is also at least somewhat ritualistic. Courtship rituals are known in many vertebrate and in every human society. In the West, they are not overtly codified, but dating has a distinct form that all Westerners recognize. Typically, Western females consent to intimate body contact with males only after the appropriate and personally acceptable rituals. In almost every case, this is preceded by intimate eye contact. Eye-scan studies, which follow the movement of eyes in response to stimuli, indicate that females scan the eyes, face, shoulders, and hips and then the eyes again in the presence of new males. In the United States, the scanning of the gluteus maximus also seems to be of increasing popularity. The scanning of obvious muscular parts seems to be related to assessing the age and physical development of the male. In general, females deny intimate eye and body contact to males that they are not interested in.

For instance, when a male and female must turn sideways to pass through a narrow door at the same time, the female will turn the front of her body away from the male (males almost always turn the front of their body toward the female). Most females avoid prolonged eye contact and touching of strange males, but when females do not follow this pattern, it is usually regarded as flirting. Sexual signaling is done verbally in both males and females, but visual signaling is still significant. Despite their marital status, both males and females dress to be attractive and impressive to both sexes. As with other species, obtaining mates involves both attraction and competition.

It is interesting to note that in animals where there is a sexual dimorphism in appearance, it is usually the male that has the more elaborate visual display. Among humans, sexually dimorphic display varies tremendously, and our species cannot be easily classified as similar to any other species. In the West, there is the perception that it is males, attracted to visually displaying females, that initiate sexual behavior. In fact, normal sexual behavior begins with the participation of both sexes. The frequency of female sexual activity reaches a peak in the late twenties. Females, according to one study, are most likely to initiate sexual behavior (including masturbation) during ovulation, when they are most fertile. Human females also appear to become more active just before ovulation, and their skill at motor tasks improves during the same period. One speculation is that they are trying to impress males or initiate more contact with males by becoming more physically active. However, the highest frequency of copulation does not coincide with fertility. Seasonally, U.S. females are most likely to become pregnant during the fall and early winter of temperate climates. Sociological, seasonal, and ultimately evolutionary factors may account for this. For instance in the West, the "holiday season" leads to parties which leads to mating which results in late spring and summer births. Temperate mammals (with rutting seasons instead of parties) adhere to the same pattern. It is important in this regard to remember that although hominids are tropical mammals, the tropics in most areas are highly seasonal, especially in terms of resource availability. Females have a much more direct evolutionary interest in synchronizing mating and birth with resource availability.

Males

It has been said that among sexually reproducing primates males are expendable. This concept refers to the fact that a group can have only a few males, and yet each female can produce offspring because a single male can inseminate a number of females. Males on average mature a few years later than females. Secondary sex characteristics include the development of pubic and axial hair (as in females), the growth of facial hair, the enlargement of the penis, descent of the testicles, and the development of muscle tone and definition. Males, when encountering new females, scan the face, the breasts, the hips, the breasts again, followed by a return to the face.

Males appear to be more aggressive in initiating copulation. Like females, most males attempt to accentuate maleness. Sexually dimorphic male characters include height, muscle definition, strength, penis size, and overall size. Indeed, it has long been noted that females not only tend to marry and mate up socially, but also mate up in terms of age. In most societies, males marry females that are younger than themselves. In our own society, we have come to refer to liaisons between older males and younger females as December-spring unions, frequently resulting from "male menopause." Younger mates of older powerful males are frequently referred to as "trophy wives." The unfair fact remains that it is much easier for males to acquire new sexual partners as they get older than it is for females. In our culture, this stems to a large extent from the unfair fact that females are still often "judged" on their physical appearance, while males are judged not only on how they look, but also on their social status. In a sexually dimorphic species where males are more powerful (in the many meanings of the word), this reproductive strategy makes evolutionary if not socially equitable sense.

Homosexuality

Homosexuality is an extremely controversial subject in U.S. society. In almost every other society, it is much less controversial. In 1974, the American Psychiatric Association declared that homosexuality was not a disorder or disease and therefore neither had nor needed a "cure." Homosexuality exists in every known society. In most societies, it is taken as a natural state of affairs. The percentage of homosexuals range from 4 to 20 percent in all the groups studied. However, there are few if any known cases of exclusive homosexuality over the course of a lifetime. Nonetheless, these numbers have been cited as support for the idea that there is a biological basis to homosexuality. The problem with this explanation is that no direct genetic or hormonal correlations have been found in homosexuals. However, researchers led by Dean H. Hammer of the National Cancer Institute have announced a genetic difference in a segment of the DNA of male homosexuals that is transmitted from the mother on the X chromosome. Males have an X and a Y chromosome, while females have two X chromosomes. This means that this segment of DNA is maternally passed. A similar sex linkage occurs with color blindness in males. This is not the same as saying that this part of the DNA causes homosexuality. It is also known that prenatal exposure of female fetuses to male hormones promotes "tomboyish" behaviors in postnatal females, but differences in the blood chemistry of homosexuals are undetectable. The few cases where hormonal differences have been found have turned out to be fraudulent.

As mentioned above, another characteristic of homosexuals is that there are very few cases in which homosexuals have always been exclusively homosexual. Bisexual experience in otherwise heterosexual females appears to be much more common than in heterosexual males. This may be because most cultures tolerate and even encourage more public and private intimacy in females. Among homosexuals, there is also an interesting sexual dimorphism in which male homosexuals behave more like male heterosexuals and female homosexuals behave more like female heterosexuals in certain respects. Male homosexuals tend to be much more promiscuous, whether synchronously or serially. Male homosexuals are also more numerous, but this may only reflect social training, which is more tolerant of and even encourages male aggressiveness in any endeavor. Female homosexuals have far fewer and much more stable relationships. This suggests some interesting interpretations of the nature of homosexuality.

One interpretation is that the desire or urge to engage in sexual activity is innate, but that its expression is determined by enculturation and/or personal experience. This suggests that, with the possible exception of prenatal exposure to hormones mentioned above, homosexuals are not "born gay." However, in defense of the "born gay" position, there is some evidence suggesting that repeated crossdressing of boys is indicative of future homosexual behavior, but "tomboyishness" among females is not correlated with adult sexual gender preference. The question of a genetic or cultural basis for homosexuality should have nothing to do with whether it is permitted by society. We have already seen that few societies tolerate the public display of any form of overt sexuality. However, the cultural definition of overt sexuality varies tremendously. Homophobia seems to be especially Western.

Thailand is an interesting case study in human sexuality. It has become infamous as one of the sex capitals of the world, at least in the eyes of Western tourists, most of whom do not speak the language and rarely spend more than a few weeks there. Thais are tolerant of both extramarital sexual activity (especially among men) and homosexual activity (among both sexes). Transvestites are considered a source of amusement and not a behavior to be derided. A similar attitude toward gender switching is found among many Native American cultures in the form of berdaches or two spirits. Ninety percent of Thai male adolescents have visited a Thai prostitute by the time they are fourteen years of age. Until very recently, marriage was a strictly contractual matter that could last from one day to years. Also until recently, women were generally treated as chattel, yet a Thai woman still has the quasi-legal right to cut off a man's penis and feed it to the ducks if she catches him having sex with another woman. Magazines depicting naked women, such as *Playboy* and *Penthouse,* are strictly illegal, yet live sex shows of any kind are performed publicly for tourists. At the same time, almost no respectable Thai woman and a majority of Thai men would participate in any public display of affection, let alone sex. Most Thai women are virgins before they marry, though this seems to be changing.

What this example illustrates is that it is very hard to characterize the sexual practices of any cultural group. Thai mores may also be another example of the Mead factor, which recognizes that people do not consistently do what they say they do or that what they publicly support as an ideal or objective is often very different from what actually happens. After her study in Samoa, Margaret Mead came to believe that rape and premarital sex were rare in that society. As mentioned previously, a subsequent researcher with more experience with the culture felt that Mead had been fooled. Perhaps more than anything, what these differences and the example of Thailand illustrate is that all kinds of sexual behavior occur in all human societies. Homosexuality and other variants on sexual behavior are no exception. American society was apparently duped by the now infamous "Kinsey Report," many aspects of which were fabricated.

It is difficult to characterize sexual behavior in humans given the immensity of cultural variation. From an evolutionary point of view, it is possible to make a few observations about the uniqueness of human sexuality. Human sexuality is more integrated into nonreproductive behavior than in any other primate and probably any other vertebrate. It is difficult to separate it from social organization, economics, sports, and perhaps most of what we do on a daily basis. World attitudes about copulation range from regarding it as a kind of social support through considering it sacred to considering it degrading. As with many other human characteristics, there is as much variation within a culture as there is between cultures. There are rules about sexual behavior in every culture, and yet those rules are routinely broken by individuals.

Rape

Rape also seems to occur in all societies. Scientific studies in our society have emphasized that the act of rape is really a form of aggression and not sexuality. In many societies, including our own, rape need not involve sexual activity forced on the female. Sex with underage females constitutes rape in our own society. In other societies, simply being alone with an unmarried female is tantamount to rape. As with all forms of sexual abuse, the perpetrator was usually abused as a child. This suggests that such behavior is learned and not genetically based.

In the history of "civilized countries," rape has been closely associated with military victory as one of the "spoils of war." It may be that rape has always been an important means of gene flow between cultures, but this does not mean that it is genetically based or that nothing should or can be done to prevent it. Like war, it seems to be permitted in special situations where one group or even individual is engaged in antagonistic activities against another.

As is the case with other forms of human sexual behavior, rape is embedded in a constellation of behaviors that are unrelated in other animals. However, I believe it is too simplistic to view it as just another form of interpersonal aggression. Among humans, the lack of sexual activity can enhance the desire for sexual activity. Coupled with intoxicants, the desire for sexual contact can take socially unacceptable forms such as rape. A much more fundamental question is why is it that some individuals come to violate the norms of their own societies? We know that situations such as war, crowding, isolation, repression, and the other terrible things that humans are capable of doing to each other can easily result in behaviors that are normal for our species as a whole.

Love

Human beings recognize that there are many kinds of love and that a single definition of love is impossible. Here we treat love as it relates to sex and reproduction. I mentioned previously that falling in love frequently produces what would otherwise be considered childlike behavior in adults. Changes in mood, appetite, ability to concentrate, personal spacing behavior, and general feelings of well-being occur when one is "falling in love." There is some evidence that endorphins also play an important part in love. These natural opioids impart a feeling of well-being that could perhaps be described as a "natural high."

Another internally produced substance that has been implicated in love is oxytocin. However, it has been suggested that oxytocin is involved in bonding love. Oxytocin levels rise with the onset of childbirth and remain high for some days or even weeks after birth. It may stimulate imprinting and has also been implicated in the postinfatuation phase of "comfortable love" characteristic of long-term human pair bonds.

The state of being in love also seems to be a means of accomplishing imprinting between family members such as siblings and offspring. In the case of most forms of sexual love, two adult people imprint on each other. This is logical given the childlike behaviors usually associated with a time in the human life cycle when we are learning behaviors that will be important as adults. In adults, this period is seldom permanent or at least it does not maintain the same characteristics throughout a relationship. Interestingly enough, a survey of the males and females of those strange animals known as American college students reveals that "love at first sight" is a very rare phenomenon. However, "lust at first sight" is a very common phenomenon among both sexes. Sexual dimorphism about attitudes toward love also exists in this same group. Men fall in love faster than women, but women fall in love for longer periods. Almost paradoxically, women are most likely to end a bad relationship, while men will hang on to it longer. There is no way to generalize these findings for humankind as a whole, but these findings provide fruitful areas for future intercultural research. No obvious evolutionary function or advantage is obvious in these findings, but they are generally consistent with the fact that human females inherently must invest more of their physical biological resources into reproduction.

The importance of love is reflected in a survey of navy personnel reported by Rahe (1972) and quoted by Reynolds (1980). Of life events that were most likely to negatively affect one's health the top three were death of a spouse, divorce, and marital separation. Pregnancy was ranked twelfth. Losing a job or being jailed were far below. Again, these findings are based largely on U.S. men, but they indicate how female biology and social relationships are closely tied to human males. The lesson seems to be that the separation of sexuality from close social bonds is not easily attained among humans.

Beginning at the end of the nineteenth century, there arose a growing interest in how each sex selected the other. It is now fairly well agreed that males are innately more aggressive than females. They account for a much higher percentage of aggressive crimes and other antisocial behaviors in all cultures. Specifically, it has been suggested that human females have selected more aggressive ("demonic") males for reasons of defense and resources acquisition. It has further been suggested that females have paradoxically also favored promiscuous males as mates. This interpretation is based on the observation that sperm becomes more numerous and motile after mating. Following this reasoning, females that receive the sperm of a male that has recently mated have a reproductive advantage over females with faithful mates. The selection for an absent and aggressive male does not make much sense for a female with offspring to nurture. This seems especially true when it is remembered that human infants are more vulnerable for a longer period than any other terrestrial animal.

Freudian Thought

Freudian theory holds that adult sexuality grows out of the infant's concern with the physical relationship with their mother's and father's sexuality. According to the theory, during the course of maturation, males come to want to have sexual relations with their mothers and eventually realize that their father is a sexual competitor. Daughters want to sleep with their fathers, whose possession of a penis makes them envious. The son's realization that he is in sexual competition with his father results in feelings of guilt, generally referred to as the *Oedipus complex.* Females develop *penis envy* when they discover that, like their mother, they have less prominent external genitalia. The female then comes to perceive herself in competition for her father. These basic sexual concerns form the basis of subsequent personality development including neuroses. In Freud's scheme, all humans experienced inevitable sexual problems that have to be worked out over the course of a lifetime. Maturation is thus presented as a series of inevitable psychological stages that will not end in satisfaction unless an individual learns to admit that the Freudian perspectives are correct.

It is now thought by most psychologists that Freud's interpretation of human sexuality is probably more related to Freud's own Victorian world and his personal sexual perspectives than to any innate or inevitable human sexual psychology. Another of Freud's ideas, *projection,* maintained that people can become obsessed with some particular problem to the point where they project their own neuroses onto the actions of other people. This leads to a paradox in which Freud's concern with sex becomes only a projection of his own sexuality. Perhaps the main problem with Freud's interpretation of human sexuality is that it is neither testable nor falsifiable.

For Freudians, the most important means of dealing with sexual problems is through psychoanalysis, which involves dream therapy and other techniques. As we will discuss later, most people enjoy talking about their dreams. Exposing one's feelings to friends and trusted individuals is so much a part of the human condition that it is easy to understand why periodic trips to psychoanalysts help. Paying a professional large sums of money for brief periods of attentiveness seems to further enhance the effectiveness of psychoanalysis. The development of sexual obsessions from the infant experience seems unlikely because intimate contact between parent and infant ceases in most societies long before the infant develops an interest in copulation. It is true that the sexual response (erection resulting either spontaneously or from touching) is present from birth, but the sexual fixation (to borrow and probably misuse a Freudian term) is not supported by the Coolidge effect, which is present in most humans and other mammals. Furthermore, attributing a sexual basis to almost every human emotion and experience just does not fit well with what we know from other cultures. As mentioned previously, which body parts are regarded as sexual and the attractiveness of nakedness varies tremendously between cultures. From an evolutionary perspective, perhaps the most unbelievable aspect of Freudian sexual theory is that after so many millions of years of selective pressure, sexuality would still cause major adaptive problems in the normal functioning and therefore reproduction of humans.

In retrospect, what is truly remarkable about Freud's views on human nature and especially human sexuality is how thoroughly he ignored the Darwinian perspective. Writing in an era when Darwinian thought was being much discussed and genetics was being discovered, it is remarkable that one researcher's opinion about human sexuality could have been taken so seriously as to form the foundation of psychiatric thinking for the generations that followed. Freud recognized early childhood as a formative period in the development of personality but, in my mind, overemphasized its importance in the development of sexuality. I believe he did perhaps suspect that aspects of sexuality permeate many facets of adult life. Freud's perspective differed from the modern evolutionary biologist in its lack of interest in the system in which humans perpetuate the system. What we see from the vantage of one hundred years since is that Freud was right in concluding that individual variation in sexual behavior is exceedingly great in its details.

Sex and Sociobiology

Sociobiological theory maintains that the principle of inclusive fitness dictates that males and females have different reproductive strategies that have been canalized by millions of years of evolution. Specifically, because the number of offspring a male can produce is theoretically unlimited and the maximum a female can produce is limited by the length of gestation, females have inherently different "strategies" to maximize their inclusive fitness. Theoretically, the number of off-spring a female can produce is finite. In humans, this means a female can theo-retically produce only one offspring for every year of her life after menarche. In fact, few females have ever lived up to this potential, though the maximum record seems to be over one hundred for a ninety-year-old woman who had a tendency to give birth to twins.

By way of review, males can produce an infinite number of offspring a year (again, theoretically). Therefore, males and females have evolved fundamentally different reproductive strategies that underlie male–female sexual relationships. Sociobiologists suggest that because inclusive fitness drives behavior that each individual behaves so as to maximize their own contribution of DNA in the next generation. Because males are potentially unlimited in the amount of DNA they can leave, their mating strategy involves impregnating as many females as pos-sible. It has been suggested that there is a so-called male promiscuity gene that causes males to seek out many more opportunities for mating. Males in effect practice a "shotgun" strategy and have developed sociosexual behavior to achieve this end. Males are not necessarily responsible for any aspect of reproduction and rearing after mating. Therefore, their reproductive energies can be most efficiently concentrated on mating and not childrearing. From a sociobiological perspective, it would be most effective for males to help rear their first offspring while still continuing to impregnate as many females as possible. This is especially true because of the reality of "paternal uncertainty," which emphasizes that males can never be sure that their mate's offspring carries their own DNA. Males should be less selective about who they mate with because their basic strategy is sup-posedly quantity and not quality. For the female, the opposite should be true. The sociobiological model encounters a paradox resulting from the fact that the male allocation of resources, or at least the promise of such, is often a prerequisite to female consent. The United States has many recent laws designed to deal with "dead-beat dads," who are an increasing problem throughout the world.

One recent study of male and female attitudes toward mate selection found that both males and females had equally high standards of what they were looking for in a mate. Douglas T. Kendrik, a psychologist at Arizona State University, found that both sexes wanted "attractive, agreeable and emotionally stable" mates that they perceived as being closer to their own qualities. A difference emerged between males and females in assessment of the qualities for one-time encounter matings or "one-night stands." Females tended to maintain the same high standards that they had for selecting a permanent mate. Males, on the other hand, significantly lowered the standards of who they would consent to mate with for a short time. Sociobiological theory explains this difference on the basis of the fact that it is the female who must bear the offspring. She therefore has a much greater need to carefully assess all potential mates. The male simply treats one-time mating events as another chance to pass on their DNA without committing his own energy and resources.

Females, by virtue of the fact that it is they that give birth, must necessarily devote a considerable amount of energy to postmating nourishment and care of the offspring. Females in almost all cultures also put most of the postnatal care into what has facetiously been called the "little parasite." Because the energy requirements are so great, sociobiologists reason that females have developed behavioral strategies for getting males to also invest energy in the raising of the offspring. As part of this strategy, females have developed mechanisms for evaluating the male's willingness to invest time and energy in the offspring before mating. To support this goal, females have evolved a "coyness gene." Essentially, this behavior says that mating will not be allowed until the female receives some indication or assurance that the male will help in childrearing. Among humans, this can take the form of promises, a formal engagement, or ultimately the public commitment we call marriage.

Sociobiologists believe that this biological situation explains a number of cross-cultural courting, mating, and marriage behaviors. This is, for instance, why it is that males are the "sexual aggressors" and why it is that females will not have sex with strange males. This also supposedly explains why it is that males in courting or precourting rituals and behaviors are the ones that are expected to show their willingness to expend resources by paying for the date. This may also explain the widespread existence of a bride price that is given to the female's relatives. A dowry, which comes with the bride on marriage, is also common in many cultures. In general, there is evidence that most societies have some mechanism for insuring that future offspring will have the resources that they need to be raised to maturity. Sociobiological perspective also suggests that the institution of marriage has benefits for both sexes. For a female, the immediate benefit is a public social commitment to providing aid for the rearing of the offspring. For the male, marriage increases the chances of assured paternity of his offspring. The inclusive fitness advantage of this is that males cannot be "tricked" into putting energy and resources into the propagation of DNA that is not his own.

We noted in a previous chapter that a concern with ancestry is reflected in male-directed insults, while female insults involve criticism of casual or profitable sexual activity and infertility.

One of the implications of the sociobiological perspective on human sexuality is that the social double standard that severely punishes female promiscuity and tolerates male promiscuity is biologically adaptive and "natural" for our species. The formalization of sexual access in human society also (according to this perspective) creates a niche for reproductive "cheaters" who take advantage of a sociosexual system. If the female's main goal is the acquisition of resources and energy for raising her offspring as the goal of sanctioned mating, then sociobiology also presents an explanation of why males with more resources should be preferred over those with less to offer. One would logically expect that males would have the same preference, but it can be argued that because the male strategy is one of quantity and not quality, he is more interested in acquiring a number of younger and obviously healthy partners as signaled by nubility.

Sociobiologists also have an explanation for the seemingly nonadaptive (in terms of inclusive fitness) behavior of homosexuality. It has been suggested that by withdrawing their personal DNA from future generations, homosexuals decrease competition with the DNA of their siblings. Furthermore, because they are not engaged in actual sexual competition, they are also available to aid in the care and nurture of their siblings and other relatives' offspring. The fact is that in most societies, homosexuals often do not perform such functions. Just as much time is devoted to sexual competition for sexual partners as in heterosexuals. Until recently, the common pattern of homosexuality in Western society usually required the declared homosexual to move out of his or her parental household.

A more ominous implication of the application of sociobiological theory to human sexuality is the inescapable conclusion that rape is just another way for males to optimize their inclusive fitness. This suggests that rape offers the maximum return in inclusive fitness for a minimal investment of time and energy—it is the ultimate form of cheating. Based on the logic of sociobiology, anti-abortion laws maximize the advantage of cheaters. In a similar vein, proponents of sociobiology suggest that infanticide is also related to male attempts to maximize their inclusive fitness. Sarah Hrdy studied langurs and concluded that invading males from another troop routinely kill the offspring that they did not sire to bring the females into estrus. A similar phenomenon has been reported for lions. Thus, male-generated infanticide is supposedly adaptive for certain individuals. One problem with both this and the sociobiological explanation of rape is that human behavior does not conform to principles developed on the bases of nonhuman studies. Heterosexual rape does not usually result in the production of offspring. Among humans, infanticide is almost always the prerogative of the female, who must in fact delete an individual carrying 50 percent of her DNA from the next generation.

Sociobiological theory might also logically predict that incest would be the preferred choice in reproduction because genetically healthy offspring from consanguineous matings are arguably much more the rule than normal. The incest taboo should then be a rarity instead of the rule that is found among all peoples. Once again the Coolidge principle strongly suggests that recombination with more distantly related individuals has been reinforced by natural selection.

Sociobiological theory proposes that human sexual behavior is optimized for inclusive fitness. According to this way of thinking, many of the sexual behaviors that most societies regard as aberrant are in fact adaptive for individuals who carry out such behaviors. Although many sociobiologists would deny that they support this interpretation, their central premise of inclusive fitness and sexual dimorphism in male and female reproductive objectives leads inescapably to this conclusion. The suggestion of a female coyness gene and a male promiscuity gene makes a little more sense, but this interpretation says little about the conscious motivations for courtship, mating, and bonding. Sociobiological theory maintains that volitional behavior is irrelevant to inclusive fitness, but such a "paradigm" does little to help us in understanding an animal such as humans, whose behavior is overwhelmingly conscious and volitional.

Summary

Human sexuality is unique in the absence of three characteristics: visually displayed estrus in females, the great amount of time spent in mating that does not produce offspring, and the extension of mating well past the fertile period of the female life cycle. The emphasis on mating as opposed to simple reproduction may be related to the maintenance of a long-term male–female bond in which the male aids in the rearing of offspring by supplying resources and energy. As part of this process, humans have come to classify sexuality as a form of play. [The process of falling in love probably also aids in the formation of long-term but not necessarily lifelong bonds, which no longer span an entire lifetime because humans now live much longer than in even the recent historic past of the last few thousand years.] In humans, courtship involves a reversion to childlike behavior that is reflected in language, mental states, interpersonal contact, and other behaviors. In general, this state exhibits characteristics that probably promote interpersonal imprinting.

Freudian theory interprets human sexuality as resulting from inborn conflicts inherently arising out of infancy and childhood. However, the ubiquitous presence of these conflicts in all human societies is impossible to demonstrate. Sociobiologists relate sexuality directly to inclusive fitness and point out that because males and females have very different potentials for the number of offspring they can leave, male and female strategies are different. They maintain that males have evolved to become promiscuous and that females have evolved to be more reticent in their acceptance of mating partners. For females, the problem is identifying and obtaining males who will help raise the offspring. For this reason, they tend to mate only with males that have shown indications of future help. Males, on the other hand, supposedly take advantage of most mating opportunities and therefore more actively pursue females. Sociobiologists also explain rape and homosexuality as an instance of an open niche for "cheaters" in the first instance and as a means by which nonreproducing individuals can help care for individuals sharing some of their own DNA in the second instance. The behaviors predicted by these models do not conform very well with actual behaviors in most human societies.

There can be no final meaningful comparison of human sexuality with other mammals. Culture is so intertwined with reproduction that few if any analogs exist in other species. It is still safe to say that the brain is the largest and most important sexual organ in both males and females. As such, the brain is programmable by culture and personal experience. All sexual dimorphism, including mating strategies, derives from the fact that, by definition, the female must invest more of her biological resources in the offspring.

QUESTIONS FOR REVIEW

1. How is human sexuality different from that of other mammals?

2. What differences in reproductive and mating strategies do sociobiologists perceive between male and female humans? Why?

3. How can marriage be defined in a way that is recognizable in every culture?

4. How do people that are "falling in love" behave?

5. Is there a universality to sexual attraction?

6. What are men and women looking for in potential mates?

MIND AND BODY EXPERIMENTS

1. Observe how parties mostly comprising couples differ from parties mostly composed of single people.

2. Walk through a narrow doorway with someone of the opposite sex. Observe the orientation of both bodies.

3. Ask divorced people why they got divorced. Try to obtain specific answers about recurring problems in the relationship. Is there a pattern?

4. Ask people what physical parts of a potential mate they notice first.

5. Find out the age differences between couples that you know. Plot them on a graph using age differences (in months) and income (males and females) as the axes.

SUGGESTED READINGS

Aberle, D. F., Bronfenbrenner, U., Hess, E. H., Miller, D. R., Schneider, D. H., and Spuhler, J. N. 1963. The Incest Taboo and the Mating Patterns of Animals. *American Anthropologist* 65: 253–265.

Akil, H., Watson, S. J., Young, E., Lewis, M. E., Khachaturian, H., and Walker, J. M. 1984. Endogenous Opioids: Biology and Function. *Annual Review of Neuroscience* 7: 223–255.

Bischof, N. 1975. Comparative Ethology of Incest Avoidance. In R. Fox (ed.), *Biosocial Anthropology.* New York: Wiley and Sons.

Bower, B. 1993. Genetic Clue to Male Homosexuality Emerges. *Science News* 37.

Burd, M. 1986. Sexual Selection and Human Evolution: All or None Adaptation? *American Anthropologist* 88: 167–72.

Cabanac, M. 1971. Physiological Role of Pleasure. *Science* 173: 1103–1107.

Campbell, B. G. 1972. *Sexual Selection and the Descent of Man.* Chicago: Aldine.

Cant, J. 1981. Hypothesis for the Evolution of Human Breasts and Buttocks. *American Naturalist* 117: 99–204.

Crawford, C., and Galdikas, B. M. F. 1986. Rape in Nonhuman Animals: An Evolutionary Perspective. *Canadian Psychology* 27: 215–230.

Daly, M., and Wilson, M. I. 1978. *Sex, Evolution and Behavior.* North Scituate, MA: Duxbury.

Fedigan, L. M. 1983. Dominance and Reproductive Success. *Yearbook of Physical Anthropology* 26: 91–129.

Fedigan, L. M. 1986. The Changing Role of Women in Models of Human Evolution. *Annual Review of Anthropology* 15: 25–56.

Freud S. 1938. Three Contributions to the Theory of Sex. A.A. Brill (ed). In the basic writings of Sigmund Freud. New York: Modern Library.

Goody, J. 1976. *Production and Reproduction: A Comparative Study of the Domestic Domain.* Cambridge: Cambridge University Press.

Goody, J. 1983. *The Development of the Family and Marriage in Europe.* Cambridge: Cambridge University Press.

Hausfater, G., and Hrdy, S. B. (eds.). 1984. *Infanticide, Comparative and Evolutionary Perspectives.* New York: Aldine.

Hetherington, E. M. 1972. Effects of Father Absence on Personality Development in Adolescent Daughters. *Developmental Psychology* 7: 313–326.

Kinsey A., Pomeroy, W. and Martin, C. 1948. *Sexual behavior in the human male.* Philadelphia: Saunders.

Kinsey A., Pomeroy, W. and Martin, C. 1953. *Sexual behavior in the human female.* Philadelphia: Saunders.

Kinzey, W. G. (ed.). 1987. *The Evolution of Human Behavior: Primate Models.* Albany: State University of New York Press.

Low, B. S., Alexander, R. D., and Ninin, K. M. 1987. Human Hips, Breasts, and Buttocks: Is Fat Deceptive? *Ethology & Sociobiology* 8: 249–257.

Marcia-Lees, F. E., Relethford, J. H., and Sorger, T. 1986. Evolutionary Perspectives on Permanent Breast Enlargement in Human Females. *American Anthropologist* 88(2): 423–428.

Masters, W. H., and Johnson, V. E. 1971. The Sexual Response Cycles of the Human Male and Female: Comparative Anatomy and Physiology. In B. Lieberman (ed.), *Human Sexual Behavior.* New York: Wiley and Sons.

Morbeck M. E., Galloway, A., and Zihlman, A. (eds.). 1997. *The Evolving Female.* Princeton: Princeton University Press.

Morgan, E. 1972. *The Descent of Woman.* New York: Stein and Day.

Parker, S. T. 1987. A Sexual Selection Model for Hominid Evolution. *Human Evolution* 2: 235–253.

Wrangham, R. 1983. Ultimate Social Structures Determining Social Structure. In R. Hindle (ed.), *Primate Social Relationships: An Integrated Approach,* pp. 255–261. Sunderland, MA: Sinauer Associates.

Wuethrich, B. 1993. Evolutionists Pick Up on One Night Stands. *Science News.*

Yalon, I., Green, R., and Fisk, F. 1973. Prenatal Exposure to Female Hormones: Effect on Psychosexual Development in Boys. *Archives of General Psychiatry* 28: 554–561.

CHAPTER

8 Intelligence, Learning, and Memory

This second-order learning capacity, which enables animals to produce novel "emergent" responses by reusing information in new contexts, has been shown to correlate with brain size, but not encephalization.

—Terrence Deacon

From the perspective of interspecific comparison, larger brains are better at developing novel responses to new situations. All animals can learn and do so as a part of normal maturation. However, whatever it is that we mean by intelligence seems to be the ability to learn more things throughout a longer period of the life span. Intelligence, along with consciousness, is perhaps the most difficult aspect of human behavior to define and identify. It is not necessarily a behavior and is most certainly not a single entity. Furthermore, there is no consensus about whether intelligence can be considered distinct from such other aspects of thinking as memory, emotion, or perception. It also now seems apparent that these three arbitrary categories not only have their own levels of complexity, but also that the distinctiveness of the categories is largely the product of the human mind. The twentieth-century West has been particularly obsessed by the single entity concept and its relationship to social behavior. Just as the Greek intellect was preoccupied with truth and the Roman with virtue, U.S. public thought has emphasized intelligence, especially as it relates to race, sex, and genetics. Throughout the last century, the growth of genetics paralleled and became intertwined with an interest in intelligence. Every day human animals make judgments about their conspecifics based on race, sex, and intelligence, and yet scientists continue to treat these characteristics as separate dimensions of human behavior.

There is also now widespread scientific agreement that there is at least some genetic component of intelligence that is heritable. Furthermore, there is a growing trend in the psychological literature to fuse the concept of memory, cultural, and personal experience with the concept of intelligence. At least part of the reason for this is that the term *intelligence* has a long history of misuse and abuse that has been used to justify social policies, some of which have been blatantly racist. This is best illustrated by a consideration of the history of IQ tests.

Henry Jerrison tackled the question of interspecific differences in intelligence. He quantified the observation that humans have a relatively larger brain in his EQ (*encephalization quotient*), which is a great brain volume and weight in relation to body size. Humans are the most encephalized animals. The evolutionary record strongly proclaims that increasingly larger brains were associated with increasingly more complex behavior. However, beyond theories about packing and space constraints, we still do not understand how or why a larger brain is associated with complex thinking and behavior. Furthermore, attempts to estimate what constitutes relatively large brains have employed such diverse criteria as brain weight or volume to body weight, stature, somatic surface area, and gland sizes. We do know that brain size eventually outstripped the evolution of the female pelvic cavity and that physical brain expansion has probably ceased in the context of natural selection. Arguably, Neanderthals had larger cranial capacities than modern humans.

From an interspecific and evolutionary perspective, it is clear that whatever we mean by intelligence, humans have more of it. The contention that we cannot carry out meaningful interspecific comparisons is ludicrous. The idea that cats are highest in "feline intelligence" and dogs are highest in "canine intelligence" ignores the inescapable conclusion that humans are more complex than earthworms. A new though limited definition of intelligence can be found in *behavioral plasticity* (see below), which can directly relate a history of behavioral change to environmental change. To paraphrase Terrence Deacon, animals become good at paying attention to what is important to them. From an interspecific perspective, it is possible to note that more behaviorally plastic species take a longer time to reach anatomical and behavioral maturity. Because humans pay attention to a wider range of environmental detail than other species, they also take the longest time to learn those details.

IQ Tests

In the early part of this century, psychologist Alfred Binet (1857–1911) developed a test for Parisian elementary schools that would aid in identifying children who might encounter learning difficulties. He developed a series of questions concerning language, mathematics, and logical skills that were meant to determine the mental age of a child. Certain tasks that could be completed by a child were correlated with a certain chronological age in most children. His tests were never designed to assess intelligence. Instead, he intended his assessments to serve as a general guideline to help educators help children. Binet never wanted the tests to be used to categorize or exclude individuals from various types of educational programs or levels.

As Stephen J. Gould recounts in his book *The Mismeasure of Man*, H. H. Goddard, a U.S. director of a New Jersey school for the "feeble minded," devised the term *moron* for "high-grade defectives" (people with an adult mental age of between eight and twelve years). He also used Binet's scale to argue that intelligence was a single entity and that morons could be identified. He furthermore argued that if left unchecked, morons were capable of breeding and therefore endangering society. He popularized the notion that intelligence, or rather the lack of "normal" intelligence, was genetic. To protect society, he favored custodial institutions, which prevented morons from breeding. By the time Binet's approach crossed the Atlantic, intelligence had become a single genetic entity that could be used to classify an individual's suitability for breeding.

In 1916, Binet's test was modified by Stanford University psychologist Lewis Terman (1877–1956), who expanded the test to measure adults and coined the term *intelligence quotient*. This adult test eventually became known as the *Stanford-Binet Test*. As Gould has also pointed out, "correct" answers were those that recognized cultural "normalcy" to the exclusion of more creative responses. In Terman's IQ tests, an intelligence quotient is calculated by dividing a subject's mental age by the subject's chronological age. The "normal" intelligence of a ten year old who has a mental age of ten will therefore have an IQ of 100. Those that have a chronological age of five and a mental age of 10 will have an IQ of 200. For decades, genius was commonly held to be 150 and above. This "rubicon" has now been lowered to the 140s or even high 130s. Before his death, Binet wrote several essays warning about the appropriateness and possible misuses of his test. One of the obvious problems with applying the test to adults is the problem of determining the difference in mental age between a forty year old and a thirty year old. Because physiological "maturation" has essentially ceased by the age of thirty, any differences would be due at least in part to experience.

The examination of 1.75 million soldiers under the direction of Robert Yerkes (1876–1956) revealed that whites had an average mental age of thirteen and that the darker the skin (moving south from Mediterranean people to people of African descent) the lower the mental age. Blacks had a mental age of about ten and one-half. Gould has detailed the prejudices and cultural biases of these results, including the fact that illiterate nonwhites were tested in segregated environments. Some of the questions are tremendously culture-bound, requiring subjects to know such things as the names of baseball teams, the Bible, commercial brand names, and auto mechanics. Other questions simply had no objective right answer. As a result of these tests, subjects were assigned to groups labeled A, B, or C. Although these were originally designated as alternative forms of a test, these grades eventually found their way into U.S. education. In theory, a person who had done poorly or was unable to take the written Alpha test was supposed to be sent to take an alternative verbal Beta test for illiterate English speakers or nonnative English speakers. These lower stages were frequently not administered properly, if they were administered at all. However, the important result is that subjects were graded. Today, it is only in North America that students are graded with letter grades.

These tests provided the impetus for the development of the S.A.T. (scholastic aptitude test), which has now become a standard device for helping to determine admission to colleges and universities in the United States. A similar test is the G.R.E. (graduate record examination), which although slightly more restricted as to category is nonetheless essentially structured along the same lines as the S.A.T.

These tests have in common the fact that they are not designed to be finished and there is a limited time span in which to answer independently segregated sections. Since the creation of these tests, scholastic testing has become big business. Robert Sternberg finds these tests have a prediction correlation of only about 0.4-0.7 of academic performance in school and even less predictive value (0.2) of career success. Although their use has been discontinued by some universities, they remain a major consideration in college admissions as a whole. The original IQ tests led to Yerkes's conclusion that only 10 percent of those examined were capable of earning baccalaureate degrees.

In addition to their effect on academia, intelligence tests also had a profound social impact in conjunction with the *eugenics movement*, which greatly feared the impact that populations like "morons" would have on the human race if allowed to breed. As immigrants landed in the United States, they were randomly tested and given intelligence tests. Many of these immigrants did not speak English or have any idea who played baseball for what city. These factors were largely ignored. Gould has also documented the fact that female intuition frequently played a part in determining which new immigrants were to be tested. The results of these tests led to the implementation of The Immigration Act of 1924, which severely restricted the number of immigrants from Europe. In the same year, Raymond Dart identified an immature specimen of *Australopithecus africanus* as the earliest known hominid ancestor, deriving not from Asia or Europe, but from Africa.

Identification of genetically based differences in intelligence have a long history in this country and in Europe. One study that has been cited frequently is the contention of Cyril Burt (1883–1971) that there are significant racial differences in IQ. Burt studied identical twins and concluded that most of their intelligence was inherited. If the differences were inherited, then they must be genetic. If the differences are genetically based, then genetic racial differences in skin color and facial features must also be associated with genetic differences in intelligence at a racial level.

Today there are still advocates of this position. **William Bradford Shockley** (1910–1989), an electrical engineer and Nobel Prize winner in physics, advocated the position that there are racial differences in intelligence and that low IQs should be removed from the population through sterilization and restrictions on reproduction. Not only is Shockley not an expert on genetics, psychology, or anthropology, but Burt's study (often cited by advocates of eugenics) was fraudulent. Despite the fact that Burt simply made up much of his data and his test subjects, other IQ tests agree with Burt's findings.

Modern Scientific Studies of Intelligence

Scholars continue to debate the significance of IQ. Recent studies have revealed that IQ tests are not only culturally biased, but the differences within a given racial or ethnic group are as great or greater than the differences between groups.

When intelligence tests are altered so that the same problem is couched in culturally or environmentally familiar terms, ethnic minorities improve in their scores. Furthermore, it appears that a truly objective and culturally neutral test is probably impossible. Even familiarity with test taking in general varies greatly among ethnic and racial groups. Test taking is an acquired skill. In many societies, verbal and facial communication is much more important and common than writing. Many societies also put little emphasis on the mental manipulation of large quantities, numbers, and exact estimations of "countable" objects.

Multiple Intelligences

Largely as the result of neuroanatomical and clinical studies, and especially recent electronic monitoring devices, there is a growing consensus that intelligence is not a single entity but encompasses a number of abilities. There is still disagreement on the genetic or environmental components of such abilities and the number of separate intelligences. One of the common features of geniuses, however they are defined, is that of expertise in only one or two fields. One of the few examples that illustrate this is the work of Leonardo da Vinci (1452–1519), who is an exception that proves the rule. Da Vinci excelled at art, engineering, anatomy, and several other normally separate fields of creative endeavor and scientific investigation. At the same time, it is important to note that da Vinci lived during an era when the ideal man was a "uomo universal," a universal or Renaissance man skilled in many realms of education and endeavor. The icons of genius of our own age are much more limited in their work. In fact, in modern Western life, occupations are so diverse that so called geniuses are commonly recognized in every category of human behavior.

The question of whether environment or innate factors account for genius has not been settled, but two interesting observations help to shed light on this age-old problem. The first is that experiments with rodents indicate that rats that grow up in enriched environments have higher brain weights. As mentioned previously, what constitutes an enriched environment is species specific. For rats it is other rats, opportunities for social interaction, and objects and situations to explore and play with. Among humans the requirements are roughly the same, though with humans we would certainly have to add the dimension of language. There is also no doubt that early exposure to subjects greatly enhances adult abilities. However, too early an exposure to subjects is probably useless. Attempts to create "superbabies" have not been successful because they have ignored the Piagetian conclusion that there are windows of acquisition for certain kinds of knowledge.

The other interesting aspect that has been implicated in intelligence is anatomical. Though the brains of acknowledged geniuses have been dissected for decades, few anatomical differences have been diagnosed that segregate geniuses from other humans. Geniuses may have large or small brains and they do not appear to have more synaptic connections or neurons than other people. However, a dissection and study of Albert Einstein's brain revealed that he possessed 75 percent more glial cells than most humans. Glial cells are involved in the metabolic maintenance of neurons. This does not sit particularly well with the idea of separate intelligences, but instead tends to persuade that the whole brain is involved in intelligence. More specific comparisons between specific regions of the brain may one day alter this picture, but currently the connectionists are on the ascendancy.

Psychologist Howard Gardner has identified what he believes to be at least seven types of intelligence. These can be listed as linguistic, musical, logical-mathematical, spatial, kinetic, and two kinds of personal intelligences involving the ability to assess the actions of oneself and others. Another ability that might be included under Gardner's spatial ability is art. We have seen that the cortex of the right hemisphere has a special ability for the perception and appreciation of visual art. Gardner suggests that such phenomena as the very specific association of certain lesions with certain symptoms and the existence of "idiot savants" support this interpretation. *Idiot savants* are people who have astounding and very specific abilities usually associated with below-average performance in other abilities. Examples of idiot savants have included people that can do rapid large calculations, remember decades of train schedules, recall future or past dates regardless of time depth, and recall the complete contents of phone books.

Gardner's interpretation is extremely compelling for students familiar with the evolutionary record of our species. It is easy to see how particular powers of recall could have been biologically reinforced and selected for over the course of hominid evolution. Furthermore, almost all these abilities have specific association areas on the cortex whose alteration controls or mediates these particular behaviors. The location of Gardner's personal intelligences may be more difficult to localize and define, but studies of frontal lobe lesions and temporal lobe epilepsy (Van Gogh's syndrome) suggest that the frontal and temporal lobes, as well as the limbic system, are probably involved. People with *Williams syndrome* often exhibit mild retardation and "pixielike" facial features, which are associated with a highly developed musical and/or linguistic ability. Such syndromes strongly support the notion that there are "centers" or association areas for certain abilities. Multiple intelligences are thus very consistent with separate (but interconnected) biologically based human behaviors.

Another major theory of multiple intelligence has been proposed by Robert Sternberg. Sternberg suggests that there are only three kinds of intelligence, which he refers to as triarchic in their organization. These are contextual, experimental, and internal intelligence. Sternberg's theory is much more general and does not have the advantage of having distinct anatomical regions that correlate with a particular intelligence. His theory further emphasizes that intelligence is really a combination of experience and genes.

The first of Sternberg's three kinds of intelligence, *contextual,* involves the ability to alter behavior or environment to solve environmental problems or cope with change. This ability involves very appropriate acts including the removal of oneself from the environment when called for. *Experimental* intelligence allows one to deal with novel situations by developing new solutions. Once the solution is developed, it is stored and is capable of being recalled without having to reformulate the steps in the solution if the same problem arises again. The last kind of intelligence is *internal*. This ability involves planning and developing solutions in anticipation of a problem. It also involves self-monitoring through feedback.

Sternberg's intelligences are much less satisfying from an evolutionary point of view than those of Gardner's. As Sternberg has described his separate intelligences, they do not appear to point to specifically human abilities and behaviors. All of these behaviors could probably be identified in chimpanzees and other mammals. Furthermore, Sternberg does not propose specific or even general anatomical areas of the brain for these behaviors. However, all of these areas are somewhat descriptive of what it is we think that the frontal lobe does. It is also hard to qualitatively separate Sternberg's intelligences, and as he has defined them they appear very similar to each other in that they generally involve learning from and adjusting to the environment. For Sternberg, intelligence is closely tied to problem solving.

Some of Gardner's intelligences are also probably well developed in chimpanzees. This is especially true of kinetic intelligence, which Gardner originally explored to account for the superb motor skills of some athletes. There is also no doubt that, in general, nonhuman primates are superb acrobats. That a special kind of kinetic intelligence should be especially developed in humans is very consistent with human abilities in the unique actions of precision throwing, gripping with the fingers, and bipedalism itself. All of these functions may have specific predispositions of the brain, but there is no doubt that environmental experience hones such innate abilities. Practice may not make perfect, but it certainly improves.

Convergent and Divergent Intelligence

Some of the people that spend their time trying to puzzle out the riddles of intelligence have suggested that individuals approach problems in two basically different ways that vary according to individual personalities and according to specific problems. One way of problem solving (and this may be what we mean by intelligence) is known as *convergent thinking*. Convergent thinking is a process of arriving at a solution to a problem by considering a number of ostensibly unrelated facts and consolidating them into a single solution. For instance, to decide what a hammer is useful for can be approached by noting its construction, its shape, the materials it is made of, and so on. One might decide that it is easy to hold, heavy, and has a flat central surface that is good for hitting other surfaces and making them move. Taken together, we know that all these qualities will accomplish what it is that we wish to do to a nail.

Divergent thinking is almost opposite in its function. Simplistically stated, divergent thinking involves considering a thing and contemplating its potentials. For instance, how many uses can a hammer be put to? It can be used for hammering, but also for throwing, a fishing weight, something to keep the door ajar, and so on.

Humans apply both strategies to different problems on a daily basis. Nonetheless, some psychologists have suggested that these two ways of problem solving delineate different basic types of personalities. Creative people, in the jargon of pop psychology, are supposedly divergent thinkers, and analytical types are supposedly convergent thinkers who solve problems rather than conceive of possibilities. As a member of our species, each of us seems to be very adept at performing both kinds of thought processes as required by the demands of our ever-changing situations. However, divergent thinking may be what we mean by creative intelligence, and convergent thinking may be what we mean by analytical intelligence. Humans are good at both but seem to be divided by personal preferences. Is deciding which bus to catch or which animal to acquire out of a herd analytical or creative? Professional artists often consider their work to be analytical, and professional analysts often consider their work to be creative. It should be remembered that professionally trained musicians process music primarily in the left hemisphere and that mathematicians employ the right hemisphere when contemplating problems with spacial dimensions. What we mean by intelligence, especially in an everyday operational sense, is clearly not easily definable.

Hormonal Bases for Intelligence

In a study of 292 children (thirteen years and younger) that scored over 700 in the S.A.T. mathematics test, Camilla Benbow discovered startling statistical differences between high scorers and the rest of the test population. She found that there were a disproportionate number of males (12:1). It was originally reasoned that because thirteen-year-old males and females would have had approximately the same number of mathematics classes, cultural and experiential differences would be minimized. In comparison with other children of their own age, these children were twice as likely to be left-handed and 60 percent of them had immune deficiencies (allergies). They were four times as likely to exhibit myopia (near-sightedness). This has been called the *Poindexter syndrome*, which refers to the myopic thick-spectacled genius stereotype portrayed in Felix the Cat cartoons.

As mentioned previously, Norman Geschwind suggested that prenatal exposure to testosterone encourages the growth of the right hemisphere while suppressing the growth of the left hemisphere. He believed that testosterone and the growth of the right hemisphere may mediate all these characteristics. At first, the superior scores of right-dominant males seems to contradict the analytical sequential functions of the brain. However, Geschwind has also suggested that it is arithmetic and not mathematical reasoning that is actually represented in the left hemisphere. If this is correct, it may be that mathematical reasoning is much more akin to the processing of spatial information than we had previously supposed.

Memory and Learning

It is a philosophical question to ask what good is intelligence without memory and learning. Like intelligence, memory and learning also seem to be compartmentalized. Most researchers recognize a number of different kinds of memories and believe that the storage of memory is mediated by the medial temporal lobe and the hippocampus. Neither of these areas seem to be involved with long-term memory, but instead seem to control the ability to enter new experiences into long-term memory and to recall short-term memory. Subjects with damage to or complete absence of the hippocampus can remember events and people from the years prior to their damage but cannot enter new information into permanent storage. They do, however, seem to possess short-term memory and carry on conversations from minute to minute, but soon after the new stimulus ceases, they have no memory of what has just occurred. A third kind of memory is called *immediate*, or *working, memory*. This is the memory one uses when engaging in immediate tasks such as driving or remembering a phone number when dialing. Some immediate memory can become committed to short-term memory and some short-term memory can be committed to long-term storage.

Two other kinds of memory are procedural and declarative. *Procedural memory* involves knowing how to do something without consciously thinking of the steps involved. These seem to be learned through practice and take much longer than declarative learning. Playing a musical instrument, skating, or riding a bike are examples of this kind of memory. Psychologist Jean Piaget suggested that the first two years of childhood involves the development of sensorimotor skills necessary for procedural learning. In this period, the child learns how to control and coordinate movements in response to stimuli. It has been further suggested that the reason we usually have no memory of these early years is that the brain has not yet developed declarative memories. The cerebellum has also been implicated in procedural memory, especially if it involves kinetic operations responses learned as the result of the conditioned reflex requiring physical action or innate response of the kind studied by physiologist Ivan Pavlov (1849–1936). His famous experiments with dogs demonstrated that environmental stimulus can elicit responses in the body by way of mental perception.

Although only a crude analogy, short-term procedural memory involving the hippocampus (part of the temporal lobe and the cerebellum) may be compared to the ROM (read only memory) of computers that allows the entering of data but not the manipulation of data into long-term memory. In humans, this data would be housed somewhere in the cortex and other parts of the brain. Without a program for data entry, data is not stored permanently. Damage to the ROM device interferes with the processing of new data but leaves previously stored data intact. The converse is also true. Though crude, the analogy is useful.

Declarative memory is the ability to recall certain information in detail. Such memories are developed quickly, for example, adults who clearly remember where they were at the time that they learned of John F. Kennedy's death. Declarative memories may also be developed as the result of eureka-type experiences. Sudden discoveries or the perception of a scientific principle constitute what the writer James Joyce called an epiphany. Declarative memories involve deducing principles from the integration of data. They entail the ability to understand how a single rule explains a seemingly diverse and unrelated number of phenomena.

From an evolutionary perspective, intelligence is of little use without long-term memory. The categories of long-term memory have probably undergone long-term selection pressures. There also seems to be sexual dimorphism in human memories. For instance, in comparison with females, males are much better at recalling the faces and names of other males. Both sexes recall past friends and lovers best. A similar phenomenon turns up in the differences between the content of male and female dreams in that males are much more likely to be involved in the dreams of both sexes. It has been suggested that it is much more important to remember male faces because males are much more dangerous than females. This is currently only speculation, but makes sense in the context of human sexual dimorphism.

The anatomical sites of long-term declarative memories are difficult to determine but almost certainly involve various areas of the cortex. As is the case with abilities, memories seem to be very specific. Declarative memory also seems to be stored through a process known as *chunking.* The classic example is that of a telephone number such as 156-9541, which is stored as separate pieces of information. Another phone number such as 123-4567 seems to be stored as a single piece of information, seven successive digits beginning with the number 1. Previously we mentioned the tremendous amount of information that is stored by recalling the word *mom.* Mnemonic devices also appear to function in this manner. Students of anatomy and law have often used such devices to recall long and complex relationships and lists. Advertisers frequently present mnemonic devices so that one will remember their product. To continue with our computer analogy, *chunking* is similar to the single icon that stores a variety of information. One does not have to remember the information from minute to minute, only that it is accessible when one needs it.

If someone in the United States hears the word *Halloween,* they know upon thinking about the word that there is a diverse amount of information stored under this icon. In fact, viewing a jack–o'–lantern can call up the same information. Deacon has emphasized that our intelligence is both iconic and "indexable." How to do things is also iconic and indexable in that we can take a procedure based on past declarative memory and apply it to new sets of problems. How to hunt animals or cook a variety of fish are good examples of such intelligence.

Interspecies Comparisons of Intelligence and Memory

There is no doubt that nonhuman animals are capable of learning and long-term memory. Such abilities seem to be related to grade among vertebrates, but we know that even one-celled animals are capable of learning. Invertebrate learning is probably unconscious, and few would argue that even chimpanzees learn in a conscious way. Chimpanzees do remember individuals they have not seen for decades. The legendary memory of elephants is supported by the limited information that is available. However, the memory of native spawning grounds by salmon has been shown to be solely biochemical. The route and destination of migratory birds is mediated by geophysical phenomena (magnetism and sunlight). These types of memories result from biochemical and electromagnetic imprinting and cannot be shown to result from conscious recall.

No one has yet proposed a widely accepted definition that allows us to make interspecific comparisons. It is difficult to say which is smarter, a cat or a dog, unless the criteria for intelligence is defined. Many researchers have maintained the question is invalid because cats are better at being cats and dogs are better at being dogs. However, as we saw earlier in a discussion of grades, such an answer begs the question of why it is that we know we are more intelligent than all other known animals. In terms of behavior, this becomes a difficult conclusion to deal with. Apart from language and a big brain, we can find few absolute differences. One thing we do not want to do is define intelligent behavior as that carried out by animals that speak and have large brains.

The cat versus dog example highlights the nature of the problem as to what constitutes greater intelligence. After years of asking students which of these animals is smarter, I have found that there is a considerable division of opinion on the subject that elicits the same general arguments from students. People who think that dogs are smarter point to the fact that dogs can be trained to do a number of "tricks" and obey both gestural and voice commands. These people point out that cats are far less trainable. The pro-cat people have often countered this with the observation that cats are too smart to be trained by humans. In fact, both animals have been selected for thousands of years to be social, especially toward humans. It may be that what domestic cats and dogs are really best at is imprinting on humans, who use sociability as a kind of litmus test of intelligence. There may be some truth to this, but other animal comparisons suggest that sociability is not what we really mean by intelligence.

Everybody agrees that whatever it is that we mean by intelligence, chimpanzees are very intelligent. However, those experienced with chimpanzees know that despite their upbringing with humans, male chimpanzees are not particularly sociable towards humans. Most chimpanzees that appear in circus acts are in fact not fully grown and when they reach adulthood, they become much less tractable. One important component of assessing interspecific intelligence must include physical and not just mental abilities. We have seen that the generalized primate body includes grasping fingers with which primates perform a variety of different tasks. The anatomical constraints of the body greatly limit an animal's behavior, no matter how intelligent it may be. Dolphins may be much more intelligent than we currently suspect, but it is safe to say they will never develop the ability to do all the complex things that primates, especially humans, do with their fingers. It will be recalled with chimpanzee language that although the impediment of lacking a humanlike vocal apparatus was removed by the use of sign language, apes still did not begin to approach humans in their linguistic abilities.

Dexterity and Intelligence

Here I propose a radical theory that suggests that the ability to physically manipulate environmental features is crucial to what it is that we mean by intelligence.

Primates, racoons, and rats are very good at manipulating objects. So are elephants, pigs, and tapirs. The commonality that unites these diverse species is prehensility, whether accomplished with the nose or free limbs with digits. Among the invertebrates, octopi have been shown to be highly adept at problem solving. The problems involve manipulative tasks such as opening a jar. Whales and dolphins also exhibit intelligent behavior, but are much less adept at manipulating objects. When dolphins do manipulate objects they do it with their snout. I suggest that "playfulness" in adulthood has been also mistaken for intelligence by human observers. However, prolonged playfulness is after all one of the biological hallmarks of humanity and is intimately involved with what it is that we mean by intelligence.

The unfused digits of primates are plesiomorphic retentions. More generalized vertebrate bodies have more generalized vertebrate brains that deal with more categories of information. It is certain that this gross generalization will prove to have some exceptions. However, this general rule is predictive. If we are ever fortunate enough to encounter extraterrestrial intelligence, it can be suggested that they will be capable of fine motor manipulations of the environment. The course of the evolution of intelligent life on Earth makes it clear that slow maturation, learning, play, and environmental manipulation are compulsory for intelligent species.

Behavioral Plasticity

It has been remarked that if a termite builds a termite mound nobody cares, but if a chimpanzee builds a tree house this is impressive. Why is this so? Perhaps we regard less instinctual or stereotyped response to particular stimuli as more intelligent. The ability to vary responses to a slightly changed stimulus seems to give one an adaptive advantage. However, the ability to produce a number of responses to the same stimulus is also a characteristic of our species. How we respond to the image of a cross can vary tremendously depending on our own internal state of mind–brain. Even more confounding is the human ability to respond to very different stimuli in the same way. This is involved in the culturally universal ability of humans to form categories of thought. For instance, many humans have a categorical opinion of how we feel about rock 'n' roll or classical music despite the fact that each category encompasses a plethora of phenomena. If a chimpanzee builds a tree house, it implies to us that it understands a category that includes complex components of particular materials and forms but also a recognizable concept of wholeness.

It is hard to take the complex and efficient organization of ant society or the directional dances of bees as an indication of intelligence. These responses are elicited by rather simple chemical and environmental clues. The same stimulus or environment will always elicit the same response. This is in no way true of humans. If humans behaved much in accordance with common stimuli, it is safe to say that economists would be much more accurate and that Madison Avenue would be even richer.

Because we cannot physically or even legitimately compare thought processes of different animals, our current stage of research limits us to what we can observe, though now we can observe live brains and not just the consequences of thinking. What we observe is that humans are plastic in their behavior no matter what standards one wishes to apply. Humans can unlearn complex procedural memories (for example, smoking, eating). Altering responses to these kind of stimuli are often difficult, but all humans can do this with virtually anything they have learned. Nonhuman animals of course can change their responses, but they have far fewer responses to unlearn no matter how much they have been trained by humans.

Generalization and Specialization of Intelligence

Humans have a paradoxical instinct for noninstinctualized behavior. Our specialization is generalization. We probably have far fewer stereotypical responses in comparison with other species. We do possess specialized processes for language, tool use and manufacture, visual discrimination, and retention of vast amounts of information from the cultural experiences that program us. The degree to which we are noninstinctual is evident in that we must learn such basic behaviors as mating and parenting, which, although acquired through learning in other species, are much more experience-based in humans. The degree to which we must learn these types of behaviors is a plesiomorphic legacy of our primate ancestry. The adaptive advantage that intelligence conveys is the ability to adapt to changing environments. Such environments can be climatic, technological, and social. Physical environments change daily, seasonally, or over the course of millions of years. Social environments can change from second to second or year to year. We are very intelligent about other people. In spite of the fact that individuals and cultures frequently misunderstand each other, we behave on a daily basis more or less accurately gauging the mental states of other people. To do this, we call on what we have treated as compartmentalized categories of thinking depending on the most relevant and appropriate classes of information that we have at our disposal. We have evolved to be generalists that retain a wider variety of categories than other species.

If one compares all the species on the planet, they can be ranked as to how specialized or generalized and as to how many kinds of information they use on a daily basis. One species must inevitably be the most generalized in the kinds of information it considers and in the kinds of actions it is capable of taking. This is why I believe that any attempts to calculate and understand intelligence must always be coupled with behavior. Natural selection constantly pushes species toward specialization, and, in this case, the analogy of the marketplace is appropriate. But following the same analogy diversification is a better long-term strategy. When other competing animals have specialized in a particular direction and when the ways of perceiving and acting become canalized, there will always be one animal that is less specialized and less dependent of stereotypical responses to the environment. Dealing with changes in the environment in learned and less somatic ways confer evolutionary flexibility. I think this is what we mean by intelligence. Behavioral plasticity explains why our species finds apes more fun to interact with than cows.

At the same time, it is difficult to explain why bacteria and cockroaches are so successful in terms of their numbers and environmental flexibility. Despite claims to the contrary, their very short life spans allow for the ability to rapidly produce new variations through the mutations of new individuals. Their environmental flexibility has come through structural changes. Humans also made a structural change, which was the ability to deal with environmental changes through the integration of a huge number of variables in rapid calculations. Life requires the extraction of chemical resources from the environment. The more alternative sources of energy that an organism can survive on builds in a selection for redundancy. Cockroaches rely on the extraction of a comparatively few resources that are ubiquitous. Humans have evolved to utilize a huge variety of resources. This means that humans ultimately come to rely on a brain that paid attention to many more things than most animals' brains. In comparison with other organisms, we are not specialized in what we pay attention to. The fact that hominid brains became relatively isolated from senses other than vision forced, according to this model, an emphasis on information processing rather the coordination of a variety of sensory inputs.

At our current stage of understanding, an ultimate definition of intelligence continues to elude us. I have suggested that it somehow refers to our species prowess at being anatomical generalists who by default and evolutionary accident never became concerted specialists at a particular way of extracting essential nutrients and reproducing. A specialization on the processing of visual information may have been, for as yet some uncomprehended reason, crucial in making us superb information processors. There is some evidence that the ability to sense photons may have been the first sense developed by organisms on this planet. Those organisms that maintained the ability to sense a wider spectrum of light may have had an advantage. Unfortunately, we have strayed into the realm of speculation and philosophy, where opinions about the nature of intelligence will no doubt remain for centuries to come.

Summary

On this planet, only humans have any interests in defining or contemplating intelligence. Within our species, recent Western thought has been particularly concerned with how to identify levels of intelligence especially at the level of the individual. Many cultures believe that "too much thinking" is responsible for everything from baldness to madness. The Judeo-Christian concern with the soul and the task of clearly separating humans from animals in the context of rapidly developing technology probably best accounts for the Western fascination with intelligence. The sustained technological explosion in the West made it easy to accept that material complexity and science must be related to intelligence. In fact, many other traditions of thought have attributed their successes (including material complexity) to such attributes as spirituality, harmony, and martial prowess. Could each of these be a separate kind of intelligence esteemed in different cultural contexts?

The traditional measures of individual variation in intelligence in the West have been written examinations, which may also involve an emphasis on manual and spatial dexterity. Variants of the IQ have far more social significance than scientific use. There does seem to be a strong genetic component to performing well on IQ tests. However, the correlations with academic success or success in life are much lower. Recent contentions that there is a correlation between socioeconomic status and IQ cannot possibly untangle test scores from social and historical factors. To do well on a test, one must learn at least to be adequately versed in the medium of the examination whether it is language, archery, or test taking itself. Should we expect a highly successful Kalahari forager to do well on a state board examination? The intelligent answer is no.

If intelligence as a single entity is highly genetic, can we breed it? The answer is no. We have been successful at breeding animals for certain qualities and temperaments, but we rarely speak of horses and dogs as being sentient. However, they are intelligences for particular tasks selected by humans. Breeders of dogs consider "working" dogs and poodles to be the most intelligent almost certainly because they are required to perform a number of different tasks such as shepherding cattle or pleasing humans. Among horse breeders, the cowboy's Western quarter horse is considered the most intelligent for exactly the same reason. This observation is not philosophically elegant, but it is pragmatic and makes sense in the context of natural selection. Furthermore, multiple intelligences are of little evolutionary value without the anatomical generalizations and specializations to put them to use. Form fits function, and both are dictated by the environment. To risk a tautology, the specialization of humans is generalization.

The concept of behavioral plasticity allows us to combine anatomy and thought to make interspecific comparisons and therefore better understand evolution. It is therefore of little surprise that the most anatomically generalized vertebrates—primates—have the greatest behavioral plasticity. Dolphins may be highly intelligent, but to confirm this we will have to study these mammals more closely because there are no obvious indications that they are on a level with humans. For instance, they do not manufacture or use an infinite variety of tools, construct dwellings or have detailed exchanges of ideas, which we define as conversation. (It probably would have been extremely difficult to discover the particular genius of Stephen Hawking if we had not used the sophisticated technology that allowed us to listen to his behavior (brain–mind).)

Humans perform so many different kinds of tasks to insure survival and reproduction that it is not surprising to see that the brain supports separate kinds of intelligences, which can be emphasized according to the natural or cultural environment. The kinds of categories of intelligence also fit extremely well with the record of hominid evolution. Scientists have yet to discover uniquely developed human abilities that make no evolutionary sense. There are no specifically human propensities for aquatic life, flying, or nocturnal insectivory, to name but a few examples of what we do not do very well. If we take what it is that humans are uniquely good at, such as language, complex social interaction, technology, the arts, and many other behaviors, we find that there are corresponding anatomical places in the brain for such behaviors. These innate propensities and predispositions are highly consistent with the fossil and archaeological record of our species. We do not find areas for telekinesis, though we are very adept at "reading" other people's minds. Various disorders illustrate that in the absence of the usual development of multiple overlapping intelligences, one or two categories can become hyperdeveloped. Perhaps the "commonsense" brain suppresses or cannot manage widespread hyperdevelopment in most individuals but can adjust biologically to particularly strong selection pressures. Cultures and individual upbringing seem capable of accomplishing a similar process. Despite the occasional Leonardo or Jefferson, the "Renaissance man" is a rare phenomenon. Positing a single intelligence for dealing with everything may be similar to developing a Theory of Everything in that the complexity of reality is best dealt with in parts.

Over the billions of years of organic evolution and by virtue of individual variation, one species had to have combined the most generalized anatomy with the most behavioral complexity in a kind of calculus that allowed the maximum flexibility. This suggests that multiple human intelligences in a single brain are the outcome of this process.

QUESTIONS FOR REVIEW

1. What assumptions are made by practitioners of IQ tests?

2. What is intelligence? What is the dichotomy between multiple and single intelligence theories?

3. How can generalization be specialization?

MIND AND BODY EXPERIMENTS

1. Make a list of friends and what they do better than anything else. Do they differ markedly?

2. How do you identify an intelligent person?

3. Ask female friends who the current leaders in the National Football League or American League are. Ask male friends how to wash woolen garments.

4. Compile a list of people you consider to be geniuses. What do they excel at?

5. What are the differences between how a thirty-year-old person "thinks" and how a twenty-year-old person "thinks"? Do some interviews.

6. What things are hard for you to remember? What parts of your life are hard to remember? Which phases are still "crystal clear" in your memory? Why do you think you have different experiences, some of which are vivid and some of which are not?

SUGGESTED READINGS

Anderson, J. R. 1983. *The Architecture of Cognition.* Cambridge, MA: Harvard University Press.

Benbow, C., and Stanley, J. 1980. Sex Differences in Mathematical Ability: Fact or Artifact? *Science* 210: 1262–1264.

Binet, A., and Simon, T. 1911. Methodes Nouvelles pour le Diagnostic du Niveque Intellecia des Arnormous. *L'Annee Psychologique* 11: 191–244.

Burt, C. 1955. The Evidence for the Concept of Intelligence. *British Journal of Educational Psychology* 25: 158–177.

Burt, C. 1963. The Genetic Determination of Differences in Intelligence: A Study of Monozygotic Twins Reared Together and Apart. *British Journal of Psychology* 57: 137–153.

Fuster, J. M. 1980. *The Prefrontal Cortex.* New York: Raven Press.

Gardner, H. 1983. *Frames of Mind: The Theory of Multiple Intelligences.* New York: Basic Books.

Griffin, D. R. 1976. *The Question of Animal Awareness: Evolutionary Continuity of Mental Experience.* New York: Rockefeller University Press.

Griffin, D. R. 1978. Prospects for a Cognitive Ethology. *Behavioral & Brain Sciences* 1: 527–538.

Jensen, A. 1973. *Educability and Group Differences.* New York: Harper and Row.

Jerrison, H. 1973. *Evolution of the Brain and Behavior.* New York: Academic Press.

Kolata, G. 1983. Math Genius May Have Hormonal Basis, *Science* 223: 1312.

Lewontin, R. C., Rose, S. P. R., and Kamin, L. J. 1984. *Not in Our Genes.* New York: Pantheon.

Lumsden, C. J., and Wilson, E. O. 1983. *Promethean Fire: Reflections on the Origin of Mind.* Cambridge, MA: Harvard University Press.

Lumsden, C. J., and Wilson, E. O. 1985. The Relation between Biological and Cultural Evolution. *Journal of Social & Biological Structures* 8: 343–359.

Parker, S. T., and Gibson, K. R. 1979. A Developmental Model for the Evolution of Language and Intelligence in Early Hominids. *Behavioral & Brain Sciences* 2: 367–408.

Penfield, W. and Rasmussen, T. 1950. *The Cerebral Cortex of Man: A Clinical Study of Localization of Function.* New York: Macmillan.

Penfield, W., and Roberts, L. 1959. *Speech and Brain Mechanisms.* Princeton, NJ: Princeton University Press.

Scarr-Salapatek, S. 1971. Unknowns in the I.Q. Equation. *Science,* 174: 1223–1228.

Scheper-Hughes, N. 1979. *Saints, Scholars and Schizophrenics.* Berkeley: University of California Press.

Shuey, A. M. 1966. *The Testing of Negro Intelligence.* New York: Social Science Press.

Sternberg, R. 1985. Beyond I.Q.: A Triarchic Theory of Human Intelligence. *Behavior & Brain Sciences.* New York: Cambridge University Press.

Terman, L. 1916. *The Measurement of Intelligence.* Boston: Houghton Mifflin.

Watson, J. B. 1926. What the Nursery Has to Say about Instincts. In C. Murcheson (ed.), *Psychologies of 1925.* Worcester, MA: Clark University Press.

Watson, J. B. 1928. *The Psychological Care of Infant and Child.* New York: Norton.

Yerkes, R. 1923. Testing the Human Mind. *Atlantic Monthly* 131: 363–364.

9

Sleep and Dreams

All men are alike when they sleep.

—Aristotle

Most people have probably had dreams which it is hard to imagine not to have been glimpses into an actually existing region of being, perhaps a corner of the spiritual world. And dreams have accordingly in all ages been regarded as revelations, and played a large part in furnishing forth mythologies and creating themes for faith to lay hold upon.

—William James

What man can remember his own dreams?

—William Shakespeare

The cultural patterning of mental life affects the patterning of dreams, visions and hallucinations.

—Marvin Harris

Most people are not all alike when they sleep, and there is very little chance that someone will spend a single night without dreaming. It is true that people have trouble remembering their dreams and that daily experiences influence nightly dreams. To function in a normal manner, all people need sleep and dreams. Sleep is covered in virtually every text dealing with psychology or neuroanatomy and physiology. Dreams, however, are seldom dealt with in these or in anthropology texts, even though the vast majority of cultures endow dreams with a specific, usually spiritual or mystical, significance. Sleep and dreams are intimately involved with other body rhythms of which there are at least two hundred types of cycles influencing the human body. Cycles are common to almost all known life-forms and are influenced by the environment. Most cycles seem to be adjustable because they can be altered in direct relation to environmental changes. These cycles are so important that the introduction of drugs, food, and disease can have significantly different effects depending on what time of day they are introduced into the body.

Dreams seem to be very important to the functioning of the normal brain. There is no known culture that regards dreams as unimportant. Almost all cultures attach considerable significance to the "messages" in dreams. Dreaming is always recognized as an experience that is separate from day-to-day reality. In the West, Freudian theory has been extensively explored in relation to a theory of dreams and symbols.

The evolutionary and adaptive significance of sleep, dreaming, and other rhythms of the body are still poorly understood. However, there is an overwhelming consensus among sleep researchers that dreams are necessary to overall well-being. At the same time, it may be possible that at least some of these cycles are teleomatic features that are connected to other essential ways of maintaining the mind and body.

Sleep and especially REM (rapid eye movement) sleep may simply be a means of saving energy. In most animals, energy consumption decreases during sleep. In humans, however, metabolism increases. We have seen that carnivores are probably the most efficient mammals in terms of conserving energy through long periods of inactivity. The fact that meat is a much more compact source of nutrients than low-energy vegetarian-based diets means that carnivores can exist with far fewer and more widely spaced meals. At the same time, hunting also requires repeated, usually fruitless, expenditures of energy. It is thus difficult to work out an accurate cost–benefit analysis between carnivores and vegetarians. Carnivores sleep from 60 to 80 percent of their adult lives; humans sleep on average about 30 percent of their adult lives. Because dreaming seems to be associated with **endothermy** in mammals, it has been suggested that the human pattern of energy use more efficiently maintains a constant internal temperature when people are asleep. Both birds and mammals are endotherms and evolved after the appearance of dinosaurs. This may suggest that REM sleep evolved independently as a common solution to the problem of maintaining a constant body temperature in an increasingly seasonal world brought about by north and south drifting continents.

Body Cycles and Rhythms

As just mentioned above, sleep and dreaming are part of a collection of at least 200 *biorhythms* that influence, govern, and organize the activity of human beings. These have been divided into three basic kinds of rhythms, which have been classified on the basis of how they fit into the human day, week, month or year. The most basic rhythm is known as a *circadian rhythm* (L. *circus*=around, *dies*=days). These biorhythms are controlled and set by external cues known as *zeitgebers* (time givers), which alert an individual to the progression of time and predictable changes in the environment. A number of cave studies in which subjects were isolated from external zeitgebers such as light and clocks indicate that people significantly lengthen their periods of both wakefulness and sleep in the absence of regulating environmental clues.

There are also internal clocks that seem to be much more independent of the environment. These include *metabolic* and *temperature cycles*. Although most circadian rhythms can be altered by external stimulus, they change very slowly. Examples of important circadian rhythms are cycles such as sleep, alertness, body temperature, and the toxicity and effectiveness of drugs. Nutrients and poisons can have dramatically different effects depending on what time of day they are ingested. In general, humans and many other animals have a roughly twenty-five-hour cycle instead of the twenty-four-hour cycle one would intuitively expect of the organisms of Earth. In a way, this makes sense because daytime and nighttime light is continually changing. Animals with an unalterable cycle probably would have difficulty in adapting to seasonal fluctuations.

Another kind of important biorhythm is known as an *ultradian rhythm*. These include cycles that span more than a day and include menstruation in females and hormonal activity in general. Most northern mammals reproduce on a seasonal cycle. In general, most populations seem to reproduce in conjunction with the availability of natural resources at the time of most births. Hibernation in many mammals is a classic but poorly understood seasonal phenomenon. Interestingly enough, studies indicate that though body metabolism and temperature are significantly depressed in hibernating mammals, they still maintain roughly twenty-five-hour clocks of other bodily functions.

In humans, disruption of circadian rhythms can have severe effects. This is especially true in relation to attentiveness, alertness, and job performance. Accidents at the nuclear plants of Chernobyl and Three Mile Island occurred between 12 A.M. and 7 A.M., when human alertness was at its daily low. Afternoon daydreaming is a well-known human phenomenon. Jet lag appears to be much more disruptive when a passenger travels from west to east than from east to west. Passengers arriving in the east find that they are awake during the time when people at their destination have been sleeping. They often arrive at the end of their day to find that they must start and participate in the new day of the easterners. Westbound travel is easier to adjust to because they can simply stay up late and then sleep longer.

The importance of light in body rhythms cannot be overestimated. This seems to be particularly true of seasonal variation in the duration and intensity of sunlight. This is underscored by *seasonal affective disorder* or SAD. People deprived of a sufficient amount of full spectrum sunlight for months at a time often develop symptoms of irritability and depression. Some even become suicidal. In arctic and other climates with short days and cold conditions requiring a lot of time spent indoors, suicidal tendencies can be an acute problem. Although often attributed to the effects of "cabin fever" (simple confinement and isolation), it is now known that full spectrum light (sunlight) is very effective in alleviating these symptoms. Other symptoms related to the lack of sunlight may involve discomfort and dementia related to the decreased production of vitamin D. It is possible that Sigmund Freud's theory of psychoanalysis was developed at least in part on the observations of Victorian Parisian women who developed a complex of symptoms known as *gran mal*, which are very similar to those of SAD. They may have resulted from the widespread tendency of nineteenth-century women to cover their skin and stay indoors.

The *pineal gland* is the master clock of the body and the brain. This tiny, fingertip-sized gland, located on the hypothalamus just above the fibers that carry light-generated signals on the *suprachiasmic nucleus,* sets body rhythms. In birds and small vertebrates with thin skulls, light is able to penetrate the skull and directly affect the pineal gland. In humans, the light must come through the eyes. The pineal gland controls the release of the neurotransmitter hormone *melatonin*, which is pivotal in inducing sleep. It may also be related to healing functions that take place during sleep. *Cortisol,* another chemical that aids in healing, is also released in increased amounts during sleep.

Sleep

The need for sleep evolved with the appearance of birds and mammals, and yet it seems to be controlled by areas of the brain, such as the brain stem, that are relatively ancient on the evolutionary timescale. Humans spend about one-third of their lives sleeping and about one-fifth of that is spent dreaming. During sleep and dreaming there are marked changes in brain and body activity. Reptiles' periods of inactivity do not coincide with a change in brain activity. Higher vertebrates enter distinct stages of brain activity that have their own particular characteristics. In all animals that sleep, the process is restorative. The body benefits from sleep. By not being used, muscles dissipate the lactic acid that accumulates during physical activity. The brain, however, requires sleep. As with other human behaviors, there is a great range of variation in the sleep that each individual requires. Infants sleep more than adults, and older adults sleep less than younger adults. Some (usually older) individuals need only one to two hours of sleep per night. The amount of sleep required may change drastically (and literally overnight) as the result of rapid shifts in schedules and geography. Cases of jet lag are examples of this. On the other hand, the "Roman nap" was a technique used in classical times in which people claimed to have derived the full benefits of several hours of sleep by training themselves to fall quickly into a deep but brief sleep lasting less than half an hour.

In the early decades of sleep research, it was speculated that sleep might simply result from the lack of sensory input during the night. It is now known that there are specific anatomical areas and specific neurotransmitters that trigger both sleep and alertness. The *raphe (seam) system*, which joins the base of the midbrain, seems to be active in inducing sleep, while the *reticular system*, which is located on either side of the raphe, seems to be involved in wakefulness. Neither of these systems perform in simple or easily understandable ways. Neurotransmitters such as *norepinephrine* and *dopamine* are associated with wakefulness, while *serotonin*, which is utilized by the raphe system, seems to help to induce sleep.

It is becoming increasingly clear that a variety of other substances that work on the brain are also involved in sleep and wakefulness. One substance known as the *"S" factor* can be purified from sleeping animals. When it is injected into the bloodstream of other animals, it induces sleep. As is true with other brain behaviors, there is a biochemical basis to sleep and alertness that can be activated by the external world (season, temperature, social pressures, disease, and diet), but it is mediated chemically.

Stages of Sleep

Sleep in humans and other higher vertebrates is divided into four stages that are repeated every night. There seems to be a general relationship between the amount of sleep and the natural danger from predators that an animal is subjected to. Carnivores, which usually have few predators, spend much more time sleeping and dreaming. An interspecific comparison of mammals suggests that the longest periods of circadian sleep occur in those animals that are least at risk when they sleep. These are generally carnivores. Estimates for cat sleep range up to 80 percent of a twenty four-hour period. The term *cat nap* seems to more accurately describe what it is they usually do when they fall deeply asleep for many periods of time during the day. Cats do not seem to progress through the stages of sleep usually characteristic of humans. At the same time, they seem to be able to monitor certain stimuli while they are asleep. Loud noises may not awake a cat, but the smell of food often does. This effect is less common in humans, but may also be present. For humans, sleep seems to be divided into more complicated patterns and stages that do not suggest the evolutionary history of a strictly carnivorous animal. In comparison with other animals, humans require a moderate amount of sleep.

Prior to falling asleep, people exhibit a period of relaxation characterized by *alpha waves* (slow even rhythms of electrical brain waves). This state can be controlled consciously and enhanced through a number of techniques including biofeedback and meditation. Body temperature, heart rate, respiration, metabolic activity, and brain activity become progressively slower as a sleeper progresses into the successive stages of sleep, and muscles become more flaccid.

Normal relaxed wakefulness gives way to stage 1 of sleep, which is characterized by spikes of activity that when they occur together are known as *spindles.* During this stage of sleep, neurons may fire independently in response to stimuli such as light, sound, and touch. If sleepers are awakened during Stage 1 sleep, they frequently deny having slept at all. By stage 2 of sleep, spindles become more frequent, and it is more difficult to awake the sleeper. Stage 3 is characterized by an accentuation of all these tendencies. Brain activity becomes even slower. External stimuli such as noise can cause a subject to cease their progression into further stages of sleep and return to stages 1 or 2. In stage 4, a sleeper enters into *deep sleep* in which brain waves are much slower than in the previous stages. Sleepers awakened during this phase of sleep are usually disoriented and groggy. Sleep walking and sleep talking tend to occur in stages 3 and 4. Sleep talking is not necessarily associated with dreams or REM sleep, and dreams can occur during other stages of sleep. Brain activity takes place in slow waves, abbreviated as *SWS* (slow wave sleep). In this stage of sleep, response to external stimuli is minimized and the neurons that are active become synchronous. During wakefulness, separate neurons are processing separate external stimuli independently.

The final sequence of sleep was first noticed by W. Dement and N. Kletiman, who observed that REM sleep is associated with dreaming. With the exception of one primitive marsupial, the spiny anteater, all mammals and birds exhibit REM sleep. In general, those species that spend the longest times in REM sleep are also the ones that spend the longest times in sleep overall. Sleep deprivation studies show that subjects deprived of all sleep make it up the next night if allowed to. However, people first make up the non-REM sleep before making up REM sleep. During the REM phase of sleep, heart and respiration rates increase and the brain becomes more active. At the same time, the muscles of the body become essentially paralyzed. This phase of sleep is also referred to as *paradoxical sleep* because the brain is highly active and yet the body is immobilized. Because the brain is active and the body is immobilized, the distinction between light sleep and deep sleep has been blurred. It is during the REM phase that it is most difficult to arouse a sleeper. Another characteristic of this kind of sleep is that neuronal firing becomes desynchronized. Muscle twitches of the fingers and face also characterize this part of a night's sleep. In short, the body seems to be asleep, while the brain is very active. New born infants begin life by spending one-third of their twenty-four-hour cycle in REM sleep, one-third of their time in non-REM sleep, and one-third of their time awake. Premature babies spend much more of their first few weeks in REM sleep. For normally maturing people, the amount of all kinds of sleep decreases as they age.

As of yet, we do not have a good evolutionary explanation for the necessity of sleep. Among mammals, species that seem to use their nervous system and muscles more intensely for short periods of time apparently require more sleep. Hibernation is not just a form of sleep because it involves a cycle that transcends circadian rhythms.

Dreams

It is during REM sleep that people most often report dreams, especially vivid visual ones. Sound and sensations are also a common part of dreams. Even people who say they do not dream almost always report a dream if they are awakened during REM sleep. The initial progression through the first three stages of sleep takes from ninety to one hundred minutes, but as the night's sleep continues, REM sleep becomes progressively longer. The average person goes through the entire cycle about four or five times a night. The last episode of REM sleep ends in awakening.

REM awakening research has also established the likelihood that we dream in real time, meaning that when a dream seems like it was ten minutes long, it probably was. Furthermore, even if REM sleep is longer than 15 minutes, sleepers do not seem to be able to remember more than 15 minutes of their dreams. In fact, dreams do not seem to be conducive to memory retention. There is, for instance, very little support for the idea that we can learn through "sleep teaching." At the same time, there is evidence that stimuli presented to the sleeper are incorporated in dreams as are the day's events. People can also be trained to remember their dreams more accurately and thoroughly through self-suggestion. The common report of the sensation of falling, floating, or flying may result from the fact that the inner ear, which mediates balance and body orientation, is in a horizontal position in the sleeper. Another common feeling is one of helplessness, probably stemming from the fact that the major muscle groups are largely paralyzed during REM. One common report is that of knowing someone is in the same room, but being unable to awake and communicate with them. The explanation of the perception of paralysis and helplessness as the result of paradoxical sleep has been criticized because people also dream about moving. The inner ear input may be responsible for this, but another more speculative mechanism, related to the phantom limb of amputees, may also be at work. The brain may somehow try to make sense of the paralysis by attempting to create a coherent explanation for the paralysis.

A number of evolutionary explanations has been advanced to account for the adaptiveness of sleep and dreams. Whatever sleep is, there is a large body of scientific and clinical evidence that indicates that sleep is restorative. Muscle repair and growth increases during sleep. This is true in spite of the fact that normally functioning adults seem to require vastly different amounts of sleep. Requirements also change with both age and conscious activity.

Paradoxical sleep may be a response of the body's need to keep some neural circuits open at all times. Paradoxical sleep may help avoid detection by nocturnal predators and keep people from injuring themselves by disabling the ability to activate major muscle groups needed for locomotion. Specifically, I suggest that in the evolutionary past such checks would be especially helpful to animals that slept in trees or other places from which they might fall if they acted out what they were dreaming about.

The Meaning and Function of Dreams

Freudian Theory

A number of general theories have been advanced about the function of dreams. Sigmund Freud believed that dreams allowed the mind to consider unconscious or subconscious thoughts that were too unpleasant to consider during wakefulness. These problems often revolved around sexuality and the Oedipus complex mentioned in Chapter 7. Nearly all psychologists and psychoanalysts believe that each dreamer's dream is a product of their own experience and personality. The information that Freud used to develop his theory of dreams was often based on dreams that were recounted sometime after they had occurred. This approach not only neglected the fact that most dreams are forgotten soon after they occur, but it also failed to take into account the fact that daily conscious experience undoubtedly influences recollections of dreams and many other memories. When dreamers are roused during or just after a dream, the details of any particular dream are generally much more vivid and complete. Probably more important, the psychoanalyst's interpretation of what a dream means is the dreamer's own interpretation. It is probably safe to say that all people have a dream that they would like to talk about given the opportunity. Furthermore, there is good anecdotal evidence that people like talking about their dreams so much that they will go out of their way to do so. As the result of more than twenty years of classroom evaluations of my teaching by my students in the college classroom, I have found that the student evaluations are always higher when, as part of the battery of questions, they are asked to recount the last dream they can remember. Many times, the students cannot remember the dreams, but the evaluations are always higher. This phenomenon suggests to me that it is not just difficult or unpleasant thoughts that are being considered in dreams. For Freud, thoughts would not have occurred in the form of dreams unless they were unpleasant.

Freud believed that another means of considering unpleasant thoughts was the use of symbolism in dreams. Psychiatrist Carl Gustav Jung (1875–1961) later expanded on this theory, postulating certain standardized symbols that he strongly implied were universal, regardless of the culture in which the dream occurred. The idea that certain symbols have a common universal meaning regardless of their cultural context has received little support from anthropological research. It is true that all cultures use similar geometric symbols such as triangles, circles, and squares. The phallic symbol or shape is also widespread among many cultures, and it is easy to understand how symbolic representations of parts of the body may have arisen. This is a different statement from saying that long cylindrical objects always refer to sexual content in a dream. The truth of the old psychology joke that "sometimes a dream about a banana is just a dream about a banana" seems obvious to someone who, like myself, has spent more than twenty years among tropical cultures. A banana dream is much more likely to represent a subconscious concern with breakfast than sex.

The sexual content of dreams is an important part of Freudian theory. However, the fact that men develop penile erection and women experience swelling of the genitals during sleep is probably not related to the sexual content of dreams, but is due to the fact that blood collects in the extremities during periods of prolonged inactivity. The phenomenon of erection is also a well-known feature of hanged men and surely has nothing to do with sexually exciting thoughts experienced by the condemned.

In defense of psychoanalytical explanations and explications of dreams, people who consciously explore remembered dreams do seem to feel better as the result of sessions with their psychoanalyst. Although slightly more speculative, it is quite possible that people do employ some symbols in their dreams. This is certainly in keeping with the greater right hemisphere of the brain involvement with the processing of space and form. A dreamer's own opinion of what the symbols or objects that appear in their dreams mean seems to be relevant to a dreamer's conscious thought. Symbols have personal as well as cultural referents developed over the course of an individual's lifetime.

Somewhat related to this phenomenon may be the fact that very few (if any) cultures attribute no significance to dreams. Their importance in folklore, history, literature, and science is legendary. Almost all cultures consider dreams to be an extraordinary experience that provides access to normally unavailable information about the past or future. Rarely do dreams concern the present. One phenomenon that has been reported several times throughout history, at least in anecdotal form, is the ability for the brain to awake from sleep with the solution to a problem that has been on the mind of the dreamer. Several inventors have reported this phenomenon. This may be a variation of Freud's explanation, but the brain is not exclusively considering problems that are too unpleasant to be consciously considered. If the "mind" is in fact contemplating problems encountered during consciousness, it may be that they are too complicated to be resolved with an obvious and simple answer. Alternatively, some may be best solved from the perspective of an overall gestalt or intuitive conclusion, which the dreaming right hemisphere seems to be best at.

If the dreaming brain is actually working out difficult problems that it does not tackle while conscious, one has to also consider the fact that people can go through an entire day thinking that a dream has actually happened. There are many cases of normal people proceeding on the basis of mistaking a dreamed event as actually having taken place. Usually the dreamer encounters reality in the form of tangible proof in the waking world that indicates that the dream could not have been true. Individuals of many non-Western cultures experience both induced and accidental dreams involving mythical or imagined components, whose elements cannot be readily checked against the natural world. There also seems to be much less importance placed on separating dream reality from waking reality in non-Western cultures. Many societies, for instance Native Americans, often require a dream or a vision before moving on to new phases of their life, such as adulthood.

Memory Consolidation

Memory consolidation is a theory of the function of dreams, which holds that dreams somehow mediate the storage of memory and aid in the acquisition of knowledge. It is true that people deprived of both REM and non-REM sleep do report increased problems with memory and learning. However, infant data is somewhat at odds with this theory, as infants spend much more time in REM but do not have memories until they reach two to three years of age. It is difficult to believe that REM sleep is serving the function of the storage of memory, but REM sleep may play some part in the sensiomotor development, which is crucial to the normal maturation of infants. Infants also learn to recognize their mother's face and voice as well as distinguish between certain syllables soon after birth. As with adults, alertness peaks shortly after sleep. However, there is no strong evidence linking REM sleep specifically with memory consolidation.

"Trash Theory"

Somewhat related to the memory consolidation theory is the "trash theory" of Crick and Mitchison, which postulates that the function of dreams is to allow the brain to cast off unneeded or trivial information. This supposedly keeps the memory from becoming cluttered with unimportant information. One of the problems with this interpretation is that what is useful information is often determined by future events. Minute details that are considered of little importance when they are initially remembered may become of considerable utility the next day.

Activation–Synthesis Theory

Another teleomatically based theory is that of activation–synthesis put forward by Hobson and McCarley. This theory suggests that stimulation of processing areas normally involved in processing stimuli arising from both the activation of internal centers and from outside sources are "turned on" for some reason during sleep and dreaming. The problem arises when centers that are normally active in processing these stimuli find that a quiet dark environment provides little input. One variant of this theory suggests that the brain compensates for the lack of external stimuli by drawing on memories. In doing so, the brain attempts to explain or rationalize the stimuli into a coherent story or scenario. If this is so, the brain is not very good at doing so because one of the usual characteristics of dreams is that they are oddly proportioned and bizarre in comparison with normal conscious behavior. Moreover, the part of the brain that has been strongly implicated in the creation of rationalizations is the left hemisphere, which seems to be far less involved in dreaming. One speculation about why the brain keeps certain centers active may be the need not to completely shut down. It may be necessary for the prevention of comalike states from which arousal is very difficult. The teleonomic function of this system may be to retain stem alertness, while dreams simply are a teleomatic product of this process.

Summary

Sleep is an essential part of human existence. It is plesiomorphic for warm-blooded vertebrates. It is one of the several internally generated and externally cued body rhythms that regulate human behavior. From an evolutionary perspective, it may have evolved as an energy-saving mechanism for conserving bodily resources during periods of the twenty-four-hour day when the body had the smallest chance of replenishing itself. The fact that carnivores sleep most and that they subsist on single daily or less than daily meals of concentrated protein supports this interpretation. Carnivores also have the least to fear from other dangerous animals when they sleep.

The human requirement for sleep is hard to assess, but it does not follow carnivore patterns. Instead, the human sleep pattern falls somewhere between herbivores and carnivores, which is consistent with our omnivorous diet. The stages of human sleep are biologically and not culturally determined. Several centers in the brain biologically control sleep, wakefulness, and alertness with the aid of neurotransmitters.

The function of dreams is much less clear. I have suggested here that they are teleomatic. At the same time, it is very clear that dream deprivation is detrimental to normal functioning. Most cultures attach special significance to dreams, and some cultures accord them properties that anthropologists usually associate with spiritual beliefs. Freud's psychoanalytic interpretations do not seem to be well supported by modern dream research. The contention that unpleasant thoughts (including sexuality) or symbolic thoughts constitute the basic reality of dreams is not supported by comparative ethnographic data.

QUESTIONS FOR REVIEW

1. How are various body cycles regulated?

2. What are the stages and characteristics of sleep?

3. What are some of the problems with Freud's theory of dreams?

4. What are some of the non-Freudian theories of the evolutionary function of dreams?

5. What is paradoxical sleep? What selection pressures might account for it?

MIND AND BODY EXPERIMENTS

1. Before going to bed, consciously concentrate on trying to remember your dreams. Do you remember them better the next morning?

2. Ask people about a dream they had once. Do they recount it with enthusiasm?

3. Interview people about nightmares or "weird dreams." Are there any commonalities of vision and emotional feeling? What constitutes a nightmare?

4. Interview people and ask them when they feel they are most alert in their twenty-four-hour cycles. Represent the combined results as a graph.

5. Ask people how long they sleep each night on average. Do the lengths correlate with age? Sex? Ethnicity? Test scores? Other factors?

SUGGESTED READINGS

Bridgeman, B. 1988. *The Biology of Behavior and Mind*. New York: Wiley and Sons.

Crick, F. and Mitchison, G. 1986. REM sleep and neural nets. *Journal of Mind and Behavior* 7: 229–249.

Dement, W. 1960. The Effect of Dream Deprivation. *Science* 131: 1705–1707.

Dement, W. 1974. *Some Must Watch While Some Must Sleep*. San Francisco: Freeman.

Dement, W., and Kleitman, N. 1957. Cyclic Variations in EEG During Sleep and Their Relation to Eye Movements, Body Motility and Dreaming. *Electroencephlography & Clinical Neurophysiology* 9: 673–690.

Hobson, J. 1994. *The Chemistry of Conscious States: How the Brain Changes Its Mind*. Boston: Little, Brown.

Hobson, J. 1995. *Sleep*. New York: Scientific American Library.

Freud, S. 1933. *New Introductory Lectures in Psychoanalysis*. New York: Norton.

Rose, S. P. R. 1976. *The Conscious Brain*. Harmondsworth, Eng.: Penguin Books.

Taub, J. M., and Berger, R. J. 1969. Extended Sleep and Performance: The Rip Van Winkle Effect. *Psychonomic Science* 16: 204–205.

CHAPTER

10

The Bottom Line

The affinities of all beings of the same class have sometimes been represented by a great tree. I believe this simile largely speaks the truth.
—Charles Darwin

Human behavior is a composite of both old and relatively new operational modes that store and act on information that has been crucial to the survival of our species. To use a computer analogy, the data which is entered, retained, and acted on is infinitely variable, but the categories or classes of information are not. Culture became crucial to hominid existence to such an extent that we cannot exist without it. The kinds of knowledge that motivate and guide us exist as a result of our evolutionary history. This history is recorded in the form of our current and fossil anatomy and in the details of the archaeological record. We are vertebrates, mammals, primates, and lastly hominids who evolved as the result of a series of "revolutions" and "successful" experiments through which most of the now dominant forms of life on this planet passed. All individuals of our species share certain characteristics because we have common ancestors at the various levels of evolutionary organization through which we have passed. Humans eventually came to depend on extra somatically transmitted forms of knowledge, known today as culture, which outstripped all competing forms of terrestrial life in its capacity to rapidly adapt to changing environments and situations. The details of our adaptations are so complex that any list of these life ways can only be a mere outline of obvious human characteristics. Nonetheless, it is exactly this that this text has attempted to present.

Understanding human evolution and behavior inevitably involves many gray areas in which the dominance of genetics and experience is not obvious. At every level, whether cellular, anatomical, or cultural, the workings of the human organism are so complex that firm conclusions about the future are still impossible. We do not behave as simply as chemical systems, but we rely on our cultural machines to deal with the complexity that our organic selves have created. In our evolution, we evolved to pay attention to what was important to the survival of the various species stages through which we passed. For some as yet uncomprehended advantages, human ancestors evolved an extreme dependence on visual processing, then bipedalism, and finally a reliance on intense communication that took the form of language. These developments have structured the categories that we use to think. Consciousness has become part of our way of dealing with the world. However, if we had to consciously design ourselves, we could not do it without reference to the specific evolutionary history of *Homo sapiens*.

This book is a crude blueprint for what nature has already built without the aid of sapient minds. The overall process by which we came to be, although almost infinitely complex, is no longer a mystery because of the insight of Darwin and others who thought that the evolution of people out of necessity must obey natural laws that govern the universe. The exact details of the origin and time of our characteristics continue to be debated. What is much more difficult to contest is the evidence that such a thing as human nature exists that characterizes all people everywhere.

The Past

I have emphasized the element of time in understanding the evolution of human behavior. A very important temporal approach to understanding the biology of human behavior seeks to order the appearance and identify the antiquity of particular behaviors. I have pointed out that there are two broadly contrasting schools of thought in this regard. Some evolutionary biologists believe that modern human behaviors arose rapidly and recently in a punctuated manner. Others believe that the hallmarks of our species arose in a gradualistic manner. Regardless of the temporal contexts that one accepts, both viewpoints agree that new traits and complexes are selected for through the process of natural selection. This is Darwin's lasting, brilliant, and largely unifying contribution.

A new approach, that of sociobiology, accepts this same process but has altered the unity of the concept of selection from that of the individual to that of the DNA molecule. Sociobiologists believe that the recognition of DNA as the ultimate level of selection explains and predicts all behavior. The problem that I have found with this approach is that it provides no suggestions for falsifying its central premise. Any data, no matter how seemingly contradictory, can be accommodated in sociobiological theory. The fundamental fault of sociobiological theory (also shared with other nomothetic explanations of the natural world) is that it cannot specify the conditions of its own falsifiability.

Most social scientists have taken a decidedly antithetical approach to the innate behavior of humans and tend to operate on the premise that environment and experience account for the vast majority of the configurations of human thought and action. Somewhat in between the two poles of sociobiology and environmental preeminence are the biopsychologists, whose recent progress makes it clear that biology can no longer be ignored as a major factor in human behavior. In fact, all human thought, behavior, and action is de facto based in biology. There is no alternative to this conclusion.

The nature versus nurture controversy continues unabated, but I have the distinct feeling that the tabula rasa people lose ground every time a new article appears in a biopsychology journal. I also believe that the sociobiologists lose ground every time the diversity of human behavior is further documented in the form of new ethnographies, which continue to expand on unlimited diversity of the human species. At the same time, it is also now clear that while diversity in its detail is unlimited, the categories of diversity are not. I here reaffirm the analogy of "old bottles and new wine," which refers to the fact that details of the wine have infinite permutations, but the containers that the wine is stored in only change their capacities and shapes as the result of millions of years of selection and evolution. I know of no better example of this than language, which, like other cultural universals, can take unlimited forms that share common characteristics and attributes. This is one of the paradoxes of the behavior of organisms. Other crucial cultural universals are perhaps more flexible, but one has to wonder why the same basic categories of perceptions and divisions for organizing the world of human perception and action are present in every culture. No matter what the kinship, artistic, social, or moral system, the fact remains that these kinds of systems are always present and recognizable to any human inhabitant of the planet. In the end, one has to turn to the specific evidence that details what we know of the course of evolution of the brain and body.

The behavioral (archaeological) and anatomical (paleontological) records of our species are of paramount importance in this regard. The anatomical and behavioral changes that made the eventual appearance of a large-brained, bipedal hominid possible originated with ecological problems that all life had to solve in a series of innovations. Changes in physiological mechanisms, locomotion, and reproduction began with the lowest invertebrates and continued through the first mammals and primates.

In the course of hominid evolution, the first major changes were in the form of transformations. The shift from quadrupedalism to bipedalism was the major metamorphosis that inevitably determined how selection pressures would influence the future development of our species. Bipedalism transformed not only the means in which our ancestors moved across the landscape, but also the way in which we perceived the world. A reduced sense of olfaction and an increased dependence on vision in conjunction with prehensile appendages allowed bipedalism. At some time, probably in conjunction with bipedalism itself, our nutrient resource began to expand from that of a frugivore to that of a far-ranging omnivore, which included meat eating.

The effect of freeing the front limbs from locomotion continues to be debated. Tool use, gestural communication, social communication, social structure, and reproduction were strongly influenced by this unique mode of locomotion. The original selective advantage of bipedalism continues to be the subject of numerous prime mover theories of human evolution. These kinds of theories no doubt will multiply as the years go on. What is certain is that bipedalism, and not a large brain, was the crucial development in setting humans on the path to intelligence. Bipedalism allowed hominids to cover long distances and search for an unprecedented range of resources. In contrast with other animals, crucial hominid resources included not only food and water but also raw materials for tool manufacture.

I believe that human consciousness, symbolic thinking, and ultimately language arose as the needs of a visually specialized animal to process a great deal of information as it ranged far and wide over ancient African landscapes. The primate predisposition for visual emphasis existed millions of years prior to bipedalism; of this there is no doubt. Although a few other omnivores are known, none of them have as a diverse resource base or as large a home range as hominids.

Selection for a larger brain came much later in the course of human evolution and was coincident with the advent of stone tool manufacture. I believe that symbolic thinking and language intensified at this time. It may be that it would have never come at all if the hands were not already freed by the unknown selection pressure that created bipedalism. This text has tried to make it clear that intelligence confers little selective advantage if there is no physical means with which to act on intelligent perceptions. Free hands and the ability to travel long distances must have resulted in competitive advantages, which have so far not been discovered in the archaeological record. Sociosexual advantages have also been postulated by many workers; unfortunately, these will for some remain just that—postulations. We are still searching for an explanation of why a slow animal the size of a chimpanzee with a brain the size of a chimpanzee could have survived the predators of the African savanna and ultimately have emerged as the most knowledgeable and dangerous animal on the planet. We are so desperate to explain this unlikely history that scientists have invoked theories ranging from increased reproductive efficiency to superior strategies of resource procurement.

When stone tools and brain enlargement do finally appear in the paleoanthropological record, it becomes easier to ascribe the hominid advantage to increased intelligence and technological efficiency. The dental evidence suggests that from the times of *Australopithecus afarensis* there was an increasing tendency toward a widening of the hominid resource base, which included carnivory. The continuation and emphasis of this adaptive niche in *Homo habilis* may have been the principal reason for the extinction of the purely vegetarian robust australopithecines, who may have been outcompeted or even consciously preyed on by the first members of our genus. Evidence of the humanity of *Homo habilis* has been disputed. They may have had home bases and shared food. The division of labor may have already been present, but the evidence for these behaviors still remains equivocal. Whether they scavenged or hunted food also remains debatable, but hunting in organized ways should no longer be taken as the hallmark of humanity or our uniqueness because a comparison with other vertebrates reveals that few meat eaters, regardless of their perceived intelligence, are strictly scavengers or predators.

It is with *Homo erectus* that we see the first unequivocal indications of cerebral reorganization (handedness and indications of speech), standardization of artifacts (symmetrically, bifacially worked artifacts), use of fire, increased mobility (in the form of transcontinental migration), and a systematic exploitation of big game (Zhoukoudian Locality 1, Torralba, and Ambrona). The widespread climatic and geographic distribution of this species strongly implies that technology had advanced substantially over that of its immediate ancestors. The anatomical function of *Homo erectus* morphology remains elusive, but for some reason thick cranial architecture was characteristic of this species. The latest representatives had evolved a brain that was three-fourths the size of anatomically modern humans.

Many morphologically intermediate forms are now known between the last specimens of *Homo erectus* and the earliest specimens of *Homo sapiens*. Although these forms are morphologically distinct and similar to the living peoples of the various geographic regions in which they have been found, very little is known about their culture and behavior. It is only with Neanderthals (*Homo sapiens neanderthalensis*) that indications of ritual, religion, increased social complexity, and highly standardized technology emerge.

However, it is only with anatomically modern humans that undoubted indications of humanness such as art emerge. The reasons for when, where, and why the Upper Paleolithic revolution in human complexity took place are still hotly debated. Some workers have suggested that the details of cultural complexity simply take time to accumulate: "Rome was not built in a day." Others have suggested that a major biological change in the brain took place at approximately 0.035 to 0.05 mya. Biologists and paleontologists can find no support in either the modern anatomy of the brain or the paleontological record for this scenario. I believe that complexity simply builds itself.

It is very important to emphasize that all the available evidence indicates that while biological transformation was very important in the beginning of our species, the remainder of human evolution is much more accurately described as an additive process. This is reflected in the archaeological record, which documents that new stone tools were simply added to the repertoire of existing tools over the course of the last 2 million years. This observation is also in agreement with the way in which the brain itself seems to have evolved. The triune brain model fits extremely well with what we know of vertebrate evolution as a whole. The sudden flowering of human potential as represented by the archaeological record from Europe strongly suggests a major change in hominid behavior, but once again no evidence currently suggests a biological change. The contention for a recent advent of language is not supported by the anatomical evidence. Suggestions that Neanderthals possessed less of a capacity for speech than modern humans have been exaggerated and are simply not supported by either modern linguistic knowledge or the fossil record. Instead, it is clear that some form of language was characteristic of the genus *Homo* by at least 1.5 mya and probably earlier.

With the advent of agriculture, humans began to live a life that they were not biologically adapted to. Problems included crowding, disease, and other stresses arising from the fact that population pressure and the increased ease with which disease is spread are characteristic of sedentary existence. Despite our current Western living conditions, we retain a number of cultural universals or biological predispositions that were developed in the course of our almost 4 million years of existence as hunters and gatherers.

The Present

The lifestyle that most agriculturally based cultures live is at odds with our evolutionary biology. We meet in a single day more people than most hunters and gatherers saw in a single lifetime. At the same time, we deal with only a few people each day in a truly "hunter and gatherer" kind of way. That is, intimate interaction and communication is limited to a few individuals. In comparison with hunters and gatherers, the length of interaction is very short. In the modern industrial world, people are often required to develop solutions to problems in a matter of minutes. I believe that this emphasis on rapid performance is also reflected in the intelligence tests that are still administered en mass to students in our society. We have developed the belief that rapidity is akin to intelligence and competence. One of the most defamatory statements that people can make about other people is the observation that they are "slow" or "not too swift." The pace of life in a city is at odds with our physiology and emotional makeup.

Although we have the biology of a nomad, we have the lifestyle of a sedentary agriculturalist. Problems that we used to solve in a physical way are now solved by mental effort and social skill. Most tasks do not require the emergency utilization of cholesterol through physical activity. Violent crime (which requires physical activity) is growing at an epidemic rate, especially among teenagers. At the same time, it is becoming increasingly clear that programs for inner-city youths that emphasize physical activity are the ones that have the most chance of success. The societal "carrots" that such programs hold out are also in large part due to the social opportunities that basketball and other sports programs offer. However, it is also important to remember that such programs are tapping into the deep roots of our evolutionary past. Physical activity and planning in a highly social environment is the sine qua non of human existence.

Crowding is a phenomenon that produces aggression in any vertebrate. The competition for resources is another manifestation of the same phenomenon that is mediated by a biology that supports the periodic use of aggression in order to survive. Physical space is such an important requirement of human biology that we should not be surprised by the fact that crowded places are stressful and violent places. As the human population continues to increase, the biologically based tendency to reproduce will continue to exacerbate our biologically based desire for adequate space. The result will continue to be a violent manifestation of human behavior. At the same time, we know that the requirement for space is mediated by social upbringing and cultural standards. Thus, both the observation of cultural norms and an awareness of innate biology are very important parameters of human behavior. The important point to emphasize is that there will always be a biologically determined requirement for a minimal amount of physical space in normally functioning organisms.

John B. Calhoun conducted a now famous experiment in which he confined breeding rats in a finite space and allowed them to reproduce as rodents have for millions of years. The result came to resemble many of our large cities. Groups of juveniles terrorized adults; the equivalent of rat day care centers appeared;

and homosexuality, rape, and murder became much more frequent. In general, the best description of how animals were behaving can be best described as a reaction to stress. This analogy is too simple for most psychologists, but it makes perfect and consistent sense to students of the hominid fossil record.

An experiment that was conducted on human beings also reveals the importantance of cultural content of human behavior. Psychologist John Millgram constructed an experiment in which subjects were told to administer painful electric shock to other individuals if they did poorly on a particular task. People pretending to be authoritarian scientists advised the volunteers in charge of administering the shock that they should carry out their assignment despite the verbal protestations of the "learner." Although the sham learner would make it clear that he "had a bad heart" or that he was in great pain, subjects still followed the directives of the sham scientist. Millgram was eventually censured by the scientific community for his experiment because of the guilt and emotional pain that his colleagues decided that the test subjects suffered every time they took responsibility for inflicting pain on the sham learners. Experiments now require potential researchers to be sure that human subjects will not be subjected to unethical pressures.

Millgram took his experiment to other countries and discovered that there were substantial cultural differences between how long a subject would follow the instructions of dictators. The degree to which people would "follow orders" appears, according to Millgram's results, to break down along national lines. In the end, Millgram concluded that U.S subjects were comparatively resistant to following the orders of authoritarian figures and that certain cultures, as represented by the people he tested in Germany, would push the alleged voltage way past the danger mark.

This study is an eloquent illustration of the interplay between biology and culture. The propensity to follow orders or resist authority seems to be an integral part of all human beings. However, the degree to which individuals will conform or tailor their lives to such propensities seems to be strongly dependent on the cultural programming. The bottom line is that humans are neither innately aggressive nor innately cooperative. Communism and fascism have failed to comprehend human nature. What humans are is highly adaptable. After years of study, I believe that one of the fundamental characteristics of the human animals is a desire to improve one's own lot in life. Sometimes this takes the form of temporary cooperation with others. Sometimes self-gain necessitates individual action and achievement. Neither of these alternatives constitutes a dominant mode of human behavior. I further believe that cultural areas of the planet that emphasize one mode of behavior over the other will always encounter problems with long-term social stability. Human behavior is not polarized toward aggressiveness or peacefulness. Instead, it is polarized toward flexibility and resilience. Governments around the world need to realize that human rights are not a political construct but a biological necessity. Human needs are just that, biological requirements for normal existence. The great socioeconomic failures of the twentieth century have been fascism and communism. Systems of human repression, whether sociosexual, expressive, or ideational, will always fail eventually. At the same time, minimally regulated social systems will always be in danger of coming apart at the seams because it seems humans require rules for living together. All social species have such rules. Real democracies have never existed for very long on this planet. Those successful systems will be those that have rules and values in accordance with our biological past. The things that make children happy such as security, love, play, imagination, social interaction, and achievement are the same things that make adults happy.

Such human universals as play and sexuality are similar in their evolutionary structure. The fact that every human will engage in play and develop sexual preferences is "built in" to our own and many other species. The specific behavioral manifestations that these activities will take is determined, to a very large part, by one's cultural and personal experience. As this text has tried to emphasize, play is an integral part of the behavioral development of all mammals, especially primates. In keeping with the general human tendency to extend maturation and increase the length of infant dependency, human play is present in adulthood. Furthermore, there is a decidedly human tendency to fuse sexual and play activity. These are all characteristic of highly intelligent primates. Play should never be thought of as wasteful. In fact, we should probably continue to emphasize the importance of fun in educating both the old and young members of our species. Our knowledge of neuroanatomy strongly supports the idea that enjoyment is an integral part of effective learning. Socialness or group interaction is not only a requirement for normal behavioral development, but it may also be a principal component of enjoyment. Next to death, exile, banishment, and solitary confinement are the worst punishments that societies impose on their members. Voluntary solitude is so remarkable that most societies designate people such as monks, nuns, and hermits as individuals worthy of special recognition.

Western society, and in particular U.S. society, has a public concern with sexuality. Our emphasis on sexuality is in no way a purely cultural phenomenon, and most nonhuman primates are similarly interested by sex. In nonhuman primates, the line between play, sex, and social behavior is blurred. The same seems to be true of humans. All societies regulate sexual behavior through moral or legal guidelines and laws. Humans have a universal incest taboo, but the form it takes varies between cultures. The most common form of the incest taboo is that which forbids sexual intercourse between members of the nuclear family. This strongly suggests that over millions of years natural selection has acted against consanguineous matings.

At the same time, pornography is a multibillion dollar business. What is considered pornographic or even sexy varies greatly from culture to culture, and all cultures regulate sexual activity. Primate studies indicate that our closest animal relatives are interested in both viewing and participating in sexual activity. Primates are highly visually dependent animals. In Western society, explicate sexual activity is officially forbidden (as it is in most societies) and has been driven underground where it has become associated with other "underground" activities such as drugs, violence, exploitation, and prostitution.

Prostitution is ubiquitous in human society. The definition of prostitution varies between cultures. Some cultures recognize little difference between prostitution and marriage. Both prostitution and marriage require the exchange of economic goods and responsibilities for sexual access. A cross-cultural comparison of what constitutes prostitution will leave any objective researcher bewildered. However, if one has a good grasp of the nonhuman primate behavioral data and the fossil record, it is clear a symbiotic relationship between males and females involving resources and sexual availability is probably a primal constituent of our order as a whole. This text offers no advice about what to do (if anything) about either male or female prostitution, but I suggest that trading resources for sexual access has always been and will always be with us as long as our species continues to exist and reproduce.

We should think about recreation and cities. Just as we once considered play to be a waste of time, we should now realize that normal humans require the basic daily conditions that molded their biology. We have seen such environmental components as color, sound, and animals affect our emotions and therefore our intellects. If modern neuroanatomical and psychological studies have agreed on anything, it is the fact that recreation and play are crucial to human well-being and that access and availability to facilities for these very human needs should be an important component of the increasingly larger cities that dot our planet's landscapes.

The Future

For most of our evolutionary history, we were a species that lived in small groups that could exploit any resource to its maximum extent without endangering the future existence of that resource. We could cut down forests and eat meat with no prospect of driving either resource off the face of the planet. That all changed with the advent of agriculture. We are now a bull that lives in a china shop. There are now too many people, and our technology has grown so effective that we have the capability of destroying most life on the planet.

One of the questions most often asked of me as a teacher of human evolution is what the future holds. Are we still evolving? Will we look very different in the future? Will we have the enormous brains often portrayed in science fiction? There are no answers to these questions except the observation that we will be what we want to be. Because culture now outstrips natural selection in setting the pace of biological change, there is no doubt that any physical change that is to come will occur as the result of cultural decisions. In the process, there is a good chance that we might also eliminate genetic diversity, though I think the chance of this happening is small. No one will object to eliminating the cruel biological killers of humankind. The elimination of certain personality types (if there is such a thing) and certain levels of intelligence is another matter. An appreciation of organic diversity (gained through programs of instruction such as this one) will hopefully prevent the reoccurrence of past hysteria such as the eugenics and "racial cleansing" movements of this century.

My graduate advisor and friend F. Clark Howell once pointed out, over the noise of a political demonstration outside the classroom, that "Anybody who has really thought about important things realizes that the important questions of life are biological." The truth of this statement is indisputable. Wars, political movements, social reforms are all generated by biological concerns. There are certain innate properties of our species. Just as all animals mate, human beings seek sexual partners. Like all animals, human beings can be made to act aggressively. They differ from other animals in that they have at their command weapons that are capable of devastating the entire biology of our planet. We are still subject to the forces of natural selection, and driving everything we do is a combination of what we have learned and the biological cause of why we have learned it.

Human culture is made possible by biology. Human biology both makes possible and extends our capacity for learning to an extent that far exceeds any other organism on our planet. As part of our biology, we have an intense need to communicate, socialize, play, mate, and inquire. Some of this intensity is shared with other animals, but all of these predispositions are a result of our unique evolutionary history. Normal humans require these activities just as much as they require food, water, and oxygen. Parents, teachers, and governments need to treat these behaviors as fundamental facts of human existence. To ignore them is to insure failure in any human endeavor.

On Philosophers and the Infinite

As originally proposed in the science fiction classic *Forbidden Planet*, there are "monsters from the Id." We carry these as a daily legacy of our unconscious and highly emotional vertebrate beginnings. At the same time, the proposal by the fictitious Harry Seldon of Isaac Asimov's *Foundation* series that the past can predict the future is the lesson that justifies our study of human nature. The Seldon Plan relied on the fact that innovation and novelty tended to emerge from the periphery of systems and that biological behavior behaves in predictable ways if the circumstances of its existence are reasonably well known. Modern biological sciences will soon reach the same conclusions. We will never become magicians, but if we try, we can become much better engineers.

The important decisions of the future will be moral and not technological ones. Although a person of the nineteenth century would possibly have had trouble imagining all that we have achieved technologically in the twentieth century, no educated person of the time in which we now live would have trouble in believing any technological innovation of the next century. There will be no more technological surprises in the history of human consciousness. Culture and technology has permanently outstripped biological evolution, and, barring a massive and disastrous planetary war, technology will produce anything we decide that we want within the boundary of physical laws.

The issue of the coming next thousand years will not be what we can accomplish, but rather what we should do. In large part this will concern what I call "soft technology"—that is, the ability to make our machines fit with the way we want to live. In fact, the new machines of the future will not be constructed as much as they will be grown. This will intensify the already present problem of creating organisms that function as devices. Few people have a problem with the creation of oil-eating microbes, but how close does animal DNA have to be to chimpanzees for us to declare that it has biological rights? Artificial hominoids are already within the range of modern technology, and some of us suspect that the recombination of chimpanzee and human DNA has already been carried out. The questions of the future will come to increasingly focus not on the question of how, but on the question should we?

It is extremely important to emphasize that an understanding of our own species is the only way that we shall be able to say what it is that we should do with the extraordinary influence that we have on Earth. It is not enough to be humble and regard our own species' existence as essentially as important as earthworms. We have a dawning realization of the interdependence of all species, but now we have a consciousness of the importance of our biological responsibility. Part of this consciousness, when enlightened through education and experience, tells us that we are simultaneously the greatest danger and greatest hope of the planet. To make rational decisions about the fate of the entire planet, we should try as much as possible to preserve the environments and life ways to which we have adapted over the course of millions of years. In short, we need a nice office in which to make executive decisions about the solar system.

This book would be a waste if it did not conclude with a sermon such as this. Studying life for the sake of life itself, though fascinating, is wasted if we do not become motivated to do something about the predicament in which we have inevitably placed ourselves. It is difficult for most of humanity to think outside of their own particular group or culture. Indeed, we have seen that, for a very long time, we have evolved to act and think in exactly this kind of encultured manner. We are not predisposed toward cooperation or aggression, but we can so easily become polarized in one direction or the other. We have watched communism and its assumption that all people would cooperate for the common good fail. Mao Zedong tried to eradicate the Chinese family for over two generations. He failed not only because there is a biological need for the family, but also because the family is a strongly culturally programmed institution in Chinese society. The template for the importance of the family already existed, but the specific configuration and strength of this social institution was reinforced by the specifics of the "Chinese experience."

Similarly, early capitalists tried to invoke a broad interpretation of Darwin's theory as justification for the socioeconomic plundering and genocide that Western colonial powers were committing against other populations. Their justifications in many cases were based on an incomplete or biased understanding of human evolution. They failed to realize that in dealing with humans, they were dealing with biocultural systems whose variables are essentially infinite. They also believed that if there were laws of physics, there were laws for every phenomena. We need to move away from philosophy and toward making decisions about governing that are consistent with the specific record of human nature. This may be true, but discovering the local laws of human behavior are still beyond scientists to the point that none can accurately predict what it is that our species will do in the future.

The effective programs and decisions of the future will be those that are "soft." That is, they will be compatible with human nature. They will realize that any form of sociopolitical organization will only be a temporary experiment if our evolutionary nature is not taken into account. Truly far-reaching plans will realize that change and the quality of being temporary are an integral part of existence and that humans are no exception.

As far as we know, we are the only example of intelligent life in the universe. This thought is truly terrifying considering the distinct possibility that we have the undoubted ability to destroy ourselves. One small consolation is that the probabilities and distances of the universe suggest that we are not really alone, but that we have just not been fortunate enough to encounter extraterrestrial life forms. Our failure to survive our evolutionary infancy may one day be looked on by other beings as a tragic childishness that must have embarrassed a life-form that had so much potential. If we fail to survive until we are able to contact intelligent life, perhaps our knowledge will survive. If so, it will be clear to any future archaeologists that we at least developed an understanding of the principles that govern the evolution of all life-forms anywhere. When other beings become aware of our understanding of organisms, they cannot help but know that we discovered that natural selection is a fundamental force of existence that governs the creation and extinction of all organisms. They may wonder why we could know this fact and yet still have become extinct.

The Organic and the Superorganic—Admonitions about Rain Gods

The table that follows the end of this text (Table 10.1) summarizes in a somewhat exploratory way what it is that I think we can and cannot at this point say about the evolution of human behavior. What I have not listed as one of our recent achievements is that we are on the threshold of being able to finally discard explanations of human behavior that ignore biological data. *Organic explanations,* like the laws of physics, relate perception and measurement of physical structure and processes. *Superorganic explanations* believe that there is literally more to life than that which can ever be perceived. In other words, the whole of certain phenomena is greater than the sum of its parts. Sometimes referred to as *emergentism* or *essentialism,* this philosophy emphasizes the belief that even a complete knowledge of all of a system's parts would not predict the nature of the functioning whole. In Western philosophy, the soul represents one of the most outstanding examples of an emergent human quality. Things like love, aggression, and altruism traditionally have been thought to represent other examples of essentialistic human properties. In keeping with this approach, one of the most often-cited aphorisms suggests that a thorough knowledge of the properties of hydrogen and oxygen would not predict the properties of water (H_2O). At an early stage of our knowledge, we failed to predict the properties of water because we did not know enough about its constituent elements. So much is now known about hydrogen, oxygen, and carbon that we can now predict the parameters of life in spite of the fact that we cannot specify all permutations within those parameters.

According to the emergent perspective, a study of the brain would not predict "the mind." Over the course of thousands of years, whenever superorganic explanations of natural phenomena have been proposed, they have either turned out to be wrong or untestable. Although superorganic theories still abound in the social sciences, they are increasingly being abandoned as our ability to explore and catalog reality increases. What is becoming apparent is the ironic prospect that our very concern with superorganic explanations probably has an organic basis. What we have begun to master are not new philosophies, but rather better ways of comprehending complexity.

For instance, we still cannot predict the weather perfectly in spite of the fact that we have an extremely detailed knowledge of atmospheric physics. Yet we do not attribute our inability to superorganic, essentialistic, and emergent properties of weather systems. As scientists, we know that the reason that our knowledge of the parts does not add up to a predictive whole is because the system has more variables than we supposed and the possible permutations of the known variables exceed our technology's ability to identify and track them.

The mind behaves a lot like a weather system. On a daily basis, we discover more and more that behavioral correlates have sometimes very specific anatomical and neurophysiological substrates. Statements such as, "There is a vast amount about behavior we don't understand," are far different from statements such as, "There is a vast amount we will never understand." Just as weather prediction has improved, so has our understanding of brain-generated behavior. We no longer call on rain gods, and one day we shall abandon the concept of "mind" as separate from "brain." Our existence will be no less rich. The new belief does require the adoption of a mechanistic worldview, but it does not dictate biological determinism. The behavioral parameters of any organism are more than vast enough to accommodate free will and the individual variation on which Darwin based his theory of natural selection.

Perhaps a future alien philosopher will regret the fact that creatures with the capacity for the infinite, in spite of their great knowledge, failed to deal adequately with the present. This text has tried to convey and emphasize the fact that the present must be understood in terms of past evolutionary history or else there will be no future. We have to understand why it is we do the things that we do. Even more important, we must come to believe that we still do things that though once adaptive no longer are. Above all, we must isolate these tendencies and try to do something about them. I suspect that our primal characteristics and our intelligences and the lessons gained of experience are still the keys to being around when we finally have the opportunity to compare our own evolutionary legacy with that of beings from other planets.

Table 10.1   The Bottom Line

The Bottom Line

I.   Evolution
    A.   Evolution is a fact.
    B.   Humans were not specially created by God.
    C.   We are a collection of evolutionary old and new characteristics.
    D.   Theory of sociobiology does not specify how it can be falsified.

II. Primate Evolution
    A.   Humans are descended from lower primates and share many anatomical and behavioral traits in common with them.
    B.   Chimpanzees, gorillas, and humans all descend from a geologically recent ancestor.
    C.   Human sexuality is unusual.

III. The Origin of Hominids
    A.   Bipediality preceded all other important anatomical changes, while large brain developed only recently.
    B.   Humans were never meant to be exclusive vegetarians.
    C.   The earliest known hominids are found in Africa.

IV. The Fossil and Behavioral Record
    A.   Encephalization lagged behind bipedalism by at least 2 mya.
    B.   Brain enlargement begins when stone tool use begins, which is roughly correlated with the appearance of *Homo habilis*.
    C.   Some form of language, handedness, and cerebral reorganization appeared with *Homo erectus*.
    D.   *Homo erectus* immigrated from Africa and used fire.
    E.   Neanderthals were *Homo sapiens* who possessed sophisticated lithic technology, religion, and language.

The Gray Line

I.   Evolution
    A.   The rate at which evolution proceeds is debatable and perhaps not constant in speed.
    B.   God may have created humans and all animals.
    C.   Which traits are important anatomically is debatable.
    D.   Some concepts of sociobiology may apply to humans.

II. Primate Evolution
    A.   Why primates arose in the first place is a hotly contested topic.
    B.   Why we are so behaviorally different yet genetically similar to African apes is poorly understood.
    C.   The advantage that our reproductive strategy gave us is unknown.

III. The Origin of Hominids
    A.   The advantages that bipedality conferred can only be guessed at.
    B.   Why we became so omnivorous is unknown, as is the question of whether early hominids were primarily scavengers or hunters.
    C.   The hominoid group that gave rise to hominids may have lived outside of Africa, but this unlikely.

IV. The Fossil and Behavioral Record
    A.   The initial impetus for brain enlargement is unknown.
    B.   Hominids may have relied extensively on nonlithic tools before they began to manufacture stone tools.
    C.   Language, handedness, and cerebral reorganization may date back to the australopithecines.
    D.   Exactly when the immigration took place and when fire was first used is still debated.
    E.   The extent of these developments is debatable, but some form of language was almost certainly present.

The Bottom Line

V. Language and Communication
   A. All vertebrates and perhaps all animals communicate.
   B. Although they also vocalize, scent and visual communication are much more important in nonhuman primates.
   C. No primates have language, though chimpanzees show some protolinguistic abilities.
   D. Human language is dependent on uniquely developed neural anatomical structures.
   E. Immature hominids learn language easily without formal instruction.

VI. Cultural Universals
   A. Most, if not all, human cultural universals are absent among other animals.
   B. Hunters and gatherers provide the best living human models for early hominid ecology and social organization.
   C. Many cultural universals have neuroanatomical correlates, including language, art, and music.

VII. The Triune Brain and Bilateral Brain
   A. The vertical structure of the brain grossly reflects reptilian, mammalian, and human stages in vertebrate evolution.
   B. The brain is also divided into left and right hemispheres, which show differential dominance for certain functions.
   C. The linguistic superiority of the left hemisphere and the spacial superiority of the right hemisphere may be due to different amounts and arrangements of myelinated and unmyelinated neurons.

The Gray Line

V. Language and Communication
   A. Cetacean communication may be protolinguistic.
   B. Some primate vocalizations may have semantic referents, but the degree to which this is true is debatable.
   C. Chimps may exhibit some nonlimbic communication, though the evidence for this is dubious at best.
   D. When speech became fully modern is unknown, but there is no known evidence that limits speech to only anatomically modern humans.
   E. Despite intense attempts at teaching apes language, none has surpassed the level of a three-year-old child, though some trainers still debate this.

VI. Cultural Universals
   A. Some cultural universals may be nonbiologically based.
   B. The degree to which modern hunters and gatherers have been influenced by agricultural neighbors is debatable in most instances.
   C. Religion may also have biological bases. Other universals such as the incest taboo, the division of labor, food sharing, and play may also have neuroanatomical correlates, but these may be more somatically mediated.

VII. The Triune Brain and Bilateral Brain
   A. How these levels influence each other is only generally understood, but the neocortex may be the "master control" level with managing the brain as a whole.
   B. This kind of organization is arguably present in a very few nonhuman animals but may be more common than has been previously suspected. Furthermore, we still do not understand the evolutionary reason for this type of organization.
   C. Right and left differentiation may result from the telomatic effects of testosterone.

The Bottom Line

    D. Sexual dimorphism of the brain is well established and was probably selected for by the division of labor.

VIII. Love, Sex, and Reproduction
    A. Human sexuality is highly unusual, if not unique, among primates, for its prolonged duration, lack of female estrus, and the nonsynchronization of mating with fertility. These features usually have been interpreted as a means of bringing about permanent monogamous pair bonding.
    B. Love is an at least partially physiological state that induces pedogenic behavior and mediates imprinting.
    C. Freud's theory of sexuality is highly improbable. Most of Freud's interpretations reflect much more about his own personal experience than universal sexual traits of human beings.
    D. Little evidence suggests that homosexuality is mediated primarily by genes, though certain hormonal influences can be shown to affect adults exposed to opposite sex hormones at a young age.
    E. In terms of numbers of partners, male homosexuals behave like male heterosexuals; female homosexuals behave like most female heterosexuals.
    F. Homophobia is much more prevalent in North America than in almost any other region.
    G. Rape is a cultural universal that is almost always an act of aggression.

IX. Intelligence, Learning, and Memory
    A. Intelligence is not a single entity and assumptions that it is has led to misleading and inaccurate estimations of human abilities.
    B. Gardner's theory of multiple intelligences is most in accord with the neuroanalytical evidence.

The Gray Line

    D. The degree and importance of human sexual dimorphism in the brain is still poorly understood.

VIII. Love, Sex, and Reproduction
    A. Human pair bonding may be neither permanent nor monogamous in the context of increasing longevity brought about by technological means.
    B. Endorphins may be involved in love, but novelty is important in both sex and love.
    C. Psychoanalysis does seem to help resolve some sociosexual problems, but the reasons for these successes seem to have little to do with the validity of psychoanalytical theory. It may be that simple attention and communication are more important than innate sexual problems.
    D. Recent, though very limited, evidence suggests a potential genetic link to homosexuality.
    E. Though highly debatable and poorly understood, the degree to which culture, personal experience, and socialization influence sexual preference is probably substantial.
    F. Ways of dealing with homophobia are intensely debated. Outside of North America, most cultures are much more tolerant of homosexuality.
    G. Some sociobiologists maintain that rape can be adaptive.

IX. Intelligence, Learning, and Memory
    A. The degree to which IQ and other intelligence tests are correlated with success in life is very debatable.
    B. The degree to which one kind of intelligence influences another is very poorly understood.

The Bottom Line

C.   There is a definite genetic and biochemical component to intelligence.
D.   Interspecies comparisons of intelligence should emphasize behavioral plasticity in relation to evolutionary adaptations.

X.   Sleep and Dreams
  A.   Sleep is one of the most poorly understood human phenomena.
  B.   Sleep is one of many body rhythms.
  C.   Sleep is required for normal health in nearly all mammals.
  D.   Dreams are considered spiritually significant by most cultures but seldom in the manner that Freud maintained. The physiology of dreaming accounts best for the very similar cross-cultural characteristics of dreams.

XI. The Bottom Line
  A.   There is no bottom line.

The Gray Line

C.   The genetic correlates of the neurophysiological bases of intelligence are very poorly understood. The degree to which enriched environments influence intelligence may be substantial.
D.   The degree to which sensory and somatic configurations influence apparent intelligence is difficult to objectively measure.

X.   Sleep and Dreams
  A.   The need for sleep varies tremendously between individuals and throughout life. The reason for this is very poorly understood.
  B.   All rhythms may depend on both external and internal cues and stimuli.
  C.   The degree to which the lack of sleep affects performance may be significant.
  D.   Dreams may be telomatic. If they are not, no one has yet put forward a convincing explanation of their evolutionary significance.

XI. The Bottom Line
  A.   There may be a bottom line.

GLOSSARY

Acheulian industry A Paleolithic tool kit usually associated with *Homo erectus* characterized by so-called hand axes and cleavers. These tools represent the earliest evidence of symmetry in the Lower Paleolithic.

acquired characteristics Lamarck's incorrect theory that traits acquired in an individual's lifetime are passed on to one's own offspring.

actualistic Nontheoretical investigations (experiments) of data in real time and space as opposed to theoretical or deductive reconstructions of phenomena.

adaptations Adjustments in form, function, or behavior that animals make to their changing environments. The adjustments may be genetically or experientially based.

adaptive radiation The rapid (in terms of geological time) appearance and diversification of new species and resulting lineages.

age-graded A social organization in which status is at least partly determined by individual age.

Age of Mammals The Cenozoic, a time from about 65 mya to the present in which warm-blooded, viviparous, and more encephalized vertebrates diversified and dominated the planet.

aggression Antagonistic behavior that most higher organisms are capable of in situations of competition or fear.

agriculture A sedentary or transient means of producing food and other plant crops, which relies on the planting, harvesting, and tending. Societies practicing intensive agriculture usually develop complex social stratification and many other characteristics not associated with a hunting and gathering way of life.

Agta A tribal group from the Philippines that supposedly does not use division of labor and in which women hunt as much as men.

alliances In primatology, a term referring to cooperation between individuals, which may be transient or lifelong in groups of social organisms.

allocthonous In taphonomy, the term used to refer to a fossil organism that was transported from its original living or dying locality to the place of its discovery by paleontologists.

allopatric speciation Reproductive isolation brought about by geographic separation, which eventually results in the appearance of new and distinct species.

altrical In evolutionary studies, an emphasis on postnatal growth and development rather than extensive prenatal development in the womb or egg.

Ambrona (see Torralba).

Amerinds Native Americans, or East Asian-derived populations, living in the New World.

amniotic egg An egg that contains its own fluid inside a protective covering.

amphibians Lower vertebrates that depend on water for reproduction but carry out other activities in terrestrial environments.

anagenic evolution So-called straight-line evolution in which members of a single lineage change sufficiently enough from their ancestors to be considered a different species.

Andaman Islanders Occupants of Islands in Southeast Asia that at the time of the first reports of Europeans supposedly did not know how to make fire.

angiosperms   Plants that bear their seeds inside protective coverings; many of these seeds have evolved to be consumed and transported by animals. All arboreal fruits are angiosperms.

Ante-Neanderthals   A term used to refer to European hominids of uncertain taxonomic affinities that lived before Neanderthals.

anterior tooth loading   A biomechanical term referring to a relatively great force placed on the front teeth during mastication or the use of the front teeth in other activities such as biting, clamping, and holding; using the front teeth as a "third hand."

apical   Sharp and pointed.

apomorphic   Characters removed from their original evolutionary and morphological state.

arboreal adaptation   Adjusted for life in trees.

archaeology   The study of artifacts, their contexts, and uses, and relationships to each other. In general, the study of the remains of anything created by hominids.

archaic *Homo sapiens*   An informal term used to refer to hominids that (unconsensually) is used to refer to fossil hominids that resemble modern humans in their overall morphology but differ enough so as to be recognizably distinct.

Ardipithecus ramidus   The earliest species of hominids based currently on very incomplete fossils, which are nonetheless held by some workers to be a distinct taxon.

artifacts   Any artificial trace left intentionally or unintentionally by hominids including tools, trash, and modifications of the environment.

artifact and faunal scatters   In archaeology, a term used to describe and refer to the spatial distribution of artifacts and bones at a locality.

association areas   In neuroscience, the observation that certain areas of the cortex of the brain are associated with certain functions, perceptions, and actions.

asteroid theory   The theory that approximately 65 mya Earth was impacted by a meteor or comet that caused the extinction of dinosaurs and other life-forms.

atlatl   A spear thrower. A wood or bone artifact used to increase the throwing power of spears.

Aurignacian   One of many local European names used to refer to Upper Paleolithic tool kits.

Australian aborigines   The first and oldest native people of Australia who reached that continent over water at least 40,000 years ago.

australopithecines   The informal name given to the several species included in the genus *Australopithecus* that existed in Africa between at least 1 to 4 mya.

Australopithecus aethiopicus   A hyper-robust australopithecine from Ethiopia that antedates *A. boisei*.

Australopithecus afarensis   An early species of gracile australopithecine discovered at Hadar (Afar), Ethiopia; and Laetoli, Tanzania. Also the species to which Lucy and the First Family belong.

Australopithecus africanus   A species of australopithecine first discovered in South Africa by Raymond Dart that lived between approximately 2 to 3 mya.

Australopithecus anamensis   Another reported early australopithecine recognized on the basis of fragmentary material.

Australopithecus boisei   So-called robust australopithecine exhibiting massive chewing adaptations for a specialized vegetarian diet. Also informally called "Nutcracker Man," "*Zinjanthropus*" or hyper-robust australopithecine.

Autapomorphic   Morphological or behavioral traits unique to a single species.

Autochthonous   in taphonomy, fossils that lived in the area in which they are found.

behaviorism   An early twentieth-century school of psychology that emphasized the extreme importance of environment and experience in the determination of psychological traits.

Bergman's and Allen's rules   The observations named for two biologists that observed respectively that bodies of animals tend to reduce the surface area to volume and have stockier bodies with shorter limbs in cold climates.

bicameral mind   The concept that because the brain is physically composed of two hemispheres, the "mind" is also composed of two basic divisions.

bifacially flaked   In archaeology, a stone or bone artifact (and more rarely other materials) that have been worked on or struck on two sides.

binomial nomenclature   In taxonomy, the practice of assigning each organism a genus and species name (for example, *Homo sapiens*). Originally developed by Linnaeus.

bioaltruism   A sociobiological term that emphasizes the opinion that charitable or helpful behavior actually benefits the inclusive fitness of the organism seemingly performing an altruistic act.

biopsychology   An as yet imprecisely defined field that realizes that biology, anatomy, and experience must be considered together in attempts to understand human behavior and thought.

bipedal   Locomotion on two legs.

bipolar   In neuroscience, a term used to describe a disorder in which mania and depression manifest themselves alternately.

Bodo   An early (perhaps the earliest known) archaic *Homo sapien* from Bodo, Ethiopia. Notable for evidence of facial cut marks interpreted as evidence of "defleshing."

body adornment   The tendency of all humans to add artificial decoration to the body. These include clothing, color, jewelry, tattoos, and other signals.

bonobos   Scientifically known as *Pan paniscus*, these small-sized chimpanzees have recently received increased scientific attention for their behavioral similarities to humans.

bony palate   A structure forming the roof of the mouth that provides support for eating and breathing.

bottleneck   A term used in evolutionary biology to describe the rapid reduction of populations to relatively few individuals.

brain–mind dichotomy   The long persistent idea that the mind (thought) can be understood as distinct from the physiology and anatomy of the body.

brainwashing   A term that came into popular use after the Korean War, which refers to a process in which fundamental beliefs and thought can be altered through torture and other psychological manipulations and physical deprivations. Basically a means of inducing imprinting.

bride price   In sociocultural anthropology, the practice of a prospectus groom offering goods and/or services to the relatives of an intended bride.

Broca's area   An area of the neocortex of humans (usually on the posterior frontal lobe of the left hemisphere) that mediates the production of speech.

bunodunt   Cusps of teeth that are more rounded and blunt rather than sharp and piercing.

butchery sites   In archaeology, a place where hominids dismembered animals.

buzz-bow-wow   An implausible linguistic theory that suggests that language is the result of mimicking and producing onomatopoeic representations of natural sounds.

canalization   The inevitable and strictly controlled development of a behavioral or anatomical trait.

canines   The long pointed teeth used for grabbing, tearing, or piercing, the "eye teeth."

carnivorous   Meat eating.

cave bear clan   An interpretation of Neanderthal culture that argues that the involvement with extinct European cave bear (*Ursus spaeleus*) was a focal point of Neanderthal religious belief.

Cenozoic   (See Age of Mammals.)

cerebral asymmetry   In neuroscience, the well-established idea that the left and right hemispheres are alternatively dominant for certain neurological functions.

Chatelperronian   A local Upper Paleolithic European industry.

Chesowanja, Kenya   Dating to about 2 mya, disputably one of the earliest localities with evidence of hominid-produced fire.

chimpanzee   A general term for an African species of great ape belonging to the genus *Pan spp.*

chopper-chopping tools   A misnomer for Paleolithic artifacts from the Far East that differ from presumably contemporary Acheulian hand axe industries in their lack of symmetry.

chromosomes   Microscopic protein tubes of DNA found in every cell.

chronospecies   Species that undergo evolutionary change to such a degree that they are assumed to be incapable of producing viable offspring with their ancestors, even if those ancestors were extant.

clade   A line or lineage of organisms that has "split" from its ancestral population.

cladistics   An approach to the classification of organisms that emphasizes reproductive isolation departing in morphology from ancestors.

cladogenic   Splitting evolution.

Class   In biology, a large category including diverse organisms with a common anatomical organization.

classic Neanderthals   Neanderthals from Europe exhibiting more pronounced or exaggerated morphological features in comparison with Neanderthals from the Middle East.

clavicle   Collar bone. In extant vertebrates, retained only by primates.

claviculate   Having a clavicle.

common chimpanzee   *Pan troglodytes.*

comparative ethnography   The science of comparing the nature, traits, and details of different cultures.

connectionism (connectionists)   In the neurosciences, an approach that emphasize the importance of globally separated areas of the brain of a particular response or behavioral task.

consort pair   In primatology, individuals that spend time together for the purpose of mating.

conspecifics   Organisms belonging to the same species.

continuously sexually receptive   The theoretical idea that among primates, human females are willing to copulate at virtually any time.

core tools   Paleolithic tools that are more massive and thicker than the flakes that were removed from them.

corpus callosum   A dense mass of neural fibers that allow communication between the two hemispheres of the brain.

craft specialization   In anthropology, the idea that agricultural societies (usually intensively) develop specialized occupations and socioeconomic "guilds."

creationist   A pseudoscientific view that holds that the world was created exactly as the creationists interpret the Bible.

creation myth   Stories and explanations purporting to explain the origin of people, things, and existence in general.

creative explosion   John Pfeiffer's characterization of the appearance of art and complex material culture in Upper Paleolithic Europe.

crepuscular   Active at dawn or dusk.

Cretaceous   The geological period preceding the Cenozoic when dinosaurs were dominant.

crossopterygian   A surviving though rare species of fish that possesses limblike lobes. Also called a "living fossil." Their significance in evolutionary studies is that their fins are attached to muscles, which are assumed to be the precursors of exclusively terrestrial locomotion.

cultural capacity   In paleoanthropology, the idea that the degree to which a species relies on culture is biologically determined and/or circumscribed.

cultural ecology   An approach to anthropology that emphasizes the importance of understanding the resource–energy equation bases of culture.

cultural materialism   In anthropology, the idea that cultures can be understood with special reference to the goods that they produce and utilize.

cultural triad   A term used in this book to refer to the common association of art, religion, and music.

cultural universals   Categories of social and personal behavior, thought, and attitude that are common to every culture or human.

culture   The learned, shared, and acted-on component of human behavior including material, mental, linguistic, and many other aspects of humanity.

curation   In archaeology, a term used to refer to the repair and conservation of tools implying reuse.

Darwin, Charles Robert   One of the co-discoverers, along with A. R. Wallace, of the mechanism of organic evolution (natural selection).

Darwinian fitness   The concept that organisms that leave the most viable offspring are by definition the most "fit."

death and life assemblages   In archaeology, paleontology, and taphonomy, a collection of ancient artifacts or fossils occurring at a particular locality or site.

debitage   In archaeology, a French term referring to discarded waste flakes not intended for use as a tool.

deconstructism   In sociocultural anthropology, the concept that one must totally irradiate one's own cultural prejudices and values to truly understand another culture.

deep structures   In sociocultural anthropology, the idea that the brain has innate biological-based infrastructure and categories that are exhibited by all human societies.

Deluge   A term for the Noachian flood. Also used in reference to the "Antediluvian" time period. Not recognized in geology as a scientifically valid term.

dental apes   A term used to refer to Miocene and Pliocene primates that exhibit a tooth morphology similar to extant hominoids but that postcranially resemble anthropoids.

dental caries   Cavities in the teeth caused by bacterial activity.

dental formula   A numerical notation system for specifying how many kinds of teeth an animal has. (for example, human dental formula = 2/2 1/1 2/2 3/3 signifying 2 incisors, 1 canine, 2 premolars, 3 molars on one-half the maxilla and the mandible).

depositional environment   In taphonomy and paleontology, the geological circumstances in which a fossil becomes preserved.

developed Oldowan   A term used by Mary Leakey to describe a phase of Oldowan culture in which more formalized tools supposedly became more standardized and recognizable.

differential reproduction   The Darwinian observation that some individuals leave more offspring than others.

digitgrade   A term that refers to the fact that some organisms retain distinct and separate appendages known as fingers and toes, especially characteristic of primates.

dinosaurs   Usually large (by mammalian standards) reptilianlike animals that radiated and dominated the earth before the age of mammals.

diversification   In evolutionary biology, the idea that species tend to increase their numbers by specializing in increasingly different adaptive niches. In this process many new species can arise from a single ancestral species.

division of labor   In anthropology, the observation that all human societies divide up work along sexual lines or gender-specific categories.

DNA   Deoxyribonucleic acid is an organic molecule found in every cell that contains the codes for the production of proteins and the replication of itself.

dominance   In primatology, the concept that certain individuals have preferential access to certain resources such as food, mates, and space.

dominance hierarchies   In ethology, a structured hierarchy or "pecking order" in primate societies that is age-graded and based on physical strength and social alliances.

dryopithecine adaptive radiation   A time in which a group of Miocene–Pliocene hominids diversified into a number of species in Africa and Eurasia.

ecology   The study of the relationships and adaptations of organisms occupying the same environment by specializing in different means of exploiting resources.

econiche   In ecology, the particular specialization and adaptation of an organism; the way in which it makes a living.

economic cannibalism   In anthropology and related biological sciences, the eating of one conspecific by another as a usual means of fulfilling dietary requirements.

Ecthothermy   In biology, organisms which depend on external sources of heat, such as sunlight, to regulate their internal body temperature.

edge-to-edge bite   The occlusion or articulation of upper and lower teeth with the opposing surfaces in complete contact. Rare in modern humans, but common in extinct hominids.

egalitarian   In social sciences, the idea that members of a society have approximately equal social position, influence rights, and access to valued resources.

emergent properties   The concept in philosophy and science that the combination of physical components can result in supraorganic phenomena (for example, the soul, magic).

encephalized   Organisms that exhibit a relatively larger brain size in relation to body size, weight, or stature.

endothermic   In biology, the ability of organisms to generate their own internal heat.

Eoanthropus dawsoni   "Piltdown Man," a fraudulent find from England that combined human and ape remains. It was defended as indicating (incorrectly) that a large human-sized brain evolved in the course of human evolution.

Eskimo (Esquimau) A general (and some argue outmoded) term referring to Native Americans adapted to severe arctic environments in the Northern Hemisphere.

ethnicity In sociocultural anthropology, the particular cultural perspectives, thoughts, and actions that differentiate human cultures.

ethnocentric In sociocultural anthropology, the realization that perceptions are often influenced from the perspective of one's own culture.

ethnography The recording and depiction of cultures.

ethnology The comparative study of cultures.

ethology In modern biology, the study of species-specific behavior, but also behavior in general.

Eusocial In sociobiology, the theory that truly social organisms participate in the care and nurture of related offspring.

eutheria (eutheres) So-called true beasts or placental mammals.

Eve hypothesis In paleoanthropology, a variously titled and informal term purporting to explain modern human origins that postulates the human descent from a single, recent African female. A highly debated and controversial theory.

evolutionary psychology As defined in this volume, a new science that emphasizes that many modern behaviors and thought have been selected for and reinforced by natural selection.

exogamous Marriage or mating with distantly related or nonrelated individuals.

eyelid flash An inversion of the eyelid that signals aggression in some primates. However in humans, an expression conveying greeting or interest.

femur The thigh bone.

fictive kin People recognized or acknowledged as close "blood" relations even though there is no close genetic relationship.

fingernails Flat keratinous, hard tissue that replaces claws in primates.

First Family In paleoanthropology, the informal name given to a group of eleven to fourteen individuals of *A. afarensis* discovered at Hadar (Afar), including both sexes and individuals ranging in ages from children to adults.

fission In sociocultural anthropology, the tendency of individuals to separate in the absence of abundant resources. In ethology, the tendency of animals to go their separate ways or break into smaller groups in response to various environmental pressures, especially the lack of resources.

flexed burials In archaeology, individuals that are buried in the so-called prenatal position with knees and arms drawn up against the chest.

follivores Consumers of flowers and leaves.

food taboos In sociocultural anthropology, the idea that all cultures identify foods that should not be eaten.

foragers Synonymous with hunters and gatherers.

foramen magnum The large opening in the base of the braincase through which the spinal cord passes.

fusion In ethology, the repeated tendency of foraging species (including humans) to come together in the presence of abundant resources such as food, water, shelter, and potential mates.

gender The sociosexual roles that a society proscribes for its members.

genes Portions of DNA that code for certain traits in organisms.

genetic drift   The tendency of isolated populations to depart from the genetic frequencies of the parent population through inbreeding and adaptation.

genotype   The genetic makeup (code) of an individual.

geronticide   The killing of the old.

Gigantopithecus blacki   A large extinct Miocene–Pleistocene ape. The largest hominoid ever discovered.

Gombe Stream, Tanzania   Jane Goodall's (and lately others) site in Tanzania for studying chimpanzee behavior.

Gondwana   The southern half of the Pangean supercontinent including Africa, South America, portions of Asia, and possibly portions of Australia.

gorilla   *Gorilla gorilla*, the largest of the African great apes. Groups are dominated by a "silverback" male living with a "harem" of females and their offspring.

gracile australopithecine   A colloquial term for a species of early hominids that occupied East and South Africa between at least 1 to 4 mya.

gradualism   The contention that evolutionary change proceeds in a slow steady mode of change as opposed to rapid leaps.

graminivorous   An adjective that describes a diet of small particles including seeds and other small hard bits of food.

grammar   The structure and rules of how to use language.

Gravettian   In archaeology, a local European Upper Paleolithic industry.

greater infant dependency   In ethological studies and especially primatology, the concept that more encephalized species require more time for maturation, development, and parental investment

grinding stones   Stones used in a mortar and pestle manner to reduce grain to flour, which first appear in the Neolithic.

grooming   The physical interaction of primates involving the removal of dead skin, vermin, and other debris, which also functions as a social bonding mechanism.

grooming claws   In primatology, modified fingernails in some prosimians that have evolved to secondarily resemble claws.

gymnosperms   Plants that disperse their seed or spores externally without the use of fleshy coverings.

habitual bipedalism   A relatively rare form of mammalian locomotion in which animals move by walking only on two feet (appendages). In primatology and paleoanthropology, a descriptive term of how it is that humans and only humans walk.

hamadryas baboon   *Papio hamadryas*. A native of Ethiopian arid lands having a foraging mating group of a dominant male and females that must be constantly managed by the single dominant male to insure group cohesion and prevent mating with other males.

hand axe   In archaeology, a variably tear-dropped or oval-shaped bifacially worked core tool, blunted or unworked at one end and pointed at the other. In spite of the term, its actual use remains a matter of speculation. Although usually associated with *H. erectus*, no actual association has ever been confirmed.

harems   In primatology, a mating group of several females and one male.

heterodont   Teeth that have specific differing morphologies for different masticatory functions.

historical particularism Frans Boas's idea that cultural facts and history are the best way of understanding human behavior. According to this approach, theory must be secondary to the collection of cultural fact.

home base In paleoanthropology, the interpretation that early hominid places of residency or campsites were the focus of more than transient social interactions and life.

homeothermy The ability to maintain a constant internal body temperature.

Hominidae Hominoids that locomote by habitual striding bipedalism. Including both extinct ancestors and extant humans.

Homo The genus to which modern humans and other extinct species belong. Originating in Africa approximately 2.5 mya (by current estimates), its appearance is characterized by brain enlargement and subsequent geographic expansion into all parts of the world.

Homo erectus A species of hominid originating approximately 1.5 mya in Africa that subsequently spread to Asia and possibly (though much more uncertainly) to Europe. Characterized anatomically by thick cranial bones, a heavy brow ridge, and other protuberant aspects of the skull. The species became extinct by 0.2 mya.

homodont Teeth that all have the same shape and function.

Homoplasy In evolutionary studies, systems or traits that evolve within the same parameters.

Homo sapiens neanderthalensis A taxonomic designation of Neanderthal that denoted the opinion that they were a subspecies and not a separate species within the genus *Homo*.

hunters and gatherers In anthropology, people also referred to as foragers, a mobile means of subsistence relying on the collection, harvesting, and hunting of resources for survival. Usually thought to be the best living model for understanding the life ways of early hominids.

hydraulic hypothesis In anthropology, the theory that civilizations arose as the result of intensified use of water supplies, especially swamps and rivers.

Hylobatidae So-called lesser apes, gibbons, and siamangs occupying mainland and islands of Southeast Asia. Gibbons are specialized brachiators, highly arboreal, and dwell in nuclear family groups only.

hyper-robust hominid (see robust australopithecines)

hypotheses Literally "below knowing." A tentative supposition that may explain a particular phenomenon.

I'k In Africa, a group sometimes cited as an example of the breakdown of normal social structure as the result of environmental stress.

imprinting The idea in many social and biological sciences that animals develop intense emotional and psychological attachments to other individuals (and other phenomena) during certain periods of their development and life.

incest taboo The universal human prohibition against mating with close relatives, the most common of which involves members of the nuclear family.

incisors The large anterior nipping teeth in primates for eating fruit.

inclusive fitness The sociobiological concept that emphasizes the idea that maximizing one's own DNA is more important than maximizing the number of offspring generation as the measure of evolutionary fitness.

industry In archaeology, a term used to refer to the total tool kit associated with a particular culture.

Infanticide The intentional killing of infants, broadly defined here as also including intentional abortion.

insectivorous   Relying on insects as the principle component of the diet.

interspecific aggression   Violent or threatening interactions between different species.

intraspecific aggression   Violent or threatening interactions between members of the same species.

intraspecific competition   Competition for resources between members of the same same species.

Iroquois   In anthropology, a much-discussed Native American group noted for their seemingly unusual gender and psychological qualities, which allow females greater sociopolitical power as the result of male absence resulting from war and frequent participation in hunting parties.

ischial callosites   Patches of toughened skin on the buttocks of monkeys enabling them to spend a great deal of time sitting upright.

isolating mechanisms of speciation   Circumstances that preclude the mating of individuals and species long enough to result in the production of separate species. Primary mechanisms are behavioral, geographic, and temporal barriers.

Kenyapithecus wickeri   An African Miocene hominoid once considered by Louis Leakey to be an early tool-using hominid.

kin recognition   In sociobiological theory, the supposedly innate ability to identify those that are more closely genetically related to you.

Klasies River Mouth, South Africa   A cave locality that has been cited (arguably) as preserving the earliest evidence of anatomically modern humans.

KNM-ER 1470   One of the best-preserved cranium of *H. habilis*.

KNM-ER 1813   A well-preserved cranium of *H. habilis*, or another species of early *Homo* according to some workers.

KNM-ER 3733   The best-preserved cranium of early African *H. erectus* exhibiting all the commonly known traits except for thick cranial bone.

knuckle walking   A mode of locomotion practiced by chimpanzees in which the weight of the body is divided by all four limbs with the knuckles flexed.

Krapina, Croatia   A cave site in the former Yugoslavia that has been interpreted as preserving convincing evidence for Neanderthal cannibalism.

K/T boundary   The Cretaceous–Tertiary boundary at approximately 65 mya dividing the age of dinosaurs from the age of mammals.

Laetoli, Tanzania   One of the earliest (but not the earliest) sites preserving fossils and footprints of *A. afarensis*.

Lascaux, France   A French Upper Paleolithic cave site renowned for its paintings depicting Ice Age animal and other representations that had been much discussed in a variety of disciplines concerned with the human mind.

leaf sponge   A nonlithic tool created by chimpanzees by mashing up a leaf and using it to soak up water from hollows in tree trunks.

Levallois technique   A Middle Paleolithic technique for producing stone points, usually associated with Neanderthal but also thought to be associated with later peoples. Essentially, the technique evolved the trimming of cores before the detachment of a point with a single blow.

limbic   Emotional.

linguistics   The study of any aspect of language.

living floors   Places on the landscape where early hominids were thought to have dwelt. First suggested by Louis and Mary Leakey on the bases of sites at Olduvai Gorge.

locality 1 at Zhoukoudian, China   The so-called Peking Man site. A stratified karst cave accumulation spanning the last 0.2 to 0.8 mya (at least) documenting a living site utilized for hundreds of thousands of years by *H. erectus*.

locomotion   How an animal moves from place to place in the environment.

Lower Paleolithic   A period of time beginning approximately 2.5 mya and ending approximately 0.125 mya including Olduwan, Acheulian, and the other industries characterized a progression from unformalized to more formalized tools (in Africa and Europe).

lung fish   *Crossopty rigian.*

Magdalenian   A local Upper Paleolithic European industry.

mammal-like reptiles   Extinct reptiles that may have possessed hair, warm-bloodedness, and heterodont dentitions.

mandible   Lower jaw.

manuports   Unmodified natural objects (usually stone) transported to a site.

marginal environments   Inhospitable habitats with a scarcity of resources.

marsupials   Pouched mammals including kangaroos, opossum, and bandicoot.

mass extinction   The rapid extinction of a diverse number of organisms.

Materialist–non materialistic arguments   In biological philosopy, polarized opinions which hold that thinking can or cannot be understood in terms of the anatomical and biochemical phenomena which make concepts such as thought, mind, and soul possible.

matrifocal   In sociocultural anthropology, a term used to refer to cultures that emphasize the importance of females and their lineages.

matrilineal   In sociocultural anthropology, a term used to refer to an emphasis on the mother's line of descent.

mechanics   A movement that in the seventeenth and eighteenth centuries discovered and elucidated "laws" that govern the physical universe.

megafaunal extinctions   The disappearance of many large-bodied mammals in the late Pleistocene, which in the New World may have been associated with the arrival of modern humans and/or climatic change.

mental template   A plan, a way of doing things, envisioning a preconceived procedure, form or pattern.

Messinian salinity crisis   A period from roughly 10-8 mya when the Straits of Gibralter became dry land and blocked the flow of Atlantic water to the Mediterranean Sea. This blockage resulted in the exposure of land bridges with Africa and an increase in the salinity of the Mediterranean as indicated by salt deposits at Messina.

metatheres   Marsupials.

Middle Paleolithic   A general term referring to stone tool kits usually, but not just, associated with Neanderthals. Spanning a period from perhaps 0.04 to 0.2 mya, these tool kits emphasized a prepared core technique.

Middle Stone Age   See Middle Paleolithic.

midfacial prognathism   The anterior projection of the area of the face surrounding the nasal region usually characteristic of Neanderthals.

Miocene   The geological Epoch dated to between 22.5-5.2 mya, characterized by extensive moist warm forests.

mitochondrial DNA   DNA housed in the mitochondria organelles of cells whose mutations have been treated as a "molecular clock" by some researchers.

molars   Crushing and grinding teeth located at the back of the jaws.

molecular clock   The concept that an average mutation rate can be discerned for DNA and the number of differences between populations can be compared and assigned as approximate age in years which "dates" the time of divergence and reproductive isolations of populations.

monotremes   Egg-laying mammals in which the passage for the excretion of waste and reproduction are the same.

morphocline   The concept in evolutionary biology that physical traits can be arranged on a scale of opposite poles.

mosaic evolution   In evolutionary biology, the concept that different parts of an organism evolve at different rates in response to different selection pressures. Thus organisms are a collection of old and new parts.

Mousterian   In archaeology, first recognized at the archaeological locality of Le Moustier, France. Generally associated with the Middle Paleolithic and Neanderthals.

Movius line   In archaeology, first recognized by Hallam Movius, a roughly defined border dividing the hand axe industry of South Asia from the "cruder" chopper-chopping tools of the Far East.

"the muddle in the Middle"   Glynn Isaac's informal characterization of the difficulties of dating Middle Pleistocene hominid and archaeological sites.

Multiregional Hypothesis   (see regional continuity)

multimodal   In the study of communication among organisms, the concept that animals employ visual, auditory, olfactory, and chemical paths for conveying information to each other.

mutation   In genetics, a change in the genetic sequences of DNA. Generally divided into deleterious, beneficial, and neutral mutations.

nasovomer   A bone associated with a nasal organ that detects scent.

natural selection   Darwin's (and others) principle that the environment determines the reproductive success of organisms without divine intervention.

natural theology   A scientific-religious movement whose practitioners sought to further their understanding of God by closely studying the natural world.

nature versus nuture   A long-standing debate about whether innate characteristics (genetic) or experience is more important in the determination of behavior.

Neanderthal   Now spelled Neandertal in more recent German orthography, a term used to refer to a Late Pleistocene group of anatomically distinct hominids that once occupied Europe and the Middle East.

neocarnassial   A new term used in this text to describe the meat-slicing function of hominid premolars (bicuspids).

New and Old World monkeys   New World anthropoids occupying South and Central America are distinguished from Old World monkeys by being almost exclusively arboreal and more removed from human ancestry.

New World   North and South America.

Ngandong (Solo)   A site in Java that has yielded a number of fossil hominids from Java, Indonesia, variously assigned to *H. erectus* or early *H. sapiens*.

niche   In ecology, the French word for *shelf* generally understood in biological studies to denote the particular adaptation of an organism.

nonlimbic   Unemotional.

nonlithic   A term used to describe tools not made of stone.

normative research   Scientific investigation that proceeds according to widely accepted paradigms and problems emphasized by mainstream research.

nuchal torus   A bar or thickening of the occipital bone where posterior nuchal muscles attach and are especially well developed in *H. erectus*.

nuclear family   A living group consisting of a mother, father, and offspring.

nuclear winter   A theoretical concept that sufficiently large conflagration that would inject and circulate debris in the atmosphere to the point where sunlight reaching the earth would be greatly reduced. Such an effect has been hypothesized for periods of volcanic activity, meteorite impact, and nuclear bombs.

occipital bun   A swelling of the posterior brain case characteristic of Neanderthals.

Oedipal   In psychoanalytical theory, a term referring to the Oedipus tragedy in which sons desire sexual intercourse with their mothers and resent their fathers.

Oligocene   In geology the Epoch spanning ca. 33-23 mya.

Oldowan   In archaeology, the name of the earliest and simplest Paleolithic industries first recognized at Olduvai Gorge, Tanzania.

olfaction   Scent and smell.

omnivorous   In biology, organisms that eat both animals and plants.

opportunistic omnivores   In anthropology, ethology, and biology, the observation that some animals will eat both vegetable and animal protein given the opportunity.

optimal foraging theory   In ecological theory, the idea that sustained acquisition of food will not be possible if an organism expends more energy than it takes in.

Order Primates   The group of vertebrates, including prosimians, monkeys, apes, and humans. Characterized by encephalization, free digits, and emphasis on vision and delayed maturation.

organized big game hunting   In anthropology, the idea that planned and coordinated group hunting implies complex social organization, foresight, and intelligence.

orthograde   Anatomically structured with bones and organs perpendicular to the ground.

os mentum   The chin.

osteodontokeratic culture   Raymond Dart's incorrect interpretation that nonhuman animal bones associated with early hominids (australopithecines) were fashioned into artifacts. Today this so-called archaeological culture is recognized as almost exclusively the remains of carnivore predation.

paleoneurology   The study of the anatomy of fossil endocasts of the brain.

paleontology   The study of fossils.

paleospecies   Extinct organisms that are sufficiently distinct to have been considered reproductively isolated.

Pangea   In geology, the name of the single ancient continent in which all the modern continents were joined in a single super continent.

Pan paniscus   Bonobos or "pygmy" chimpanzees.

Pan troglodytes   The so-called common chimpanzee of large body size.

paradigm A shared set of beliefs and procedures employed by a community of scientists and laypeople.

parallel evolution Refers to distantly related organisms that developed similar adaptations to similar ecological problems.

paraprimates Early Paleocene mammals thought by some to morphologically mimic true primates but that should not be included in the order.

parental investment The time and energy that parents put into their offspring.

paternal uncertainty The idea that a male can never know with certainty that a female's offspring carries his own DNA.

patrifocal In anthropology, a term for societies that emphasize the importance of the male or father's side of the family.

patrilineal In anthropology, the emphasis on the importance of the father's side of the family and ancestry.

pebble tools In archaeology, an informal term used to refer to relatively simple artifacts whose manufacture requires a minimum skill to remove flakes.

petrosal bulla A part of the osseous inner ear comprising in part of the petrosal bone, a defining characteristic of primates.

phenotype The physical appearance of an organism.

pheromones Airborne hormones.

phylogenies Ancestor–descendent relationships graphically portrayed as lineages.

physical anthropologist Scientists that study the anatomy and function of hominids, living or dead.

Pima A Native American (Amerind) group living in and adapted to the Sonoran Desert of the Southwest United States and Northern Mexico.

Pithecanthropus erectus A now invalid scientific designation for *Homo erectus* discovered by Eugène Dubois in Java, Indonesia.

placenta A membrane evolved to protect and nurture the fetus of warm-blooded mammals.

plantigrade A term referring to locomotion with the sole of the feet or palms of the hands in contact with the ground.

plate tectonics The now well-accepted realization that continents float over the surface of the earth, sometimes colliding and sometimes breaking apart.

Pleistocene In geology the Epoch spanning the time between ca. 1.85-0.01 mya, divided by shifting consensus into Early (1.85-0.73 mya); Middle (0.73-0.126) and Late (0.125-0.011 mya).

Pliocene The geological Epoch between 5.2 and ca. 1.89 mya.

plesiomorphic The original or "primitive" condition of a trait.

Pliotrophy The condition in which one or a few genes influence or control a number of seemingly separate traits.

polyandrous In mating groups, the extremely rare condition of many males mating with one female.

polygamous In ethology, many females and males mating without long-term pair bonds.

polygenic traits Anatomical traits determined by a number of genes.

polygynous Mating groups in which one male mates with several females.

Pongo pygmaeus Orangutan ("forest man" in Malaysian).

population pressure Adverse conditions brought on by too many organisms competing for too few resources.

postcranial   In anatomy, below the head.

postorbital bar   A bar of bone that protects the eye sockets located on the lateral side of the orbit.

postorbital constriction   In paleoanthropology, the "pinched" appearance of the frontal bone behind the bony eye sockets as viewed from above.

preadaptation   In evolutionary theory, the concept that organisms adapted to one set of environmental selection pressures may also be adapted to a new set of pressures when the environment changes.

precision grip   The ability, especially developed in primates, to grasp objects between the thumb and forefinger. Hominids are especially adept at fingertip-to-thumb-tip gripping.

predation   Usually the killing of one species by another for food. Much less frequently among terrestrial vertebrates, cannibalism or intraspecific killing.

predator defense   Defenses to prevent those who want to eat you from doing so.

predisposition   A biological based tendency to do certain things.

prehensile   The ability to grip things with an appendage such as a hand, tail or nose (trunk in elephants and tapirs).

premasticatory food processing   Breaking down food before ingestion, i.e. cooking, cutting, and other kinds of processing.

premolars   Referred to as bicuspids by most dentists; two teeth on each side of the lower and upper jaw anterior to the three grinding molars.

prenatal position   The position that unborn infants assume in the womb characterized by arms and legs drawn up against the chest in humans and other animals.

prepared core technique   In archaeology, usually associated with Neanderthals and later hominids, a stone making tradition in which a piece of stone is first trimmed before a final point is removed.

primatology   The study of the evolution and behavior of prosimians, monkeys, and apes.

probable mutation effect   Loring Brace's idea that mutations of little adaptive value will be deleted from the gene pool. "Use it or lose it" is a fair way of describing it.

promiscuous troops   In primatology, groups of primates that form only transient sexual relationships.

Prosimians   Lower primates retaining some characteristics of other mammals such as vibrissae, a naked rhinarium; largely nocturnal and arboreal.

protein synthesis   One of two DNA functions in the construction and coding for substances in the body that have specific structural and functional roles in the growth and maintenance of the organism.

protocultural   A theoretical state of behavior postulated for organisms that seem to pass on some learned behavior from generation to generation.

prototheres (monotremes)   The lowest grade of mammals including duck-billed platypus and the echidna. They are egg layers but warm-blooded and hairy.

provisioning   The practice of some organisms (birds and some social carnivores) of providing and sharing food with helpless offspring. Also, the specific theory of C. Owen Lovejoy that postulates that early hominids practiced a mating strategy in which males traded meat for sexual intercourse.

psychic unity   In anthropology, also similar to the idea of "deep structures," a term that maintains that humans have innate categories of perception and thought.

punctuated equilibrium In evolutionary biology, the interpretation that evolutionary change proceeds in leaps of rapid morphological change followed by periods of morphological stasis.

quarry sites In archaeology, localities where hominids obtained raw materials to make artifacts, especially certain kinds of stone.

racial senescence An outmoded and little supported concept that races are destined to a fixed period of existence before they cease to exist.

racism The widespread, if not universal, practice of ascribing behavioral characteristics to groups of humans based on their appearance.

radiational cooling In biology, the dispersal and loss of body heat by organisms.

rafting In paleontology and biozoology, the observation that organisms can be transported across bodies of water on floating vegetation.

Ramapithecus punjabicus A Miocene primate found in the Siwalik Hills of India, once ardently defended in some scientific circles as the earliest hominid.

ray-finned fish Fish whose bony fins are not attached to muscled lobes as in lobe-finned fish.

recombination In genetics, the paring of different segments of DNA from different individuals.

red ochre Iron oxide, used by past and present people all over the world as a coloring agent.

reductionist A philosopher or philosophical argument that reduces complex arguments to a single or few components.

regional continuity In paleoanthropology, an interpretation that maintains that many local fossil populations in certain regions evolved into and are the direct ancestors of populations inhabiting the same regions today (also known as the multiregional hypothesis).

regional differentiation In biology, an interpretation espoused by Darwin and others that species will come to be different as a function of their geographical distribution.

relict populations Isolated remaining groups of organisms that were previously widely spread in their geographic distribution.

replacement model In paleoanthropology, the idea that anatomically modern humans arose only in Africa and then outcompeted regional hominid populations outside of Africa.

replication One of DNA's two functions, that of making copies of itself.

reproductively isolated populations Groups (populations) that mate and reproduce only with others of their own kind.

reptiles Cold-blooded, usually egg-laying terrestrial vertebrates.

retromolar space A space on the mandible of Neanderthals separating the last molar (M3) from the anterior edge of the ascending ramus indicative of pronounced midfacial prognathism.

rhinarium Nose.

ricochetal brachiation A means of locomotion practiced by hylobotids (gibbons) relying on rapid grasping of tree limbs combined with swift propulsion to the next branch.

rifle An informal concept characterizing a great parental investment in offspring.

ring-tailed lemur Prosimians confined to Madagascar and noted for their atypical terrestrial, diurnal adaptations.

robust australopithecines A general term including early large body hominids with massive masticatory structure adapted for a largely or entirely vegetarian diet requiring crushing and grinding.

rods and cones   Structures within the eye that allow the perception of color and form.

sagittal crest   An anterior–posterior running crest of bone situated on the top of the skull to which the temporalis muscles attach in the robust australopithecines and other primates.

sagittal keel   A thickening of the cranial bone along the sagittal suture in *H. erectus*.

Sasquatch, Big Foot, or Yeti   A legendary primate supposedly inhabiting Asia and North America which some scientists have speculated to be a surviving *Gigantopithecus blacki*.

scansorial   Scurrying motion.

sectorial premolar   A unicuspid premolar that hones or sharpens the opposing upper canine.

sedentary   In anthropology, a settled, nonmobile lifestyle usually associated with agriculture.

selection pressures   All the environmental circumstances that determine Darwinian fitness.

self-mimicry   In paleoanthropology, the idea that human female anatomical features such as large breasts, red lips, and the navel mimic the female body as seen from a posterior view.

sexual dimorphism   Difference in anatomy and behavior between males and females.

shamanism   The belief that certain individuals have the power to interact with supernatural powers on behalf of a client.

shotgun theory   As used in this text, the idea that leaving many offspring without investment may be more adaptive than leaving one or a few offspring who receive more concentrated parental investment.

Sinanthropus pekinensis   The now scientifically invalid name of the so-called Peking Man included in *H. erectus*.

single dentary   In paleontology, separate jaw bones that fuse to form a single bone.

single species hypothesis   A now abandoned idea that robust australopithecine and gracile australopithecine were simply and respectively males and females of the same species.

sivapithecines   A group of Miocene apes that occupied the Far East and eastern Europe.

slow quadrupedal climbing   A description of one form of primate locomotion involving the careful positioning of all four limbs.

social carnivores   Meat-eating animals that hunt cooperatively.

social endothermic model   In paleontology, the interpretation that early mammals evolved and emphasized socialness in conjunction with the maintenance of a constant internal body temperature.

socialness   The biological necessity for species to mature and interact with others of their own kind.

social stratification   In anthropology, the observation that agriculturally based societies develop social classes with different privileges and power.

sociobiology   A biological theory that holds that organisms have evolved to maximize the inclusion of their own DNA and not necessarily viable offspring in each generation.

soft punch technique   In archaeology, a technique of stone tool manufacture that employs bone or wood implements on stone to "press" stone flakes off of a stone core.

spacing   In ethology, the observation that animals tend to maintain certain distances between individuals according to the species and situations.

species   Reproductively isolated populations that mate and reproduce viable offspring only with others of their own kind.

species specific   In ethology, attributes, behavioral or anatomical, that are characteristic of a particular organism.

speech A form of communication only found in humans that incorporates both vocalizations and other forms of language.

stable core In primatology, the controversial idea that certain individuals maintain stable social alliances throughout their lifetimes.

stereoscopic vision The ability to perceive space in three dimensions made possible by the overlapping fields of vision of both eyes.

stone caches In archaeology, the interpretation that some concentrations of stones result from the accumulations of rocks saved by hominids for use in hunting.

stone ring In archaeology, Mary Leakey's characterization and recognition of a round stone structure at Olduvai Gorge as a home base or campsite.

structuralists In anthropolgoy, a school of thought that perceives the human mind as composed of innate categories.

suborder In biology, variously defined and usually arbitrary subdivisions of orders.

subsistence continuum In anthropology, the idea that obtaining food in different cultures may range from hunting, gathering, horticulture and agriculture in various combinations.

supraorbital torus In paleoanthropology, an anatomical term referring to a thick bony bar above the orbits (eye sockets).

supraorganic In philosophy and anthropology, the concept that there are influences and forces acting on beings that cannot be readily perceived or tested by people.

suspensory feeding In primatology, the practice of hanging suspended while eating.

sympathetic magic In anthropology, the belief among most cultural groups that the intentions of certain individuals (curses, blessings) can affect the physical well-being of others.

sympatric In evolutionary studies, two species or more that occupy the same area.

symplesiomorphic Shared "primitive," original characters.

synapomorphic Unique characters shared between two or more species.

synthetic theory of evolution The combination of Darwinian natural selection theory with the principles of genetics as the paradigm of all biological sciences.

taphonomic agents Forces that transport, preserve, or alter living organisms that become fossils.

taphonomy The study of the many ways in which fossils come to be.

Tasaday A tribal group in the Philippines reputed to have little sexual division of labor, origin myth or other traits, originally describe but not accepted by most researchers as a relict "Stone Age tribe."

Taung In paleoanthropology, a limestone–karst quarry that yielded *Australopithecus africanus*, recognized by Raymond Dart as the earliest human ancestor in 1924.

taurodontism Taking the form of a hollowed pulp cavity in Neanderthal teeth.

taxonomy The science of classifying organisms.

T-complex In primatology, Clifford Jolly's theory relating the orthognathic chewing of *Therapithecus* to a graminivorous diet and the reduction of hominid canine size so as to allow a rotary grinding motion of the upper and lower jaws.

temporal fossa The space behind the zygomatic arch that accommodates the temporalis muscle, one of the primary muscles of mastication.

temporalis muscle Attaching to the braincase and inserted on the mandible, this main muscle of mastication was hypertrophied in robust and hyper-robust australopithecines. In humans, it is greatly reduced.

termite stick   Twigs modified by chimpanzees to "fish" for termites.

Thecodont   Teeth rooted in distinct sockets in the jaws.

therapsids   Mammal-like reptiles.

threat yawn   In primatology, the exposure of the dentition as an aggressive warning to others.

tibia   Largest lower leg bone.

tonal   In linguistics, the fact that in many languages the timber and pitch of pronunciation changes the meaning of a word.

tool dependent   In paleoanthropology, the concept that only hominids rely on tool use for survival.

tooth comb   A modified set of procumbent incisors used by some prosimians to groom their fur.

Torralba (Ambronia)   Archaeological sites in Spain preserving evidence of Acheulian tool manufacture and big game hunting.

trading niche   In anthropology, the observation that some human groups depend on trading foraged resources for agricultural products.

transhumance   In anthropology, an adaptation emphasizing constant movement of human groups across the landscape, usually associated with herding and pastoralism.

tribosphenic molar   An early type of cusp arrangement in which three cusps are arranged in a triangular or "delta wing" shape.

tritubercular   Having three cusps on at least some of the teeth.

turbinate bones   Scroll-like and "curly" bones of the inner nose that perceive olfactory chemicals.

uniformitarianism   The concept that the natural forces at work on the earth today are the same ones that have always been at work.

Upper Paleolithic   In archaeology, the period between approximately 0.01 to 0.04 mya in which archaeological assemblages become much more complex in comparison with earlier tool kits.

ventral–ventral sex   Face-to-face sexual intercourse.

Venuses   In archaeology, an informal term used to refer to Upper Paleolithic figurines depicting naked women.

vertebrates   Animals with limb bones and backbones.

viable offspring   Offspring that are fertile and able to reproduce.

vibrissae   Sensory facial hairs (whiskers).

visually directed predation   In primatology, the idea that many primate traits can be related to the visual detection of food.

visually displayed estrus   In primatology, the observation that most female primates and other mammals signal fertility and willingness to copulate through physical changes (swelling of the genital area) that are perceived by males.

Wernicke's area   In neurosciences, an area of the human neocortex associated with the comprehension of language.

zygomatic arches   The cheekbones, which form an arch around the temporalis muscle.

BIBLIOGRAPHY

Aberle, David F., Bronfenbrenner, U., Hess, E. H., Miller, D. R., Schneider, D. H., and Spuhler, J. N. 1963. The Incest Taboo and the Mating Patterns of Animals. *American Anthropologist* 65: 25–265.

Akil, H., Watson, S. J., Young, E., Lewis, M. E., Khachaturian, H., and Walker, J. M. 1984. Endogenous Opioids: Biology and Function. *Annual Review of Neuroscience* 7: 223–255.

Anderson, J. R. 1983. *The Architecture of Cognition*. Cambridge, MA: Harvard University Press.

Averill, J. 1982. *Anger and Aggression: An Essay on Emotion*. New York: Springer-Verlag.

Axelrod, R., and Dion, D. 1988. The Further Evolution of Cooperation. *Science* 242: 1385–1390.

Axelrod, R., and Hamilton, W. D. 1981. The Evolution of Cooperation. *Science* 211: 1390–1396.

Barash, D. P. 1982. *Sociobiology and Behavior* (2nd ed.). New York: Elsevier.

Barkow, J. H. 1967. Causal Interpretation of Correlation in Cross-Cultural Studies. *American Anthropologist* 69: 506–510.

Barkow, J. H. 1973. Darwinian Psychological Anthropology: A Biosocial Approach. *Current Anthropology* 14: 373–388.

Barkow, J. H. 1977. Human Ethology and Intra-individual Systems. *Social Science Information* 16: 133–145.

Barkow, J. H. 1978. Culture and Sociobiology. *American Anthropologist* 80: 5–20.

Barkow, J. H. 1980a. Sociobiology: Is This the New Theory of Human Nature?" In A. Montagu (ed.), *Sociobiology Examined*, pp. 171–192. New York and London: Oxford University Press.

Barkow, J. H. 1980b. Biological Evolution of Culturally Patterned Behavior. In J. Lorckard (ed.), *The Evolution of Human Social Behavior*, pp. 227–296. New York: Elsevier.

Barkow, J. H. 1980c. Prestige and self-esteem: A biosocial interpretation. In D. R. Omark, F. F. Strayer, and D. G. Freedman (eds.), *Dominance Relations: An Ethological View of Human Conflict and Social Interaction*, pp. 319–332. New York: Garland.

Barkow, J. H. 1983. Begged Questions in Behavior and Evolution. In G. Davey (ed.), *Animal Models of Human Behavior*, pp. 205–222. Chichester and New York: Wiley and Sons.

Barkow, J. H. 1989a. *Darwin, Sex, and Status: Biological Approaches to Mind and Culture*. Toronto: University of Toronto Press.

Barkow, J. H. 1989b. The Elastic between Genes and Culture. *Ethology and Sociobiology* 10: 1129.

Barkow, J., Cosmides, L., and Tooby, J. (eds.). 1995. *The Adapted Mind, Evolutionary Psychology and the Generation of Culture* (2nd ed.). New York: Oxford University Press.

Benbow, C., and Stanley, J. 1980. Sex Differences in Mathematical Ability: Fact or Artifact? *Science* 210: 1262–1264.

Berlin, B., and Kay, P. 1969. *Basic Color Terms: Their Universality and Evolution*. Berkeley: University of California Press.

Bickerton, D. 1984. The Language Bioprogram Hypothesis. *Behavioral & Brain Sciences* 7: 173–221.

Binet, A., and Simon, T. 1911. Methodes Nouvelles pour le Diagnostic du Nivequ Intellecia des Arnormous. *L'Annee Psychologique* 11: 191–244.

Binford, L. 1981. *Bones: Ancient Men and Modern Myths*. New York: Academic Press.

Binford, L. 1983. *In Pursuit of the Past*. London: Thames and Hudson.

Bischof, N. 1975. Comparative Ethology of Incest Avoidance. In R. Fox (ed.), *Biosocial Anthropology*. New York: Wiley and Sons.

Boas, Franz. 1966. *Race, Language and Culture*. New York: The Free Press.

Bonner, J. T. 1980. *The Evolution of Culture in Animals*. Princeton, NJ: Princeton University Press.

Bower, B. 1993. Genetic Clue to Male Homosexuality Emerges. *Science News* 37.

Brace, C. Loring, and Ashley Montagu, M. F. 1977. *Human Evolution: An Introduction to Biological Anthropology* (2nd ed.). New York: Macmillan.

Braidwood, R. J., 1960. The Agricultural Revolution. *Scientific American* 203: 130–141.

Bridgeman, B. 1988. *The Biology of Behavior and Mind*. New York: Wiley and Sons.

Brothwell, D., and Brothwell, P. 1969. *Food in Antiquity. A Survey of the Diet of Early Peoples*. London: Thames and Hudson.

Brown, R. 1973. *A First Language: The Early Stages*. Cambridge, MA: Harvard University Press.

Brown, R., and McNeill, D. 1966. The "Tip of the Tongue" Phenomenon. *Journal of Verbal Learning & Verbal Behavior* 5: 325–337.

Brues, A. M. 1977. *People and Races*. New York: Macmillan.

Burd, M. 1986. Sexual Selection and Human Evolution: All or None Adaptation? *American Anthropologist* 88: 167–172.

Burt, C. 1955. The Evidence for the Concept of Intelligence. *British Journal of Educational Psychology* 25: 158–177.

Burt, C. 1963. The Genetic Determination of Differences in Intelligence: A Study of Monozygotic Twins Reared Together and Apart. *British Journal of Psychology* 57: 137–153.

Cabanac, M. 1971. Physiological Role of Pleasure. *Science* 173: 1103–1107.

Calhoun, J. B. 1962. Population density and social pathology. Scientific America 206, 139–148.

Campbell, B. G. 1972. *Sexual Selection and the Descent of Man*. Chicago: Aldine.

Campbell, D. T. 1983. The Two Distinct Routes beyond Kin Selection to Ultrasociality: Implications for the Humanities and Social Sciences. In D. L. Bridgeman (ed.), *The Nature of Prosocial Development*. New York: Academic Press.

Cann, R. 1987. In Search of Eve. *The Sciences* 27: 30–32.

Cant, J. 1981. Hypothesis for the Evolution of Human Breasts and Buttocks. *American Naturalist* 117: 99–204.

Cartmill, M. 1974. Rethinking Primate Origins. *Science* 184: 436–443.

Cartmill, M. 1975. *Primate Origins*. Minneapolis: Burgess.

Chagnon, N. A. 1988. *Yanomamo(diar): The Fierce People* (3rd ed.). New York: Holt, Rinehart and Winston.

Chagnon, N. A., and Irons, W. (eds.). 1979. *Evolutionary Biology and Human Social Behavior*. North Scituate, MA: Duxbury Press.

Chalmers, D. 1996 *The Conscious Mind: In Search of a Fundamental*. Oxford: Oxford University Press.

Changeux, J. 1985. *Neuronal Man: The Biology of Mind*. New York: Pantheon.

Cheney, D. L., Seyfarth, T., and Smuts, B. 1986. Social Relationships and Social Cognition in Nonhuman Primates. *Science* 234: 1361–1366.

Childe, V. G. 1936. *Man Makes Himself*. London: Watts.

Chomsky, N. 1965. *Aspects of the Theory of Syntax*. Cambridge, MA: MIT Press.

Chomsky, N. 1972. *Language and Mind*. New York: Harcourt, Brace, Jovanovich.

Chomsky, N. 1980. *Rules and Representations*. New York: Columbia University Press.

Ciochon, R. L., and Fleagle, J. G. (eds.). 1987. *Primate Evolution and Human Origins*. Hawthorne, NY: Aldine de Gruyter.

Cohen, M., and Armelegos, G. (eds.). 1984. *Paleopathology and the Origins of Agriculture*. Orlando, FL: Academic Press.

Cosmides, L., and Tooby, J. 1987. From Evolution to Behavior: Evolutionary Psychology as the Missing Link." In J. Dupre (ed.), *The Latest on the Best: Essays on Evolution and Optimality,* pp. 277–306. Cambridge, MA: MIT Press.

Crawford, C., and Galdikas, B. M. F. 1986. Rape in Nonhuman Animals: An Evolutionary Perspective. *Canadian Psychology* 27: 215–230.

Crick, F., and Koch, C. 1990. Towards a Neurobiological Theory of Consciousness. *Seminars in the Neurosciences* 2: 263–275.

Crook, J. H. 1980. *The Evolution of Consciousness.* Oxford: Clarendon Press.

Dahlberg, F. (Ed.). 1981. *Woman the Gatherer.* New Haven: Yale University Press.

Daly, M., and Wilson, M. I. 1978. *Sex, Evolution and Behavior.* North Scituate, MA: Duxbury Press.

Daly, M., and Wilson, M. I. 1989. Homicide and Cultural Evolution. *Ethology & Sociobiology* 10: 99–110.

Dart, R. 1925. *Australopithecus africanus*: The Man Ape of South Africa. *Nature* 155: 195–199.

Darwin, C. 1936. *The Descent of Man and Selection in Relation to Sex.* New York: Random House. (Original work published 1871.)

Darwin, C. 1950. *On the Origin of Species by Means of Natural Selection.* London: Watts. (Original work published 1859.)

Dawkins, R. 1976. *The Selfish Gene.* Oxford: Oxford University Press.

Dawkins, R. 1982. *The Extended Phenotype: The Gene as the Unit of Selection.* Oxford and San Francisco: W. H. Freeman.

Deacon, T. 1997. *The Symbolic Species, the Co-evolution of Language and the Brain.* New York: W. W. Norton.

Delgado, J. M. R. 1969a. Offensive–Defensive Behavior in Free Monkeys and Chimpanzees Induced by Radio Stimulation of the Brain. In S. Garattini and E. Sigg (eds.), *Aggressive Behavior.* New York: Wiley and Sons.

Delgado, J. M. R. 1969b. *Physical Control of the Mind.* New York: Harper and Row.

Dement, W. 1960. The Effect of Dream Deprivation. *Science* 131: 1705–1707.

Dement, W. 1974. *Some Must Watch While Some Must Sleep.* San Francisco: Freeman.

Dement, W., and Kleitman, N. 1957. Cyclic Variations in EEG during Sleep and Their Relation to Eye Movements, Body Motility and Dreaming. *Electroencephlography & Clinical Neurophysiology* 9: 673–690.

DeVore, I. (Ed.). 1965. *Primate Behavior: Field Studies of Monkeys and Apes.* New York: Holt, Rinehart and Winston.

Durham, W. H. 1982. Interactions of Genetic and Cultural Evolution: Models and Examples. *Human Ecology* 10: 289–323.

Eccles, J. C. 1958. The Physiology of Imagination. *Scientific American* 135–146.

Eccles, J. C. 1964. *The Physiology of Synapses.* New York: McGraw-Hill.

Edey, M. and the Editors of Time-Life. 1972. *The Missing Link.* New York: Time-Life.

Ehrlich, P. R., and Ehrlich, A. H. 1970. *Population, Resources, Environment.* San Francisco: Freeman.

Eibl-Eibesfeldt, I. 1975. *Ethology: The Biology of Behavior* (2nd ed.). New York: Holt, Rinehart and Winston.

Eiseley, L. 1958. *Darwin's Century: Evolution and the Men Who Discovered It.* New York: Doubleday.

Evans, W. 1968. *Communication in the Animal World.* New York: Crowell.

Falk, D. 1975. Comparative Anatomy of the Larynx in Man and the Chimpanzee: Implications for Language in Neanderthal. *American Journal of Physical Anthropology* 43(1): 123–132.

Falk, D. 1987. Human Paleoneurology. *Annual Review of Anthropology* 16: 13–30.

Fedigan, L. M. 1983. Dominance and Reproductive Success. *Yearbook of Physical Anthropology* 26: 91–129.

Fedigan, L. M. 1986. The Changing Role of Women in Models of Human Evolution. *Annual Review of Anthropology* 15: 25–56.

Firth, R. 1957. *Man and Culture: An Evaluation of Bronislaw Malinowski.* London: Routledge.

Fleagle, J. G. 1988. *Primate Adaptation and Evolution.* New York: Academic Press.

Fortes, M. 1969. *Kinship and the Social Order: The Legacy of Lewis Henry Morgan.* Chicago: Aldine.

Fossey, D. 1983. *Gorillas in the Mist.* Boston: Houghton Mifflin.

Fouts, R., Fouts, D., and van Cantfort, T. 1989. The Infant Louis Learns Signs from Cross-Fostered Chimpanzees. In R. Gardner, B. Gardner, and T. van Cantfort (eds.), *Teaching Sign Language to Chimpanzees.* pp. 280–292 Albany: State University of New York Press.

Freedman, D. G. 1979. *Human Sociobiology: A Holistic Approach.* New York: The Free Press.

Freeman, D. 1983. *Margaret Mead and Samoa: The Making and Unmaking of an Anthropological Myth.* Cambridge, MA: Harvard University Press.

Freud, S. 1933. *New Introductory Lectures in Psychoanalysis.* New York: Norton.

Friedl, E. 1975. *Women and Men: An Anthropologist's View.* New York: Holt, Rinehart and Winston.

Fritsch, G., and Hitzig, E. 1969. On the Electrical Excitability of the Cerebrum. In K. H. Pribran (ed.), *Brain and Behavior: Vol. 2. Perception and Action.* Harmondsworth, Eng. and Baltimore: Penguin. (Original work published 1870.)

Fuster, J. M. 1980. *The Prefrontal Cortex.* New York: Raven Press.

Galdikas, B. 1979. Orangutan Adaptation at Tanjung Puting Reserve; Mating and Ecology. In D. Hamburg and E. R. McGown (eds.), *The Great Apes,* pp. 195–233. Menlo Park, CA: Benjamin/Comming Publishing Co.

Gardner, B. T., and Gardner, R. A. 1975. Evidence for Sentence Constituents in the Early Utterances of Child and Chimpanzee. *Journal of Experimental Psychology: General* 104: 244–267.

Gardner, H. 1983. *Frames of Mind: The Theory of Multiple Intelligences.* New York: Basic Books.

Gardner, R. A., and Gardner, B. T. 1969. Teaching Sign Language to a Chimpanzee. *Science* 165: 664–672.

Garn, S. M. 1970. *Human Races* (3rd ed.). Springfield, IL: Charles C. Thomas.

Gazzaniga, M. 1970. *The Bisected Brain.* New York: Appleton-Century-Crofts.

Gazzaniga, M. 1983. Right Hemisphere Language Following Brain Bisection: A 20-Year Perspective. *American Psychologist* 38: 525–537.

Gazzaniga, M. S. 1985. *The Social Brain.* New York: Basic Books.

Geertz, C. 1962. The Growth of Culture and the Evolution of Mind. In J. M. Scher (ed.), *Theories of Mind.* Glencoe, IL: The Free Press.

Geschwind, N. 1965. Disconnexion Syndromes in Animals and Man. *Brain* 88: 237–294, 585–644.

Geschwind, N. 1970. "The Organization of Language and the Brain. *Science* 170: 940–944.

Goodall, J. 1986. *The Chimpanzees of Gombe: Patterns of Behavior.* Cambridge, MA: Belknap Press of Harvard University Press.

Goodall-Van Lawick, J. 1972. *In the Shadow of Man.* New York: Dell.

Goody, J. 1976. *Production and Reproduction: A Comparative Study of the Domestic Domain.* Cambridge: Cambridge University Press.

Goody, J. 1983. *The Development of the Family and Marriage in Europe.* Cambridge: Cambridge University Press.

Gould, S. J. 1980. Sociobiology and Human Nature: A Postpanglossian Vision. In A. Montagu (ed.), *Sociobiology Examined,* pp. 283–290. New York and London: Oxford University Press.

Gould, S. J. 1981. *The Mismeasure of Man*. New York: W. W. Norton.

Gould, S. J., and Eldredge, N. 1977. Punctuated Equilibria: The Tempo and Mode of Evolution Reconsidered. *Paleobiology* 3: 115–151.

Gowlett, J., Harris, J. W. K., Walton, D., and Wood, B. A. 1981. Early Archeological Sites, Hominid Remains and Traces of Fire from Chesowanja, Kenya. *Nature* 294: 125–129.

Graham, S. Brandt. 1979. Biology and Human Social Behavior: A Response to van den Berghe and Barash. *American Anthropologist* 81(2): 357–360.

Greenfield, L. O. 1980. A Late Divergence Hypothesis. *American Journal of Physical Anthropology* 52: 351–366.

Giffon, B. 1984. The Ethnography of Southeastern Cagayan Agta Hunting. Masters thesis, University of the Philippines.

Griffin, D. R. 1976. *The Question of Animal Awareness: Evolutionary Continuity of Mental Experience*. New York: Rockefeller Universiy Press.

Griffin, D. R. 1978. Prospects for a Cognitive Ethology. *Behavioral & Brain Sciences* 1: 527–538.

Hall, K. R. L., and De Vore, I. 1965. Baboon Social Behavior. In I. DeVore (ed.), *Primate Behavior*. New York: Holt, Rinehart and Winston.

Hamilton, W. D. 1964. The Evolution of Social Behavior, *Journal of Theoretical Biology* 7: 1–52.

Hamilton, W. D. 1970. Selfish and Spiteful Behavior in an Evolutionary Model. *Nature* 228: 1218–1220.

Hamilton, W. D. 1975. Innate Social Aptitudes of Man: An Approach from Evolutionary Genetics. In R. Fox (ed.), *Biosocial Anthropology*, pp. 133–155. New York: Wiley and Sons.

Hampshire, S. 1978. The Illusion of Sociobiology. Review of E. O. Wilson, *On Human Nature*, in *New York Review* 25 (12 October): 64–69.

Harkness, C. An Interpretation of Developmental Changes in Verbal Communication within a Sociobiological Framework. In J. H. Barkow, L. Cosmides, and J. Tooby (eds.), *The Adapted Mind: Evolutionary Psychology and the Generation of Culture*. New York: Oxford University Press.

Harlow, H. F. 1962. Social Deprivation in Monkeys. *Scientific American* 206: 1–10.

Harlow, H., and Zimmerman, R. 1958. The Development of Affectional Responses in Infant Monkeys. *Proceedings: American Philosophical Society* 102: 501–509.

Harlow, J. 1868. Recovery from the Passage of an Iron Bar through the Head. *Publications of Massachusetts Medical Society* (Boston) 2: 327–346.

Harpending, H. 1980. Perspectives on the Theory of Social Evolution. In J. H. Mielke and M. H. Crawford (eds.), *Current Developments in Anthropological Genetics* (vol. 1). New York and London: Plenum Press.

Harris, M. 1965. The Cultural Ecology of India's Sacred Cattle. *Current Anthropology* 7: 51–66.

Hausfater, G., and Hrdy, S. B. (Eds.). 1984. *Infanticide, Comparative and Evolutionary Perspectives*. New York: Aldine.

Haviland, W. A. 1990. *Anthropology* (6th ed.). Fort Worth: Holt, Rinehart and Winston.

Hayes, J. K., and Hayes, C. 1952. Imitation in a Home-Raised Chimpanzee. *Journal of Physiology & Psychology* 45: 450–459.

Heffner, H. E., and Heffner, R. 1984. Temporal Lobe Lesions and Perception of Species-Specific Vocalizations by Macaques. *Science* 226: 75–76.

Hering, E. 1977. *The Theory of Binocular Vision* (B. Bridgeman, trans.; B. Bridgeman and L. Stark, eds.). New York: Plenum Publishing. (Original work published 1868.)

Hetherington, E. M. 1972. Effects of Father Absence on Personality Development in Adolescent Daughters. *Developmental Psychology* 7: 313–326.

Hewes, G. W. 1973. Primate Communication and the Gestural Origin of Language. *Current Anthropology* 14: 5–24.

Hickerson, N. P. 1980. *Linguistic Anthropology.* New York: Holt, Rinehart and Winston.

Hobson, J. 1994. *The Chemistry of Conscious States: How the Brain Changes Its Mind.* Boston: Little, Brown.

Hobson, J. 1995. *Sleep.* New York: Scientific American Library.

Holloway, R. L. 1980. The O. H. 7 (Olduvai Gorge, Tanzania) Hominid Partial Brain Endocast Revisited. *American Journal of Physical Anthropology* 53: 267–274.

Holloway, R. L. 1981a. The Indonesian *Homo erectus* Brain Endocast Revisited. *American Journal of Physical Anthropology* 55: 503–521.

Holloway, R. L. 1981b. Volumetric and Asymmetry Determinations on Recent Hominid Endocasts: Spy I and II, Djebel Jhroud 1, and the Salb *Homo erectus* specimens, with Some Notes on Neanderthal Brain Size. *American Journal of Physical Anthropology* 55: 385–393.

Holloway, R. L. 1983. Human Paleontological Evidence Relevant to Language Behavior. *Human Neurobiology* 2: 105–114.

Howell, F. C. 1970. *Early Man.* New York: Time-Life.

Hrdy, S. Blaffer. 1980. *The Langurs of Abu: Female and Male Strategies of Reproduction.* Cambridge, MA: Harvard University Press.

Hrdy, S. Blaffer. 1981. *The Woman That Never Evolved.* Cambridge, MA: Harvard University Press.

Hsu, F. L. K. 1971. Psychological Homeostasis and Jen: Conceptual Tools for Advancing Psychological Anthropology. *American Anthropologist* 73: 23–44.

Huang Wanpa, Ciohon, R., Gu Yumin, Larick, P. Fang Qien, Schwarcz, H., Yong, C., deVos J., and Rink, W. 1995. Early *Homo* and Associated Fauna from Asia. *Nature* 378:275–278.

Irwin, C. J. 1985. Sociocultural Biology: Studies in the Evolution of Some Netsilingmiut and Other Sociocultural Behaviors. Doctoral dissertation, Syracuse University.

Irwin, C. J. 1987. A Study of the Evolution of Ethnocentrism. In V. Reynolds, V. Falger, and I. Vine (eds.), *The Sociobiology of Ethnocentrism: Evolutionary Dimensions of Xenophobia, Discrimination, Racism and Nationalism,* pp. 131–156. London and Sydney: Croom Helm.

Isaac, G. L. 1978a. The Archaeological Evidence for the Activities of Early Hominids, In C. J. Jolly (ed.), *Early Hominids in Africa,* pp. 219–254. New York: St. Martin's.

Isaac, G. L. 1978b. The Food-Sharing Behavior of Protohuman Hominids. *Scientific American* 238: 90–108.

Jaynes, J. 1978. *The Origin of Consciousness in the Breakdown of the Bicameral Brain*: Boston: Houghton Mifflin.

Jennings, Jesse D. 1974. *Prehistory of North America* (2nd ed.). New York: McGraw-Hill.

Jensen, A. 1973. *Educability and Group Differences.* New York: Harper and Row.

Jerrison, H. 1973. *Evolution of the Brain and Behavior.* New York: Academic Press.

Johanson, D., White, T., and Coppens, Y. 1979. A New Species of the Genus *Australopithecus* (Primates: Hominidae). In *The Pliocene of Eastern Africa.* Kirtlandia 28: 1–14.

Jolly, C. J. 1970. The Seed Eaters: A New Model of Hominid Differentiation Based on a Baboon Analogy. *Man* 5: 5–26.

Kaplan, D. 1968. The Superorganic: Science or Metaphysics. In R. Manners and D. Kaplan (eds.), *Theory in Anthropology: A Sourcebook.* Chicago: Aldine.

Kaplan, D. 1972. *Culture Theory.* Englewood Cliffs, NJ: Prentice-Hall.

Kay, R. F. 1981. The Nut-Crackers—A New Theory of the Adaptations of the Ramapithecinae. *American Journal of Physical Anthropology* 55: 141–151.

Kimura, D. 1973. The Asymmetry of the Human Brain. *Scientific American* 228: 70–78.

Kinzey, W. G. (Ed.). 1987. *The Evolution of Human Behavior: Primate Models*. Albany: State University of New York Press.

Koestler, A. 1967. *The Ghost in the Machine*. London: Hutchinson.

Kolata, G. 1983. Math Genius May Have Hormonal Basis. *Science* 223: 1312.

Kortlandt, A. 1980. "How Might Early Hominids Have Defended Themselves against Large Predators and Food Competition?" *Journal of Human Evolution* 9: 79–112.

Kroeber, A. 1958. Totem and Taboo: An Ethnologic Psychoanalysis. In W. Lessa and E. Z. Vogt (eds.), *Reader in Comparative Religion: An Anthropological Approach*. New York: Harper & Row.

Kuhn, T. 1968. *The Structure of Scientific Revolutions*. Chicago: University of Chicago Press [International Encyclopedia of Unified Science, 2 (27)].

Kummer, H. 1971. *Primate Societies: Group Techniques of Ecological Adaptation*. Chicago: Aldine.

LaBarre, W. 1945. Some Observations of Character Structure in the Orient: The Japanese. *Psychiatry* 8: 319–342.

Lancaster, J. B. 1975. *Primate Behavior and the Emergence of Human Culture*. New York: Holt, Rinehart and Winston.

Laughlin, W. S. 1968. Hunting: An Integrating Biobehavior System and Its Evolutionary Importance. In R. B. Lee and I. DeVore (eds.), *Man the Hunter*, pp. 304–320. Chicago: Aldine.

Leakey, L. S. B. 1967. Development of Aggression as a Factor in Early Man and Prehuman Evolution. In C. Clements and D. Lundsley (eds.), *Aggression and Defense*. Los Angeles: University of California Press.

Lee, R. B. 1969. !Kung Bushman Subsistence: An Input-Output Analysis. In A. P. Vayda (ed.), *Environment and Cultural Behavior*, pp. 47–49. Garden City, NY: Natural History Press.

Lee, R. B. 1984. *The Dobe !Kung: Foragers in a Changing World*. New York: Holt, Rinehart and Winston.

LeMay, M. 1975. The Language Capability of Neanderthal Man. *American Journal of Physical Anthropology* 43(1): 9–14.

Leroi-Gourhan, A. 1968. The Evolution of Paleolithic Art. *Scientific American* 218: 58ff.

Levine, S. 1966. Sex Differences in the Brain. *Scientific American* 84–90.

Lévi-Strauss, C. 1963. *Structural Anthropology*. New York: Basic Books.

Lévi-Strauss, C. 1966. *The Savage Mind*. Chicago: University of Chicago Press.

Lewin, R. 1983. Is the Orangutan a Living Fossil? *Science* 222: 1223.

Lewin, R. 1986. Myths and Methods in Ice Age Art. *Science* 234: 938.

Lewin, R. 1987a. The Earliest Humans Were More Like Apes. *Science* 236: 106–163.

Lewin, R. 1987b. Four Legs Bad, Two Legs Good. *Science* 235: 969–971.

Lewin, R. 1987c. Why Is Ape Tool Use So Confusing? *Science* 236: 776–777.

Lewin, R. 1988. Molecular Clocks Turn a Quarter Century. *Science* 235: 969–971.

Lewontin, R. C., Rose, S. P. R., and Kamin, L. J. 1984. *Not in Our Genes*. New York: Pantheon.

Liberman, A. M. 1974. The Specialization of the Language Hemisphere. In F. O. Schmitt and F. G. Worden (eds.), *The Neurosciences: Third Study Program*. Cambridge, MA: MIT Press.

Liberman, A. M. 1982. On Finding That Speech Is Special. *American Psychologist* 37: 148–167.

Lieberman, P. 1975. *On the Origins of Language: An Introduction to the Evolution of Human Speech*. New York: Macmillan.

Lieberman, P. 1979. Hominid Evolution, Supralaryngeal Vocal-Tract Physiology and the Fossil Evidence for Reconstructions. *Brain & Language* 7: 101–126.

Lieberman, P. 1984. *The Biology and Evolution of Language*. Cambridge, MA: Harvard University Press.

Lieberman, P., Crelin, E. S., and Klatt, D. H. 1972. Phonetic Ability and the Related Anatomy of the Newborn, Adult Human, Neanderthal Man, and the Chimpanzee. *American Anthropologist* 74: 287–307.

Linton, R. 1936. *The Study of Man: An Introduction*. New York: Appleton.

Locke, J. 1937. An Essay Concerning Human Understanding. *The English Philosophers from Bacon to Mill*. New York: Modern Library. (Original work published 1690.)

Lorenz, K. 1965. *Evolution and Modification of Behavior*. Chicago: University of Chicago Press.

Lorenz, K. 1971. *Studies in Animal and Human Behavior* (vol. II). Cambridge, MA: Harvard University Press.

Lovejoy, C. O. 1981. Origin of Man. *Science* 211: 341–350.

Low, B. S., Alexander, R. D., and Noonan, K. M. 1987. Human Hips, Breasts, and Buttocks: Is Fat Deceptive? *Ethology & Sociobiology* 8: 249–257.

Lumley, H. de. 1969. A Paleolithic Camp at Nice. *Scientific American* 220(5): 42–49.

Lumsden, C. J. 1989. Does Culture Need Genes? *Ethology & Sociobiology* 10: 11–28.

Lumsden, C. J., and Wilson, E. O. 1983. *Promethean Fire: Reflections on the Origin of Mind*. Cambridge, MA: Harvard University Press.

Lumsden, C. J., and Wilson, E. O. 1985. The Relation between Biological and Cultural Evolution. *Journal of Social & Biological Structures* 8: 343–359.

Luria, A. R. 1964. Factors and Forms of Aphasia. In A. V. S. de Reuch and M. O'Connor (eds.), *Disorders of Language*. Boston: Little, Brown.

Luria, A. R. 1966. *Higher Cortical Functions in Man*. London: Tavistock.

Luria, A. R. 1970. The Functional Organization of the Brain. *Scientific American* March: 66–79.

MacDonald, K. B. 1988. Sociobiology and the Cognitive-Developmental Tradition in Moral Development Research. In K. B. MacDonald (ed.), *Sociobiological Perspectives on Human Development*, pp. 140–167. New York: Springer-Verlag.

MacLean, P. D. 1958. Contrasting Functions of Limbic and Neocortical Systems of the Brain and Their Relevance to Psychophysiological Aspects of Medicine. *American Journal of Medicine* 25: 611–626.

MacLean, P. D. 1973. *A Triune Concept of the Brain and Behavior*. Toronto: University of Toronto Press.

MacLean, P. D. 1978. The Evolution of Three Mentalities. In S. L. Washburn and E. R. McCown (eds.), *Human Evolution. Biosocial Perspectives*, pp. 3–57. Menlo Park, CA: Benjamin/Cummings.

Mair, L. 1969. *Witchcraft*. New York: McGraw-Hill.

Marshack, A. 1972. *The Roots of Civilization: A Study in Prehistoric Cognition; The Origins of Art, Symbol and Notation*. New York: McGraw-Hill.

Mascia-Lees, F. E., Relethford, J. H., and Sorger, T. 1986. Evolutionary Perspectives on Permanent Breast Enlargement in Human Females. *American Anthropologist* 88(2): 423–428.

Masters, W. H., and Johnson, V. E. 1971. The Sexual Response Cycles of the Human Male and Female: Comparative Anatomy and Physiology. In B. Lieberman (ed.), *Human Sexual Behavior*. New York: Wiley and Sons.

Mayr, E. 1982. *The Growth of Biological Thought, Diversity, Evolution and Inheritance.* Cambridge, MA: Belknap Press of Harvard University Press.

McGuire, M. T., and Taylor, C. E. (Eds.). 1988. Reciprocal Altruism: 15 Years Later. Special number of *Ethology & Sociobiology* 9(2–4): 67–256.

McHenry, H. 1975. Fossils and the Mosaic Nature of Human Evolution. *Science*, 190: 524–431.

Mead, M. 1928. *Coming of Age in Samoa.* New York: Morrow.

Mead, M. 1963. *Sex and Temperament in Three Primitive Societies* (3rd ed.). New York: Morrow.

Middleton, J. (Ed.). 1970. *From Child to Adult: Studies in the Anthropology of Education.* Garden City, NY: Natural History Press (American Museum Source Books in Anthropology).

Millgram, S. 1974. *Obedience to Authority.* New York: Harper and Row.

Montagu, A. 1964a. *The Concept of Race.* London: Macmillan.

Montagu, A. 1964b. *Man's Most Dangerous Myth: The Fallacy of Race* (4th ed.). New York: World Publishing.

Morbeck, M. E., Galloway, A., and Zihlman, A. (Eds.). 1997. *The Evolving Female.* Princeton: Princeton University Press.

Morgan, E. 1972. *The Descent of Woman.* New York: Stein and Day.

Morgan, L. H. 1877. *Ancient Society.* New York: World Publishing.

Morris, D. 1967. *The Naked Ape.* New York: Dell.

Morrison, A. R. 1983. A Window on the Sleeping Brain. *Scientific American* April: 94–102.

Murdock, G. P. 1967. *Ethnographic Atlas.* Pittsburgh: University of Pittsburgh Press.

Murdock, G. P., and White, D. R. 1969. Standard Cross-Cultural Sample. 1. *Ethnology* 8: 329–369.

Needham, R. 1972. *Belief, Language and Experience.* Chicago: University of Chicago Press.

O'Keefe, J., and Nadel, L. 1978. *The Hippocampus as a Cognitive Map.* Oxford: Clarendon Press.

Oswalt, W. H. 1972. *Other Peoples Other Customs: World Ethnography and Its History.* New York: Holt, Rinehart and Winston.

Panksepp, J. 1982. Toward a General Psychobiological Theory of Emotions. *Behavioral & Brain Sciences* 5: 407–467.

Parker, S. T. 1987. A Sexual Selection Model for Hominid Evolution. *Human Evolution* 2: 235–253.

Parker, S. T., and Gibson, K. R. 1979. A Developmental Model for the Evolution of Language and Intelligence in Early Hominids. *Behavioral & Brain Sciences* 2: 367–408.

Patterson, F. and Linden, E. 1981. *The Education of Koko.* New York: Holt, Rinehart and Winston.

Pavlov, I. 1927. *Conditioned Reflexes.* New York: Oxford University Press.

Penfield, W., and Rasmussen, T. 1950. *The Cerebral Cortex of Man: A Clinical Study of Localization of Function.* New York: Macmillan.

Penfield, W., and Roberts, L. 1959. *Speech and Brain Mechanisms.* Princeton, NJ: Princeton University Press.

Peters, C. R. 1979. Toward an Ecological Model of African Plio-Pleistocene Hominid Adaptations. *American Anthropologist* 81(2): 261–278.

Pfeiffer, J. 1982. *The Creative Explosion.* Ithaca: Cornell University Press.

Piaget, J. 1924. *The Language and Thought of a Child.* New York: Harcourt, Brace and World.

Piaget, J. 1954. *The Construction of Reality in the Child.* New York: Basic Books.

Piaget, J. 1973. *The Child and Reality.* New York: Penguin Books.

Pinker, S. 1994. *The Language Instinct: How the Mind Creates Language*. New York: William Morrow.

Pope, G. G. 1989. Bamboo and Human Evolution. *Natural History*, October: pp. 48–57.

Popper, K. R., and Eccles, J. C. 1977. *The Self and Its Brain*. Berlin: Springer-Verlag.

Porter, R. H. 1987. Kin Recognition: Functions and Mediating Mechanisms. In C. Crawford, M. Smith, and D. Krebs (eds.), *Sociobiology and Psychology: Ideas, Issues and Applications*, pp. 175–203. Hillsdale, NJ: Lawrence Erlbaum Associates.

Potts, R. 1984. Home Bases and Early Hominids. *American Scientist* 72(4): 338–347.

Premack, A. J., and Premack, D. 1972. Teaching Language to an Ape. *Scientific American* 277(4): 92–99.

Premack, D., and Premack, A. 1983 *The Mind of an Ape*. New York: W. W. Norton.

Pribram, K. H. 1971. *Languages of the Brain*. Englewood Cliffs, NJ: Prentice-Hall.

Pribram, K. H. 1981. Emotions. In S. Filskov and T. Boll (eds.), *Handbook of Clinical Neuropsychology*. New York: Wiley and Sons.

Prideaux, T., and the Editors of Time-Life. 1973. *Cro-Magnon Man*. New York: Time-Life.

Rahe, R. 1972. Subjects' Recent Life Changes and Their Near-Future Illness Susceptability. In F. Reichsman (ed.), *Advances in Psychosomatic Medicine*, vol. 8. Basel: Karger.

Raichle, M. E. 1996/1997. Visualizing the Mind. In B. M. Jubilan (ed.), *Biopsychology 96/97* 2nd ed., pp. 6–13.

Read-Martin, C. E., and Read, D. W. 1975. Australopithecine Scavenging and Human Evolution: An Approach from Faunal Analysis. *Current Anthropology* 16(3): 359–368.

Reid, J. J., Schiffer, M. B., and Rathje, W. L. 1975. Behavioral Archaeology: Four Strategies. *American Anthropologist* 77: 864–869.

Reynolds, V. 1980. *The Biology of Human Action* (2nd ed.). Oxford and San Francisco: W. H. Freeman and Co., Ltd.

Reynolds, V., Falger, V., and Vine, I. (Eds.). 1987. *The Sociobiology of Ethnocentrism: Evolutionary Dimensions of Xenophobia, Discrimination, Racism and Nationalsim*. London and Sydney: Croom Helm.

Romer, A. S. 1974. *The Vertebrate Story*. Chicago: University of Chicago Press.

Rose, R. M., Gordon, T. P., and Bernstein, I. S. 1972. Plasma Testosterone Levels in the Male Rhesus: Influences of Sexual and Social Stimuli. *Science* 178: 643–645.

Rose, S. P. R. 1976. *The Conscious Brain*. Harmondsworth, Eng.: Penguin Books.

Ross, W. 1984. Beyond the Biological Model: New Directions in Bisexual and Homosexual Research. *Journal of Homosexuality* 10: 63–69.

Rozin, P., Poritsky, S., and Sotski, R. 1971. American Children with Reading Problems Can Easily Learn to Read English Represented by Chinese Characters. *Science* 171: 1264–1267.

Rumbaugh, D. (Ed.). 1977. *Language Learning by a Chimpanzee: The Lana Project*. New York: Academic Press.

Rumbaugh, D., Savage Rumbaugh, S., and Scanlons, S. 1982. The Relationship between Language in Apes and Human Beings, In I. King and J. Forbes (eds.), *The Lance Project*. 38: 361–385. New York: Academic Press.

Rushton, J. P., Fulker, D. W., Neale, M. C., Nias, D. K. B., and Eysenck, H. J. 1986. Altruism and Aggression: The Heritability of Individual Differences. *Journal of Personality & Social Psychology* 50(6): 1192–1198.

Sahlins, M. 1961. The Segmentary Lineage: An Organization of Predatory Expansion. *American Anthropologist* 63: 322–343.

Sahlins, M. 1976. *The Use and Abuse of Biology: An Anthropological Critique of Sociobiology*. Ann Arbor: University of Michigan Press.

Sapir, E., 1917. Do We Need a Superorganic? *American Anthropologist* 19: 441–447.

Sarich, V., and Cronin, J. 1976. Molecular Systematics of the Primates. In M. Goodman and R. Tashian (eds.), *Molecular Anthropology: Genes and Proteins in the Evolutionary Ascent of Primates*, pp. 141–171. New York: Plenum.

Scarr-Salapatek, S. 1971. Unknowns in the I.Q. Equation. *Science* 174: 1223–1228.

Schaller, G. B. 1963. *The Mountain Gorilla*. Chicago: University of Chicago Press.

Schaller, G. B. 1971. *The Year of the Gorilla*. New York: Ballantine.

Scheper-Hughes, N. 1979. *Saints, Scholars and Schizophrenics*. Berkeley: University of California Press.

Seaborg, D. 1984. Sexual Orientation, Behavioral Plasticity, and Evolution. *Journal of Homosexuality* 10: 153–159.

Searle, J. 1980. Minds, Brains, and Programs. *Behavioral & Brain Sciences* 3: 417–457.

Seyfarth, R. M. 1981. Do Monkeys Rank Each Other? *Brain & Behavior Sciences* 4: 447–448.

Seyfarth, R. M., Cheney, D. L., and Marler, P. 1980. Monkey Responses to Three Different Alarm Calls. *Science* 210: 801–803.

Shipman, P. 1997. Taphonomy. In F. Spencer (ed.), *History of Physical Anthropology*, vol. 2, M-Z, pp. 1019–1022. New York: Garland.

Shuey, A. M. 1966. *The Testing of Negro Intelligence*. New York: Social Science Press.

Simons, E. L. 1989. Human Origins. *Science* 245: 1343–1350.

Simpson, G. G. 1949. *The Meaning of Evolution*. New Haven: Yale Universtiy Press.

Simpson, G. G. 1953. *The Major Features of Evolution*. New York: Columbia University Press.

Skeels, H. M. 1942. A Study of the Differential Stimulation on Mentally Retarded Children: A Follow Up. *American Journal of Mental Deficiency* 46: 340–345.

Skeels, H. M. 1966. Adult Status of Children with Contrasting Early Life Experiences: A Follow Up Study. *Monographs of the Society for Research in Child Development* 31(3).

Skinner, B. F. 1948. *Waldon Two*. New York: Macmillan.

Skinner, B. F. 1953. *Science and Human Behavior*. New York: Macmillan.

Skinner, B. F. 1957. *Verbal Behavior*. New York: Appleton-Century-Crofts.

Slobin, D. I. 1971. *Psycholinguistics*. Glenview, IL.: Scott, Foresman.

Smith, P. E. L. 1976. *Food Production and Its Consequences* (2d ed.). Menlo Park, CA: Cummings.

Smuts, B. 1987. What Are Friends For? *Natural History* 96(2): 41.

Spencer, H. 1886. *Principles of Sociology*. New York: Appleton.

Sperry, R. 1974. Lateral Specialization in the Surgically Separated Hemispheres. In F. O. Schmitt and F. G. Worden (eds.), *The Neurosciences: Third Study Program*. Cambridge, MA: MIT Press.

Sperry, R., Gazzaniga, M., and Bogen, J. 1969. Interhemispheric Relationships: The Neocortical Commisures—Syndromes of Hemisphere Disconnection. In P. Vinken and G. Bruyn (eds.), *Handbook of Clinical Neurology*, vol. 4. Amsterdam: North-Holland.

Spuhler, J. N. (Ed.). 1959. *The Evolution of Man's Capacity for Culture*. Detroit: Wayne State University Press.

Squire, L. 1982. The Neuropsychology of Human Memory. *Annual Review of Neuroscience* 5: 241–273.

Squire, L. 1986. Mechanisms of Memory. *Science* 232: 1612–1619.

Stahl, A. Brower. 1984. Hominid Dietary Selection before Fire. *Current Anthropology* 25: 151–168.

Stanley, S. M. 1981. *The New Evolutionary Timetable*. New York: Basic Books.

Steklis, D., and Harnad, S. 1976. From Hand to Mouth: Some Critical Stages in the Evolution of Language. In D. Steklis and S. Harnad (eds.), *Origins and Evolution of Language and Speech, Annals of the New York Academy of Sciences* 280: 445–454.

Sternberg, R. 1985. Implicit theories of intelligence, creativity and wisdom. *Journal of Personality and Social Psychology* 49: 607–627.

Strickberger, M. W. 1996. *Evolution*. Sudbury, MA: Jones and Bartlett.

Stringer, C. B., and Andrews, P. 1988. Genetic and Fossil Evidence for the Origin of Modern Humans. *Science* 239: 1263–1268.

Susman, R. L., Stern, J. T., and Jungers, W. L. 1984. Aborablity and Bipedality in Hadar Hominids. *Folia Primatogia* 43: 113–156.

Swadesh, M. 1959. Linguistics as an Instrument of Prehistory. *Southwestern Journal of Anthropology* 15: 20–35.

Swishe III, C., Curtis, G., Jacob, T., Getty, G., Suprijo, A., and Widasmoro T. 1994. Age of the earliest known hominids in Java, Indonesia. *Science* 263: 1181–1121.

Symons, D. 1979. *The Evolution of Human Sexuality*. New York: Oxford University Press.

Taub, J. M., and Berger, R. J. 1969. Extended Sleep and Performance: The Rip Van Winkle Effect. *Psychonomic Science* 16: 204–205.

Terenius, L. 1982. Endorphins, Perception, and Schizophrenia. In G. Hemmings (ed.), *Biological Aspects of Schizophrenia and Addiction*. New York: Wiley and Sons.

Terenius, L., and Walstrom, A. 1975. Morphine-like Ligand for Opiate Receptors in Human CSF. *Life Sciences* 16: 1759–1764.

Terman, L. 1916. *The Measurement of Intelligence*. Boston: Houghton Miffin.

Terrace, H. 1979. *NIM*. New York: Knopf.

Teuber, H. L. 1964. "The Riddle of Frontal Lobe Function in Man. In J. M. Warren and K. Akert (eds.), *The Frontal Granular Cortex and Behavior*. New York: McGraw-Hill.

Tooby, J., and DeVore, I. 1987. The Reconstruction of Hominid Behavioral Evolution through Strategic Modeling. In W. G. Kinzey (ed.), *The Evolution of Human Behavior: Primate Models*, pp. 183–237. Albany: State University of New York Press.

Toth, N. 1985. Archeological Evidence for Preferential Right-handedness in the Lower and Middle Pleistocene, Its Possible Implications. *Journal of Human Evolution* 14: 607.

Trigger, B. 1989. *A History of Archeological Thought*. Cambridge, Eng.: Cambridge University Press.

Trivers, R. L. 1971. The Evolution of Reciprocal Altruism. *Quartlery Review of Biology* 46: 35–37.

Trivers, R. L. 1972. Parental Investment and Sexual Selection. In B. Campbell (ed.), *Sexual Selection and the Descent of Man, 1871–1971*, pp. 136–179. Chicago: Aldine.

Trivers, R. L. 1985. *Social Evolution*. Menlo Park, CA: Benjamin/Cummings.

Turnbull, C. M., 1961. *The Forest People*. New York: Simon & Schuster.

Ucko, P. J., and Rosenfeld, A. 1967. *Paleolithic Cave Art*. New York: McGraw-Hill.

Vayda, A. P., and R. Rappaport. 1968. Ecology, Cultural and Noncultural. In J. A. Clifton (ed.), *Introduction to Cultural Anthropology*. Boston: Houghton Mifflin.

Vincent, J. 1979. On the Special Division of Labor, Population, and the Origins of Agriculture. *Current Anthropology* 20(2): 422–425.

De Waal, F., and Lanting, F. 1997. *Bonobo, The Forgotten Ape*. Berkeley: The University of California Press.

Wada, J., and Rasmussen, T. 1960. Intracarotid Injection of Sodium Amytal for the Lateralization of Cerebral Speech Dominance: Experimental and Clinical Observations. *Journal of Neurosurgery* 17: 266–282.

Washburn, S. L. 1959. Speculations on the Inter-relations of the History of Tools and Biological Evolution. In J. N. Spuhler (ed.), *The Evolution of Man's Capacity for Culture*. Detroit: Wayne State University Press.

Washburn, S. L. 1960. Tools and Human Evolution. *Scientific American* 63: 413–419.

Washburn, S. L., and Lancaster, C. S. 1968. The Evolution of Hunting. In S. L. Washburn and P. C. Jay (eds.), *Perspectives on Human Evolution*, pp. 213–229. New York: Holt, Rinehart and Winston.

Washburn, S. L., and Moore, R. 1980. *Ape into Human: A Study of Human Evolution* (2nd ed.). Boston: Little, Brown.

Watson, J. B. 1926. What the Nursery Has to Say About Instincts. In C. Murcheson (ed.), *Psychologies of 1925*. Worcester, MA: Clark University Press.

Watson, J. B. 1928. *The Psychological Care of Infant and Child*. New York: W. W. Norton.

Weiss, M. L., and Mann, A. E. 1990. *Human Biology and Behavior* (5th ed.). Boston: Little, Brown.

Westermarck, E. A. 1926. *A Short History of Marriage*. New York: Macmillan.

Whelehan, P. 1985. Review of Incest, a Biosocial View. *American Anthropologist* 87: 678.

White, L. 1940. The Symbol: The Origin and Basis of Human Behavior. *Philosophy of Science* 7: 451–463.

White, T. D. 1979. Evolutionary Implications of Pliocene Hominid Footprints. *Science* 208: 175–176.

Wilson, A. K., and Sarich, V. M. 1969. A Molecular Time Scale for Human Evolution. *Proceedings of the National Academy of Science* 63: 1089–1093.

Wilson, E. O. 1975a. *Sociobiology: The New Synthesis*. Cambridge, MA: Belknap Press of Harvard University Press.

Wilson, E. O. 1975b. Some Central Problems of Sociobiology. *Social Science Information* 14: 5–18.

Wrangham, R. 1983. Ultimate Social Structures Determining Social Structure. In R. Hindle (ed.), *Primate Social Relationships: An Integrated Approach*, pp. 255–261. Sunderland, MA: Sinauer Associates.

Wranghan, R., and Peterson, D. 1996. *Demonic Males: Apes and the Origins of Human Violence*. Boston: Houghton Mifflin.

Wurtman, R. 1982. Nutrients That Modify Brain Function. *Scientific American* 50–59.

Wynne-Edwards, V. C. 1962. *Animal Dispersion in Relation to Social Behavior*. Edinburgh: Oliver and Boyd.

Wynne-Edwards, V. C. 1971. Intergroup Selection in the Evolution of Social Systems. In G. C. Williams (ed.), *Group Selection*, pp. 93–104. Chicago: Aldine-Atherton.

Yalon, I., Green, R., and Fisk, F. 1973. Prenatal Exposure to Female Hormones: Effect on Psychosexual Development in Boys. *Archives of General Psychiatry* 28: 554–561.

Yerkes, R. 1923. Testing the Human Mind. *Atlantic Monthly* 131: 363–364.

Zaidel, A. 1983. A Response to Gazzaniga: Language in the Right Hemisphere, Convergent Perspectives. *American Psychologist* 38: 542–546.

Zivin, G. (Ed.). 1985. *The Development of Expressive Behavior. Biology-Environment Interaction*. Orlando, FL: Academic Press.

INDEX

Acheulean industry, 114
acquired characteristics, 8
activation-syntehsis theory, 274
adaptations, 27
  shifts, 28
  radiations, 28
age-graded, 63
aggression, 63, 161
agriculture, 135
Agta, 148
altruism, 16
Ambrona, 117, 280
Andaman Islanders, 152
anthropoids, 64
apes, 67–70
apomorphic, 31
Aquatic Theory, 95
archaeology, 6, 33–34
archaic *Homo sapiens*, 113, 121
Ardipithecus ramidus, 86
art, 130, 157, 219
artifacts, 34
association areas, 117, 169
asteroid theory, 47
Aurignacian, 129
australopithecines, 99–100
    gracile, 100–101
    robust, 101–102
Australopithecus aethiopicus, 101–102
Australopithecus afarensis, 78, 80, 84–85, 95, 100–101, 280
Australopithecus africanus, 49, 82, 84–85, 100–102
Australopithecus anamensis, 86
Australopithecus boisei, 83, 101–103
autapomorphic, 31
Bakker, Robert, 52
behaviorism, 3
Benbow, Camilla, 255
Benedict, Ruth, 38
Bergman's and Allen's rules, 123
bipedalism, 87–99
Binet, Alfred, 38, 249
bioaltruism, 16
"Black Hole" period, 90
Boas, Franz, 38

Bodo, Africa, 126
Brace, Loring, 20
brain lobes, 177
brain-mind dichotomy, 3, 41
Broca, Paul, 179
Broca's area, 179
Broom, Robert, 82, 101
Buckland, William, 49
Burt, Cyril, 251
butchery sites, 108
Calhoun, John B., 282
Campbell, Bernard, 92–93
canalization, 37
Carley, Adam, 189
Cartmill, Matt, 62
cerebral asymmetry, 117
Chalmers, David, 189
Chatelperronian, 129
chimpanzees, 68, 70–74, 257–258
China, 119, 124, 125, 149, 151
Chomsky, Noam, 196
chronospecies, 26
cladistics, 5, 21, 23, 29, 31
Clark, William Le Gros, 109
classification, 21
Coca-Cola principle, 33
communication, 196
comparative ethnography, 35
competitive exclusion, 27
computers, 4
convergent intelligence, 254
Coolidge effect, 229
Copernicus, Nicolaus, 9
creationists, 5
creative explosion, 129
Crick, Francis, 188
crime, 160
cultural ecology, 38
cultural, materialism, 38
cultural universals, 35
culture, 35
Cuvier, Georges, 8, 10, 28, 45–46, 48, 57
da Vinci, Leonardo, 252
dancing, 158, 218–219
Dart, Raymond, 49, 91, 101, 251